EARTH ALIVE

Readings in Environmental Ethics

First Edition

Edited by

David Skrbina

Detroit
CREATIVE FIRE PRESS
2021

Design, layout, and conception: Copyright © 2021 by Creative Fire Press
A division of *The Walden Group*, a Michigan non-profit educational corporation

Production manager: Charlie Clendening

Contents copyright original sources (see Appendix). Material is reproduced here under the U. S. Fair Use Doctrine (17 U.S.C., section 107, 1976), in accordance with the publication of non-profit, educational material.

No part of this publication may be reproduced, stored in a retrieval system, or transmitted, in any form or by any means, electronic, mechanical, photocopying, recording, or otherwise.

Library of Congress Cataloging-in-Publication Data

Earth Alive: Readings in Environmental Ethics / edited by David Skrbina - 1st ed.
      p.   cm.
Includes bibliographical references.
ISBN 978-1737-4461-01 (pbk.: alk. paper)
Philosophy. I. Skrbina, David

Interior & cover design by:
David G. Barnett

Printing number: 9 8 7 6 5 4 3 2 1

Printed in the United States of America on acid-free paper.

CONTENTS

INTRODUCTION
    Scott Russell Sanders
        A Fleet of Arks   7

    Herman Hesse
        Siddhartha   13

PART I: HISTORICAL CONTEXT

    Plato
        Phaedrus, Philebus, Timaeus, Critias, Laws   17

    Aristotle
        Politics, Parts of Animals, De Anima, On the Heavens   21

    Bible
        Genesis, Psalms   23

    St. Francis
        Canticle of the Sun   25

    Bacon and Galileo
        Origins of the mechanistic worldview   27

    Benedict Spinoza
        Ethics   29

    Lynn White, Jr.
        Historical Roots of our Ecologic Crisis   33

    Henryk Skolimowski
        Knowledge and Values   43

PART II: TWENTIETH CENTURY ENVIRONMENTALISTS

Aldo Leopold
Thinking Like a Mountain, The Land Ethic   55

Rachel Carson
Silent Spring   69

Henryk Skolimowski
Ecological Humanism   79

James Lovelock
Quest for Gaia, 'Bad news'   83

PART III: PHILOSOPHICAL DEVELOPMENT

Christopher Stone
Should Trees have Standing?   93

Joel Feinberg
Rights of Animals and Unborn Generations   105

Roderick Nash
Do Rocks Have Rights?   119

Derrick Jensen
Strangely Like War   133

Kenneth Goodpaster
On Being Morally Considerable   147

Andrew Brennan
Moral Standing of Natural Objects   155

PART IV: ECO-PHILOSOPHY AND DEEP ECOLOGY

Gregory Bateson
Steps to an Ecology of Mind   171

Arne Naess
    The Shallow and the Deep, Long-range Ecology Movement   181

Matthew Fox
    Deep Ecology: A New Philosophy of our Time?   185

B. Devall and G. Sessions
    Deep Ecology   191

Henryk Skolimowski
    Eco-philosophy and Deep Ecology   199

PART V: APPLIED ECO-ETHICS

John Seymour
    Age of Healing   207

Theodore Roszak
    Ecopsychology since 1992   211

Gregory Bateson
    The Roots of Ecological Crisis   219

P. Ehrlich and J. Holdren
    I = PAT   223

Fact Sheets on Population   225

'Goodbye Cruel World', Ecological Footprint   229

Garrett Hardin
    Lifeboat Ethics   235

Fact Sheets on Land Use   244

'Livestock a Major Threat to Environment', Earthsave Report   247

Eric Schlosser
    What's in the Meat?   253

Sprawl City   267

'Don't Panic, But...'   269

Dave Foreman
    Defending the Earth   273

Earth Liberation Front (ELF)
    Web page, diary, communiqué   296

Ivan Illich
    Energy and Equity   301

Ted Kaczynski
    Industrial Society and its Future 311

APPENDICES

A: Overview of major environmental groups   323

B: Copyright acknowledgments   325

INTRODUCTION: A FLEET OF ARKS

SCOTT RUSSELL SANDERS (2003)

At dawn one morning in July, police showed up with bulldozers, chainsaws and guns to force a band of protesters out of a 40-acre wood in my hometown of Bloomington, Indiana. The sheriff and his deputies were upholding a ruling by the county council, which gave a developer the right to turn these woods into an apartment complex. The protesters were upholding the right of the woods to remain as woods, one of the last parcels of big trees left within the noose of roads encircling our city. A few protesters had lived for months up in the trees on temporary platforms, while local people took turns bringing them food and drink. The tree-sitters were arrested along with a number of their supporters, sixteen in all, and they are now awaiting trial. As I write, the trees are falling, and a private security firm guards the perimeter of the vanishing woods.

The police had the law on their side, of course, but they also had the banks, building contractors, real-estate agents, merchants, utility companies, fast-food vendors, newspaper owners, and countless other boosters that stood to make money from the development. The protesters set against that power their unarmed bodies and their unfashionable convictions. They believe there are values more important than money. They believe that red oaks and red foxes and all the creatures of the woods deserve a home. They believe that a civilized community must show restraint by leaving some land alone, to remind ourselves of the wild world on which our lives depend and to keep ourselves humble and sane.

Similar conflicts are taking place around the globe. By and large, the developers are winning. Yet it's plain to many people that the Earth cannot long support the extravagant way of life so common in rich countries, nor can it support the spreading of that extravagance to poor countries. Sooner or later we'll burn up all the cheap oil, we'll pump the aquifers dry, carve up the last big forests and fish out the seas, plough up the last arable land and taint the last clean air. Endless consumption is ruinous to the planet and bound to fail. The question is not whether it will fail but when, and how the end of our spree will come—by choice, or by catastrophe.

Knowing all this, how should we act? We might shrug off the knowledge, pretend we can go on building houses, driving cars, shopping around the clock, wiping out other species, fouling the atmosphere, polluting water, and squandering soil forever. We might admit the gravity of our situation, while counting on scientists and engineers to come up with a technical fix. We might place our faith in the free market, believing it will somehow furnish a second, unspoiled Earth for our use, once the price is right. We might concede that neither economics nor technology will enable us to pursue infinite growth on a finite globe, and so decide to live it up while we can, leaving future generations to figure out how to survive on a ransacked planet. Or we might seek to live more lightly, reducing our demands on the Earth, devising or recovering simple, elegant, durable practices that could serve our descendants long after the current binge of consumption has withered away.

The first four responses to Earth's limits are by far the most visible. Those who strive to live more simply are harder to see. They don't crowd the malls or fast-food shops. Occasionally they make news by defending trees from bulldozers, but they rarely show up on talk shows or the covers of magazines. Instead, largely invisible except to one another, they go about learning the skills and mastering the tools necessary for meeting basic human needs. They grow food. They build shelters. They make clothes. They draw energy from sun and wind and wood. They get by with fewer possessions, and learn to repair the ones they have. They create much of their own entertainment, and derive pleasure from good work, human company, and the perennial show of Nature. As far as possible, they rear their children away from television and advertising. They buy as little as they can from the global economy, and instead support local economies based on co-operation, barter and sharing. They protect and restore woods, prairies, rivers and swamps, making room for wildness.

I think of these people as builders of arks, for their ways and works are vessels designed to preserve from extinction not merely our fellow creatures, as on Noah's legendary ark, but also the wisdom necessary for dwelling in place generation after generation without diminishing either the place or the planet. In their efforts to conserve skilful means and wild lands, they point the way beyond the rising flood of extinction—the ecological cataclysm precipitated by growth in human population and consumption—toward a new, durable civilization.

The forest that the tree-sitters were trying to save is called Brown's Woods, after the local speculator who owned it. Bill Brown—who is by all accounts a decent, prosperous man—could have sold or even donated the woods to a land trust or the city of Bloomington, but he stood to make a tidy sum by selling it to the developer, so that is what he did. The arguments for turning Brown's Woods into the Canterbury House Apartments are familiar: people need somewhere to live; people need jobs; investors deserve a return on their capital; the city must grow. We can always think of reasons for subduing land to our desires.

Whatever the arguments, the upshot is that the felling of Brown's Woods has diminished our commonwealth, and those who live here after us will inherit a grimmer, grimier place. We are not the only ones hurt. The hawks, coyotes, toads and salamanders, the butterflies and beetles will all have to leave, if they can outrun the bulldozers, and if they can find another haven anywhere near the sprawling city. The red oaks and shagbark hickories have no such chance, nor do the trout lilies and dogtooth violets, the bloodroot and chanterelles. These neighbors have no say over the future of the neighborhood. They write no checks, cast no votes. They have no voice in how we use the land—unless some of us speak up for them.

You may recall that God sends the Biblical flood in punishment for human corruption, sparing only the upright Noah, Noah's family, and a breeding pair of "every living thing" (Genesis 6:19). God instructs Noah to build an ark and take refuge there along with a male and female of each species. Then come forty days and forty nights of rain. "And all flesh died that moved upon the earth, birds, cattle, beasts, all swarming creatures that swarm upon the earth, and every man; everything on the dry land in whose nostrils was the breath of life." You might wonder why all the crows and crickets and other innocent breathers must drown for sins committed by humans, but the Bible does not say.

When the skies clear, Noah sends forth a dove to search for dry land. The dove comes back empty-billed on its first flight, returns bearing an olive leaf on the second flight, and after the third flight does not return at all. Reassured, Noah and his fellow passengers drift to shore and step onto solid earth. Pleased by Noah's obedience, God vows, "I will never again curse the ground because of man, for the imagination of man's heart is evil from his youth; neither will I ever again destroy every living creature as I have done. While the earth remains, seedtime and harvest, cold and heat, summer and winter, day and night shall not cease." It's a beautiful promise, one that softens considerably the image of the tyrant who sent the flood.

But the promise has a dark side, from which we are still suffering. For God says to Noah, "Be fruitful and multiply, and fill the earth. The fear of you and the dread of you shall be upon every beast of the earth, and upon every bird of the air, upon everything that creeps on the ground and all the fish of the sea; into your hand they are delivered. Every moving thing that lives shall be food for you; and as I gave you the green plants, I give you everything." The passage may be read as merely stating the plain truth: all beasts *do* live in dread of us, because we are clever enough to displace, capture, or kill every other species. Understood in this light, God's charge to Noah may be taken as a warning not to abuse our power. But the same words may also be read as justifying our utter dominion over Nature. If every animal and plant was created to serve our needs, if everything has been given into our hands, then we may use the Earth as we see fit. Read in this way, the passage becomes a license to loot the planet.

While such a reading might appeal to the most reckless of developers, it is firmly contradicted by the rest of Noah's story. A few verses later, we find a third variation on the promise, one that clearly limits our dominion. "Behold," God tells Noah, "I establish my covenant with you and your descendants after you, and with every living creature that is with you, the birds, the cattle, and every beast of the earth with you, as many as came out of the ark. I establish my covenant with you, that never again shall all flesh be cut off by the waters of a flood, and never again shall there be a flood to destroy the earth." The God who speaks here sounds chastened, as if regretting the slaughter of so many innocent beings. This God is the creator and protector of crickets and crows, rattlesnakes and rotifers. This God cherishes *all* creatures, whether or not they go about on two legs, and by implication Noah is being told to cherish them as well.

The lesson we draw from the Biblical flood depends on which part of this story we embrace. One tradition blesses humans alone, conveying the whole Earth to our use; the other blesses all creatures alike, granting to each species its own right to survive and flourish. The first view instructs us to fill the Earth with our kind and to impose our will on all living things; the second instructs us to honor our fellow creatures, to show restraint in our uses of the Earth, and to take our place modestly in the household of Nature.

By and large, those who wield the levers of power in the global economy hold the first view. They insist on the sovereignty of human appetite. Nothing has value in their eyes except insofar as it can be bought or sold or otherwise used. They scorn the idea that animals or plants could have rights, even the right to survive. While they fight against protections for endangered species—mocking those who defend rare fish or birds—they support the engineering and patenting of new life forms, which can more conveniently be turned into cash. They resist every effort to preserve wilderness; they regard public land as an arena for private plunder; they reject any limits to growth; they seek to overthrow every barrier to drilling, mining, logging, road-building, polluting, or profit-making. By largely controlling the delivery of news, advertising and entertainment, they tell us what to believe and what to buy, and they force-feed us a lethal vision of the good life.

Clearly, humans could not have survived without making use of the Earth. Our ancestors hunted and fished, they gathered berries and seeds and roots, they fashioned clothing from skins and fibers, they cleared fields and planted grains, they domesticated animals, they cut down trees and dug up rocks and baked clay into bricks to build shelters, they harnessed fire and smelted ore into metal. The question is not whether we should use the Earth, but to what degree and to what end. With only stone-tipped weapons, our ancestors drove many species of large animals to extinction; with hand-tools, they felled enough trees to create deserts. Our need for prudence has grown along with the power of our technology, as stone points have given way to nuclear weapons, as bone hooks on fishing lines have given way to ocean-going trawlers pulling miles-long seines, as digging sticks have given way to draglines capable of stripping the tops from mountains in the search for coal. Likewise, as our population has grown from the few million people alive at Noah's time to the more than six billion today, so has our need for an ethic of restraint.

Noah's story offers us such an ethic in the call to protect *all* creatures on the ark. Those who hear this call insist that human beings are not the sovereign rulers. They insist that we belong to the community of soil, water, air, and all living things, and they seek to live in such a way as to preserve and enhance the health of this greater community. They accept limits to growth and limits to human population. Whether or not they've read the Bible, their actions are in keeping with God's command to Noah, which was to save not only those species that would be useful to humans, but *everything*—the creepers and crawlers, the stingers and biters, the predators and parasites. From a religious perspective, this abundance is all the handiwork of God, who loves the Creation and wishes to preserve it. From an ecological perspective, each species is vital because it embodies an irreplaceable store of knowledge accumulated over millions of years, and it interacts with other species in ways far more intricate than we could ever fathom, let alone recreate. Religion and ecology alike instruct us to honor all life. And so, recognizing that the Earth has suffered great damage because of our carelessness, and realizing that many other species besides our own are in danger, those who believe the solidarity of living things have set about building arks.

«««—»»»

A Fleet of Arks

A book may be an ark, as *Walden* and *Small Is Beautiful* and *The One-Straw Revolution* clearly are, ferrying an ethical vision through stormy times. Organic farming, solar designing and other practices that protect the fertility and abundance of Earth may be arks. A co-op for sharing food or housing or tools might be an ark, and so might be a community chorus, an arts centre, a backyard garden, a children's science museum, a yoga class, a school—any human structure, invention or gathering that conserves the wisdom necessary for meeting our needs without despoiling the planet.

Among the builders and tenders of arks, the ones who come closest to fulfilling Noah's task are the people who work at protecting and restoring wild lands. Some devote a portion or even the whole of their own land to providing habitat for other creatures. Others join together to protect land through legal restrictions, donation, or outright purchase. In my own county, the Sycamore Land Trust has combined gifts, grants and federal and state funds to protect a 270-acre parcel of wet forest along Beanblossom Creek, which is home to a colony of great blue herons. Every time I see one of these magisterial birds wading in a nearby lake or flying overhead with long legs trailing, I realize they might not be here at all without the Beanblossom Refuge.

Whether protected by government, trusts, or individuals, natural lands offer the last resort for other species as well as for those of our own species who crave contact with wildness. These preserves need not be large to be valuable: every scrap of ground can serve as an ark. Quite a few people in my city have dug up their lawns and planted their gardens with native flowers, shrubs and ferns. As one garden after another goes native, the roar and stink of mowers give way to the songs of birds and the smell of flowers. In summer, monarch butterflies on migration stop to nectar on blossoms, and in winter raccoons leave their tracks in the snow. All year, people walking by these exuberant yards pause on the sidewalks to gaze and listen, caught by a feral scent, a startling shape, a flash of life.

Every unsprayed garden and unkempt yard, every meadow, marsh and woods may become a reservoir for biological possibilities, keeping alive creatures who bear in their genes a wealth of evolutionary discoveries. Every such refuge may also become a reservoir for spiritual possibilities, keeping alive our connection with the land, reminding us of our origins in the green world.

Ark-builders realize, however, that nothing is gained by creating refuges in one place, if we behave in such a way as to contribute to the pillaging of land somewhere else. If we're going to build arks, we should do everything we can to avoid swelling the flood. This means living more lightly, and it means nurturing local economies, since the global economy cares neither for the fate of the Earth nor for the health of particular places. By protecting wild land, the ark-builders are helping to preserve the biological heritage—the seed stock, the diversity of species, the intricate web of fertility—that we will need to replenish the Earth after the flood recedes.

When the tree-sitters were arrested in Brown's Woods, the sheriff was quoted in the paper as saying, "We want to do this slow and easy, so no one gets injured—so everybody has their say and can get on with their lives." What he didn't seem to grasp was that the protesters *were* getting on with their lives. They were expressing their love for a piece of the Earth. In this dispute over Brown's Woods, one side has its say by sending in police and bulldozers, and by throwing the protesters in jail; the other side has its say by weaving yarn among the trees and speaking plain words on behalf of the community of all beings.

If I were in the dock—as by rights I should be, given my sympathies—I would testify that we must protect the remaining wild lands, especially in our cities, because we desperately need the companionship of other species. We need them for pleasure, for instruction, for inspiration. We need them to recall us from the frenzy of our lives. We need the birds, butterflies, frogs and snakes to help us monitor the health of our home places. We need the trees and other plants to purify our water and air. We need wild lands as reminders of the natural cycles and deep time out of which we have evolved and on which we depend. These untrammeled spaces offer us relief from the hard, temporary, sometimes ugly shapes of human constructions. They serve as reservoirs from which other parts of the city and countryside might be repopulated with wild creatures. They give us a chance to glimpse the shaping intelligence in Nature, to sense the ultimate mystery from which all things rise, and to align our lives with that power.

The defenders of Brown's Woods and the other people I am calling ark-builders don't belong to a single political party. They don't follow one particular religion, or perhaps any religion at all. They don't come from one age bracket, ethnic group, or educational background. They don't obey a master plan, nor do they pretend to have a remedy for all the ills of our day. Instead, they're bound together by a certain joy and boldness in seeking to preserve the diversity of living things and the essentials of human knowledge and art. What they share is a moral vision, one informed by an understanding of ecology and a reverence for life.

Building an ark when the floodwaters are rising is not an act of despair: it's an act of hope. To build an ark is to create a space within which life in its abundance may continue. But no refuge can be sealed off entirely from the worldwide flood. Acid rain may leach it; ultraviolet radiation pouring through the ozone hole may bleach it; invasive insects or viruses may attack it; pollution from adjoining land may wash over it. In any case, no single refuge is large enough to contain the full array of species. The big predators, such as lions and wolves, need more space, as do grazing animals such as bison. And the animals that migrate, from caribou to cranes, need sanctuaries stretching across entire continents for feeding, resting, and bearing young. Even thousands of sanctuaries, blooming across our cities and countryside, will not be spacious enough if the rest of the planet becomes an industrial wasteland.

Ultimately, there will be no security for life on Earth unless we see the whole planet as an ark. We are not the captains of this vessel, although we may flatter ourselves by thinking so. We are common passengers, and yet because we are both clever and numerous, we bear a unique responsibility to do everything we can to assure that this one precious ark will stay afloat, with all the least and greatest of our fellow-travelers safely on board.

SIDDHARTHA

HERMANN HESSE (1922)

Siddhartha stooped down, picked up a stone from the ground, and weighed it in his hand.

"This," he said effortlessly, as if at play, "is a stone, and within a certain time it will perhaps be earth, and from earth it will become a plant or an animal or a person. Now, in the past I would have said: 'This stone is merely a stone, it is worthless, it belongs to the world of *maya*; but, because in the cycle of transformations it may also become a person and a mind, I assign some value even to it.' That is how I might once have reasoned."

"But today I think: This stone is a stone, it is also an animal, it is also a god, it is also Buddha; I do not revere and love it because it may some day become one thing or another, but because it has, *for a long time, always, been everything*—and it is precisely the fact of its being a stone, of its appearing to me as a stone now and today, that makes me love it and see value and meaning in each of its veins and cavities, in the yellow, in the gray, in its hardness, in the ring it emits when I strike it, in the dryness or moistness of its surface. There are stones that feel like oil or soap to the touch, and others like leaves, others like sand; and each one is special and prays *'Om'* in its own way, each one is *Brahman*; but, at the same time and just as much, it is a stone, it is oily or soapy; and that is precisely what I like and find marvelous and worthy of adoration."

"—But do not let me say any more about this. Words do no good to the secret meaning; everything always immediately becomes a little different when you express it, a little falsified, a little foolish—... I am perfectly contented that one person's treasure of wisdom always sounds like foolishness to someone else."

Govinda listened in silence.

"Why did you tell me that about the stone?" he asked hesitantly, after a pause.

"I did it unintentionally. Or perhaps it was intended to show that I love the stone, and the river, and all these things we look at and can learn from. I can love a stone, Govinda, and also a tree or a piece of bark. They are physical things, and things can be loved..."

Govinda said: "But is that which you call 'physical things' something real, something substantial? Is that not merely a ruse of *maya*, merely an image and an illusion? Your stone, your tree, your river—are they realities?"

Siddhartha said: "That does not trouble me very much, either. Things may be illusory or not; if they are, I, too, am illusory, and so they continue to be of the same nature as myself. That is what makes them so dear and worthy of reverence to me: they share my nature. Therefore I can love them."

«««—»»»

And if the Earth no longer knows your name,
Whisper to the silent Earth: I'm flowing.
To the flashing water say: I am.

— Rainer Maria Rilke

PART I: HISTORICAL CONTEXT

REFLECTIONS ON THE ENVIRONMENT

PLATO

On the one hand, Plato has been criticized for both his *dualism* (the world of phenomena vs. the world of the Forms), and for his emphasis on the *individual* in his ethical theories ('egocentrism').

On the other hand, we find a number of passages that support a respect for nature, that indicate an awareness of environmental degradation, and that see the cosmos as alive and ensouled:

CRITIAS (110e-111e)

[In ancient times,] the land was the best in the world, and was therefore able in those days to support a vast army, raised from the surrounding people. ... Many great deluges have taken place during the nine thousand years, for that is the number of years which have elapsed since the time of which I am speaking; and during all this time and through so many changes, there has never been any considerable accumulation of the soil coming down from the mountains, as in other places, but the earth has fallen away all round and sunk out of sight. The consequence is, that in comparison of what then was, there are remaining only the bones of the wasted body, as they may be called, as in the case of small islands, all the richer and softer parts of the soil having fallen away, and the mere skeleton of the land being left. But in the primitive state of the country, its mountains were high hills covered with soil, and the plains of Phelleus were full of rich earth, and there was abundance of wood in the mountains.

Of this last the traces still remain, for although some of the mountains now only afford sustenance to bees, not so very long ago there were still to be seen roofs of timber cut from trees growing there, which were of a size sufficient to cover the largest houses; and there were many other high trees, cultivated by man and bearing abundance of food for cattle. Moreover, the land reaped the benefit of the annual rainfall, not as now losing the water which flows off the bare earth into the sea, but, having an abundant supply in all places, and receiving it into herself and treasuring it up in the close clay soil, it let off into the hollows the streams which it absorbed from the heights, providing everywhere abundant fountains [i.e. springs] and rivers, of which there may still be observed sacred memorials in places where fountains once existed; and this proves the truth of what I am saying. Such was the natural state of the country...

PHAEDRUS

[T]he priests of the temple of Zeus at Dodona say that the first prophecies were the words of an oak. Everyone who lived at that time, not being as wise as you young ones are today, found it rewarding enough in their simplicity to listen to an oak or even a stone, so long as it was telling the truth... (275b)

TIMAEUS

We may call these plants 'living things' on the ground that anything that partakes of life has an incontestable right to be called a 'living thing'. And in fact, what we are talking about now [i.e. the plant] partakes of the third type of soul... This type is totally devoid of opinion, reasoning, or understanding, though it does share in sensation, [both] pleasant and painful, and desires. (77b)

Of the gods that have come to be within the universe, Earth ranks as the foremost, the one with greatest seniority. (40c).

[D]ivine providence brought our world [i.e. the cosmos] into being as a truly living thing, endowed with soul and intelligence. (30c).

PHILEBUS

[T]he body of the universe which has the same properties as our [body], but more beautiful in all respects...possesses a soul. (30a).

LAWS (Book X, 903c)

The ruler of the universe has ordered all things with a view to the excellence and preservation of the whole, and each part, as far as may be, has an action and passion appropriate to it. ... And one of these portions of the universe is thine own, unhappy man, which, however little, contributes to the whole; and you do not seem to be aware that this and every other creation is for the sake of the whole, and in order that the life of the whole may be blessed; and that you are created for the sake of the whole, and not the whole for the sake of you.

Mahoney (1997) summarizes the argument for an ecological view of Plato as follows:

[A]ccording to Plato the natural world is a single living organism in which the well-being of all the parts is harmonized. As part of nature, each human's well-being is coordinated with the well-being of nature as a whole: to pursue one's own good is the very same thing as to contribute to the good of the whole natural organism.   To attain one's own good, one must contribute to the good of the whole of which one is a part, that is, one must be just.

Because humans are rational beings, they can understand the true character of the spatiotemporal world and how their well-being is enmeshed in the web of the well-being of the world as a whole. That is, humans can understand themselves and their own good as natural beings. ... Thus, according to Plato, ...human well-being requires acting justly, that is, making one's contribution to the good of the natural world.

REFLECTIONS ON THE ENVIRONMENT

ARISTOTLE

On the one hand, some statements by Aristotle seem to *oppose* the notion of intrinsic value, and support merely instrumental value:

POLITICS (Book I, Part 8)

Again, there are many sorts of food, and therefore there are many kinds of lives both of animals and men; they must all have food, and the differences in their food have made differences in their ways of life. For of beasts, some are gregarious, others are solitary; they live in the way which is best adapted to sustain them, accordingly as they are carnivorous or herbivorous or omnivorous: and their habits are determined for them by nature in such a manner that they may obtain with greater facility the food of their choice. But, as different species have different tastes, the same things are not naturally pleasant to all of them; and therefore the lives of carnivorous or herbivorous animals further differ among themselves.

In the lives of men too there is a great difference. The laziest are shepherds, who lead an idle life, and get their subsistence without trouble from tame animals; their flocks having to wander from place to place in search of pasture, they are compelled to follow them, cultivating a sort of living farm. Others support themselves by hunting, which is of different kinds. Some, for example, are bandits, others, who dwell near lakes or marshes or rivers or a sea in which there are fish, are fishermen, and others live by the pursuit of birds or wild beasts. The greater number obtain a living from the cultivated fruits of the soil...

Property, in the sense of a bare livelihood, seems to be given by nature herself to all, both when they are first born, and when they are grown up. For some animals bring forth, together with their offspring, so much food as will last until they are able to supply themselves...; the viviparous [live-bearing] animals have up to a certain time a supply of food for their young in themselves, which is called milk.

In like manner we may infer that, after the birth of animals, plants exist for their sake, and that the other animals exist for the sake of man, the tame for use and food, the wild, if not all at least the greater part of them, for food, and for the provision of clothing and various instruments. Now if nature makes nothing incomplete, and nothing in vain, the inference must be that she has made all animals for the sake of man. (1256a19-b22)

On the other hand, we find passages that support a respect for all life and even all nature, and that promote an 'organismic' view of the universe:

ON THE PARTS OF ANIMALS (Book 1, part 5)

Having already treated of the celestial world, as far as our conjectures could reach, we proceed to treat of animals, without omitting, to the best of our ability, any member of the kingdom, however ignoble. For if some have no graces to charm the sense, yet even these, by disclosing to intellectual perception the artistic spirit that designed them, give immense pleasure to all who can trace links of causation, and are inclined to philosophy. Indeed, it would be strange if [images] of them were attractive, because they disclose the skill of the painter or sculptor, and the original realities themselves were not more interesting, to all at any rate who have eyes to discern the reasons that determined their formation. We therefore must not recoil with childish aversion from the examination of the humbler animals. Every realm of nature is marvelous.

And as Heraclitus, when the strangers who came to visit him found him warming himself at the furnace in the kitchen and hesitated to go in, reported to have bidden them not to be afraid to enter, as even in that kitchen divinities were present, so we should venture on the study of every kind of animal without distaste; for each and all will reveal to us something natural and something beautiful. Absence of haphazard and conduciveness of everything to an end are to be found in Nature's works in the highest degree, and the resultant end of her generations and combinations is a form of the beautiful. (645a4-25)

ON THE SOUL (*De Anima*) (Book 1, part 5)

It seems that the principle found in plants is also a kind of soul; for this is the only principle which is common to both animals and plants. (411b27)

ON THE HEAVENS (Book 2, part 2)

[W]e have already decided...that the heaven is alive [*empsychos*] and contains a principle of motion. (285a)

THE BIBLE

NEW KING JAMES VERSION

Genesis 1

[26] Then God said, "Let Us make man in Our image, according to Our likeness; let them have dominion over the fish of the sea, over the birds of the air, and over the cattle, over all the earth and over every creeping thing that creeps on the earth."

[27] So God created man in His own image; in the image of God He created him; male and female He created them.

[28] Then God blessed them, and God said to them, "Be fruitful and multiply; fill the earth and subdue it; have dominion over the fish of the sea, over the birds of the air, and over every living thing that moves on the earth."

Genesis 9

[1] So God blessed Noah and his sons, and said to them: "Be fruitful and multiply, and fill the earth.

[2] And the fear of you and the dread of you shall be on every beast of the earth, on every bird of the air, on all that move on the earth, and on all the fish of the sea. They are given into your hand.

[3] Every moving thing that lives shall be food for you. I have given you all things, even as the green herbs."

Psalm 8

[4] What is man that You are mindful of him, And the son of man that You visit him?

[5] For You have made him a little lower than the angels, And You have crowned him with glory and honor.

⁶ You have made him to have dominion over the works of Your hands; You have put all things under his feet,

⁷ All sheep and oxen — Even the beasts of the field,

⁸ The birds of the air, And the fish of the sea That pass through the paths of the seas.

Job 12

⁷ But ask the beasts, and they will teach you; the birds of the air, and they will tell you;

⁸ Or speak to the Earth, and it will teach you; and the fish of the sea will declare to you.

⁹ Who among all these does not know that the hand of the Lord has done this?

THE CANTICLE OF THE SUN

ST. FRANCIS OF ASSISI (1182-1226)

Most high, all-powerful, all good, Lord!
All praise is yours, all glory, all honor
And all blessing.

To you, alone, Most High, do they belong.
No mortal lips are worthy
To pronounce your name.

All praise be yours, my Lord, through all that you have made,
And first my lord Brother Sun,
Who brings the day; and light you give to us through him.

How beautiful is he, how radiant in all his splendor!
Of you, Most High, he bears the likeness.

All praise be yours, my Lord, through Sister Moon and Stars;
In the heavens you have made them, bright and precious and fair.

All praise be yours, my Lord, through Brothers Wind and Air,
And fair and stormy, all the weather's moods,
By which you cherish all that you have made.

All praise be yours, my Lord, through Sister Water,
So useful, lowly, precious and pure.

All praise be yours, my Lord, through Brother Fire,
Through whom you brighten up the night.
How beautiful is he, how gay!
Full of power and strength.

All praise be yours, my Lord, through Sister Earth, our mother,
Who feeds us in her sovereignty and produces
Various fruits with colored flowers and herbs.

All praise be yours, my Lord, through those who grant pardon
For love of you; through those who endure

Earth Alive

Sickness and trial.
Happy those who endure in peace,
By you, Most High, they will be crowned.

All praise be yours, my Lord, through Sister Death,
From whose embrace no mortal can escape.
Woe to those who die in mortal sin!
Happy those She finds doing your will!
The second death can do no harm to them.

Praise and bless my Lord, and give him thanks,
And serve him with great humility.

ORIGINS OF THE MECHANISTIC WORLDVIEW

BACON AND GALILEO

<u>Francis Bacon</u> (1561-1626) – English philosopher, one of the first major thinkers of the Renaissance. Bacon was influenced by the literal Biblical view in which man is given dominion over the Earth. He took it as humanity's mission to examine, explore, and manipulate the natural world to achieve human ends. But we cannot do this without the proper *knowledge* of nature; knowledge gives us the power to act as we choose in the world.

His most famous work is the <u>Novum Organum</u> (1620):

Book I.1: "Man is Nature's agent and interpreter."

I.3: "Human *knowledge* and human *power* come to the same thing, because ignorance of cause frustrates effect. For *Nature is conquered only by obedience*; and that which in thought is a cause, is like a rule in practice."

I.129: "And it would not be irrelevant to distinguish three kinds and degrees of human ambition. [The first is personal ambition; the second is the ambition to conquer other nations.] But if anyone attempts to renew and extend the power and empire of the human race itself *over the universe of things* [i.e. nature], his ambition is without a doubt both more sensible and more majestic than the others'. And the empire of man over things lies solely in the arts [i.e. technology] and sciences. ... Let man recover the *right over nature* which belongs to him by God's gift..."

This is the basis for the famous Baconian belief that *'knowledge is power.'* No one prior to Bacon viewed knowledge in quite this way.

«««—»»»

<u>Galileo Galilei</u> (1564-1642) – Italian astronomer, scientist, and philosopher. Invented the telescope, and used it to justify belief in the Copernican system, which argued that the Earth revolved around the sun. The Church disagreed, tried Galileo for heresy, and confined him to house arrest in 1633 for the remainder of his life.

According to him, everything in nature could be *quantified*, or measured, and thus expressed mathematically. As he wrote in <u>The Assayer</u> (1623):

"Philosophy is written in this grand book, the universe, which stands continually open to our gaze. But the book cannot be understood unless one first learns to comprehend the language and read the characters in which it is written. It is written in the language of *mathematics*, and its characters are triangles, circles, and other geometric figures without which it is humanly impossible to understand a single word of it; without these one is wandering in a dark labyrinth."

The implication is, that anything not expressible in mathematics is either *unreal*, or, at best, *unimportant*.

ETHICS

SPINOZA

Spinoza's book The Ethics (1677) is arranged in five parts, of which the first two, 'On God' and 'On the Nature and Origin of the Mind', are considered the most important. Using a logical, almost mathematical procedure, he proceeds to argue that all of existence – the entire universe and everything in it – is a 'single substance', something he calls "God, or Nature" (see Part IV, Preface – below). This approach is called *metaphysical monism*.

Further, since this 'one substance' of the universe is taken as 'God', Spinoza's view is called *pantheism* – 'all is God':

Part I – "On God"

Definition 3: By *substance*, I mean that which is in itself, and is conceived through itself; in other words, that of which a conception can be formed independently of any other conception.

Def. 6: By *God*, I mean a being absolutely infinite—that is, a substance consisting in infinite attributes, of which each expresses an eternal and infinite essence.

Axiom 1: Everything which exists, exists either in itself or in something else.

Proposition 5: There cannot exist in the universe two or more substances having the same nature or attribute.

Prop 8: Every substance is necessarily infinite.

Prop 11: "God", or a substance consisting of infinite attributes, of which each expresses an eternal and infinite essence, necessarily exists.

("Proof"— If this be denied, conceive, if possible, that God does not exist: then his essence does not involve existence. But this is absurd. Therefore God necessarily exists.)

Therefore, there exists at least one 'infinite substance' (called 'God'), which has all possible attributes. Incidentally, we humans can only grasp *two* of these attributes – "extension" (matter and space), and "thought" (mind). All other attributes are beyond our comprehension.

Furthermore, there cannot exist a second substance, since it would have to have at least one attribute in common with 'God'. But, by Prop 5, this is impossible. Hence, there exists only <u>one</u> infinite substance, 'God':

> <u>Prop 14</u>: Besides God no substance can be granted or conceived.

«««—»»»

As mentioned above, 'God' is in fact equated with 'Nature'. For example:

> For the eternal and infinite Being, which we call *God or Nature*, acts by the same necessity as that whereby it exists. For we have shown, that by the same necessity of its nature, whereby it exists, it likewise works. The reason or cause why *God or Nature* exists, and the reason why he acts, are one and the same. Therefore, as he does not exist for the sake of an end, so neither does he act for the sake of an end; of his existence and of his action there is neither origin nor end. ... (Part IV, Preface)

So God/Nature simply 'is', and does not exist or act toward any pre-established ends or purposes. Similarly, the things of the natural world – animals, plants, minerals – are not made for any purpose, let alone for *human* purpose. He attacks the "misconception" that things were made by God for man:

> All such opinions spring from the notion commonly entertained, that all things in nature act as men themselves act, namely, with an end in view. It is accepted as certain, that God himself directs all things to a certain end, for they say that God has made all things for man, and man that he might worship God. ...
>
> Further, as [men] find in themselves and outside themselves many means which assist them...in their search for what is useful, for instance, eyes for seeing, teeth for chewing, herbs and animals for yielding food, the sun for giving light, the sea for breeding fish, etc., they consider all natural things as means to their own advantage. Now as they are aware, that they found these conveniences and did not make them, they think they have cause for believing that some other being has made them for their use. As they look upon things as means, they cannot believe them to be self-created; but, judging from the means which they are accustomed to prepare for them-

selves, they are bound to believe in some ruler or rulers of the universe, endowed with human freedom, who have arranged and adapted everything for human use. (Part I, Appendix)

There is an important point of distinction here, however. Spinoza is not objecting to the use of natural things, but rather to the notion that 'God made things for us'. Spinoza still believes that it is acceptable, for example, to kill animals for human purposes:

> [I]t is plain that the law against the slaughtering of animals is founded rather on vain superstition and womanish pity than on sound reason. The rational quest of what is useful to us further teaches us the necessity of associating ourselves with our fellowmen, but not with beasts, or things, whose nature is different from our own; we have the same rights in respect to them as they have in respect to us. Nay, as everyone's right is defined by his virtue, or power, men have far greater rights over beasts than beasts have over men. Still I do not deny that beasts feel: what I deny is, that we may not consult our own advantage and use them as we please, treating them in the way which best suits us; for their nature is not like ours, and their emotions are naturally different from human emotions. (Part IV, Prop 37, Note 1).
>
> Besides men, we know of no particular thing in Nature in whose mind we may rejoice, and whom we can associate with ourselves in friendship or any sort of fellowship; therefore, whatsoever there be in Nature besides man, a regard for our advantage does not call on us to preserve, but to preserve or destroy according to its various capabilities, and to adapt to our use as best we may. (Part IV, Appendix 26)

«‹‹—›»›

The final point of significance relates to Spinoza's theory of *mind*. Notice in the last two passages above he says, "I do not deny that beasts feel"; and he implies that, "besides men", other natural things have "minds" (though not of the same level of sophistication).

Spinoza in fact believed that *all* things possess 'minds', that everything is animate. This is clearly stated in Part II, Prop 13 (Scholium):

> We thus comprehend, not only that the human mind is united to the body, but also the nature of the union between mind and body. However, no one will be able to grasp this adequately or distinctly, unless he first has adequate knowledge of the nature of our body.

31

> The propositions we have advanced hitherto have been entirely general, applying not more to men than to other individual things, all of which, though in different degrees, are animated [*animata*].

As we said, God/Nature has infinitely many attributes, but only two of these – "thought" and "extension" – are knowable. 'Mind' is a part of thought, and 'body' is a part of extension. But humans are not unlike other natural things; we are all manifestations of "one substance", we all exist "in God", and therefore *we all possess all attributes* (as does God/Nature).

Just as our body has an 'image' within the attribute of thought (that which we call our 'mind'), so too all things have an 'image' in thought – their 'minds'. In this sense, *all things are animated*: 'panpsychism.'

«««—»»»

The fact that all things have minds does not mean that they all can 'think' or 'reason'. They can, however, act in at least two related ways: the first is to *seek to preserve themselves*. This is Spinoza's theory of *conatus* (a tendency or striving):

> Part III, Prop 6: Everything, in so far as it is in itself, endeavors to persist in its own being.

The second effect of mind is to *enhance the power of the body*:

> Part III, Prop 12: The mind as far as it can, strives to imagine those things that increase or aid the body's power of acting.

The meaning of these two tendencies is reasonably clear for living things, but is rather cryptic with respect to, say, a stone or a mountain.

Thus Spinoza seems to offer *two* justifications for seeing a kind of intrinsic value in all things:

pantheism: everything is part of a single, divine substance (God/Nature), and
panpsychism: everything has a mind.

This said, we are still justified (on his view) in our use and even destruction, when warranted, of other things in nature. So clearly their intrinsic value is not an ultimate value; it is still seen as subservient to human values and wants.

THE HISTORICAL ROOTS OF OUR ECOLOGIC CRISIS

LYNN WHITE, JR. (1967)

A conversation with Aldous Huxley not infrequently put one at the receiving end of an unforgettable monologue. About a year before his lamented death he was discoursing on a favorite topic: Man's unnatural treatment of nature and its sad results. To illustrate his point he told how, during the previous summer, he had returned to a little valley in England where he had spent many happy months as a child. Once it had been composed of delightful grassy glades; now it was becoming overgrown with unsightly brush because the rabbits that formerly kept such growth under control had largely succumbed to a disease, myxomatosis, that was deliberately introduced by the local farmers to reduce the rabbits' destruction of crops. Being something of a Philistine, I could be silent no longer, even in the interests of great rhetoric. I interrupted to point out that the rabbit itself had been brought as a domestic animal to England in 1176, presumably to improve the protein diet of the peasantry.

All forms of life modify their contexts. The most spectacular and benign instance is doubtless the coral polyp. By serving its own ends, it has created a vast undersea world favorable to thousands of other kinds of animals and plants. Ever since man became a numerous species he has affected his environment notably. The hypothesis that his fire-drive method of hunting created the world's great grasslands and helped to exterminate the monster mammals of the Pleistocene from much of the globe is plausible, if not proved. For 6 millennia at least, the banks of the lower Nile have been a human artifact rather than the swampy African jungle which nature, apart from man, would have made it. The Aswan Dam, flooding 5000 square miles, is only the latest stage in a long process. In many regions terracing or irrigation, overgrazing, the cutting of forests by Romans to build ships to fight Carthaginians or by Crusaders to solve the logistics problems of their expeditions, have profoundly changed some ecologies. Observation that the French landscape falls into two basic types, the open fields of the north and the *bocage* of the south and west, inspired Marc Bloch to undertake his classic study of medieval agricultural methods. Quite unintentionally, changes in human ways often affect nonhuman nature. It has been noted, for example, that the advent of the automobile eliminated huge flocks of sparrows that once fed on the horse manure littering every street.

The history of ecologic change is still so rudimentary that we know little about what really happened, or what the results were. The extinction of the European aurochs as late as 1627 would seem to have been a simple case of overenthusiastic hunting. On more intricate matters it often is impossible to find solid information. For a thousand years or more the Frisians and Hollanders have been pushing back the

North Sea, and the process is culminating in our own time in the reclamation of the Zuider Zee. What, if any, species of animals, birds, fish, shore life, or plants have died out in the process? In their epic combat with Neptune have the Netherlanders overlooked ecological values in such a way that the quality of human life in the Netherlands has suffered? I cannot discover that the questions have ever been asked, much less answered.

People, then, have often been a dynamic element in their own environment, but in the present state of historical scholarship we usually do not now exactly when, where, or with what effects man-induced changes came. As we enter the last third of the 20th century, however, concern for the problem of ecologic backlash is mounting feverishly. Natural science, conceived as the effort to understand the nature of things, had flourished in several eras and among several peoples. Similarly, there had been an age-old accumulation of technological skills, sometimes growing rapidly, sometimes slowly. But it was not until about four generations ago that Western Europe and North America arranged a marriage between science and technology, a union of the theoretical and the empirical approaches to our natural environment. The emergence in widespread practice of the Baconian creed that scientific knowledge means technological power over nature can scarcely be dated before about 1850, save in the chemical industries, where it is anticipated in the 18th century. Its acceptance as a normal pattern of action may mark the greatest event in human history since the invention of agriculture and perhaps in nonhuman terrestrial history as well.

Almost at once the new situation forced the crystallization of the novel concept of ecology; indeed, the word ecology first appeared in the English language in 1873. Today, less than a century later, the impact of our race upon the environment has so increased in force that it has changed in essence. When the first cannons were fired, in the early 14th century, they affected ecology by sending workers scrambling to the forests and mountains for more potash, sulfur, iron ore, and charcoal, with some resulting erosion and deforestation. Hydrogen bombs are of a different order: a war fought with them might alter the genetics of all life on this planet. By 1285 London had a smog problem arising from the burning of soft coal, but our present combustion of fossil fuels threatens to change the chemistry of the globe's atmosphere as a whole, with consequences which we are only beginning to guess. With the population explosion, the carcinoma of planless urbanism, the now geological deposits of sewage and garbage, surely no creature other than man has ever manages to foul its nest in such short order.

There are many calls to action, but specific proposals, however worthy as individual items, seem too partial, palliative, negative: ban the bomb, tear down the billboards, give the Hindus contraceptives and tell them to eat their sacred cows. The simplest solution to any suspect changes is, of course, to stop it, or, better yet, to revert to a romanticized past: make those ugly gasoline stations look like Anne Hathaway's cottage or (in the Far West) like ghost-town saloons. The "wilderness area" mentality invariably advocates deep-freezing an ecology, whether San Gimignano or the High Sierra, as it was before the first Kleenex was dropped. But neither atavism nor prettification will cope with the ecologic crisis of our time.

What shall we do? No one yet knows. Unless we think about fundamentals, our

The Historical Roots of Our Ecologic Crisis

specific measures may produce new backlashes more serious than those they are designed to remedy.

As a beginning we should try to clarify our thinking by looking, in some historical depth, at the presuppositions that underlie modern technology and science. Science was traditionally aristocratic, speculative, intellectual in intent; technology was lower-class, empirical, action-oriented. The quite sudden fusion of these two, towards the middle of the 19th century, is surely related to the slightly prior and contemporary democratic revolutions which, by reducing social barriers, tended to assert a functional unity of brain and hand. Our ecologic crisis is the product of an emerging, entirely novel democratic culture. The issue is whether a democratized world can survive its own implications. Presumably we cannot unless we rethink our axioms.

The Western Traditions of Technology and Science

One thing is so certain that it seems stupid to verbalize it: both modern technology and modern science are distinctively *Occidental*. Our technology has absorbed elements from all over the world, notably from China; yet everywhere today, whether in Japan or in Nigeria, successful technology is Western. Our science is the heir to all the sciences of the past, especially perhaps to the work of the great Islamic scientists of the Middle Ages, who so often outdid the ancient Greeks in skill and perspicacity: al-Razi in medicine, for example; of ibn-al-Haytham in optics; or Omar Khayam in mathematics. Indeed, not a few works of such geniuses seem to have vanished in the original Arabic and to survive only in medieval Latin translations that helped to lay the foundations for later Western developments. Today, around the globe, all significant science is Western in style and method, whatever the pigmentation or language of the scientists.

A second pair of facts is less well recognized because they result from quite recent historical scholarship. The leadership of the West, both in technology and in science, is far older than the so-called Scientific Revolution of the 17th century or the so-called Industrial revolution of the 18th century. These terms are in fact outmoded and obscure the true nature of what they try to describe—significant stages in two long and separate developments. By A.D. 1000 at the latest—and perhaps, feebly, as much as 200 years earlier—the West began to apply water power to industrial processes other than milling grain. This was followed in the late 12th century by harnessing of wind power. From simple beginnings, but with remarkable consistency of style, the West rapidly expanded its skills in the development of power machinery, labor-saving devices, and automation. Those who doubt should contemplate that most monumental achievement in the history of automation: the weight-driven mechanical clock, which appeared two forms in the early 14th century. Not in craftsmanship but in the basic technological capacity, the Latin West of the later Middle Ages far outstripped its elaborate, sophisticated, and esthetically magnificent sister cultures, Byzantium and Islam. In 1444 a great Greek ecclesiastic, Bessarion, who had gone to Italy, wrote a letter to a prince in Greece. He is amazed by the superiority of Western ships, arms, textiles, glass. But above all he is astonished by the spectacle of waterwheels sawing timbers and pumping the bellows of blast furnaces. Clearly, he had seen nothing of the sort in the Near East.

By the end of the 15th century the technological superiority of Europe was such that its small, mutually hostile nations could spill out over all the rest of the world, conquering, looting, and colonizing. The symbol of this technological superiority is the fact that Portugal, one of the weakest states of the Occident, was able to become, and to remain for a century, mistress of the East Indies. And we must remember that the technology of Vasco da Gama and Albuquerque was built by pure empiricism, drawing remarkably little support of inspiration from science.

In the present-day vernacular understanding, modern science is supposed to have begun in 1543, when both Copernicus and Besalius published their great works. It is no derogation of their accomplishments, however, to point out that such structures as the *Fabrica* and the *De revolutionibus* do not appear overnight. The distinctive western tradition of science, in fact, began in the late 11th century with a massive movement of translation of Arabic and Greek scientific works into Latin. A few notable books—Theophrastus, for example—escaped the West's avid appetite for science, but within less than 200 years effectively the entire corpus of Greek and Muslim science was available in Latin, and was being eagerly read and criticized in the new European universities. Out of criticism arose new observation, speculation, and increasing distrust of ancient authorities. By the late 13th century Europe had seized global scientific leadership from the faltering hands of Islam. It would be as absurd to deny the profound originality of Newton, Galileo, or Copernicus as to deny that of the 14th century scholastic scientists like Buridan or Oresme on whose work they built. Before the 11th century, science scarcely existed in the Latin West, even in Roman times. From the 11th century onward the scientific sector of Occidental culture has increased in a steady crescendo.

Since both our technological and our scientific movements got their start, acquired their character, and achieved world dominance in the Middle Ages, it would seem that we cannot understand their nature or their present impact upon ecology without examining fundamental medieval assumption and developments.

Medieval View of Man and Nature

Until recently, agriculture has been the chief occupation even in "advanced" societies; hence, any change in methods of tillage has much importance. Early plows, drawn by two oxen, did not normally turn the sod but merely scratched it. Thus, cross-plowing was needed and fields tended to be squarish. In the fairly light soils and semiarid climates of the Near East and Mediterranean, this worked well. But such a plow was inappropriate to the wet climate and often sticky soils of northern Europe. By the latter part of the 7th century after Christ, however, following obscure beginnings, certain northern peasants were using an entirely new kind of plow, equipped with a vertical knife to cut the line of the furrow, a horizontal share to slice under the sod, and a moldboard to turn it over. The friction of this plow with the soil was so great that it normally required not two but eight oxen. It attacked the land with such violence that cross-plowing was not needed, and fields tended to be shaped in long strips.

The Historical Roots of Our Ecologic Crisis

In the days of the scratch-plow, fields were distributed generally in units capable of supporting a single family. Subsistence farming was the presupposition. But no peasant owned eight oxen: to use the new and more efficient plow, peasants pooled their oxen to form large plow-teams, originally receiving (it would appear) plowed strips in proportion to their contribution. Thus, distribution of land was based no longer on the needs of a family but, rather, on the capacity of a power machine to till the earth. Man's relation to the soil was profoundly changed. Formerly man had been part of nature; now he was the exploiter of nature. Nowhere else in the world did farmers develop any analogous agricultural implement. Is it coincidence that modern technology, with its ruthlessness toward nature, has so largely been produced by descendants of these peasants of northern Europe?

This same exploitive attitude appears slightly before A.D. 830 in Western illustrated calendars. In older calendars the months were shown as passive personifications. The new Frankish calendars, which set the style for the Middle Ages, are very different: they show men coercing the world around them—plowing, harvesting, chopping trees, butchering pigs. Man and nature are two things, and man is master.

These novelties seem to be in harmony with larger intellectual patterns. What people do about their ecology depends on what they think about themselves in relation to things around them. Human ecology is deeply conditioned by beliefs about our nature and destiny—that is, by religion. To western eyes this is very evident in, say, India or Ceylon. It is equally true of ourselves and of our medieval ancestors.

The victory of Christianity over paganism was the greatest psychic revolution in the history of our culture. It has become fashionable today to say that, for better or worse, we live in "the post-Christian age." Certainly the forms of our thinking and language have largely ceased to be Christian, but to my eye the substance often remains amazingly akin to that of the past. Our daily habits of action, for example, are dominated by an implicit faith in perpetual progress which was unknown either to Greco-Roman antiquity of to the Orient. It is rooted in, and is indefensible apart from, Judeo-Christian teleology. The fact that Communists share it merely helps to show what can be demonstrated on many other grounds: that Marxism, like Islam, is a Judeo-Christian heresy. We continue today to live, as we have lived for about 1700 years, very largely in a context of Christian axioms.

What did Christianity tell people about their relations with the environment?

While many of the world's mythologies provide stories of creation, Greco-Roman mythology was singularly coherent in this respect. Like Aristotle, the intellectuals of the ancient West denied that the visible world had had a beginning. Indeed, the idea of a beginning was impossible in the framework of their cyclical notion of time. In sharp contrast, Christianity inherited from Judaism not only a concept of time as nonrepetitive and linear but also a striking story of creation. By gradual stages a loving and all-powerful God had created light and darkness, the heavenly bodies, the earth and all its plants, animals, birds, and fishes. Finally, god had created Adam and, as an afterthought, Eve to keep man from being lonely. Man named all the animals, thus establishing his dominance over them. God planned all of this explicitly for man's benefit and rule: no item in the physical creation had any purpose save to serve man's purposes. And, although man's body is made of clay, he is not simply pat of nature: he is made in God's image.

Especially in its Western form, Christianity is the most anthropocentric religion the world has seen. As early as the 2nd century both Tertulian and Saint Irenaeus of Lyons were insisting that when God shaped Adam he was foreshadowing the image of the incarnate Christ, the Second Adam. Man shares, in great measure, God's transcendence of nature. Christianity in absolute contrast to ancient paganism and Asia's religions (except perhaps Zoroastrianism), not only established a dualism of man and nature but also insisted that it is God's will that man exploit nature for his proper ends.

At the level of the common people this worked out in an interesting way. In Antiquity every tree, every spring, every stream, every hill had it's own *genius loci*, its guardian spirit. These spirits were accessible to men, but were very unlike men; centaurs, fauns, and mermaids show their ambivalence. Before one cut a tree, mined a mountain, or dammed a brook, it was important to placate the spirit in charge of that particular situation, and to keep it placated. By destroying pagan animism, Christianity made it possible to exploit nature in a mood of indifference to the feelings of natural objects.

It is often said that for animism the Church substituted the cult of saints. True; but the cult of saints is functionally quite different from animism. The saint is not *in* natural object; he may have special shrines, but his citizenship is in heaven. Moreover, a saint is entirely a man; he can be approached in human terms. In addition to saints, Christianity of course also had angels and demons inherited from Judaism and perhaps, at one remove, from Zoroastrianism. But these were all as mobile as the saints themselves. The spirits *in* natural objects, which formerly had protected nature from man, evaporated. Man's effective monopoly on spirit in this world was confirmed, and the old inhibitions to the exploitation of nature crumbled.

When one speaks in such sweeping terms, a note of caution is in order. Christianity is a complex faith, and its consequences differ in differing contexts. What I have said may well apply to the medieval West, where in fact technology made spectacular advances. But the Greek East, a highly civilized realm of equal Christian devotion, seems to have produced no marked technological innovation after the late 7th century, when Greek fire was invented. The key to the contrast may perhaps be found in a difference in the tonality of piety and thought which students of comparative theology find between the Greek and the Latin Churches. The Greeks believed that sin was intellectual blindness, and that salvation was found in illumination, orthodoxy—that is, clearly thinking. The Latins, on the other hand, felt that sin was moral evil, and that salvation was to be found in right conduct. Eastern theology has been intellectualist. Western Theology has been voluntarist. The Greek saint contemplates; the Western saint acts. The implications of Christianity for the conquest of nature would emerge more easily in the Western atmosphere.

The Christian dogma of creation, which is found in the first clause of all the Creeds, has another meaning for out comprehension of today's ecologic crisis. By revelation, God had given man the Bible, the Book of Scripture. But since God had made nature, nature also must reveal the divine mentality. The religious study of nature for the better understanding of God was known as natural theology. In the early Church, and always in the Greek East, nature was conceived primarily as a symbolic system through which God speaks to men: the ant is a sermon to sluggards; rising flames are the symbol of the soul's aspiration. This view of nature was essentially artistic rather than scientific. While Byzantium preserved and copied great numbers of ancient Greek scientific texts, science as we conceive it could scarcely flourish in such an ambience.

However, in the Latin West by the early 13th century natural theology was following a very different bent. It was ceasing to be the decoding of the physical symbols of God's communication with man and was becoming the effort to understand God's mind by discovering how his creation operates. The rainbow was no longer simply a symbol of hope first sent to Noah after the Deluge: Robert Grosseteste, Friar Roger Bacon, and Theodoric of Freiberg produced startlingly sophisticated work on the optics of the rainbow, but they did it as a venture in religious understanding. From the 13th century onward, up to and including Leibniz and Newton, every major scientist, in effect, explained his motivations in religious terms. Indeed, if Galileo had not been so expert an amateur theologian he would have got into far less trouble: the professionals resented his intrusion. And Newton seems to have regarded himself more as a theologian than as a scientist. It was not until the late 18th century that the hypothesis of God became unnecessary to many scientists.

It is often hard for the historian to judge, when men explain why they are doing what they want to do, whether they are offering real reasons or merely culturally acceptable reasons. The consistency with which scientists during the long formative centuries of western science said that the task and the reward of the scientist was "to think God's thoughts after him" leads one to believe that this was their real motivation. If so, then modern Western science was cast in a matrix of Christian theology. The dynamism of religious devotion, shaped by the Judeo-Christian dogma of creation, gave it impetus.

An Alternative Christian View

We would seem to be headed toward conclusions unpalatable to many Christians. Since both *science* and *technology* are blessed words in our contemporary vocabulary, some may be happy at the notions, first, that, viewed historically, modern science is an extrapolation of natural theology and, second, that modern technology is at least partly to be explained as an Occidental, voluntarist realization of the Christian dogma of man's transcendence of, and rightful mastery over, nature. But, as we now recognize, somewhat over a century ago science and technology—hitherto quite separate activities—joined to give mankind powers which, to judge by many of the ecologic effects, are out of control. If so, Christianity bears a huge burden of guilt.

I personally doubt that disastrous ecologic backlash can be avoided simply by applying to our problems more science and more technology. Our science and technology have grown out of Christian attitudes toward man's relation to nature which are almost universally held not only by Christians and neo-Christians but also by those who fondly regard themselves as post-Christians. Despite Copernicus, all the cosmos rotates around out little globe. Despite Darwin, we are *not*, in our hearts, part of the natural process. We are superior to nature, contemptuous of it, willing to use it for our slightest whim. The newly elected Governor of California, like myself a churchman but less troubled than I, spoke for the Christian tradition when he said (as is alleged), "when you've seen one redwood tree, you've seen them all." To a Christian a tree can be no more than a physical fact. The whole concept of the sacred grove is alien to Christianity and to the ethos of the West. For nearly 2 millennia Christian missionaries have been chopping down sacred groves, which are idolatrous because they assume spirit in nature.

What we do about ecology depends on our ideas of the man-nature relationship. More science and more technology are not going to get us out of the present ecologic crisis until we find a new religion, or rethink our old one. The beatniks, who are the basic revolutionaries of our time, show a sound instinct in their affinity for Zen Buddhism, which conceives of the man-nature relationship as very nearly the mirror image of the Christian view. Zen, however, is as deeply conditioned by Asian history as Christianity is by the experience of the West, and I am dubious of its viability among us.

Possibly we should ponder the greatest radical in Christian history since Christ: Saint Francis of Assisi. The prime miracle of Saint Francis is the fact that he did not end at the stake, as many of his left-wing followers did. He was so clearly heretical that a General of the Franciscan Order, Saint Bonaventura, a great and perceptive Christian, tried to suppress the early accounts of Franciscanism. The key to an understanding of Francis is his belief in the virtue of humility—not merely for the individual but for man as a species. Francis tried to depose man from his monarchy over creation and set up a democracy of all God's creatures. With him the ant is no longer simply a homily for the lazy, flames a sign of the thrust of the soul toward union with God; now they are Brother Ant and Sister Fire, praising the Creator in their own ways as Brother man does.

Later commentators have said that Francis preached to the birds as a rebuke to men who would not listen. The records do not read so: he urged the little birds to praise God, and in spiritual ecstasy they flapped their wings and chirped rejoicing. Legends of saints, especially the Irish saints, had long told of their dealings with animals but always, I believe, to show their human dominance over creatures. With Francis it is different. The land around Gubbio in the Apennines was being ravaged by a fierce wolf. Saint Francis, says the legend, talked to the wolf and persuaded him of the error of his ways. The wolf repented, died in the odor of sanctity, and was buried in consecrated ground.

What Sir Steven Runciman calls "the Franciscan doctrine of the animal soul" was quickly stamped out. Quite possibly it was in part inspired, consciously or unconsciously, by the belief in reincarnation held by the Cathar heretics who at that time teemed in Italy and southern France, and who presumably had got it originally from India. It is significant that at just the same moment, about 1200, traces of metempsychosis are found also in western Judaism, in the Provencal *Cabbala*. But Francis held neither to transmigration of souls nor to pantheism. His view of nature and of man rested on a unique sort of panpsychism of all things animate and inanimate, designed for the glorification of their transcendent Creator, who, in the ultimate gesture of cosmic humility, assumed flesh, lay helpless in a manger, and hung dying on a scaffold.

The Historical Roots of Our Ecologic Crisis

I am not suggesting that many contemporary Americans who are concerned about our ecologic crisis will be either able or willing to counsel with wolves or exhort birds. However, the present increasing disruption of the global environment is the product of a dynamic technology and science which were originating in the Western medieval world against which Saint Francis was rebelling in so original a way. Their growth cannot be understood historically apart form distinctive attitudes toward nature which are deeply grounded in Christian dogma. The fact that most people do not think of these attitudes as Christian is irrelevant. No new set of basic values has been accepted in our society to displace those of Christianity. Hence we shall continue to have a worsening ecologic crisis until we reject the Christian axiom that nature has no reason for existence save to serve man.

The greatest spiritual revolutionary in Western history, Saint Francis, proposed what he thought was an alternative Christian view of nature and man's relation to it: he tried to substitute the idea of the equality of all creatures, including man, for the idea of man's limitless rule of creation. He failed. Both our present science and our present technology are so tinctured with orthodox Christian arrogance toward nature that no solution for our ecologic crisis can be expected from them alone. Since the roots of our trouble are so largely religious, the remedy must also be essentially religious, whether we call it that or not. We must rethink and refeel our nature and destiny. The profoundly religious, but heretical, sense of the primitive Franciscans for the spiritual autonomy of all parts of nature may point a direction. I propose Francis as a patron saint for ecologists.

KNOWLEDGE & VALUES

HENRYK SKOLIMOWSKI (1975)

> Where is the wisdom
> We have lost in knowledge?
> Where is the knowledge
> We have lost in information?
> —T. S. Eliot

Let us begin with certain distinctions that are fundamental to the scientific world-view and are at the same time responsible for many of our present problems, conceptual and otherwise. One is the distinction between knowledge and values. The separation of these two was a momentous event in the intellectual history of the West, leading as it did to the emancipation of specialized scientific disciplines from the body of natural philosophy. But it was a perilous event, too, in that it led in the long run to a conception of the universe as a clock-like mechanism and to the gradual elimination of these elements of our knowledge which disagreed with that mechanistic view — including intrinsic values, which were replaced by instrumental values.

Logically there would seem to have been two different processes involved: intense exploration of the physical world on the one hand and the slow disappearance of intrinsic human values on the other. This logical separation is misleading, however, for what we witness here are two aspects of the same process. The quest for scientific explanations and the growth in importance of the physical sciences coincided with, indeed took place in the context of a decline in the importance of intrinsic values. Our vast store of knowledge of the physical world can thus be said to have been accumulated at the expense of human values. This is a large claim, and the present essay will attempt to justify it. Also, I shall argue that there appears to be a see-saw relationship between factual knowledge and intrinsic human values: as one goes up, the other is pushed down. If this perception is correct, then it would follow that the resurrection of intrinsic values and their reinstatement at the centre of our lives may indeed come about but that it will be at the expense of our adulation of science and of the physical fact, which we have exaggeratedly elevated to the status of deities.

Basic Historical Positions

Historically we can distinguish at least four basic positions regarding the relation of values to knowledge.

The first is the position of classical antiquity as exemplified by Plato: values and knowledge are fused together; one does not become dominant or subservient to the other. As we know, Plato believed in the unity of truth, goodness and beauty. Within his universe values and knowledge are two aspects of the same thing. No knowledge is then value-free; and no values can be regarded as void of knowledge. According to Plato, to possess superior knowledge is to lead a superior life. Knowledge is a vital part of the network of life. Most sins are the fruits of ignorance.

In the Middle Ages we can distinguish the second position: knowledge is fused with values, but at the same time it is subordinated to values which are determined by the Church. Knowledge is then in the service of values and must agree with values a priori accepted as supreme. To grasp God's design, God's order, and the values that follow from this order sometimes required faculties stronger than the mere human intellect, which at times saw discrepancies between natural reason and God's order. Hence revelation was accepted as a mode of cognition, for it allowed one to transcend reason and to find a justification for the fusion of knowledge and values under the supremacy of values.

The remaining two positions can be clearly discerned in the post-Renaissance period. The third position separates knowledge from values, without, however, giving supremacy to either. This position is perhaps best represented by Immanuel Kant (1720-1804), who clearly saw in Newtonian physics indubitable knowledge governing the behaviour of the physical universe—a separate realm unto itself; but who, at the same time, would not submit the autonomy and sovereignty of man to any deterministic set of physical laws. Hence he summarised the autonomy of both realms by announcing: "The starry heavens above you and the moral law within."

The fourth position is, of course, the one held by classical empiricism and its more recent extensions: 19th century positivism and 20th century logical empiricism. This position separates values from knowledge and, by attaching a supreme importance to physical knowledge and by ruling that values are not proper knowledge, it ipso facto establishes the primacy of knowledge over values. This tradition is so near to us and envelops so constantly and consistently that we are often unable to see through it so as to assess its impact on us.

In summary, the four basic positions are:

- Plato — the fusion of knowledge with values without ascertaining the primacy of one over the other;
- Christianity — the fusion of the two by ascertaining the primacy of values;
- Kant — the separation of the two without censure of either;
- empiricism — the separation of values from knowledge while ascertaining the primacy of (factual) knowledge over values.

It is, of course, the empiricist position, or the empiricist tradition that we want to examine in some detail, for this is the tradition that looms largest on our intellectual horizons; this is the tradition that has become our intellectual orthodoxy, the tradition that, so to speak, has been programmed into our ways of thinking and judging, the tradition that has brought the value-vacuum to our society, to our universities, to our individual lives. These are large claims and need to be substantiated. We cannot substantiate them by taking a textbook on philosophy, inspecting the content of empiricist doctrines, and then attempting to determine in what way these doctrines are affecting our lives and our views.

The life of cultures and societies is an exceedingly complex affair. What we must do is to unravel the multitude of causes and effects and then see how the original visions and insights (of Bacon, Galileo, Descartes, etc.) have given rise to larger doctrines, been channeled into various tributaries of learning and life, reinforced and strengthened in process; and how it still feeds upon itself by outlining the boundaries of its territory and maintaining a rigid control on what is legitimate within the territory and what is illegitimate. To give two specific examples: the research into chemical warfare is "legitimate", for it is an extension of "objective knowledge" into the sphere of "some chemicals"; the research on acupuncture is not "legitimate", because the phenomenon itself seems to undermine more of the fundamental tenets of the empiricist world view. The connection between a particular phenomenon, or a particular strategy, and the basic tenets of the world view is indirect and is usually several steps removed, but it is there, if we have the patience and perseverance to look for it.

As strange as it may seem, this connection is often more readily grasped by intellectually "unsophisticated" rebellious youth than by the "sophisticated" minds that govern present academia. It is rather remarkable that, on the basis of some inner moral feedback, young people can sometimes react with strong moral revulsion, and the certitude of their moral stand, to abuses of knowledge in academia and elsewhere while academia itself seems often oblivious of the fact.

I have sketched the line from Francis Bacon to B. F. Skinner as if it were one uninterrupted, homogeneous development; as if the present predicament were the result of some inexorable logical process. The process was far from homogeneous. What is really startling is the fact that, in spite of a great variety of opposing intellectual forces, the scientific-empiricist world view has prevailed so remarkably.

Quite parallel to the empiricist tradition that has prevailed, there ran and still does run, the other tradition, which for the lack of a better term we shall call anti-empiricist. This tradition was represented by minds at least as powerful and superlative as was the empiricist. Pascal, Leibniz and Spinoza in the 17th century, Rousseau and Kant in the 18th century, Hegel and Nietzsche in the 19th century were all seeking a world liberated from the constraints of scholastic theology, but which would not be reduced to quantity and measure.

Pascal's case is particularly illuminating, for he, more clearly than perhaps anyone else in the 17th century, saw the great value and the great attraction of science and, at the same time, the great danger in unconditional submission to science. He wrote: "Knowledge of physical science will not console me for ignorance of morality in time of affliction, but knowledge of morality will always console me for ignorance of physical science." (*Pensees*, 23)

Equally illuminating is Spinoza's case. His *Ethics* is the work in which he argues that the good is everything which furthers knowledge, and vice versa. Happiness consists solely in knowledge. Virtue itself is knowledge. "Happiness is not a reward for virtue, but virtue itself." He further argues that love can be conceived as the perfectibility of man through knowledge, for knowledge induces love — a position not far removed from Plato's. What is most curious about Spinoza's *Ethics* is that it attempts to prove its propositions as if it were a textbook of geometry. Though profoundly departing from the scientific tradition which later was to prevail, Spinoza paid lip service to it (and more than that), attempting to give geometrical (scientific?) demonstrations to his ethical convictions.

In the 18th century Rousseau and Kant defended, in their respective ways, the autonomy of the human world against the encroachment of the mechanistic world view and the spreading wave of empiricism. Of the two, Rousseau was the flamboyant one, while Kant was the incisive one. Rousseau eloquently, and sometimes dramatically, protested against "civilization", which he thought estranged man from his essence and from his fellow men. The "artificial" ways that civilization imposes on us are at the source of individual and social alienation. This was a prelude to 20th century outcries against science and technology imposing on us their artificial ways.

The Eclipse of Values in the 19th Century

The 19th century marks the triumph of science and technology and the unprecedented spread of the scientific world view. The aggressive assertion of positivism and materialism, of which Marxism was a part; of scientific rationality and technological efficiency; of the age of industrialisation, which, alas, happened to be the age of environmental devastation, were all pointing to a brave new world in which traditional (intrinsic) values are sent to limbo. We need to examine this process more closely in order to understand why the triumphs of science had to signify an eclipse of values.

Science did not develop in a social vacuum but as part of the unfolding new culture. The battle against petrified aspects of institutionalised religion was going on in the 17th and 18th centuries, as well as, and indeed with greater intensity, in the 19th century, which was more aggressive and successful in containing the influence of religion in the realm of thought than was true in the previous two centuries. The secular, rational, science-based world view mounted itself firmly onto the stage. The rest seemed merely a matter of implementation. The time appeared to be near when paradise on earth would prevail.

The battle between science and religion was by no means limited only to intellectual matters, to means of interpreting the world around us. It was also an ideological battle; and it was an eschatological battle, for what was at stake were the ends of man's life. Religion represented the status quo, it was turned inward, it urged man to perfect himself, and to seek the ultimate reward in the afterlife. Science represented the on-going process of change, it was turned outward, and it promised salvation here on earth. In this process religion was often in an alliance with intrinsic values, supported them and was supported by them. On the other hand, science was in an alliance with progress. The corollaries of the two opposing forces of religion and science—intrinsic values on the one hand, and progress on the other—were themselves construed as adversaries. Indeed "progressive" and "revolutionary" individuals of the 19th century debunked with equal vehemence both traditional religion and traditional values, which they somehow identified with the feudal and bourgeois ethos, thus regarding them unworthy of the new epoch, in which toughness, rationality and a no-nonsense pragmatic attitude were called for.

In this climate intrinsic values were somehow regarded as the vestiges of the obsolete world. It is therefore no wonder that new doctrines concerning values attempted, implicitly or explicitly, to serve the scientific world view and to justify its supremacy. Utilitarianism was the doctrine which announced that the basis for our ethics and action should be the principle: the greatest good for the greatest number. Formulated in this way utilitarianism does not seem to signify the submission of ethics to the dictates of science. However, the principle was soon vulgarised to mean: the biggest number of material goods to the largest possible number of people. This is indeed the underlying ethos of the technological, or consumptive society. Thus we can see that utilitarianism has become an adjunct to material progress, its ethical justification; material progress itself is an essential part of the scientific-technological world view. A scrupulous historian might object that this interpretation does violence to the historical meaning of utilitarianism, as expounded by Jeremy Bentham and John Stuart Mill. Ethical doctrines are what they become in actual practice. The ease with which utilitarianism was "instrumentalised" and integrated into the technological society only shows how much it was attuned to the increasingly homogenised brave new world. After all, Bentham and Mill were 19th century empiricists par excellence. Their views embodied all the limitations characteristic of empiricists.

Nihilism and scientism, on the other hand, overtly preached the gospel of Science, enshrined Facts as deities, and condemned all the products of the human spirit as "meaningless" or reactionary.

The intellectual climate of the 20th century — that is of the Western economically developed countries — not only favoured the rise and dominance of materialism. It also somehow inhibited all other individuals from considering values as one of the central concerns of human thought and human life.

One of the great misfortunes of Western thought of the last centuries was to link intrinsic values with institutionalized religion. The bankruptcy of one form of institutionalised religion was tantamount, in the eyes of many, to the bankruptcy of religion as such, and of intrinsic values woven into this religion. This identification was based on a faulty logic. Religion, and especially intrinsic values, are not the tools of the clergy to keep the masses in control (though occasionally they are used to such purposes) but are the forms and structures, worked out over the millennia of human experience, through which the individual can transcend himself and thereby make the most of himself or herself as a human being, through which man's spirituality and humanity can acquire its shape and maintain its vitality, through which we define ourselves as self-transcending beings. As such, as I have argued before, intrinsic values outline and define the scope of our humanity.

Information-Knowledge-Wisdom

Something happened between 1700 and 1900. We divided man into halves. We separated man's knowledge from his essence, from his values, from his transcendental concerns. Knowledge became isolated, put into a special container called brain. This container came to be regarded as a chest of tools: we pick up from this chest this or that tool for the task at hand. There is no longer the unity of man and his knowledge. There are only specialised tools to handle specialised tasks. At this point knowledge becomes mere information. Soon it becomes translated into "bits" of computerised information. The whole process is de-personalised, mechanised, computerised.

The separation of facts from values, of man from his knowledge, of physical phenomena from all "other" phenomena, resulted in the atomisation of the physical world, as well as of the human world. The process of isolation, abstraction and estrangement (of one phenomenon from other phenomena), a precondition of the successful practice of modern natural science, was in fact a process of *conceptual alienation*. This conceptual alienation became in turn human alienation: man estranged himself from his knowledge and his values. Thus the primary cause of contemporary alienation is a mistaken conception of the universe in which everything is separated and divided and in which the human being is equally atomised and divided.

The present compartmentalisation is *unnatural*. In order to restore our sanity and to recompose our divided selves we have to rethink some of the basic premises. To begin with, we have to realise that *the state of one's knowledge is an important characteristic of the state of one's being*. This is a re-statement of the view of knowledge held by Plato, Augustine and Copernicus. This view is still held among primitive societies, notably among some tribes of the American Indians.

The statement that our knowledge is an important aspect of our being, that as total bio-social organisms, we cannot and do not act independently of our knowledge, is not an expression of nostalgia for paradise lost. It is a statement describing the human condition. How can we validate such a claim, particularly in our times when knowledge seems to be so divorced from life? If the integration of relevant knowledge is indispensible for the coherence of one's life, then it simply follows that to deprive people of this knowledge may be the source of confusion and incoherence in their lives. One does not have to be an astute observer to perceive that this is exactly what has happened in the contemporary period. Young people (and not only the young) are lost, confused and alienated because they do not have relevant knowledge to guide them; they do not have a compass, a sense of centre that would make sense of the world around them. Instead they are furnished with bits of information and data, with expertise which they so often find to be irrelevant knowledge.

This is a pathological situation: knowledge does not render enlightenment but confusion: the amassing of information only furthers the process of alienation. The situation is especially pathological because never in the history of mankind has learning (and supposedly knowledge) been pursued on such a vast scale as today, and never has the estrangement of man from the world, and from his fellow man, been greater than today. The cause must lie, then, in the nature of the knowledge we pursue. Knowledge alienated from the human mind and human values in turn de-sensitizes and alienates people who acquire this knowledge.

But let us be very careful when we say that this knowledge is "irrelevant". For in one sense it is very relevant: it is relevant to the economic system which is mainly interested in the maximisation of profit. It is relevant to the technological society as we have known it. It is relevant to the conception of the world as a factory. The system of economic, ecological and human exploitation is not interested in knowledge, let alone wisdom. But it is vitally interested in information and expertise; it is interested in its smooth functioning, which is based on technological efficiency. For this reason we furnish our students and ourselves with information and expertise, not with knowledge.

Let us ask ourselves a most general question at this point. Is there one, underlying reason for this eclipse of values and other pathologies that follow from it? Perhaps the most succinct answer to this question was given by Max Scheler, who said: "To conceive the world as value-free is a task which men set themselves on account of a value: the vital value of mastery and power over things." We realise nowadays that this mastery has been an illusion, that we cannot subdue the world to our will without destroying, or at least seriously impairing ourselves. However, we still maintain and perpetuate the system which was designed for this grand, but ultimately pitiful, folly.

There is another general question which should be raised, namely, the question of the relation of theory to practice. The separation of values from knowledge may be seen as an abstract philosophical matter on one level. But this separation is an indispensable part of the process of turning people into materialists, in order to maintain the present consumptive society and the conception of the world as a factory. Let us not complain that there is no relation between theory and practice. There is: ingenious theories have been created and maintained in order to justify and maintain parasitic practices with regard to other people and nature at large. It should be emphasised that the system is equally parasitic on people and nature at large. It is of the utmost importance that we understand the relation between the economic forces of a society and its conception of nature and of the universe, between our daily practices and the outlook on the world we hold. These larger outlooks, or world views, imposed on us subtly and sometimes insidiously, justify and motivate our daily practices.

And let us be clear that if we accept the scientific world view with its underlying rationality and its extension modern technology — we have lost straight away. For this world view generates and justifies: turning knowledge into information, values into economic commodities, people into experts. The perilous aspect of modern science lies in the consequences it has led to, lies in the requirements and demands that it implicitly makes on people and the eco-system. It is useless to argue that it is not science that did the harm but the people who applied it. Knowledge is inseparable from people. Science has moulded people's minds to as great a degree as people have moulded science. The twilight of scientific reason, which we are witnessing nowadays, is not necessarily the twilight of humanity. Scientific reason will have to wane and to release us from its overpowering tentacles so that we can restore the strained relation between knowledge and values.

Which brings us once more to the phenomenon of knowledge as an inherent aspect of one's being. This phenomenon manifests itself not only in frustrated and alienated youth, whose knowledge does not guide them because they are filled with irrelevant bits of information, but also in the opposite phenomenon: our veneration of and craving for wise people. Wise people are the ones whose knowledge matters, are those who are in the state of being in which knowledge matters, are the integrated ones, in the sense that their knowledge serves them as human beings. We envy them because it is a state difficult to achieve in the contemporary world. Their wisdom is simply the integration of knowledge with values; it is a demonstration that knowledge is not a futile store of information but a vital force that sustains life on all levels of human existence; it is a resurrection of the universal property of knowledge, which can be seen in all animals and pre-industrial societies, namely the unity of life and knowledge.

The re-integration of knowledge with values will have to take place not in order to make each of us a sage, but in order to assure the survival of humanity. It should be transparently clear to us that we shall not be able to cope with the plethora of problems which the present (scientific-technological) mode of our interaction with nature and other people has originated, until we again arrive at a stage in which our knowledge will matter to us as human beings. This will be a knowledge intertwined with values and at their service. This knowledge will be a re-embodiment, on a new level, of Plato's and Augustine's contention that to think correctly is the condition of behaving well; with this proviso however, that to think correctly is not merely an abstract characteristic of the brain but an expression of a state of being; a combination of the intellectual insight and moral power.

This state of being, which is still maintained in wise people, is something akin to the state of grace. The term "grace" is extremely loaded. All "respectable intellectuals" avoid it. But its past religious connotation should not deter us from making good use of it, for this term makes us clearly aware that to think well is not to think dexterously, ruthlessly, logically: to think well requires a special state of mind and of the entire being. This state of mind needs to be cultivated and nurtured as much as we cultivate — in long years of abstract thinking — the mind geared to "scientific objectivity."

We have a great deal to learn from oriental cultures, from the past history of our own civilisation, and from primitive societies alive today, in understanding, acquiring and maintaining this state of mind in which "thinking well is a pre-condition of behaving well." To emphasise, what is at stake is not, the acquisition of another piece of knowledge — or how "other" societies thought and acted — which we shall append to our existing knowledge, but a change in the structure of our knowledge and in the structure of our mind which will lead, so we should like to hope, to the healing of the value knowledge split and to the elimination of a great deal of present alienation.

Should anyone attempt to call this attitude, which we tentatively call "grace", a return to prescientific prejudices, obscurantism or the like, we should reply: why should the state of mind in which abstract entities called "facts" are enshrined as deities be preferable to the state of mind in which intrinsic values are so enshrined? For the state of grace, of which, we have spoken, is another expression for the state of mind in which intrinsic values are enshrined. When we say: "the human being — it sounds noble"; "dignity is an essential component of being human"; "freedom is a necessary requirement of the concept of humanity", we in fact "engrace" man. We have to change the world around us, and the frame of our minds, and the structure of our knowledge so that these expressions are not phrases empty of meaning.

Should this discourse strike someone as too philosophical and abstract, and too difficult to implement, let me answer that there are no easy remedies for the present predicament, the present value-vacuum in particular, which we have brought onto ourselves by pursuing certain philosophical abstractions and then fallen victims to.

Knowledge & Values

During the past three centuries we have redefined the world around ourselves and these redefinitions resulted in the violation of the world around us, and of ourselves. We have to doubt our previous wisdom; specifically we have to discard a great deal of the "wisdom" of the prophets of material progress, for this progress is leading us to doom. We have to obliterate many spurious dichotomies and distinctions, for they are often at the root of alienation in the present world. Above all, we have to restore the unity of knowledge and values.

PART II: TWENTIETH CENTURY ENVIRONMENTALISTS

A SAND COUNTY ALMANAC

ALDO LEOPOLD (1949)

THINKING LIKE A MOUNTAIN

A deep chesty bawl echoes from rimrock to rimrock, rolls down the mountain, and fades into the far blackness of the night. It is an outburst of wild defiant sorrow, and of contempt for all the adversities of the world.

Every living thing (and perhaps many a dead one as well) pays heed to that call. To the deer it is a reminder of the way of all flesh, to the pine a forecast of midnight scuffles and of blood upon the snow, to the coyote a promise of gleanings to come, to the cowman a threat of red ink at the bank, to the hunter a challenge of fang against bullet. Yet behind these obvious and immediate hopes and fears there lies a deeper meaning, known only to the mountain itself. Only the mountain has lived long enough to listen objectively to the howl of a wolf.

Those unable to decipher the hidden meaning know nevertheless that it is there, for it is felt in all wolf country, and distinguishes that country from all other land. It tingles in the spine of all who hear wolves by night, or who scan their tracks by day. Even without sight or sound of wolf, it is implicit in a hundred small events: the midnight whinny of a pack horse, the rattle of rolling rocks, the bound of a fleeing deer, the way shadows lie under the spruces. Only the ineducable tyro can fail to sense the presence or absence of wolves, or the fact that mountains have a secret opinion about them.

My own conviction on this score dates from the day I saw a wolf die. We were eating lunch on a high rimrock, at the foot of which a turbulent river elbowed its way. We saw what we thought was a doe fording the torrent, her breast awash in white water. When she climbed the bank toward us and shook out her tail, we realized our error: it was a wolf. A half-dozen others, evidently grown pups, sprang from the willows and all joined in a welcoming melee of wagging tails and playful maulings. What was literally a pile of wolves writhed and tumbled in the center of an open flat at the foot of our rimrock.

In those days we had never heard of passing up a chance to kill a wolf. In a second we were pumping lead into the pack, but with more excitement than accuracy: how to aim a steep downhill shot is always confusing. When our rifles were empty, the old wolf was down, and a pup was dragging a leg into impassable slide-rocks.

We reached the old wolf in time to watch a fierce green fire dying in her eyes. I realized then, and have known ever since, that there was something new to me in those eyes — something known only to her and to the mountain. I was young then, and full of trigger-itch; I thought that because fewer wolves meant more deer, that no wolves would mean hunters' paradise. But after seeing the green fire die, I sensed that neither the wolf nor the mountain agreed with such a view.

Since then I have lived to see state after state extirpate its wolves. I have watched the face of many a newly wolfless mountain, and seen the south-facing slopes wrinkle with a maze of new deer trails. I have seen every edible bush and seedling browsed, first to anemic destitute, and then to death. I have seen every edible tree defoliated to the height of a saddlehorn. Such a mountain looks as if someone had given God a new pruning shears, and forbidden Him all other exercise. In the end the starved bones of the hoped-for deer herd, dead of its own too-much, bleach with the bones of the dead sage, or molder under the high lined junipers.

I now suspect that just as a deer herd lives in mortal fear of its wolves so does a mountain live in mortal fear of its deer. And perhaps with better cause, for while a buck pulled down by wolves can be replaced in two or three years, a range pulled down by too many deer may fail of replacement in as many decades.

So also with cows. The cowman who cleans his range of wolves does not realize that he is taking over the wolf's job of trimming the herd to fit the range. He has not learned to think like a mountain. Hence we have dustbowls, and rivers washing the future into the sea.

We all strive for safety, prosperity, comfort, long life, and dullness. The deer strives with his supple legs, the cowman with trap and poison, the statesman with pen, the most of us with machines, votes, and dollars, but it all comes to the same thing: peace in our time. A measure of success in this is all well enough, and perhaps is a requisite to objective thinking, but too much safety seems to yield only danger in the long run. Perhaps this is behind Thoreau's dictum: *In wildness is the salvation of the world.* Perhaps this is the hidden meaning in the howl of the wolf, long known among mountains, but seldom perceived among men.

«««—»»»

THE LAND ETHIC

When god-like Odysseus returned from the wars in Troy, he hanged all on one rope a dozen slave-girls of his household whom he suspected of misbehavior during his absence.

This hanging involved no question of propriety. The girls were property. The disposal of property was then, as now, a matter of expediency, not of right and wrong.

Concepts of right and wrong were not lacking from Odysseus' Greece: witness the fidelity of his wife through the long years before at last his black-prowed galleys clove the wine-dark seas for home. The ethical structure of that day covered wives, but had not yet been extended to human chattels. During the three thousand years which have since elapsed, ethical criteria have been extended to many fields of conduct, with corresponding shrinkages in those judged by expediency only.

The Ethical Sequence

This extension of ethics, so far studied only by philosophers, is actually a process in ecological evolution. Its sequences may be described in ecological as well as in philosophical terms. An ethic, ecologically, is a limitation on freedom of action in the struggle for existence. An ethic, philosophically, is a differentiation of social from anti-social conduct. These are two definitions of one thing. The thing has its origin in the tendency of interdependent individuals or groups to evolve modes of co-operation. The ecologist calls these symbioses. Politics and economics are advanced symbioses in which the original free-for-all competition has been replaced, in part, by co-operative mechanisms with an ethical content.

The complexity of co-operative mechanisms has increased with population density, and with the efficiency of tools. It was simpler, for example, to define the anti-social uses of sticks and stones in the days of the mastodons than of bullets and billboards in the age of motors.

The first ethics dealt with the relation between individuals; the Mosaic Decalogue is an example. Later accretions dealt with the relation between the individual and society. The Golden Rule tries to integrate the individual to society; democracy to integrate social organization to the individual.

There is as yet no ethic dealing with man's relation to land and to the animals and plants which grow upon it. Land, like Odysseus' slave-girls, is still property. The land relation is still strictly economic, entailing privileges but not obligations.

The extension of ethics to this third element in human environment is, if I read the evidence correctly, an evolutionary possibility and an ecological necessity. It is the third step in a sequence. The first two have already been taken. Individual thinkers since the days of Ezekiel and Isaiah have asserted that the despoliation of land is not only inexpedient but wrong. Society, however, has not yet affirmed their belief. I regard the present conservation movement as the embryo of such an affirmation.

An ethic may be regarded as a mode of guidance for meeting ecological situations so new or intricate, or involving such deferred reactions, that the path of social expediency is not discernible to the average individual. Animal instincts are modes of guidance for the individual in meeting such situations. Ethics are possibly a kind of community instinct in-the-making.

The Community Concept

All ethics so far evolved rest upon a single premise: that the individual is a member of a community of interdependent parts. His instincts prompt him to compete for his place in that community, but his ethics prompt him also to co-operate (perhaps in order that there may be a place to compete for).

The land ethic simply enlarges the boundaries of the community to include soils, waters, plants, and animals, or collectively: the land.

This sounds simple: do we not already sing our love for and obligation to the land of the free and the home of the brave? Yes, but just what and whom do we love?

Earth Alive

Certainly not the soil, which we are sending helter-skelter downriver. Certainly not the waters, which we assume have no function except to turn turbines, float barges, and carry off sewage. Certainly not the plants, of which we exterminate whole communities without batting an eye. Certainly not the animals, of which we have already extirpated many of the largest and most beautiful species. A land ethic of course cannot prevent the alteration, management, and use of these 'resources,' but it does affirm their right to continued existence, and, at least in spots, their continued existence in a natural state.

In short, a land ethic changes the role of Homo sapiens from conqueror of the land-community to plain member and citizen of it. It implies respect for his fellow members, and also respect for the community as such.

In human history, we have learned (I hope) that the conqueror role is eventually self-defeating. Why? Because it is implicit in such a role that the conqueror knows, ex cathedra, just what makes the community clock tick, and just what and who is valuable, and what and who is worthless, in community life. It always turns out that he knows neither, and this is why his conquests eventually defeat themselves.

In the biotic community, a parallel situation exists. Abraham knew exactly what the land was for: it was to drip milk and honey into Abraham's mouth. At the present moment, the assurance with which we regard this assumption is inverse to the degree of our education.

The ordinary citizen today assumes that science knows what makes the community clock tick; the scientist is equally sure that he does not. He knows that the biotic mechanism is so complex that its workings may never be fully understood.

That man is, in fact, only a member of a biotic team is shown by an ecological interpretation of history. Many historical events, hitherto explained solely in terms of human enterprise were actually biotic interactions between people and land: The characteristics of the land determined the facts quite as potently as the characteristics of the men who lived on it.

Consider, for example, the settlement of the Mississippi valley. In the years following the Revolution, three groups were contending for its control: the native Indian, the French and English traders, and the American settlers. Historians wonder what would have happened if the English at Detroit had thrown a little more weight into the Indian side of those tipsy scales which decided the outcome of the colonial migration into the cane-lands of Kentucky. It is time now to ponder the fact that the cane-lands, when subjected to the particular mixture of forces represented by the cow, plow, fire, and axe of the pioneer, became bluegrass. What if the plant succession inherent in this dark and bloody ground had, under the impact of these forces, given us some worthless sedge, shrub, or weed? Would Boone and Kenton have held out? Would there have been any overflow into Ohio, Indiana, Illinois, and Missouri? Any Louisiana purchase? Any transcontinental union of new states? Any Civil War?

Kentucky was one sentence in the drama of history. We are commonly told what the human actors' in this drama tried to do, but we are seldom told that their success, or the lack of it, hung in large degree on the reaction of particular soils to the impact of the particular forces exerted by their occupancy. In the case of Kentucky, we do not even know where the bluegrass came from-whether it is a native species, or a stowaway from Europe.

Contrast the cane-lands with what hindsight tells us about the Southwest, where the pioneers were equally brave, resourceful, and persevering. The impact of occupancy here brought no bluegrass, or other plant fitted to withstand the bumps and buffetings of hard use. This region, when grazed by livestock, reverted through a series of more and more worthless grasses, shrubs, and weeds to a condition of unstable equilibrium. Each recession of plant types bred erosion; each increment to erosion bred a further recession of plants. The result today is a progressive and mutual deterioration, not only of plants and soils, but of the animal community subsisting thereon. The early settlers did not expect this: on the *cienegas* of New Mexico some even cut ditches to hasten it. So subtle has been its progress that few residents of the region are aware of it. It is quite invisible to the tourist who finds this wrecked landscape colorful and charming (as indeed it is, but it bears scant resemblance to what it was in 1848).

This same landscape was 'developed' once before, but with quite different results. The Pueblo Indians settled the Southwest in pre-Columbian times, but they happened not to be equipped with range livestock. Their civilization expired, but not because their land expired.

In India, regions devoid of any sod-forming grass have been settled apparently without wrecking the land, by the simple expedient of carrying the grass to the cow, rather than vice versa. (Was this the result of some deep wisdom, or was it just good luck? I do not know.)

In short the plant succession steered the course of history; the pioneer simply demonstrated, for good or ill, what successions inhered in the land. Is history taught in this spirit? It will be, once the concept of land as a community really penetrates our intellectual life.

The Ecological Conscience

Conservation is a state of harmony between men and land. Despite nearly a century of propaganda, conservation still proceeds at a snail's pace; progress still consists largely of letterhead pieties and convention oratory. On the back forty we still slip two steps backward for each forward stride.

The usual answer to this dilemma is 'more conservation education.' No one will debate this, but is it certain that only the volume of education needs stepping up? Is something lacking in the content as well?

It is difficult to give a fair summary of its content in brief form but, as I understand it, the content is substantially this: obey the law, vote right, join some organizations, and practice what conservation is profitable on your own land; the government will do the rest.

Is not this formula too easy to accomplish anything worth-while? It defines no right or wrong, assigns no obligation, calls for no sacrifice, implies no change in the current philosophy of values. In respect of land use, it urges only enlightened self-interest. Just how far will such education take us? An example will perhaps yield a partial answer.

By 1930 it had become clear to all except the ecologically blind that southwestern

Earth Alive

Wisconsin's topsoil was slipping seaward. In 1933 the farmers were told that if they would adopt certain remedial practices for five years, the public would donate CCC labor to install them, plus the necessary machinery and materials. The offer was widely accepted, but the practices were widely forgotten when the five-year contract period was up. The farmers continued only those practices that yielded an immediate and visible economic gain for themselves.

This led to the idea that maybe farmers would learn more quickly if they themselves wrote the rules. Accordingly, the Wisconsin Legislature in 1937 passed the Soil Conservation District Law. This said to the farmers, in effect: We, the public, will furnish you free technical service and loan you specialized machinery, if you will write your own rules for land-use. Each county will write its own rules, and these will have the force of law. Nearly all the counties promptly organized to accept the proffered help, but after a decade of operation, no county has yet written a single rule. There has been visible progress in such practices as strip-cropping, pasture renovation, and soil liming, but none in fencing woodlots against grazing, none from excluding plow and cow from steep slopes. The farmers, in short, have selected those remedial practices which were profitable anyhow, and ignored those which were profitable to the community, but not clearly profitable to themselves.

When one asks why no rules have been written, one is told that the community is not yet ready to support them; education must precede rules. But the education actually in progress makes no mention of obligations to land over and above those dictated by self-interest, The net result is that we have more education but less soil, fewer healthy woods, and as many floods as in 1937.

The puzzling aspect of such situations is that the existence of obligations over and above self-interest is taken for granted in such rural community enterprises as the betterment of roads, schools, churches, and baseball teams. Their existence is not taken for granted, nor as yet seriously discussed, in bettering the behavior of the water that falls on the land, or in the preserving of the beauty or diversity of the farm landscape. Land-use ethics are still governed wholly by economic self-interest, just as social ethics were a century ago.

To sum up: we asked the farmer to do what he conveniently could to save his soil, and he has done just that, and only that. The farmer who clears the woods off a 75 per cent slope, turns his cows into the clearing and dumps its rainfall, rocks, and soil into the community creek, is still (if otherwise decent) a respected member of society. If he puts lime on his fields and plants his crops on contour, he is still entitled to all the privileges and emoluments of his Soil Conservation District, The District is a beautiful piece of social machinery, but it is coughing along on two cylinders because we have been too timid, and too anxious for quick success to tell the farmer the true magnitude of his obligations. Obligations have no meaning without conscience, and the problem we face is the extension of the social conscience from people to land.

No important change in ethics was ever accomplished without an internal change in our intellectual emphasis, loyalties, affections, and convictions. The proof that conservation has not yet touched these foundations of conduct lies in the fact that philosophy and religion have not yet heard of it. In our attempt to make conservation easy, we have made it trivial.

Substitutes for a Land Ethic

When the logic of history hungers for bread and we hand out a stone, we are at pains to explain how much the stone resembles bread. I now describe some of the stones which serve in lieu of a land ethic.

One basic weakness in a conservation system based wholly on economic motives is that most members of the land community have no economic value. Wildflowers and songbirds are examples. Of the 22,000 higher plants and animals native to Wisconsin, it is doubtful whether more than 5 per cent can be sold, fed, eaten, or otherwise put to economic use. Yet these creatures are members of the biotic community, and if (as I believe) its stability depends on its integrity, they are entitled to continuance.

When one of these non-economic categories is threatened, and if we happen to love it, we invent subterfuges to give it economic importance. At the beginning of the century songbirds were supposed· to be disappearing. Ornithologists jumped to the rescue with some distinctly shaky evidence to the effect that insects would eat us up if birds failed to control them. The evidence had to be economic in order to be valid.

It is painful to read these circumlocutions today. We have no land ethic yet, but we have at least drawn nearer the point of admitting that birds should continue as a matter of biotic right, regardless of the presence or absence of economic advantage to us.

A parallel situation exists in the situations of predatory mammals, raptorial birds, and fish-eating birds. Time was when biologists somewhat overworked the evidence that these creatures preserve the health of game by killing weaklings, or that they control rodents for the farmer, or that they prey on 'worthless' species. Here again, the evidence had to be economic in order to be valid. It is only in recent years that we hear the more honest argument that predators are members of the community, and that no special interest has the right to exterminate them for the sake of a benefit, real or fancied, to itself. Unfortunately this enlightened view is still in the talk stage. In the field the extermination of predators goes merrily on: witness the impending erasure of the timber wolf by fiat of Congress, the Conservation Bureaus, and many state legislatures.

Some species of trees have been 'read out of the party' by economics-minded foresters because they grow too slowly, or have too low a sale value to pay as timber crops: white cedar, tamarack, cypress, beech, and hemlock are examples. In Europe, where forestry is ecologically more advanced, the non-commercial tree species are recognized as members of the native forest community, to be preserved as such, within reason. Moreover some (like beech) have been found to have a valuable function in building up soil fertility. The interdependence of the forest and its constituent tree species, ground flora, and fauna is taken for granted.

Lack of economic value is sometimes a character not only of species or groups, but of entire biotic communities: marshes, bogs, dunes, and 'deserts' are examples. Our formula in such cases is to relegate their conservation to government as refuges, monuments, or parks. The difficulty is that these communities are usually interspersed with more valuable private lands; the government cannot possibly own or control such scattered parcels. The net effect is that we have relegated some of them to ultimate extinction over large areas. If the private owner were ecologically minded, he would be proud to be the custodian of a reasonable proportion of such areas, which add diversity and beauty to his farm and to his community.

In some instances, the assumed lack of profit in these 'waste' areas has proved to be wrong, but only after most of them had been done away with. The present scramble to re-flood muskrat marshes is a case in point.

There is a clear tendency in American conservation to relegate to government all necessary jobs that private landowners fail to perform. Government ownership, operation, subsidy, or regulation is now widely prevalent in forestry, range management, soil and watershed management, park and wilderness conservation, fisheries management, and migratory bird management, with more to come. Most of this growth in governmental conservation is proper and logical, some of it is inevitable. That I imply no disapproval of it is implicit in the fact that I have spent most of my life working for it. Nevertheless the question arises: What is the ultimate magnitude of the enterprise? Will the tax base carry its eventual ramifications? At what point will governmental conservation, like the mastodon, become handicapped by its own dimensions? The answer, if there is any, seems to be in the land ethic, or some other force which assigns more obligation to the private landowner.

Industrial landowners and users, especially lumbermen and stockmen, are inclined to wail long and loudly about the extension of government ownership and regulation to land, but (with notable exceptions) they show little disposition to develop the only visible alternative: the voluntary practice of conservation no their own lands.

When the private landowner is asked to perform some unprofitable act for the good of the community, he today assents only with outstretched palm. If the act costs him cash this is fair and proper, but when it costs only forethought, open-mindedness, or time, the issue is at least debatable. The overwhelming growth of land-use subsidies in recent years must be ascribed, in large part, to the governments own agencies for conservation education: the land bureaus, the agricultural colleges, and the extension services. As far as I can detect, no ethical obligations toward land is taught in these institutions.

To sum up: a system of conservation based solely on economic self-interest is hopelessly lopsided. It tends to ignore, and thus eventually to eliminate, many elements in the land community that lack commercial value, but that are (as far as we know) essential to its healthy functioning. It assumes, falsely, I think, that the economic parts of the biotic clock will function without the uneconomic parts. It tends to relegate to government many functions eventually too large, too complex, or too widely dispersed to be performed by government.

An ethical obligation on the part of the private owner is the only visible remedy for these situations.

The Land Pyramid

An ethic to supplement and guide the economic to land presupposes the existence of some mental image of land as a biotic mechanism. We can be ethical only in relation to something we can see, feel, understand, love, or otherwise have faith in.

The image commonly employed in conservation education is 'the balance of nature.' For reasons too lengthy to detail here, this figure of speech fails to describe accurately what little we know about the land mechanism. A much truer image is the one employed by ecology: the biotic pyramid. I shall first sketch the pyramid as a symbol of land, and later develop some of its implications in terms of land use.

Plants absorb energy from the sun. This energy flows through a circuit called the biota, which may be represented by a pyramid consisting of layers. The bottom layer is the soil. A plant layer rests on the soil, an insect layer on the plants, a bird and rodent layer on the insects, and so on up through various animal groups to the apex layer, which consists of the larger carnivores.

The species of a layer are alike not in where they came from, or in what they look like, but rather in what they eat. Each successive layer depends on those below it for food and often for other services, and each in turn furnishes food and services to those above. Proceeding upward, each successive layer decreases in numerical abundance. Thus, for every carnivore there are hundreds of his prey, thousands of their prey, millions of insects, uncountable plants. The pyramidal form of the system reflects this numerical progression from apex to base. Man shares an intermediate layer with the bears, raccoons, and squirrels which eat both meat and vegetables.

The lines of dependency for food and other services are called food chains. Thus soil-oak-deer-Indian is a chain that has now been largely converted to soil-corn-cow-farmer. Each species, including ourselves, is a link in many chains. The deer eats a hundred plants other than oak, and the cow a hundred plants other than corn. Both, then, are links in a hundred chains. The pyramid is a tangle of chains so complex as to seem disorderly, yet the stability of the system proves it to be a highly organized structure. Its functioning depends on the co-operation and competition of its diverse parts.

In the beginning, the pyramid of life was low and squat; the food chains short and simple. Evolution has added layer after layer, link after link. Man is one of thousands of accretions to the height and complexity of the pyramid. Science has given us many doubts, but it has given us at least one certainty: the trend of evolution is to elaborate and diversify the biota.

Land, then, is not merely soil; it is a fountain of energy flowing through a circuit of soils, plants, and animals. Food chains are the living channels which conduct energy upward; death and decay return it to the soil. The circuit is not closed; some energy is dissipated in decay, some is added by absorption from the air, some is stored in soils, peats, and long-lived forests; but it is a sustained circuit, like a slowly augmented revolving fund of life. There is always a net loss by downhill wash, but this is normally small and offset by the decay of rocks. It is deposited in the ocean and, in the course of geological time, raised to form new lands and new pyramids.

The velocity and character of the upward flow of energy depend on the complex structure of the plant and animal community, much as the upward flow of sap in a tree depends on its complex cellular organization. Without this complexity, normal circulation would presumably not occur. Structure means the characteristic numbers, as well as the characteristic kinds of functions, of the component species. This interdependence between the complex structure of the land and its smooth functioning as an energy unit is one of its basic attributes.

When a change occurs in one part of the circuit, many other parts must adjust themselves to it. Change does not necessarily obstruct or divert the flow of energy; evolution is a long series of self-induced changes, the net result of which has been to elaborate the flow mechanism and to lengthen the circuit. Evolutionary changes, however, are usually slow and local. Man's invention of tools has enabled him to make changes of unprecedented violence, rapidity, and scope.

One change is in the composition of floras and faunas. The larger predators are lopped off the apex of the pyramid; food chains, for the first time in history, become shorter rather than longer. Domesticated species from other lands are substituted for wild ones, and wild ones are moved to new habitats. In this world-wide pooling of faunas and floras, some species get out of bounds as pests and diseases, others are extinguished. Such effects are seldom intended or foreseen; they represent unpredicted and often untraceable readjustments in the structure. Agricultural science is largely a race between the emergence of new pests and the emergence of new techniques for their control.

Another change touches the flow of energy through plants and animals and its return to the soil. Fertility is the ability of soil to receive, store, and release energy. Agriculture, by overdrafts on the soil, or by too radical a substitution of domestic for native species in the superstructure, may derange the channels of flow or deplete storage. Soils depleted of their storage, or of the organic matter which anchors it, wash away-faster than they form. This is erosion.

Waters, like soil, are part of the energy circuit. Industry, by polluting waters or obstructing them with dams, may exclude the plants and animals necessary to keep energy in circulation. Transportation brings about another basic change: the plants or animals grown in one region are now consumed and returned to the soil in another.

Transportation taps the energy stored in rocks, and in the air, and uses it elsewhere; thus we fertilize the garden with nitrogen gleaned by the guano birds from the fishes of seas on the other side of the Equator. Thus the formerly localized and self-contained circuits are pooled on a world-wide scale.

The process of altering the pyramid for human occupation releases stored energy, and this often gives rise, during the pioneering period, to a deceptive exuberance of plant and animal life, both wild and tame. These releases of biotic capital tend to becloud or postpone the penalties of violence.

This thumbnail sketch of land as an energy circuit conveys three basic ideas:

(1) That land is not merely soil.
(2) That the native plants and animals kept the energy circuit open; others may or may not.
(3) That man-made changes are of a different order than evolutionary changes, and have effects more comprehensive than is intended or foreseen.

These ideas, collectively, raise two basic issues: Can the land adjust itself to the new order? Can the desired alterations be accomplished with less violence?

Biotas seem to differ in their capacity to sustain violent conversion. Western Europe, for example, carries a far different pyramid than Caesar found there. Some large animals are lost; swampy forests have become meadows or plowland; many new plants and animals are introduced, some of which escape as pests; the remaining natives are greatly changed in distribution and abundance. Yet the soil is still there and, with the help of imported nutrients, still fertile; the waters flow normally; the new structure seems to function and to persist. There is no visible stoppage or derangement of the circuit.

Western Europe, then, has a resistant biota. Its inner processes are tough, elastic, resistant to strain. No matter how violent the alterations, the pyramid, so far, has developed some new *modus vivendi* which preserves its habitability for man, and for most of the other natives.

Japan seems to present another instance of radical conversion without disorganization.

Most other civilized regions, and some as yet barely touched by civilization, display various stages of disorganization, varying from initial symptoms to advanced wastage. In Asia Minor and North America diagnosis is confused by climatic changes, which may have been either the cause or the effect of advanced wastage. In the United States the degree of disorganization varies locally; it is worst in the Southwest the Ozarks, and parts of the South, and least in New England and the Northwest. Better land-uses may still arrest it in the less advanced regions. In parts of Mexico, South America, South Africa, and Australia a violent and accelerating wastage is in progress, but I cannot assess the prospects.

This almost world-wide display of disorganization in the land seems to be similar to disease in an animal, except that it never culminates in complete disorganization or death. The land recovers, but at some reduced level of complexity, and with a reduced carrying capacity for people, plants, and animals. Many biotas currently regarded as 'lands of opportunity' are in fact already subsisting on exploitative agriculture, i.e. they have already exceeded their sustained carrying capacity. Most of South America is overpopulated in this sense.

In arid regions we attempt to offset the process of wastage by reclamation, but it is only too evident that the prospective longevity of reclamation projects is often short. In our own West, the best of them may not last a century.

The combined evidence of history and ecology seems to support one general deduction: the less violent the man-made changes, the greater the probability of successful readjustment in the pyramid. Violence, in turn, varies with human population density; a dense population requires a more violent conversion. In this respect, North America has a better chance for permanence than Europe, if she can contrive to limit her density.

This deduction runs counter to our current philosophy, which assumes that because a small increase in density enriched human life, that an indefinite increase will enrich it indefinitely. Ecology knows of no density relationship that holds for indefinitely wide limits. All gains from density are subject to a law of diminishing returns.

Whatever may be the equation for men and land, it is improbable that we as yet know all its terms. Recent discoveries in mineral and vitamin nutrition reveal unsuspected dependencies in the up-circuit: incredibly minute quantities of certain substances determine the value of soils to plants, of plants to animals. What of the down-circuit? What of the vanishing species, the preservation of which we now regard as an aesthetic luxury? They helped build the soil; in what unsuspected ways may they be essential to its maintenance? Professor Weaver proposes that we use prairie flowers to reflocculate the wasting soils of the dust bowl; who knows for what purpose cranes and condors, otters and grizzlies may some day be used?

Land Health and the A-B Cleavage

A land ethic, then, reflects the existence of an ecological conscience and this in turn reflects a conviction of individual responsibility for the health of the land. Health is the capacity of the land for self-renewal. Conservation is our effort to understand and preserve this capacity.

Conservationists are notorious for their dissensions. Superficially these seem to add up to mere confusion, but a more careful scrutiny reveals a single plane of cleavage common to many specialized fields. In each field one group (A) regards the land as soil, and its function as commodity-production; another group (B) regards the land as a biota, and its function as something broader. How much broader is admittedly in a state of doubt and confusion.

In my own field, forestry, group A is quite content to grow trees like cabbages, with cellulose as the basic forest commodity. It feels no inhibition against violence; its ideology is agronomic. Group B, on the other hand, sees forestry as fundamentally different from agronomy because it employs natural species, and manages a natural environment rather than creating an artificial one. Group B prefers natural reproduction on principle. It worries on biotic as well as economic grounds about the loss of species like chestnut, and the threatened loss of the white pines. It worries about a whole series of secondary forest functions: wildlife, recreation, watersheds, wilderness areas. To my mind, Group B feels the stirrings of an ecological conscience.

In the wildlife field, a parallel cleavage exists. For Group A the basic commodities are sport and meat; the yardsticks of production are ciphers of take in pheasants and trout. Artificial propagation is acceptable as a permanent as well as a temporary recourse—if its unit costs permit. Group B, on the other hand, worries about a whole series of biotic side-issues. What is the cost in predators of producing a game crop? Should we have further recourse to exotics? How can management restore the shrinking species, like prairie grouse, already hopeless as shootable game? How can management restore the threatened rarities, like trumpeter swan and whooping crane? Can management principles be extended to wildflowers? Here again it is clear to me that we have the same A-B cleavage as in forestry.

In the larger field of agriculture I am less competent to speak, but there seem to be somewhat parallel cleavages. Scientific agriculture was actively developing before ecology was born, hence a slower penetration of ecological concepts might be expected. Moreover the farmer, by the very nature of his techniques, must modify the biota more radically than the forester or the wildlife manager. Nevertheless, there are many discontents in agriculture which seem to add up to a new vision of 'biotic farming.'

Perhaps the most important of these is the new evidence that poundage or tonnage is no measure of the food-value of farm crops; the products of fertile soil may be qualitatively as well as quantitatively superior. We can bolster poundage from depleted soils by pouring on imported fertility, but we are not necessarily bolstering food-value. The possible ultimate ramifications of this idea are so immense that I must leave their exposition to abler pens.

The discontent that labels itself 'organic farming' while bearing some of the earmarks of a cult, is nevertheless biotic in its direction, particularly in its insistence on the importance of soil flora and fauna.

The ecological fundamentals of agriculture are just as poorly known to the public as in other fields of land-use. For example, few educated people realize that the marvelous advances in technique made during recent decades are improvements in the pump rather than the well. Acre for acre, they have barely sufficed to offset the sinking level of fertility.

In all of these cleavages, we see repeated the same basic paradoxes: man as the conqueror *versus* man the biotic citizen; science the sharpener of his sword *versus* science the searchlight on his universe; land the slave and servant *versus* the collective organism. Robinson's injunction to Tristram may well be applied, at this juncture, to *Homo sapiens* as a species in geological time:

> Whether you will or not
> You are a King, Tristram, for you are one
> Of the time-tested few that leave the world,
> When they are gone, not the same place it was.
> Mark what you leave.

The Outlook

It is inconceivable to me that an ethical relation to land can exist without love, respect, and admiration for land, and a high regard for its value. By value, I of course mean something far broader than mere economic value; I mean value in the philosophical sense.

Perhaps the most serious obstacle impeding the evolution of a land ethic is the fact that our educational and economic system is headed away from, rather than toward, an intense consciousness of land. Your true modern is separated from the land by many middlemen, and by innumerable physical gadgets. He has no vital relation to it; to him it is the space between cities on which crops grow. Turn him loose for a day on the land, and if the spot does not happen to be a golf links or a 'scenic' area, he is bored stiff. If crops could be raised by hydroponics instead of farming, it would suit him very well. Synthetic substitutes for wood, leather, wool, and other natural land products suit him better than the originals. In short, land is something he has 'outgrown.'

Almost equally serious as an obstacle to the land ethic is the attitude of the farmer for whom the land is still an adversary, or a taskmaster that keeps him in slavery. Theoretically, the mechanization of farming ought to cut the farmer's chains, but whether it really does is debatable.

One of the requisites for an ecological comprehension of land is an understanding of ecology, and this is by no means co-extensive with 'education'; in fact, such higher education seems deliberately to avoid ecological concepts. An understanding of ecology does not necessarily originate in courses bearing ecological labels; it is quite as likely to be labeled geography, botany, agronomy, history, or economics. This is as it should be, but whatever the label, ecological training is scarce.

The case for a land ethic would appear hopeless but for the minority which is in obvious revolt against these 'modern' trends.

The 'key-log' which must be moved to release the evolutionary process for an ethic is simply this: quit thinking about decent land-use as solely an economic problem. Examine each question in terms of what is ethically and esthetically right, as well as what is economically expedient. A thing is right when it tends to preserve the integrity, stability, and beauty of the biotic community. It is wrong when it tends otherwise.

It of course goes without saying that economic feasibility limits the tether of what can or cannot be done for land. It always has and it always will. The fallacy the economic determinists have tied around our collective neck, and which we now need to cast off, is the belief that economics determines *all* land-use. This is simply not true. An innumerable host of actions and attitudes, comprising perhaps the bulk of all land relations, is determined by the land-users' tastes and predilections, rather than by his purse. The bulk of all land relations hinges on investments of time, forethought, skill, and faith rather than on investments of cash. As a land-user thinketh, so is he.

I have purposely presented the land ethic as a product of social evolution because nothing so important as an ethic is ever 'written.' Only the most superficial student of history supposes that Moses 'wrote' the Decalogue; it evolved in the minds of a thinking community, and Moses wrote a tentative summary of it for a 'seminar.' I say tentative because evolution never stops.

The evolution of a land ethic is an intellectual as well as emotional process. Conservation is paved with good intentions which prove to be futile, or even dangerous, because they are devoid of critical understanding either of the land, or of economic land-use. I think it's a truism that as the ethical frontier advances from the individual to the community, its intellectual content increases.

The mechanism of operation is the same for any ethic: social approbation for right actions: social disapproval for wrong actions. By and large, our present problem is one of attitudes and implements. We are remodeling the Alhambra with a steam shovel, and we are proud of our yardage. We shall hardly relinquish the shovel, which after all has many good points; but we are in need of gentler and more objective criteria for its successful use.

SILENT SPRING

RACHEL CARSON (1962)

Elixirs of Death

For the first time in the history of the world, every human being is now subjected to contact with dangerous chemicals, from the moment of conception until death. In the less than two decades of their use, the synthetic pesticides have been so thoroughly distributed throughout the animate and inanimate world that they occur virtually everywhere. They have been recovered from most of the major river systems and even from streams of groundwater flowing unseen through the earth. Residues of these chemicals linger in soil to which they may have been applied a dozen years before. They have entered and lodged in the bodies of fish, birds, reptiles, and domestic and wild animals so universally that scientists carrying on animal experiments find it almost impossible to locate subjects free from such contamination. They have been found in fish in remote mountain lakes, in earthworms burrowing in soil, in the eggs of birds—and in man himself. For these chemicals are now stored in the bodies of the vast majority of human beings, regardless of age. They occur in the mother's milk and probably in the tissues of the unborn child.

All this has come about because of the sudden rise and prodigious growth of an industry for the production of man-made or synthetic chemicals with insecticidal properties. This industry is a child of the Second World War. In the course of developing agents of chemical warfare, some of the chemicals created in the laboratory were found to be lethal to insects. The discovery did not come by chance: insects were widely used to test chemicals as agents of death for man.

The result has been a seemingly endless stream of synthetic insecticides. In being man-made—by ingenious laboratory manipulation of the molecules, substituting atoms, altering their arrangement—they differ sharply from the simpler insecticides of prewar days. These were derived from naturally occurring minerals and plant products—compounds of arsenic, copper, lead, manganese, zinc, and other minerals, pyrethrum from the dried flowers of chrysanthemums, nicotine sulphate from some of the relatives of tobacco, and rotenone from leguminous plants of the East Indies.

What sets the new synthetic insecticides apart is their enormous biological potency. They have immense power not merely to poison but to enter into the most vital processes of the body and change them in sinister and often deadly ways. Thus, as we shall see, they destroy the very enzymes whose function is to protect the body from harm, they block the oxidation processes from which the body receives its energy, they prevent the normal functioning of various organs, and they may initiate in certain cells the slow and irreversible change that leads to malignancy.

Yet new and more deadly chemicals are added to the list each year and new uses are devised so that contact with these materials has become practically worldwide. The production of synthetic pesticides in the United States soared from 124,159,000 pounds in 1947 to 637,666,000 pounds in 1960—more than a fivefold increase. The wholesale value of these products was well over a quarter of a billion dollars. But in the plans and hopes of the industry this enormous production is only a beginning.

A Who's Who of pesticides is therefore of concern to us all. If we are going to live so intimately with these chemicals eating and drinking them, taking them into the very marrow of our bones—we had better know something about their nature and their power.

Needless Havoc

As man proceeds toward his announced goal of the conquest of nature, he has written a depressing record of destruction, directed not only against the earth he inhabits but against the life that shares it with him. The history of the recent centuries has its black passages—the slaughter of the buffalo on the western plains, the massacre of the shorebirds by the market gunners, the near-extermination of the egrets for their plumage.

Now, to these and others like them, we are adding a new chapter and a new kind of havoc—the direct killing of birds, mammals, fishes, and indeed practically every form of wildlife by chemical insecticides indiscriminately sprayed on the land.

Under the philosophy that now seems to guide our destinies, nothing must get in the way of the man with the spray gun. The incidental victims of his crusade against insects count as nothing; if robins, pheasants, raccoons, cats, or even livestock happen to inhabit the same bit of earth as the target insects and to be hit by the rain of insect-killing poisons no one must protest.

The citizen who wishes to make a fair judgment of the question of wildlife loss is today confronted with a dilemma. On the one hand conservationists and many wildlife biologists assert that the losses have been severe and in some cases even catastrophic. On the other hand the control agencies tend to deny flatly and categorically that such losses have occurred, or that they are of any importance if they have. Which view are we to accept?

The credibility of the witness is of first importance. The professional wildlife biologist on the scene is certainly best qualified to discover and interpret wildlife loss. The entomologist, whose specialty is insects, is not so qualified by training, and is not psychologically disposed to look for undesirable side effects of his control program. Yet it is the control men in state and federal governments—and of course the chemical manufacturers—who steadfastly deny the facts reported by the biologists and declare they see little evidence of harm to wildlife. Like the priest and the Levite in the biblical story, they choose to pass by on the other side and to see nothing. Even if we charitably explain their denials as due to the shortsightedness of the specialist and the man with an interest this does not mean we must accept them as qualified witnesses.

The best way to form our own judgment is to look at some of the major control programs and learn, from observers familiar with the ways of wildlife, and unbiased in favor of chemicals just what has happened in the wake of a rain of poison falling from the skies into the world of wildlife.

To the bird watcher, the suburbanite who derives joy from birds in his garden, the hunter, the fisherman or the explorer of wild regions, anything that destroys the wildlife of an area for even a single year has deprived him of pleasure to which he has a legitimate right. This is a valid point of view even if it has sometimes happened, some of the birds and mammals and fishes are able to re-establish themselves after a single spraying, a great and real harm has been done.

But such re-establishment is unlikely to happen. Spraying tends to be repetitive, and a single exposure from which the wildlife populations might have a chance to recover is a rarity. What usually results is a poisoned environment, a lethal trap in which not only the resident populations succumb but those who come in as migrants as well. The larger the area sprayed the more serious the harm, because no oases of safety remain. Now, in a decade marked by insect-control programs in which many thousands or even millions of acres are sprayed as a unit, a decade in which private and community spraying has also surged steadily upward, a record of destruction and death of American wildlife has accumulated. Let us look at some of these programs and see what has happened.

During the fall of 1959 some 27,000 acres in southeastern Michigan, including numerous suburbs of Detroit, were heavily dusted from the air with pellets of aldrin, one of the most dangerous of all the chlorinated hydrocarbons. The program was conducted by the Michigan Department of Agriculture with the cooperation of the United States Department of Agriculture its announced purpose was control of the Japanese beetle.

Little need was shown for this drastic and dangerous action. On the contrary, Walter P. Nickell, one of the best-known and best-informed naturalists in the state, who spends much of his time in the field with long periods in southern Michigan every summer declared:

> For more than thirty years, to my direct knowledge, the Japanese beetle has been present in the city of Detroit in small numbers. The numbers have not shown any appreciable increase in all this lapse of years. I have yet to see a single Japanese beetle [in 1959] other than the few caught in Government catch traps in Detroit... Everything is being kept so secret that I have not yet been able to obtain any information whatsoever to the effect that they have increased in numbers.

An official release by the state agency merely declared that the beetle had "put in its appearance" in the areas designated for the aerial attack upon it. Despite the lack of justification the program was launched, with the state providing the manpower and supervising the operation, the federal government providing equipment and additional men, and the communities paying for the insecticide.

The Japanese beetle, an insect accidentally imported into the United States, was discovered in New Jersey in 1916, when a few shiny beetles of a metallic green color were seen in a nursery near Riverton. The beetles, at first unrecognized, were finally identified as a common inhabitant of the main islands of Japan. Apparently they had entered the United States on nursery stock imported before restrictions were established in 1912.

From its original point of entrance, the Japanese beetle has spread rather widely throughout many of the states east of the Mississippi, where conditions of temperature and rainfall are suitable for it. Each year some outward movement beyond the existing boundaries of its distribution usually takes place. In the eastern areas where the beetles have been longest established, attempts have been made to set up natural controls. Where this has been done, the beetle populations have been kept at relatively low levels, as many records attest.

Despite the record of reasonable control in eastern areas the Midwestern states now on the fringe of the beetle's range have launched an attack worthy of the most deadly enemy instead of only a moderately destructive insect, employing the most dangerous chemicals distributed in a manner that exposes large numbers of people, their domestic animals, and all wildlife to the poison intended for the beetle. As a result these Japanese beetle programs have caused shocking destruction of animal life and have exposed human beings to undeniable hazard. Sections of Michigan, Kentucky, Iowa, Indiana, Illinois, and Missouri are all experiencing a rain of chemicals in the name of beetle control.

The Michigan spraying was one of the first large-scale attacks on the Japanese beetle from the air. The choice of aldrin, one of the deadliest of all chemicals, was not determined by any peculiar suitability for Japanese beetle control, but simply by the wish to save money – aldrin was the cheapest of the compounds available. While the state in its official release to the press acknowledged that aldrin is a "poison," it implied that no harm could come to human beings in the heavily populated areas to which the chemical was applied. (The official answer to the query "What precautions should I take?" was "For you, none.") An official of the Federal Aviation Agency was later quoted in the local press to the effect that "this is a safe operation" and a representative of the Detroit Department of Parks and Recreation added his assurance that "the dust is harmless to humans and will not hurt plants or pets." One must assume that none of these officials had consulted the published and readily available reports of the United States Public Health Service, the Fish and Wildlife Service, and other evidence of the extremely poisonous nature of aldrin.

Acting under the Michigan pest control law, which allows the state to spray indiscriminately without notifying or gaining permission of individual landowners, the low-lying planes began to fly over the Detroit area. The city authorities and the Federal Aviation Agency were immediately besieged by calls from worried citizens. After receiving nearly 800 calls in a single hour the police begged radio and television stations and newspapers to "tell the watchers what they were seeing and advise them it was safe" according to the Detroit News. The Federal Aviation Agency's safety officer assured the public that "the planes are carefully supervised" and "are authorized to fly low." In a somewhat mistaken attempt to allay fears, he added that the planes had emergency valves that would allow them to dump their entire load instantaneously. This, fortunately, was not done, but as the planes went about their work the pellets of insecticide fell on beetles and humans alike, showers of "harmless" poison descending on people shopping or going to work and on children out from school for the lunch hour. Housewives swept the granules from porches and sidewalks, where they are said to have "looked like snow." As pointed out later by the Michigan Audubon Society, "In the spaces between shingles on roofs, in eaves-troughs, in the cracks in bark and twigs, the little white pellets of aldrin-and-clay, no bigger than a pin head, were lodged by the millions . . . When the snow and rain came every puddle became a possible death potion."

Within a few days after the dusting operation, the Detroit Audubon Society began receiving calls about the birds. According to the Society's secretary, Mrs. Ann Boyes,

> "The first indication that the people were concerned about the spray was a call I received on Sunday morning from a woman who reported that coming home from church she saw an alarming number of dead and dying birds. The spraying there had been done on Thursday. She said there were no birds at all flying in the area, that she had found at least a dozen [dead] in her backyard and that the neighbors had found dead squirrels."

All other calls received by Mrs. Boyes that day reported "a great many dead birds and no live ones... People who had maintained bird feeders said there were no birds at all at their feeders." Birds picked up in a dying condition showed the typical symptoms of insecticide poisoning—tremoring, loss of ability to fly, paralysis, convulsions.

Nor were birds the only forms of life immediately affected. A local veterinarian reported that his office was full of clients with dogs and cats that had suddenly sickened. Cats, who so meticulously groom their coats and lick their paws, seemed to be most affected. Their illness took the form of severe diarrhea, vomiting, and convulsions. The only advice the veterinarian could give his clients was not to let the animals out unnecessarily, or to wash the paws promptly if they did so. (But the chlorinated hydrocarbons cannot be washed even from fruits or vegetables, so little protection could be expected from this measure.)

Despite the insistence of the City-County Health Commissioner that the birds must have been killed by "some other kind of spraying" and that the outbreak of throat and chest irritations that followed the exposure to aldrin must have been due to "something else," the local Health Department received a constant stream of complaints. A prominent Detroit internist was called upon to treat four of his patients within an hour after they had been exposed while watching the planes at work. All had similar symptoms: nausea, vomiting, chills, fever, extreme fatigue, and coughing.

The Detroit experience has been repeated in many other communities as pressure has mounted to combat the Japanese beetle with chemicals. At Blue Island, Illinois, hundreds of dead and dying birds were picked up. Data collected by birdbanders here suggest that 80 per cent of the songbirds were sacrificed. In Joliet, Illinois, some 3000 acres were treated with heptachlor in 1959. According to reports from a local sportsmen's club, the bird population within the treated area was "virtually wiped out." Dead rabbits, muskrats, opossums, and fish were also found in numbers, and one of the local schools made the collection of insecticide-poisoned birds a science project.

Earth Alive

And No Birds Sing

Over increasingly large areas of the United States, spring now comes unheralded by the return of the birds, and the early mornings are strangely silent where once they were filled with the beauty of bird song. This sudden silencing of the song of birds, this obliteration of the color and beauty and interest they lend to our world have come about swiftly, insidiously, and unnoticed by those whose communities are as yet unaffected.

From the town of Hinsdale, Illinois, a housewife wrote in despair to one of the world's leading ornithologists, Robert Cushman Murphy, Curator Emeritus of Birds at the American Museum of Natural History:

> Here in our village the elm trees have been sprayed for several years [she wrote in 1958]. When we moved here six years ago there was a wealth of bird life; I put up a feeder and had a steady stream of cardinals, chickadees, downies and nuthatches all winter, and the cardinals and chickadees brought their young ones in the summer.
>
> After several years of DDT spray, the town is almost devoid of robins and starlings; chickadees have not been on my shelf for two years, and this year the cardinals are gone too; the nesting population in the neighborhood seems to consist of one dove pair and perhaps one catbird family.
>
> It is hard to explain to the children that the birds have been killed off, when they have learned in school that a Federal law protects the birds from killing or capture. 'Will they ever come back?' they ask, and I do not have the answer. The elms are still dying, and so are the birds. *Is* anything being done? *Can* anything be done? Can *I* do anything?

A year after the federal government had launched a massive spraying program against the fire ant, an Alabama woman wrote: "Our place has been a veritable bird sanctuary for over half a century. Last July we all remarked, 'There are more birds than ever.' Then, suddenly, in the second week of August, they all disappeared. I was accustomed to rising early to care for my favorite mare that had a young filly. There was not a sound of the song of a bird. It was eerie, terrifying. What was man doing to our perfect and beautiful world? Finally, five months later a blue jay appeared and a wren."

The autumn months to which she referred brought other somber reports from the deep South, where in Mississippi, Louisiana, and Alabama the *Field Notes* published quarterly by the National Audubon Society and the United States Fish and Wildlife Service noted the striking phenomenon of "blank spots weirdly empty of virtually *all* bird life." The *Field Notes* are a compilation of the reports of seasoned observers who have spent many years afield in their particular areas and have unparalleled knowledge of the normal bird life of the region. One such observer reported that in driving about southern Mississippi that fall she saw "no land birds at all for long distances." Another in Baton Rouge reported that the contents of her feeders had lain untouched "for weeks on end," while fruiting shrubs in her yard, that ordinarily would be stripped clean by that time, still were laden with berries. Still another reported that his picture window, "which often used to frame a scene splashed with the red of 40 or 50 cardinals and crowded with other species, seldom permitted a view of as many as a bird or two at a time." Professor Maurice Brooks of the University of West Virginia, an authority on the birds of the Appalachian region, reported that the West Virginia bird population had undergone "an incredible reduction."

One story might serve as the tragic symbol of the fate of the birds—a fate that has already overtaken some species, and that threatens all. It is the story of the robin, the bird known to everyone. To millions of Americans, the season's first robin means that the grip of winter is broken. Its coming is an event reported in newspapers and told eagerly at the breakfast table. And as the number of migrants grows and the first mists of green appear in the woodlands, thousands of people listen for the first dawn chorus of the robins throbbing in the early morning light. But now all is changed, and not even the return of the birds may be taken for granted.

The survival of the robin, and indeed of many other species as well, seems fatefully linked with the American elm, a tree that is part of the history of thousands of towns from the Atlantic to the Rockies, gracing their streets and their village squares and college campuses with majestic archways of green. Now the elms are stricken with a disease that afflicts them throughout their range, a disease so serious that many experts believe all efforts to save the elms will in the end be futile. It would be tragic to lose the elms, but it would be doubly tragic if, in vain efforts to save them, we plunge vast segments of our bird populations into the night of extinction. Yet this is precisely what is threatened.

The so-called Dutch elm disease entered the United States from Europe about 1930 in elm burl logs imported for the veneer industry. It is a fungus disease; the organism invades the water conducting vessels of the tree, spreads by spores carried in the flow of sap, and by its poisonous secretions as well as by mechanical clogging causes the branches to wilt and the tree to die. The disease is spread from diseased to healthy trees by elm bark beetles. The galleries which the insects have tunneled out under the bark of dead trees become contaminated with spores of the invading fungus, and the spores adhere to the insect body and are carried wherever the beetle flies. Efforts to control the fungus disease of the elms have been directed largely toward control of the carrier insect. In community after community, especially throughout the strongholds of the American elm the Midwest and New England, intensive spraying has become routine procedure.

What this spraying could mean to bird life, and especially to the robin, was first made clear by the work of two ornithologists at Michigan State University, Professor George Wallace and one of his graduate students, John Mehner. When Mr. Mehner began work for the doctorate in 1954, he chose a research project that had to do with robin populations. This was quite by chance, for at that time no one suspected that the robins were in danger. But even as he undertook the work, events occurred that were to change its character and indeed to deprive him of his material.

Spraying for Dutch elm disease began in a small way on the university campus in 1954. The following year the city of East Lansing (where the university is located) joined in, spraying on the campus was expanded, and, with local programs for gypsy moth and mosquito control also under way, the rain of chemicals increased to a downpour.

During 1954, the year of the first light spraying, all seemed well. The following spring the migrating robins began to return to the campus as usual. Like the bluebells in Tomlinson's haunting essay "The Lost Wood," they were "expecting no evil" as they reoccupied their familiar territories. But soon it became evident that something was wrong. Dead and dying robins began to appear on the campus. Few birds were seen in their normal foraging activities or assembling in their usual roosts. Few nests were built; few young appeared. The pattern was repeated with monotonous regularity in succeeding springs. The sprayed area had become a lethal trap in which each wave of migrating robins would be eliminated in about a week. Then new arrivals would come in, only to add to the numbers of doomed birds seen on the campus in the agonized tremors that precede death.

"The campus is serving as a graveyard for most of the robins that attempt to take up residence in the spring," said Dr. Wallace. But why? At first he suspected some disease of the nervous system, but soon it became evident that "in spite of the assurances of the insecticide people that their sprays were 'harmless to birds' the robins were really dying of insecticidal poisoning; they exhibited the well-known symptoms of loss of balance, followed by tremors, convulsions, and death."

Several facts suggested that the robins were being poisoned, not so much by direct contact with the insecticides as indirectly, by eating earthworms. Campus earthworms had been fed inadvertently to crayfish in a research project and all the crayfish had promptly died. A snake kept in a laboratory cage had gone into violent tremors after being fed such worms. And earthworms are the principal food of robins in the spring.

A key piece in the jigsaw puzzle of the doomed robins was soon to be supplied by Dr. Roy Barker of the Illinois Natural History Survey at Urbana. Dr. Barker's work, published in 1958, traced the intricate cycle of events by which the robins fate is linked to the elm trees by way of the earthworms. The trees are sprayed in the spring (usually at the rate of 2 to 5 pounds of DDT per 50-foot tree, which may be the equivalent of as much as 23 pounds per acre where elms are numerous) and often again in July, at about half this concentration. Powerful sprayers direct a stream of poison to all parts of the tallest trees, killing directly not only the target organism, the bark beetle, but other insects, including pollinating species and predatory spiders and beetles. The poison forms a tenacious film over the leaves and bark. Rains do not wash it away. In the autumn the leaves fall to the ground, accumulate in sodden layers, and begin the slow process of becoming one with the soil. In this they are aided by the toil of the earthworms, who feed in the leaf litter, for elm leaves are among their favorite foods. In feeding on the leaves the worms also swallow the insecticide, accumulating and concentrating it in their bodies. Dr. Barker found deposits of DDT throughout the digestive tracts of the worms, their blood vessels, nerves, and body wall. Undoubtedly some of the earthworms themselves succumb, but others survive to become "biological magnifiers" of the poison. In the spring the robins return to provide another link in the cycle. As few as 11 large earthworms can transfer a lethal dose of DDT to a robin. And 11 worms form a small part of a day's rations to a bird that eats 10 to 12 earthworms in as many minutes.

Not all robins receive a lethal dose, but another consequence may lead to the extinction of their kind as surely as fatal poisoning. The shadow of sterility lies over all the bird studies and indeed lengthens to include all living things within its potential range. There are now only two or three dozen robins to be found each spring on the entire 185-acre campus of Michigan State University, compared with a conservatively estimated 370 adults in this area before spraying. In 1954 every robin nest under observation by Mehner produced young. Toward the end of June, 1957, when at least 370 young birds (the normal replacement of the adult population) would have been foraging over the campus in the years before spraying began, Mehner could find only one young robin. A year later Dr. Wallace was to report: "At no time during the spring or summer [of 1958] did I see a fledgling robin anywhere on the main campus, and so far I have failed to find anyone else who has seen one there."

Part of this failure to produce young is due, of course, to the fact that one or more of a pair of robins dies before the nesting cycle is completed. But Wallace has significant records which point to something more sinister—the actual destruction of the birds' capacity to reproduce. He has, for example, "records of robins and other birds building nests but laying no eggs, and others laying eggs and incubating them but not hatching them. We have one record of a robin that sat on its eggs faithfully for 21 days and they did not hatch. The normal incubation period is 13 days... Our analyses are showing high concentrations of DDT in the testes and ovaries of breeding birds," he told a congressional committee in 1960. "Ten males had amounts ranging from 30 to 109 parts per million in the testes, and two females had 151 and 211 parts per million respectively in the egg follicles in their ovaries."

Soon studies in other areas began to develop findings equally dismal. Professor Joseph Hickey and his students at the University of Wisconsin, after careful comparative studies of sprayed and unsprayed areas, reported the robin mortality to be at least 86 to 88 per cent. The Cranbrook Institute of Science at Bloomfield Hills, Michigan, in an effort to assess the extent of bird loss caused by the spraying of the elms, asked in 1956 that all birds thought to be victims of DDT poisoning be turned in to the institute for examination. The request had a response beyond all expectations. Within a few weeks the deep-freeze facilities of the institute were taxed to capacity, so that other specimens had to be refused. By 1959 a thousand poisoned birds from this single community had been turned in or reported. Although the robin was the chief victim (one woman calling the institute reported 12 robins lying dead on her lawn as she spoke), 63 different species were included among the specimens examined at the institute.

The robins, then, are only one part of the chain of devastation linked to the spraying of the elms, even as the elm program is only one of the multitudinous spray programs that cover our land with poisons. Heavy mortality has occurred among about 90 species of birds, including those most familiar to suburbanites and amateur naturalists. The populations of nesting birds in general have declined as much as 90 per cent in some of the sprayed towns. As we shall see, all the various types of birds are affected — ground feeders, treetop feeders, bark feeders, predators.

ECOLOGICAL HUMANISM

HENRYK SKOLIMOWSKI (1974)

Oswald Spengler has written that 'Technics are the tactics for living'. This is a very useful phrase indeed. I shall take advantage of it while stating our dilemma and while searching for possible solutions.

Modern technology—or better, western technology—has failed us not because it has become economically counter productive in the long run; and not because it has become ecologically devastating, but mainly because it has forgotten its basic function, namely that all technics are, in the last resort, the tactics for living. Because modern technology has failed us as a set of the tactics for living, it has also proved in the process to be economically counter-productive and ecologically ruinous.

But this indictment also affects Alternative Technology. Alternative Technology has started rather vigorously, captured the imagination of many, and is now fizzling out. Why? Because Alternative Technology has not taken itself seriously enough, that is, as a new set of tactics for living.

When pushed to an extreme, Alternative Technology has either become an idoltry of new kinds of gadgets, or else a crass ideology of the New Left: a feverish process perpetuating itself, though perhaps empty of content. Alternative Technology has been waning (though the Establishment has just discovered it) because it did not go to its roots; it did not confront itself with the ultimate task of all technics: to become a set of tactics for living.

The tactics for living are not merely new uses of old instruments. Culture is a fundamental part of the tactics for living. Thriving and healthy, culture provides a set of dynamic structures for living. Within the western world, particularly during the last 150 years, and especially during the last 50 years, culture (as well as religion) has been systematically misunderstood, mystified, misread and distorted, and taken either to be a sickly product of decadent minds or an anachronism of the pre-technological era. In either case, culture was considered more or less spurious. But culture and religion are an inherent part of the human strategies for survival and well being.

However, the culture of the post-industrial era cannot be a simple resuscitation of some traditional cultures, for it will have to meet new contingencies of life, which means it will have to rethink the products of the human mind and spirit within a differently conceived world.

I have chosen to call this new set of tactics for living, which encompasses New Technology, New Culture and New Ideology, *Ecological Humanism*. Ecological Humanism is not a new label for old things, nor simply pouring old wine into new bottles. I must point out, in particular, that Ecological Humanism has little to do with traditional humanisms; and it quite sharply separates itself from Marxist or Socialist humanism, which calls (along with other humanisms) for the appropriation of nature to man.

Traditional humanism has emphasised the nobility of man, the independence of man, indeed the greatness of man who is cut in the Protean mould. This conception of man went hand in hand with the idea of appropriating nature to the ends and needs of man. Marx fully accepted this conception of man and the idea of the appropriation of nature (or simply using nature) to man's advantage, or, indeed, to man's content.

Ecological Humanism is based on the reversed premise. It calls for the appropriation of man to nature. We have to see man as a part of a larger scheme of things: of nature and cosmos. We have to transcend and abolish the idea of the Protean (and Faustian) man. The consequences of this reversal are quite far reaching, and I will just touch on some of them. On a more practical level, Ecological Humanism signifies, among other things, frugality, recycling, the reverence for nature, which are really three different aspects of the same thing.

I must emphasise that Ecological Humanism is not just another fancy name for saying that we should be less wasteful, for it signifies a fundamental reorientation of the multitude of things. Not many people, Marxists in particular, are aware that traditional humanism, as based on the ideal of the Protean man and the idea of the appropriation of nature (with the tacit acceptance of both present science and present technology) are simply incompatible with the ideal of harmony between the human species and the rest of nature.

Now, let me spell out some of the consequences of Ecological Humanism. On the practical level, as I have already mentioned, Ecological Humanism spells out a new kind of technology based on the idea of frugality, recycling, the reverence for nature, new economy; of which the reverence for nature is not a spurious ornament, but an intrinsic part of a new design.

On the level of the individual, Ecological Humanism signifies (that is, after we cease to be consumptive hogs) inner exuberance instead of the restless outward activity; empathy and compassion rather than ruthless competition; understanding in depth rather than merely handling of information.

On the level of the entire culture, Ecological Humanism signifies a fundamental switch from the traditional idiom, in which man asserts himself against things 'out there', tries to impress himself on the world, to the idiom, in which man will mesh himself with the things 'out there'.

It is by now clear to you, I hope, that no New Technology can provide a solution by itself, that no New Culture can provide a solution by itself, that no New Ideology can provide an answer by itself, but that each must become an aspect of a larger paradigm, an aspect, in other words, of a new set of tactics for living.

In the realm of ideology, Ecological Humanism points towards social relationships based on the ideas of sharing and stewardship, rather than owning things and fighting continuous ruthless battles in open and camouflaged social wars.

In short, Ecological Humanism is based on a new articulation of the world at large:
- it sees *the world* not as a place for pillage and plunder, an arena for gladiators, but as a *sanctuary* in which we temporarily dwell, and of which we must take the utmost care;

- it sees *man* not as an acquisitor and conquistadore, but as a *guardian* and *steward*;
- it sees *knowledge* not as an instrument for the domination of nature, but ultimately as techniques for the refinement of the soul;
- it sees *values* not in pecuniary equivalents, but in *intrinsic terms* as a vehicle which contributes to a deeper understanding of people by people, and a deeper cohesion between people and the rest of creation;
- and it sees all these above mentioned elements as a part of the new tactics for living.

"A man's reach should exceed his grasp, or what's a heaven for?" (Browning).

THE QUEST FOR GAIA

DR. JAMES LOVELOCK (1975)

Consider the following propositions:

1. Life exists only because material conditions on Earth happen to be just right for its existence;
2. Life defines the material conditions needed for its survival, and makes sure that they stay there.

The first of these is the conventional wisdom. It implies that life has stood poised like a needle on its point for over 3.5 billion years. If the temperature or humidity or salinity or acidity or any one of a number of other variables had strayed outside a narrow range of values for any length of time, life would have been annihilated.

Proposition 2 is an unconventional view. It implies that living matter is not passive in the face of threats to its existence. It has found means, as it were, of driving the point of the needle into the table of forcing conditions to stay within the permissible range. This article supports and develops this view.

The Sun, being a typical star of the main sequence, has evolved according to a standard and well-established pattern. A consequence of this is that during the Earth's existence the Sun's output of energy has increased substantially. The Earth now receives between 1.4 and 3.3 times more energy than it did just after its formation 4 billion years ago. The Earth's surface temperature at the time when life began has been calculated. These calculations take into account the solar input, the radiative properties of the surface and the composition of the atmosphere. At that time, the atmosphere probably contained ammonia and other complex molecules which acted like the glass in a greenhouse, that is, by reducing the radiation of heat and long-wave infra-red radiation from Earth. The calculations show that the surface temperature could indeed have been within the range we now know to be needed to start life off.

Once life began, it fed on the atmospheric blanket. Unless some means had existed for restoring to it heat-retaining gases such as ammonia, or of altering the Earth's surface to make it more heat-retentive, the planet would surely have become uniformly ice-bound and lifeless. The rate of increase of solar energy would have been too small to compensate. Yet the fossil record and the continuity of life gives no support to this conclusion. At the time of supposed emergence from glaciation, that is, when the radiation from the more active Sun had made up for the radiation loss due to loss of the heat-retaining gases, and when only the feeble beginnings of a new life should have been possible, complex multi-celled organisms had already evolved. Life must have found a way of keeping the temperature of the Earth's surface within the critical range of 15-30 deg C for hundreds of millions of years, in spite of drastic changes of atmospheric composition and a large increase in the mean solar flux. The calculations were wrong because they left out the effect of the defense mechanism that life uses to protect itself.

Extinction through glaciation was not the only danger. Overproduction of ammonia and other heat-retaining gases could have result in the opposite effect, known as the "runaway greenhouse", that is to a rapidly increasing surface temperature that would have scorched the Earth and left it permanently lifeless, as is the planet Venus now. The evidence that this did not happen is plain—we would not have written these words nor would you be reading them.

Has life been able to control other conditions of existence besides the surface temperature of the Earth? A most significant fact about the Earth is the composition of its atmosphere. Almost everything about its composition seems to violate the laws of chemistry. If chemical thermodynamics alone mattered, almost all the oxygen and most of the nitrogen in the atmosphere ought to have ended up in the sea combined as nitrate ion. The air we breathe cannot be a very fortunate once-off emanation from the rocks; it can only be an artifact maintained in a steady state far from chemical equilibrium by biological processes.

The significance of this was first realized some years ago when one of us, in association with Dian Hitchcock, took up the problem of deciding whether it would be possible detect life on Mars by the use only of spectroscopic observations on its atmosphere. Our suggestion was to look for any combination of constituents that was far from chemical equilibrium; if such was found life might exist there. (So far no such combination has been detected on either Mars or Venus.)

Gaia

It appeared to us that the Earth's biosphere was able to control at least the temperature of the Earth's surface and the composition of the atmosphere. Prima facie, the atmosphere looked like a contrivance put together co-operatively by the totality of living systems, to carry out certain necessary control functions. This led us to the formulation of the proposition that living matter, the air, the oceans, the land surface were parts of a giant system which was able to control temperature, the composition of the air and sea, the pH of the soil and so on so as to be optimum for survival of the biosphere. The system seemed to exhibit the behavior of a single organism, even a living creature. One having such formidable powers deserved a name to match it; William Golding the novelist, suggested Gaia—the name given by the ancient Greeks to their Earth goddess.

The past three years have been explaining and elaborating the Gaia thesis (in collaboration with Lynn Margulis) and checking its implications against fact. It has proved to be fruitful. It has led us along many paths and by-paths, and valuable insights have been gained especially about the consequences of Man's interaction with the biosphere. The following is a selection of some of the interesting things we have found on the way.

Atmospheric constituents

If Gaia is a living entity we have the right to ask questions such as "what purpose does constituent X serve in the atmosphere?" As an example, the biosphere produces 1 billion tons of ammonia a year. Why?

As already pointed out, in early times, when the Sun was cooler than it is now, ammonia served to keep the Earth warm. At present time, the need for ammonia is different and just as important, because we believe that ammonia keeps the soil near to pH 8 which is an optimum value for living processes. It is needed because a consequence of having nitrogen and sulphur-containing substances in the air in the presence of an excess of oxygen is their tendency to combine to produce strongly acid materials—thunder storms produce tons of nitric acid and if there were no regulator such as ammonia the soil would become sour and hostile to most organisms.

Another of our beliefs is that one of the purposes of the small but definite amount of methane in the atmosphere is to regulate the oxygen content. Methane is a product of anaerobic fermentation in soil and sea. Some of the methane rises into the stratosphere where it oxidizes to carbon dioxide and water, so becoming the principal source of water vapor in the upper air. The water rises further into the ionosphere and is photolyzed to oxygen and hydrogen. Oxygen descends and hydrogen escapes into space. In effect, methane production is a way of transporting hydrogen from the Earth's surface to the stratosphere in sufficient quantity to maintain oxygen concentration in the lower atmosphere.

We have also found interesting and unexpected trace gases in the atmosphere, such as dimethyl sulphide, methyl iodide and carbon tetrachloride. There is no doubt that the first two are biological emissions and they may well serve to transport the essential elements, sulfur and iodine, from the sea to the land. Carbon tetrachloride does not seem to have a biological source but its uniform distribution in the atmosphere, showing no difference between the Northern and Southern hemispheres, and other evidence suggest that it is not a man-made pollutant either. Its origins are an intriguing puzzle as is the question of its function, if any.

For more than 3.5 billion years in the face of a big increase of solar output, the mean temperature of the Earth's surface must have remained within the range of 15-30° C. How did Gaia do this? She must have used several ways to keep surface temperatures so constant. Before there was a significant amount of oxygen in the air, the emission and absorption of ammonia by simple organisms may have been the control process, so making use of its heat absorbing and retaining properties. Variations of the concentration of ammonia in the air would therefore be a means of temperature control.

There must have been other ways as well, for the failure of only one year's crop of ammonia would have led to a self-accelerating temperature decline and extinction of life. One can envisage advantage being taken of the ability of certain algae to change color from light to dark, thereby influencing the emissivity and the albedo of the surface. Later, when photosynthesizing and respiring organisms existed and oxygen became a major constituent of the air, the control of the concentration of carbon dioxide, which is also a heat absorbing and retaining gas, may have been used to play a role in stabilizing temperature.

Earth Alive

Gaia and Man

Gaia is still a hypothesis. The facts and speculations in this article and others that we have assembled corroborate but do not prove her existence but, like all useful theories right or wrong, Gaia suggests new questions which may throw light on old ones. Let us ask another. What bearing has she on pollution, population, and man's role in the living world?

Gaia has survived the most appalling of all atmospheric pollutants, namely oxygen, which was put into the atmosphere in substantial quantity about 2 billion years ago when the photosynthesizers had completed their task of oxidizing the surface and the atmosphere. Whole ranges of species must have been killed off or driven into dark, oxygen-free prisons from which they have never been released; the appearance of the whole planetary surface and its chemistry were completely changed. To appreciate the impact of oxygen, think of what would happen to us if a marine organism began to photosynthesize chlorine and was successful enough to replace oxygen in the air with chlorine. This is science fiction, but oxygen was as poisonous to the primitive ferments as chlorine would be to us today.

Man's present activity as a polluter is trivial by comparison and he cannot thereby seriously change the present state of Gaia let alone hazard her existence. But there is an aspect of man's activities more disturbing than pollution. If one showed a control engineer the graph of the Earth's mean temperature against time over the past million years, he would no doubt remark that it represented the behavior of a system in which serious instabilities could develop but which had never gone out of control. One of the laws of system control is that if a system is to maintain stability it must possess adequate variety of response, that is, have at least as many ways of countering outside disturbances as these are outside disturbances to act on it. What is to be feared is that man-the-farmer and man-the-engineer are reducing the total variety of response open to Gaia.

The growing human population of the Earth is leading us to use drastic measures to supply this population with resources, of which food has prime importance. Natural distribution of plants and animals are being changed, ecological systems destroyed and whole species altered or deleted. But any species or group of species in an ecological association may contribute just that response to an external threat that is needed to maintain the stability of Gaia. We therefore disturb and eliminate at our peril; long before the world population has grown so large that we consume the entire output from photosynthesizers, instabilities generated by lack of variety of response could intervene to put this level out of reach.

Puzzling climate

Are there any signs that we might have triggered something off already? There is at least one such possibility—the present puzzling climate. Unprecedented temperature decreases have occurred in northern regions, such as Iceland, along with many other unfamiliar manifestations, such as modified wind systems and rainfall distributions.

Many explanations of these climate trends have been put forward. Some mechanism that either reduces the amount of the Sun's radiation reaching the Earth or increases the amount radiated is required. Ecologists, not unexpectedly, place the blame on the products of man's activities. Increasing dustiness of the atmosphere, nuclear explosions, supersonic aircraft have all been proposed and considered, but within our admittedly limited theoretical understanding of what goes on, none has stood up well to criticism.

Another possibility which we are exploring is that one of the trace gas emissions such as that of nitrous oxide serves as a biological climate regulator. Nitrous oxide is produced naturally by soil micro-organisms at a rate of hundreds of millions of tons annually. The output varies however, as a result of agriculture, particularly from the use of nitrogenous fertilizers. We do not know how nitrous oxide could modify the climate, but the evidence suggests that it has been, increasing in concentration and it is known to penetrate the stratosphere where its decomposition products could affect the ozone layer.

This climatic trend may be "just another fluctuation" of the kind which has occurred before and which will cure itself. This tends to be the meteorologists' views but the uncomfortable thought remains that none of the earlier occurrences has been explained. Perhaps some unidentified activity of man has been the common factor and nowadays there are a good deal more men about, active in many more ways. The consequences this time could well be much more serious and prolonged. We await developments somewhat uneasily.

Finally, a brief prospective look at the relation between man and Gaia, which also sums up the implications of this article. Socially-organized man has the ability possessed by no other species to collect, store and process information and then to use it to manipulate the environment in a purposeful and anticipatory fashion. When our forebears became farmers they set themselves on a path, which we are still beating out, that must have had an impact on the rest of Gaia almost as revolutionary as that of the evolution of photosynthetic organisms millennia before. The area of the outside world that we, as a species, are capable of regulating to our short-term advantage has gradually expanded from the immediate locality of a settlement to vast geographical regions. This path could take us finally to the point at which the area of manipulation becomes the whole world. What happens then?

Nineteenth century technocracy would say that we would then have won the final victory in the battle against nature. The Earth would be our spaceship; we the passengers and crew; the rest of nature, living and dead, our life support system. But the price of victory might well be that we should have immobilized Gaia's control systems which she has established to keep the conditions on our planet at the level necessary for her and therefore our survival. The responsibility for the task of maintaining system stability would pass to us alone and it would be dauntingly difficult. As well as carrying technical burdens, we should also have to make agonizing social and moral decisions, such as, how many passengers the spaceship could afford to carry and whom to throw overboard to make room.

A need to survive

The easier path is to rid ourselves of 19th century technocratic thinking, to reject the idea that human existence is necessarily a battle against nature. Let us make peace with Gaia on her terms and return to peaceful co-existence with our fellow creatures. Thirty thousand years ago some of our ancestors did something like this. They abandoned primitive hunting and took up what has been called the transhumane way of life. Men lived and migrated with the animal herds, defended them against other predators and systematically culled them for food. This ensured them a more plentiful and regular supply of animal products than the random hunting mode which it superseded. But our first priority as a species is to choose from the numerous technically feasible means of limiting our own population those which are socially acceptable in social and moral terms.

Now for one more speculation. We are sure that man needs Gaia but could Gaia do without man? In man Gaia has the equivalent of a central nervous system and an awareness of herself and the rest of the Universe. Through man, she has a rudimentary capacity, capable of development, to anticipate and guard against threats to her existence. For example, man can command just about enough capacity to ward off a collision with a planetoid the size of Icarus. Can it then be that in the course of man's evolution within Gaia he has been acquiring the knowledge and skills necessary to ensure her survival?

Postscript: The News Is Very, Very Bad
James Lovelock (2006)

Imagine a young policewoman delighted in the fulfillment of her vocation; then imagine her having to tell a family whose child had strayed that he has been found dead, murdered in a nearby wood.

Or think of a young physician newly appointed who has to tell you that the biopsy revealed invasion by an aggressive metastasizing tumor.

Doctors and the police know that many accept the simple awful truth with dignity but others try in vain to deny it.

Whatever the response, the bringers of such bad news rarely become hardened to their task and some dread it.

We have relieved judges of the awesome responsibility of passing the death sentence, but at least they had some comfort from its frequent moral justification. Physicians and the police have no escape from their duty.

This article is the most difficult I have written and for the same reasons. My Gaia theory sees the Earth behaving as if it were alive, and clearly anything alive can enjoy good health, or suffer disease.

Gaia has made me a planetary physician and I take my profession seriously.

Now I, too, have to bring bad news.

The climate centres around the world, which are the equivalent of the pathology lab of a hospital, have reported the Earth's physical condition, and the climate specialists see it as seriously ill, and soon to pass into a morbid fever that may last as long as 100,000 years.

I have to tell you, as members of the Earth's family and an intimate part of it, that you—and especially civilization—are in grave danger.

Our planet has kept itself healthy and fit for life, just like an animal does, for most of the more-than 3-billion years of its existence.

The Quest for Gaia

It was ill luck that we started polluting at a time when the sun is too hot for comfort. We have given Gaia a fever and soon her condition will worsen to a state like a coma. She has been there before and recovered, but it took more than 100,000 years.

We are responsible and will suffer the consequences: as the century progresses, the temperature will rise 8°C in temperate regions and 5°C in the tropics. Much of the tropical land mass will become scrub and desert, and will no longer serve for regulation; this adds to the 40% of the Earth's surface we have depleted to feed ourselves.

Curiously, aerosol pollution of the northern hemisphere reduces global warming by reflecting sunlight back to space. This "global dimming" is transient and could disappear in a few days like the smoke that it is, leaving us fully exposed to the heat of the global greenhouse.

We are in a fool's climate, accidentally kept cool by smoke, and before this century is over billions of us will die and the few breeding pairs of people that survive will be in the Arctic where the climate remains tolerable.

By failing to see that the Earth regulates its climate and composition, we have blundered into trying to do it ourselves, acting as if we were in charge. By doing this, we condemn ourselves to the worst form of slavery.

If we chose to be the stewards of the Earth, then we are responsible for keeping the atmosphere, the ocean and the land surface right for life. A task we would soon find impossible—and something before we treated Gaia so badly, she had freely done for us.

To understand how impossible it is, think about how you would regulate your own temperature or the composition of your blood. Those with failing kidneys know the never-ending daily difficulty of adjusting water, salt and protein intake. The technological fix of dialysis helps, but is no replacement for living healthy kidneys.

My new book, *The Revenge Of Gaia*, expands these thoughts, but you still may ask why science took so long to recognize the true nature of the Earth.

I think it is because Darwin's vision was so good and clear that it has taken until now to digest it. In his time, little was known about the chemistry of the atmosphere and oceans, and there would have been little reason for him to wonder if organisms changed their environment as well as adapting to it.

Had it been known then that life and the environment are closely coupled, Darwin would have seen that evolution involved not just the organisms, but the whole planetary surface.

We might then have looked upon the Earth as if it were alive, and known that we cannot pollute the air or use the Earth's skin—its forest and ocean ecosystems—as a mere source of products to feed ourselves and furnish our homes. We would have felt instinctively that those ecosystems must be left untouched because they were part of the living Earth.

So what should we do? First, we have to keep in mind the awesome pace of change and realise how little time is left to act; and then each community and nation must find the best use of the resources they have to sustain civilisation for as long as they can. Civilisation is energy-intensive and we cannot turn it off without crashing, so we need the security of a powered descent.

On the British Isles, we are used to thinking of all humanity and not just ourselves; environmental change is global, but we have to deal with the consequences here in the United Kingdom.

Unfortunately our nation is now so urbanised as to be like a large city and we have only a small acreage of agriculture and forestry. We are dependent on the trading world for sustenance; climate change will deny us regular supplies of food and fuel from overseas.

We could grow enough to feed ourselves on the diet of World War 2, but the notion that there is land to spare to grow biofuels, or be the site of wind farms, is ludicrous. We will do our best to survive, but sadly I cannot see the United States or the emerging economies of China and India cutting back in time, and they are the main source of emissions.

The worst will happen and survivors will have to adapt to a hell of a climate. Perhaps the saddest thing is that Gaia will lose as much or more than we do. Not only will wildlife and whole ecosystems go extinct, but in human civilisation the planet has a precious resource. We are not merely a disease; we are, through our intelligence and communication, the nervous system of the planet. Through us, Gaia has seen herself from space, and begins to know her place in the universe.

We should be the heart and mind of the Earth, not its malady. So let us be brave and cease thinking of human needs and rights alone, and see that we have harmed the living Earth and need to make our peace with Gaia. We must do it while we are still strong enough to negotiate, and not a broken rabble led by brutal war lords. Most of all, we should remember that we are a part of it, and it is indeed our home.

Post-Postscript: "Frank Fenner Sees No Hope for Humans"
The Australian (June 16, 2010)

"We're going to become extinct," the eminent scientist says. "Whatever we do now is too late." Fenner is an authority on extinction. The emeritus professor in microbiology at the Australian National University played a leading role in sending one species into oblivion: the variola virus that causes smallpox.

Fenner says the real trouble is the population explosion and "unbridled consumption". The number of Homo sapiens is projected to exceed 6.9 billion this year, according to the UN. With delays in firm action on cutting greenhouse gas emissions, Fenner is pessimistic.

"We'll undergo the same fate as the people on Easter Island," he says. "Climate change is just at the very beginning. But we're seeing remarkable changes in the weather already. The Aborigines showed that without science and the production of carbon dioxide and global warming, they could survive for 40,000 or 50,000 years. But the world can't. The human species is likely to go the same way as many of the species that we've seen disappear."

"Homo sapiens will become extinct, perhaps within 100 years," he says. "A lot of other animals will, too. It's an irreversible situation. I think it's too late. I try not to express that because people are trying to do something, but they keep putting it off. Mitigation would slow things down a bit, but there are too many people here already."

PART III: PHILOSOPHICAL DEVELOPMENT

SHOULD TREES HAVE STANDING?—TOWARD LEGAL RIGHTS FOR NATURAL OBJECTS

Introduction: The Unthinkable

In *Descent of Man,* Darwin observes that the history of man's moral development has been a continual extension in the objects of his "social instincts and sympathies." Originally each man had regard only for himself and those of a very narrow circle about him; later, he came to regard more and more "not only the welfare, but the happiness of all his fellow-men"; then "his sympathies became more tender and widely diffused, extending to men of all races to the imbecile, maimed, an other useless members of society, and finally to the lower animals...."

The history of the law suggests a parallel development. Perhaps there never was a pure Hobbesian state of nature, in which no "rights" existed except in the vacant sense of each man's "right to self-defense." But it is not unlikely that so far as the earliest families (including extended kinship groups and clans) were concerned, everyone outside the family was suspect, alien, rightless. And even within the family, persons we presently regard as the natural holders of at least some rights had none.

Take, for example, children. We know something of the early rights-status of children from the widespread practice of infanticide—especially of the deformed and female. (Senicide, as among the North American Indians, was the corresponding rightlessness of the aged). The child was less than a person: an object, a thing.

The legal rights of children have long since been recognized in principle, and are still expanding in practice. Witness, just within recent time, *In re Gault*, guaranteeing basic constitutional protections to juvenile defendants, and the Voting Rights Act of 1970. We have been making persons of children although they were not, in law, always so. And we have done the same, albeit imperfectly some would say, with prisoners, aliens, women (especially of the married variety), the insane, blacks, fetuses, and Indians.

Nor is it only matter in human form that has come to be recognized as the possessor of rights. The world of the lawyer is peopled with inanimate right-holders: trusts, corporations, joint ventures, municipalities, Subchapter R partnerships, and nation-states, to mention just a few. Ships, still referred to by courts in the feminine gender, have long had an independent jural life, often with striking consequences. We have become so accustomed to the idea of a corporation having "its" own rights, and being a "person" and "citizen" for so many statutory and constitutional purposes, that we forget how jarring the notion was to early jurists. "That invisible, intangible and artificial being, that mere legal entity," Chief Justice Marshall wrote of the corporation in *Bank of the United States v. Deveaux* —could a suit be brought in *its* name?

Ten years later, in the *Dartmouth College* case, he was still refusing to let pass unnoticed the wonder of an entity "existing only in contemplation of law." Yet, long before Marshall worried over the personifying of the modern corporation, the best medieval legal scholars had spent hundreds of years struggling with the notion of the legal nature of those great public "corporate bodies," the Church and the State. How could they exist in law, as entities transcending the living Pope and King? It was clear how a king could bind *himself*—on his honor—by a treaty. But when the king died, what was it that was burdened with the obligations of, and claimed the rights under, the treaty *his* tangible hand had signed? The medieval mind saw (what we have lost our capacity to see) how *unthinkable* it was, and worked out the most elaborate conceits and fallacies to serve as anthropomorphic flesh for the Universal Church and the Universal Empire.

It is this note of the *unthinkable* that I want to dwell upon for a moment. Throughout legal history, each successive extension of rights to some new entity has been, theretofore, a bit unthinkable. We are inclined to suppose the rightlessness of rightless "things" to be a decree of Nature, not a legal convention acting in support of some status quo. It is thus that we defer considering the choices involved in all their moral, social, and economic dimensions. And so the United States Supreme Court could straight-facedly tell us in *Dred Scott* that Blacks had been denied the rights of citizenship "as a subordinate and inferior class of beings, who had been subjugated by the dominant race...."

In the nineteenth century, the highest court in California explained that Chinese had not the right to testify against white men in criminal matters because they were

> a race of people whom nature has marked as inferior, and who are incapable of progress or intellectual development beyond a certain point...between whom and ourselves nature has placed an impassable difference.

Recall, too, that it was not so long ago that the fetus was rightless. In an early suit attempting to establish a wrongful death action on behalf of a negligently killed fetus (now widely accepted practice), Holmes, then on the Massachusetts Supreme Court, seems to have thought it simply inconceivable "that a man might owe a civil duty and incur a conditional prospective liability in tort to one not yet in being."

The fact is, that each time there is a movement to confer rights onto some new "entity," the proposal is bound to sound odd or frightening or laughable. This is partly because until the rightless thing receives its rights, we cannot see it as anything but a *thing* for the use of "us"— those who are holding rights at the time. There is something of a seamless web involved: there will be resistance to giving the thing "rights" until it can be seen and valued for itself; yet, it is hard to see it and value it for itself until we can bring, ourselves to give it "rights"—which is almost inevitably going to sound inconceivable to a large group of people.

The reason for this little discourse on the unthinkable, the reader must know by now, if only from the title of the paper. I am quite seriously proposing that we give legal rights to forests, oceans, rivers and other so-called "natural objects" in the environment—indeed, to the natural environment as a whole.

As strange as such a notion may sound, it is neither fanciful nor devoid of operational content. In fact, I do not think it would be a misdescription of recent developments in the law to say that we are already on the verge of assigning some such rights, although we have not faced up to what we are doing in those particular terms. We should do so now, and begin to explore the implications such a notion would hold.

Toward Rights for the Environment

Now, to say that the natural environment should have rights is not to say anything as silly as that no one should be allowed to cut down a tree. We say human beings have rights, but—at least as of the time of this writing—they can be executed. Corporations have rights, but they cannot plead the fifth amendment; *In re Gault* gave 15-year-olds certain rights in juvenile proceedings, but it did not give them the right to vote. Thus, to say that the environment should have rights is not to say that it should have every right we can imagine, or even the same body of rights as human beings have. Nor is it to say that everything in the environment should have the same rights as every other thing in the environment.

What the granting of rights does involve has two sides to it. The first involves what might be called the legal-operational aspects; the second, the psychic and sociopsychic aspects. I shall deal with these aspects in turn.

1. The Legal-Operational Aspects

What it Means to be a Holder of Legal Rights

There is, so far as I know, no generally accepted standard for how one ought to use the term "legal rights." Let me indicate how I shall be using it in this piece.

First and most obviously, if the term is to have any content at all, an entity cannot be said to hold a legal right unless and until *some public authoritative body* is prepared to give *some amount of review* to actions that are colorably inconsistent with that "right." For example, if a student can be expelled from a university and cannot get any public official, even a judge or administrative agent at the lowest level, either (i) to require the university to justify its actions, or (ii) to compel the university to accord the student some procedural safeguards (a hearing, right to counsel, right to have notice of charges), then the minimum requirements for saying that the student has a legal right to his education do not exist.

But for a thing to be a *holder of legal rights*, something more is needed than that some authoritative body will review the actions and processes of those who threaten it. As I shall use the term, "holder of legal rights," each of three additional criteria must be satisfied. All three, one will observe, go towards making a thing *count* jurally—to have a legally recognized worth and dignity in its own right, and not merely to serve as a means to benefit "us" (whoever the contemporary group of rights-holders may be). They are, first, that the thing can institute legal actions *at its behest*; second, that in determining the granting of legal relief, the court must take *injury to it* into account; and, third, that relief must run to the *benefit of it*.

The Rightlessness of Natural Objects at Common Law

Consider, for example, the common law's posture toward the pollution of a stream. True, courts have always been able, in some circumstances, to issue orders that will stop the pollution. But the stream itself is fundamentally rightless, with implications that deserve careful reconsideration.

The first sense in which the stream is not a rights-holder has to do with standing. The stream itself has none. So far as the common law is concerned, there is in general no way to challenge the polluter's actions save at the behest of a lower riparian [someone who lives along the river]—another human being—able to show an invasion of *his* rights. This conception of the riparian as the holder of the right to bring suit has more than theoretical interest. The lower riparians may simply not care about the pollution. They themselves may be polluting, and not wish to stir up legal waters. They may be economically dependent on their polluting neighbor. And of course, when they discount the value of winning by the costs of bringing suit and the chances of success, the action may not seem worth undertaking.

The second sense in which the common law denies "rights" to natural objects has to do with the way in which the merits are decided in those cases in which someone is competent and willing to establish standing. At its more primitive levels, the system protected the "rights" of the property owning human with minimal weighing of any values. Today we have come more and more to make balances—but only such as will adjust the economic best interests of identifiable humans.

The third way in which the common law makes natural objects rightless has to do with who is regarded as the beneficiary of a favorable judgment. Here, too, it makes a considerable difference that it is not the natural object that counts in its own right. To illustrate this point, let me begin by observing that it makes perfectly good sense to speak of, and ascertain, the legal damage to a natural object, if only in the sense of "making it whole" with respect to the most obvious factors. The costs of making a forest whole, for example, would include the costs of reseeding, repairing watersheds, restocking wildlife—the sorts of costs the Forest Service undergoes after a fire. Making a polluted stream whole would include the costs of restocking with fish, water-fowl, and other animal and vegetable life, dredging, washing out impurities, establishing natural and/or artificial aerating agents, and so forth.

Now, what is important to note is that, under our present system, even if a plaintiff riparian wins a water pollution suit for damages, no money goes to the benefit of the stream itself to repair *its* damages. This omission has the further effect that, at most, the law confronts a polluter with what it takes to make the plaintiff riparians whole; this may be far less than the damages to the stream, but not so much as to force the polluter to desist.

In any case, no natural object, such as a river or stream, has any of the three cri-

Should Trees Have Standing?

teria of a rights-holder. They have no standing in their own right; their unique damages do not count in determining outcome; and they are not the beneficiaries of awards. In such fashion, these objects have traditionally been regarded by the common law, and even by all but the most recent legislation, as objects for man to conquer and master and use—in such a way as the law once looked upon "man's" relationships to African Negroes.

Even where special measures have been taken to conserve them, as by seasons on game and limits on timber cutting, the dominant motive has been to conserve them *for us*—for the greatest good of the greatest number of human beings. Conservationists, so far as I am aware, are generally reluctant to maintain otherwise. As the name implies, they want to conserve and guarantee our consumption and our enjoyment of these other living things. In their own right, natural objects have counted for little, in law as in popular movements.

Toward Having Standing in its Own Right

It is not inevitable, nor is it wise, that natural objects should have no rights to seek redress in their own behalf. It is no answer to say that streams and forests cannot have standing because streams and forests cannot speak. Corporations cannot speak either; nor can states, estates, infants, incompetents, municipalities or universities. Lawyers speak for them, as they customarily do for the ordinary citizen with legal problems.

One ought, I think, to handle the legal problems of natural objects as one does the problems of legal incompetents—human beings who have become vegetable. If a human being shows signs of becoming senile and has affairs that he is de jure incompetent to manage, those concerned with his well being make such a showing to the court, and someone is designated by the court with the authority to manage the incompetent's affairs. The guardian (or "conservator" or "committee"—the terminology varies) then represents the incompetent in his legal affairs. Courts make similar appointments when a corporation has become "incompetent"—they appoint a trustee in bankruptcy or reorganization to oversee its affairs and speak for it in court when that becomes necessary.

On a parity of reasoning, we should have a system in which, when a friend of a natural object perceives it to be endangered, he can apply to a court for the creation of a guardianship. Perhaps we already have the machinery to do so. California law, for example, defines an incompetent as any person, whether insane or not, who by reason of old age, disease, weakness of mind, or other cause, is unable, unassisted, properly to manage and take care of himself or his property, and by reason thereof is likely to be deceived or imposed upon by artful or designing persons.

Of course, to urge a court that an endangered river is "a person" under this provision will call for lawyers as bold and imaginative as those who convinced the Supreme Court that a railroad corporation was a "person" under the fourteenth amendment, a constitutional provision theretofore generally thought of as designed to secure the rights of freedmen. If such an argument based on present statutes should fail, special environmental legislation could be enacted along traditional guardianship lines. Such provisions could provide for guardianship both in the instance of public natural objects and also, perhaps with slightly different standards, in the instance of natural objects on "private" land.

2. The Psychic and Socio-Psychic Aspects

There are, as we have seen, a number of developments in the law that may reflect a shift from the view that nature exists *for men*. These range from increasingly favorable procedural rulings for environmental action groups—as regards standing and burden of proof requirements, for example—to the enactment of comprehensive legislation such as the National Environmental Policy Act and the thoughtful Michigan Environmental Protection Act of 1970.

Of such developments one may say, however, that it is not the environment *per se* that we are prepared to take into account, but that man's increased awareness of possible long range effects on himself militate in the direction of stopping environmental harm in its incipiency. And this is part of the truth, of course. Even the far-reaching National Environmental Policy Act, in its preambulatory "Declaration of National Environmental Policy," comes out both for "restoring and maintaining environmental quality *to the overall welfare and development of man*" as well as for creating and maintaining "conditions under which *man and nature can exist in productive harmony*," Because the health and well-being of mankind depend upon the health of the environment, these goals will often be so mutually supportive that one can avoid deciding whether our rationale is to advance "us" or a new "us" that includes the environment.

For example, consider the Federal Insecticide, Fungicide, and Rodenticide Act (FIFRA) which insists that, *e.g.* pesticides, include a warning "adequate to prevent injury to living man and other vertebrate animals vegetation, and useful invertebrate animals." Such a provision undoubtedly reflects the sensible notion that the protection of humans is best accomplished by preventing dangerous accumulations in the food chain. Its enactment does not necessarily augur far-reaching changes in, nor even call into question fundamental matters of consciousness.

But the time is already upon us when we may have to consider subordinating some human claims to those of the environment *per se*. One *can* say that we never know what is going to prove useful at some future time. In order to protect ourselves, therefore, we ought to be conservative now in our treatment of nature. I agree. But when conservationists argue this way to the exclusion of other arguments, or find themselves speaking in terms of "recreational interests" so continuously as to play up to, and reinforce, homocentrist perspectives, there is something sad about the spectacle. One feels that the arguments lack even their proponent's convictions. I expect they want to say something less egotistic and more emphatic but the prevailing and sanctioned modes of explanation in our society are not quite ready for it. In this vein, there must have been abolitionists who put their case in terms of getting more work out of the Blacks.

For my part, I would prefer a frank avowal that even making adjustments for esthetic improvements, what I am proposing is going to cost "us," i.e., reduce our standard of living as measured in terms of our present values.

Yet, this frankness breeds a frank response—one which I hear from my colleagues and which must occur to many a reader. Insofar as the proposal is not just an elaborate legal fiction, but really comes down in the last analysis to a compromise of *our* interests for *theirs*, why should we adopt it? "What's in it for 'us'?"

This is a question I am prepared to answer, but only after permitting myself some observations about how *odd* the question is. It asks for me to justify my position in the very anthropocentric hedonist terms that I am proposing we modify. One is inclined to respond by a counter: "couldn't you (as a white) raise the same questions about compromising your preferred rights-status with Blacks?"; or "couldn't you (as a man) raise the same question about compromising your preferred rights-status with women?" Such counters, unfortunately, seem no more responsive than the question itself. (They have a nagging ring of "yours too" about them.)

What the exchange actually points up is a fundamental problem regarding the nature of philosophical argument. Recall that Socrates, whom we remember as an opponent of hedonistic thought, confutes Thrasymachus by arguing that immorality makes one miserably unhappy! Kant, whose moral philosophy was based upon the categorical imperative, finds himself justifying, *e.g.*, promise keeping and truth telling, on the most prudential—one might almost say, commercial—grounds.

This "philosophic irony" may owe to there being something unique about ethical argument. "Ethics cannot be put into words", Wittgenstein puts it; such matters "make themselves manifest." On the other hand, perhaps the truth is that in any argument which aims at persuading a human being to action (on ethical or any other bases), "logic" is only an instrument for illuminating positions, at best, and in the last analysis it is psychological appeals to the listener's self-interest that hold sway, however "principled" the rhetoric may be.

With this reservation as to the peculiar task of the argument that follows, let me stress that the strongest case can be made from the perspective of human advantage for conferring rights on the environment. Scientists have been warning of the crises the earth and all humans on it face if we do not change our ways—radically—and these crises make the lost "recreational use" of rivers seem absolutely trivial.

The earth's very atmosphere is threatened with frightening possibilities: absorption of sunlight, upon which the entire life cycle depends, may be diminished; the oceans may warm (increasing the "greenhouse effect" of the atmosphere), melting the polar ice caps, and destroying our great coastal cities; the portion of the atmosphere that shields us from dangerous radiation may be destroyed. Testifying before Congress, sea explorer Jacques Cousteau predicted that the oceans (to which we dreamily look to feed our booming populations) are headed toward their own death: "The cycle of life is intricately tied up with the cycle of water ... the water system has to remain alive if we are to remain alive on earth." We are depleting our energy and our food sources at a rate that takes little account of the needs even of humans now living.

These problems will not be solved easily; they very likely can be solved, if at all, only through a willingness to suspend the rate of increase in the standard of living (by present values) of the earth's "advanced" nations, and by stabilizing the total human population. For some of us this will involve forfeiting material comforts; for others it will involve abandoning the hope someday to obtain comforts long envied. For all of us it will involve giving up the right to have as many offspring as we might wish.

Such a program is not impossible of realization, however. Many of our so-called "material comforts" are not only in excess of, but are probably in opposition to, basic biological needs. Further, the "costs" to the advanced nations is not as large as would appear from Gross National Product figures. GNP reflects social gain (of a sort) without discounting for the social *cost* of that gain, *e.g.,* the losses through depletion of resources, pollution, and so forth. As has well been shown, as societies become more and more "advanced," their real marginal gains become less and less for each additional dollar of GNP. Thus, to give up "human progress" would not be as costly as might appear on first blush.

Nonetheless, such far-reaching social changes are going to involve us in a serious reconsideration of our consciousness towards the environment. I say this knowing full well that there is something more than a trifle obscure in the claim: is popular consciousness a meaningful notion, to begin with? If so, what is our present consciousness regarding the environment? Has it been causally responsible for our material state of affairs? Ought we to shift our consciousness (and if so, to what exactly, and on what grounds)? How, if at all, would a shift in consciousness be translated into tangible institutional reform? Not one of these questions can be answered to everyone's satisfactions, certainly not to the author's.

It is commonly being said today, for example, that our present state of affairs—at least in the West—can be traced to the view that Nature is the dominion of Man, and that this attitude, in turn, derives from our religious traditions:

> Man is exclusively divine, all other creatures and things occupy lower and generally inconsequential stature; man is given dominion over all creatures and things; he is enjoined to subdue the earth.... This environment was created by the man who believes that the cosmos is a pyramid erected to support man on its pinnacle, that reality exists only because man can perceive it, that God is made in the image of man, and that the world consists solely of a dialogue between men. Surely this is an infantilism which is unendurable. It is a residue from a past of inconsequence when a few puny men cried of their supremacy to an unhearing and uncaring world. One longs for a psychiatrist who can assure man that his deep seated cultural inferiority is no longer necessary or appropriate.... It is not really necessary to destroy nature in order to gain God's favor or even his undivided attention.

Surely this is forcibly put, but it is not entirely convincing as an explanation for how we got to where we are. For one thing, so far as intellectual influences are to be held responsible for our present state of affairs, one might as fairly turn on Darwin as the Bible. It was, after all, Darwin's views—in part through the prism of Spencer—that gave moral approbation to struggle, conquest, and domination; indeed, by emphasizing man's development as a product of chance happenings, Darwin also had the effect—intended or not—of reducing our awareness of the mutual interdependency of everything in Nature.

SHOULD TREES HAVE STANDING?

And besides, the spiritual beliefs of the Chinese and Indians "in the unity between man and nature had no greater effect than the contrary beliefs in Europe in producing a balance between man and his environment"; in China, *tao* notwithstanding, "ruthless deforestation has been continuous." I am under the impression, too, that notwithstanding the vaunted "harmony" between the American Plains Indians and Nature, once they had equipped themselves with rifles their pursuit of the buffalo expanded to fill the technological potential.

The fact is, that "consciousness" explanations pass too quickly over the less negative but simpler view of the situation: there are an increasing number of humans, with increasing wants, and there has been an increasing technology to satisfy them at "cost" to the rest of nature. Thus, we ought not to place too much hope that a changed environmental consciousness will in and of itself reverse present trends.

Furthermore, societies have long since passed the point where a change in human consciousness on any matter will rescue us from our problems. More than ever before we are in the hands of *institutions*. These institutions are not "mere legal fictions" moreover—they have wills, minds, purposes, and inertias that are in very important ways their own, i.e., that can transcend and survive changes in the consciousnesses of the individual humans who supposedly comprise them, and whom they supposedly serve. (It is more and more the *individual human being*, with his consciousness, that is the legal fiction.)

For these reasons, it is far too pat to suppose that a western "environmental consciousness" is solely or even primarily responsible for our environmental crisis. On the other hand, it is not so extravagant to claim that it has dulled our resentment and our determination to respond. For this reason, whether we will be able to bring about the requisite institutional and population growth changes depends in part upon effecting a radical shift in our feelings about "our" place in the rest of Nature.

A radical new conception of man's relationship to the rest of nature would not only be a step towards solving the material planetary problems; there are strong reasons for such a changed consciousness from the point of making us far better humans. If we only stop for a moment and look at the underlying human qualities that our present attitudes toward property and nature draw upon and reinforce, we have to be struck by how stultifying of our own personal growth and satisfaction they can become when they take rein of us.

To be able to get away from the view that Nature is a collection of useful senseless objects is deeply involved in the development of our abilities to love—or, if that is putting it too strongly, to be able to reach a heightened awareness of our own, and others' capacities in their mutual interplay. To do so, we have to give up some psychic investment in our sense of separateness and specialness in the universe.

And this, in turn, is hard giving indeed, because it involves us in a flight backwards, into earlier stages of civilization and childhood in which we had to trust (and perhaps fear) our environment, for we had not then the power to master it. Yet, in doing so, we—as persons—gradually free ourselves of needs for supportive illusions. Is not this one of the triumphs for "us" of giving legal rights to blacks and women?

Changes in this sort of consciousness are already developing for the betterment of the planet and us. There is now federal legislation which "establishes by law," the humane ethic that animals should be accorded the basic creature comforts of adequate housing, ample food and water, reasonable handling, decent sanitation, sufficient ventilation, shelter from extremes of weather and temperature, and adequate veterinary care including the appropriate use of pain-killing drugs....

The Vietnam War has contributed to this movement, as it has to others. Five years ago a Los Angeles mother turned out a poster which read "War is not Healthy for children and other living things." It caught on tremendously—at first, I suspect, because it sounded like another clever protest against the war, *i.e.*, another angle. But as people say such things, and think about them, the possibilities of what they have stumbled upon become manifest—in its suit against the Secretary of Agriculture to cancel the registration of DDT, the Environmental Defense Fund alleged "biological injury to man and other living things."

A few years ago the pollution of streams was thought of only as a problem of smelly, unsightly, unpotable water *i.e.*, to us. Now we are beginning to discover that pollution is a process that destroys wondrously subtle balances of life within the water, and as between the water and its banks.

This heightened awareness enlarges our sense of the dangers to us. But it also enlarges our empathy. We are not only developing the scientific capacity, but we are cultivating the personal capacities *within us* to recognize more and more the ways in which nature is like us.

The time may be on hand when these sentiments, and the early stirrings of the law, can be coalesced into a radical new theory or myth of man's relationships to the rest of nature. I do not mean "myth" in a demeaning sense of the term, but in the sense in which, at different times in history, our social "facts" and relationships have been comprehended and integrated by reference to the "myths" that we are co-signers of a social contract, that the Pope is God's agent, and that all men are created equal. Pantheism, Shinto and Tao all have myths to offer. But they are all, each in its own fashion, quaint, primitive and archaic.

What is needed is a myth that can fit our growing body of knowledge of geophysics, biology and the cosmos. I do not think it too remote that we may come to regard the Earth, as some have suggested, as one organism, of which mankind is a functional part—the mind, perhaps: different from the rest of nature, but different as a man's brain is from his lungs:

> International scientific studies have shown irrefutably that the Earth as a whole is an organized system of most closely interrelated and indeed interdependent activities. It is, in the broadest sense of the term, an "organism." The so-called life-kingdoms and the many vegetable and animal species are dependent upon each other for survival in a balanced condition of planet-wide existence; and they depend on their environment, conditioned by oceanic and atmospheric currents, and even more by the protective action of the ionosphere and many other factors which have definite rhythms of operation. Mankind is part of this organic planetary whole; and there can be no

truly new global society, and perhaps in the present state of affairs no society at all, as long as man will not recognize, accept and enjoy the fact that mankind has a definite function to perform

In order to give a constructive meaning to the activities of human societies all over the globe, these activities—physical and mental—should be understood and given basic value with reference to the wholesome functioning of the entire Earth, and we may add of the entire solar system. This cannot be done (1) if man insists on considering himself an alien Soul compelled to incarnate on this sorrowful planet, and (2) if we can see in the planet, Earth, nothing but a mass of material substances moved by mechanical laws, and in "life" nothing but a chance combination of molecular aggregations.

As I see it, the Earth is only one organized "field" of activities—and so is the human person—but these activities take place at various levels, in different "spheres" of being and realms of consciousness. The lithosphere is not the biosphere, and the latter not the... ionosphere. The Earth is not *only* a material mass. Consciousness is not only "human"; it exists at animal and vegetable levels, and most likely must be latent, or operating in some form in the molecule and the atom; and all these diverse and in a sense hierarchical modes of activity and consciousness should be seen integrated in and perhaps transcended by an all-encompassing and "eonic" planetary Consciousness.

Mankind's function within the Earth-organism is to extract from the activities of all other operative systems within this organism the type of consciousness which we call "reflective" or "self"—consciousness—or, we may also say to *mentalize* and give meaning, value, and "name" to all that takes place anywhere within the Earth-field....

This "mentalization" process operates through what we call culture. To each region of, and living condition in, the total field of the Earth-organism, a definite type of culture inherently corresponds. Each region is the "womb" out of which a specific type of human mentality and culture can and sooner or later will emerge. All these cultures—past, present and future—and their complex interrelationships and interactions are the collective builders of the Mind of humanity; and this means of the *conscious Mind of the Earth*. (*Directives for New Life,* by D. Rudhyar, 1971).

As radical as such a consciousness may sound today, all the dominant changes we see about us point in its direction. Consider just the impact of space travel, of world-wide mass media, of increasing scientific discoveries about the interrelatedness of all life processes. Is it any wonder that the term "spaceship earth" has so captured the popular imagination? The problems we have to confront are increasingly the world-wide crises of a global organism: not pollution of a stream, but pollution of the atmosphere and of the ocean. Increasingly, the death that occupies each human's imagination is not his own, but that of the entire life cycle of the planet earth, to which each of us is as but a cell to a body.

To shift from such a lofty fancy as the planetarization of consciousness to the operation of our municipal legal system is to come down to earth hard. Before the forces that are at work, our highest court is but a frail and feeble—a distinctly human—institution. Yet, the Supreme Court may be at its best not in its work of handing down decrees, but at the very task that is called for: of summoning up from the human spirit the kindest and most generous and worthy ideas that abound there, giving them shape and reality and legitimacy. In the case of the environment, the Supreme Court may find itself in a position to award "rights" in a way that will contribute to a change in popular consciousness. It would be a modest move, to be sure, but one in furtherance of a large goal: the future of the planet as we know it.

THE RIGHTS OF ANIMALS AND UNBORN GENERATIONS

JOEL FEINBERG (1974)

Every philosophical paper must begin with an unproved assumption. Mine is the assumption that there will still be a world five hundred years from now, and that it will contain human beings who are very much like us. We have it within our power now, clearly, to affect the lives of these creatures for better or worse by contributing to the conservation or corruption of the environment in which they must live. I shall assume furthermore that it is psychologically possible for us to care about our remote descendants, that many of us in fact do care, and indeed that we ought to care.

My main concern then will be to show that it makes sense to speak of the rights of unborn generations against us, and that given the moral judgment that we ought to conserve our environmental inheritance for them, and its grounds, we might well say that future generations *do* have rights correlative to our present duties toward them. Protecting our environment now is also a matter of elementary prudence, and insofar as we do it for the next generation already here in the persons of our children, it is a matter of love. But from the perspective of our remote descendants it is basically a matter of justice, of respect for their rights. My main concern here will be to examine the concept of a right to better understand how that can be.

The Problem

To have a 'right' is to have a claim *to* something and *against* someone—the recognition of which is called for by legal rules or, in the case of moral rights, by the principles of an enlightened conscience. In the familiar cases of rights, the claimant is a competent adult human being, and the claimee is an officeholder in an institution or else a private individual, in either case, another competent adult human being.

Normal adult human beings, then, are obviously the sorts of beings of whom rights can meaningfully be predicated. Everyone would agree to that, even extreme misanthropes who deny that anyone in fact has rights. On the other hand, it is absurd to say that rocks can have rights, not because rocks are morally inferior things unworthy of rights (that statement makes no sense either), but because rocks belong to a category of entities of whom rights cannot be meaningfully predicated. That is not to say that there are no circumstances in which we ought to treat rocks carefully, but only that the rocks themselves cannot validly claim good treatment from us.

In between the clear cases of rocks and normal human beings, however, is a spectrum of less obvious cases, including some bewildering borderline ones. Is it meaningful or conceptually possible to ascribe rights to our dead ancestors? To individual animals? To whole species of animals? To plants? To idiots and madmen? To fetuses? To generations yet unborn? Until we know how to settle these puzzling cases, we cannot claim fully to grasp the concept of a right, or to know the shape of its logical boundaries.

One way to approach these riddles is to turn one's attention first to the most familiar and unproblematic instances of rights, note their most salient characteristics, and then compare the borderline cases with them, measuring as closely as possible the points of similarity and difference. In the end, the way we classify the borderline cases may depend on whether we are more impressed with the similarities or the differences between them and the cases in which we have the most confidence.

It will be useful to consider the problem of individual animals first because their case is the one that has already been debated with the most thoroughness by philosophers so that the dialectic of claim and rejoinder has now unfolded to the point where disputants can get to the end game quickly and isolate the crucial point at issue. When we understand precisely what is at issue in the debate over animal rights, I think we will have the key to the solution of all the other riddles about rights.

Individual Animals

Almost all modern writers agree that we ought to be kind to animals, but that is quite another thing from holding that animals can claim kind treatment from us as their due. Statutes making cruelty to animals a crime are now very common, and these, of course, impose legal duties on people not to mistreat animals; but that still leaves open the question whether the animals, as beneficiaries of those duties, possess rights correlative to them. We may very well have duties *regarding* animals that are not at the same time duties *to* animals, just as we may have duties regarding rocks, or buildings, or lawns, that are not duties to the rocks, buildings, or lawns.

Some legal writers have taken the still more extreme position that animals themselves are not even the directly intended beneficiaries of statutes prohibiting cruelty to animals. During the nineteenth century, for example, it was commonly said that such statutes were designed to protect human beings by preventing the growth of cruel habits that could later threaten human beings with harm too. Prof. Louis B. Schwartz finds the rationale of the cruelty-to-animals prohibition in its protection of animal lovers from affronts to their sensibilities:

> It is not the mistreated dog who is the ultimate object of concern. Our concern is for the feelings of other human beings, a large proportion of whom, although accustomed to the slaughter of animals for food, readily identify themselves with a tortured dog or horse and respond with great sensitivity to its sufferings.

This seems to me to be factitious. How much more natural it is to say with John Chipman Gray that the true purpose of cruelty-to-animals statutes is "to preserve the dumb brutes from suffering." The very people whose sensibilities are invoked in the alternative explanation, a group that no doubt now includes most of us, are precisely those who would insist that the protection belongs primarily to the animals themselves, not merely to their own tender feelings. Indeed, it would be difficult even to account for the existence of such feelings in the absence of a belief that the animals deserve the protection in their own right and for their own sakes.

Even if we allow, as I think we must, that animals are the intended direct beneficiaries of legislation forbidding cruelty to animals, it does not follow directly that animals have legal rights, and Gray himself, for one, refused to draw this further inference. Animals cannot have rights, he thought, for the same reason they cannot have duties, namely, that they are not genuine "moral agents."

Now, it is relatively easy to see why animals cannot have duties, and this matter is largely beyond controversy. Animals cannot be "reasoned with" or instructed in their responsibilities; they are inflexible and unadaptable to future contingencies; they are subject to fits of instinctive passion which they are incapable of repressing or controlling, postponing or sublimating. Hence, they cannot enter into contractual agreements, or make promises; they cannot be trusted; and they cannot be blamed for what would be called "moral failures" in a human being. They are therefore incapable of being moral subjects, of acting rightly or wrongly in the moral sense, of having, discharging, or breeching duties and obligations.

But what is there about the intellectual incompetence of animals (which admittedly disqualifies them for duties) that makes them logically unsuitable for rights? The most common reply to this question is that animals are incapable of *claiming* rights on their own. They cannot make motion, on their own, to courts to have their claims recognized or enforced; they cannot initiate, on their own, any kind of legal proceedings; nor are they capable of even understanding when their rights are being violated, of distinguishing harm from wrongful injury, and responding with indignation and an outraged sense of justice instead of mere anger or fear.

No one can deny any of these allegations, but to the claim that they are the grounds for disqualification of rights of animals, philosophers on the other side of this controversy have made convincing rejoinders. It is simply *not* true, says W. D. Lamont, that the ability to understand what a right is and the ability to set legal machinery in motion by one's own initiative are necessary for the possession of rights. If that were the case, then neither human idiots nor wee babies would have any legal rights at all. Yet it is manifest that both of these classes of intellectual incompetents have legal rights recognized and easily enforced by the courts. Children and idiots start legal proceedings, not on their own direct initiative, but rather through the actions of proxies or attorneys who are empowered to speak in their names.

If there is no conceptual absurdity in this situation, why should there be in the case where a proxy makes a claim on behalf of an animal? People commonly enough make wills leaving money to trustees for the care of animals. Is it not natural to speak of the animal's right to his inheritance in cases of this kind? If a trustee embezzles money from the animal's account, and a proxy speaking in the dumb brute's behalf presses the animal's claim, can he not be described as asserting the animal's *rights*?

More exactly, the animal itself claims its rights through the vicarious actions of a human proxy speaking in its name and in its behalf. There appears to be no reason why we should require the animal to understand what is going on (so the argument concludes) as a condition for regarding it as a possessor of rights.

Some writers protest at this point that the legal relation between a principal and an agent cannot hold between animals and human beings. Between humans, the relation of agency can take two very different forms, depending upon the degree of discretion granted to the agent, and there is a continuum of combinations between the extremes. On the one hand, there is the agent who is the mere "mouthpiece" of his principal. He is a "tool" in much the same sense as is a typewriter or telephone; he simply transmits the instructions of his principal. Human beings could hardly be the agents or representatives of animals in this sense, since the dumb brutes could no more use human "tools" than mechanical ones.

On the other hand, an agent may be some sort of expert hired to exercise his professional judgment on behalf of, and in the name of, the principal. He may be given, within some limited area of expertise, complete independence to act as he deems best, binding his principal to all the beneficial or detrimental consequences. This is the role played by trustees, lawyers, and ghost-writers. This type of representation requires that the agent have great skill, but makes little or no demand upon the principal, who may leave everything to the judgment of his agent. Hence, there appears, at first, to be no reason why an animal cannot be a totally passive principal in this second kind of agency relationship.

H. J. McCloskey, I believe, accepts the argument up to this point, but he presents a new and different reason for denying that animals can have legal rights. The ability to make claims, whether directly or through a representative, he implies, is essential to the possession of rights. Animals obviously cannot press their claims on their own, and so if they have rights, these rights must be assertable by agents. Animals, however, cannot be represented, McCloskey contends, and not for any of the reasons already discussed but rather because representation, in the requisite sense, is always of *interests*, and animals (he says) are incapable of having interests.

Now, there is a very important insight expressed in the requirement that a being have interests if he is to be a logically proper subject of rights. This can be appreciated if we consider just why it is that mere things cannot have rights. Consider a very precious "mere thing"—a beautiful natural wilderness, or a complex and ornamental artifact, like the Taj Mahal. Such things ought to be cared for, because they would sink into decay if neglected, depriving some human beings, or perhaps even all human beings, of something of great value. Certain persons may even have as their own special job the care and protection of these valuable objects.

But we are not tempted in these cases to speak of "thing-rights" correlative to custodial duties, because, try as we might, we cannot think of mere things as possessing interests of their own. Some people may have a duty to preserve, maintain, or improve the Taj Mahal, but they can hardly have a duty to help or hurt it, benefit or aid it, succor or relieve it. Custodians may protect it for the sake of a nation's pride and art lovers' fancy; but they don't keep it in good repair for "its own sake," or for "its own true welfare," or "well-being."

A mere thing, however valuable to others, has no good of its own. The explanation of that fact, I suspect, consists in the fact that mere things have no conative life: no conscious wishes, desires, and hopes; or urges and impulses; or unconscious drives, aims, and goals; or latent tendencies, direction of growth, and natural fulfillments. Interests must be compounded somehow out of conations; hence mere things have no interests. Consequently, they have no interests to be protected by legal or moral rules. Without interests a creature can have no "good" of its own, the achievement of which can be its due. Mere things are not loci of value in their own right, but rather their value consists entirely in their being objects of other beings' interests.

So far McCloskey is on solid ground, but one can quarrel with his denial that any animals but humans have interests. I should think that the trustee of funds willed to a dog or cat is more than a mere custodian of the animal he protects. Rather his job is to look out for the interests of the animal and make sure no one denies it its due. The animal itself is the beneficiary of his dutiful services.

Many of the higher animals at least have appetites, conative urges, and rudimentary purposes, the integrated satisfaction of which constitutes their welfare or good. We can, of course, with consistency treat animals as mere pests and deny that they have any rights; for most animals, especially those of the lower orders we have no choice but to do so. But it seems to me, nevertheless, that in general, animals *are* among the sorts of beings of whom rights can meaningfully be predicated and denied.

Now, if a person agrees with the conclusion of the argument thus far, that animals are the sorts of beings that *can* have rights, and further, if he accepts the moral judgment that we ought to be kind to animals, only one further premise is needed to yield the conclusion that some animals do in fact have rights. We must now ask ourselves for whose sake ought we to treat (some) animals with consideration and humaneness? If we conceive our duty to be one of obedience to authority, or to one's own conscience merely, or one of consideration for tender human sensibilities only, then we might still deny that animals have rights, even though we admit that they are the kinds of beings that *can* have rights.

But if we hold not only that we ought to treat animals humanely but also that we should do so for the animals' own sake that such treatment is something we owe animals as their due, something that can be claimed for them, something the withholding of which would be an injustice and a wrong, and not merely a harm, then it follows that we do ascribe rights to animals. I suspect that the moral judgments most of us make about animals do pass these phenomenological tests, so that most of us do believe that animals have rights, but are reluctant to say so because of the conceptual confusions about the notion of a right that I have attempted to dispel above.

Now we can extract from our discussion of animal rights a crucial principle for tentative use in the resolution of the other riddles about the applicability of the concept of a right, namely, that the sorts of beings who can have rights are precisely those who have (or can have) interests. I have come to this tentative conclusion for two reasons: (1) because a right holder must be capable of being represented and it is impossible to represent a being that has no interests, and (2) because a right holder must be capable of being a beneficiary in his own person, and a being without interests is a being that is incapable of being harmed or benefitted, having no good or "sake" of its own. Thus, a being without interests has no "behalf" to act in, and no "sake" to act for.

My strategy now will be to apply the "interest principle," as we can call it, to the other puzzles about rights, while being prepared to modify it where necessary (but as little as possible), in the hope of separating in a consistent and intuitively satisfactory fashion the beings who can have rights from those which cannot.

Vegetables

It is clear that we ought not to mistreat certain plants, and indeed there are rules and regulations imposing duties on persons not to misbehave in respect to certain members of the vegetable kingdom. It is forbidden, for example, to pick wildflowers in the mountainous tundra areas of national parks, or to endanger trees by starting fires in dry forest areas. Members of Congress introduce bills designed, as they say, to "protect" rare redwood trees from commercial pillage.

Given this background, it is surprising that no one speaks of plants as having rights. Plants, after all, are not "mere things"; they are vital objects with inherited biological propensities determining their natural growth. Moreover, we do say that certain conditions are "good" or "bad" for plants, thereby suggesting that plants, unlike rocks, are capable of having a "good." (This is a case, however, where "what we say" should not be taken seriously: we also say that certain kinds of paint are good or bad for the internal walls of a house, and this does not commit us to a conception of walls as beings possessed of a good or welfare of their own.) Finally, we are capable of feeling a kind of affection for particular plants, though we rarely personalize them, as we do in the case of animals, by giving them proper names.

Still, all are agreed that plants are not the kinds of beings that can have rights. Plants are never plausibly understood to be the direct intended beneficiaries of rules designed to "protect" them. We wish to keep redwood groves in existence for the sake of human beings who can enjoy their serene beauty, and for the sake of generations of human beings yet unborn. Trees are not the sorts of beings who have their "own sakes," despite the fact that they have biological propensities. Having no conscious wants or goals of their own, trees cannot know satisfaction or frustration, pleasure or pain. Hence, there is no possibility of kind or cruel treatment of trees. In these morally crucial respects, trees differ from the higher species of animals.

Yet trees are not mere things like rocks. They grow and develop according to the laws of their own nature. Aristotle and Aquinas both took trees to have their own "natural ends." Why then do I deny them the status of beings with interests of their own? The reason is that an interest, however the concept is finally to be analyzed, presupposes at least rudimentary cognitive equipment. Interests are compounded out of *desires* and *aims*, both of which presuppose something like *belief*, or cognitive awareness.

Mere brute longings unmediated by beliefs—longings for one knows not what—might perhaps be a primitive form of consciousness (I don't want to beg that question) but they are altogether different from the sort of thing we mean by "desire," especially when we speak of human beings.

If some such account as the above is correct, we can never have any grounds for attributing a desire or a want to a creature known to be incapable even of rudimentary beliefs; and if desires or wants are the materials interests are made of, mindless creatures have no interests of their own. The law, therefore, cannot have as its intention the protection of their interests, so that "protective legislation" has to be understood as legislation protecting the interests human beings may have in them.

Plant life might nevertheless be thought at first to constitute a hard case for the interest principle for two reasons. In the first place, plants no less than animals are said

The Rights of Animals and Unborn Generations

to have needs of their own. To be sure, we can speak even of mere things as having needs too, but such talk misleads no one into thinking of the need as belonging, in the final analysis, to the "mere thing" itself. If we were so deceived we would not be thinking of the mere thing as a "mere thing" after all. We say, for example, that John Doe's walls need painting, or that Richard Roe's car needs a washing, but we direct our attitudes of sympathy or reproach (as the case may be) to John and Richard, not to their possessions. It would be otherwise, if we observed that some child is in need of a good meal. Our sympathy and concern in that case would be directed at the child himself as the true possessor of the need in question.

The needs of plants might well seem closer to the needs of animals than to the pseudo-needs of mere things. An owner may need a plant (say, for its commercial value or as a potential meal), but the plant itself, it might appear, needs nutrition or cultivation. Our confusion about this matter may stem from language. It is a commonplace that the word 'need' is ambiguous. To say that X needs Y may be to say either: (1) Y is necessary to the achievement of one of X's goals, or to the performance of one of its functions, or (2) Y is good for X; its lack would harm X or be injurious or detrimental to him (or it). The first sort of need-statement is value-neutral, implying no comment on the value of the goal or function in question; whereas the second kind of statement about needs commits its maker to a value judgment about what is good or bad for X in the long run, that is, about what is in X's interests.

A being must have interests, therefore, to have needs in the second sense, but *any* kind of thing, vegetable or mineral, could have needs in the first sense. An automobile needs gas and oil to function, but it is no tragedy for it if it runs out—an empty tank does not hinder or retard its interests. Similarly, to say that a tree needs sunshine and water is to say that without them it cannot grow and survive; but unless the growth and survival of trees are matters of human concern, affecting human interests, practical or aesthetic, the needs of trees alone will not be the basis of any claim of what is "due" them in their own right. Plants may need things in order to discharge their functions, but their functions are assigned by human interests, not their own.

The second source of confusion derives from the fact that we commonly speak of plants as thriving and flourishing, or withering and languishing. One might be tempted to think of these states either as themselves consequences of the possession of interests so that even creatures without wants or beliefs can be said to have interests, or else as grounds independent of the possession of interests for the making of intelligible claims of rights. In either case, plants would be thought of as conceivable possessors of rights after all.

Consider what it means to speak of something as "flourishing." The verb *to flourish* apparently was applied originally and literally to plants only, and in its original sense it meant simply "to bear flowers: *blossom*"; but then by analogical extension of sense it came also to mean "to grow luxuriantly: increase, and enlarge," and then to "*thrive*" (generally), and finally, when extended to human beings, "to be prosperous," or to "increase in wealth, honor, comfort, happiness, or whatever is desirable." Applied to human beings the term is, of course, a fixed metaphor. When a person flourishes, something happens to his interests analogous to what happens to a plant when it flowers, grows, and spreads. A person flourishes when his interests (whatever they may be) are progressing severally and collectively toward their harmonious fulfillment and spawning new interests along the way whose prospects are also good. To flourish is to glory in the advancement of one's interests, in short, to be happy.

Nothing is gained by twisting the botanical metaphor back from humans to plants. To speak of thriving human interests as if they were flowers is to speak naturally and well, and to mislead no one. But then to think of the flowers or plants as if they were interests (or the signs of interests) is to bring the metaphor back full circle for no good reason and in the teeth of our actual beliefs. Some of our talk about flourishing plants reveals quite clearly that the interests that thrive when plants flourish are human not "plant interests."

For example, we sometimes make a flowering bush flourish by "frustrating" its own primary propensities. We pinch off dead flowers before seeds have formed, thus "encouraging" the plant to make new flowers in an effort to produce more seeds. It is not the plant's own natural propensity (to produce seeds) that is advanced, but rather the gardener's interest in the production of new flowers and the spectator's pleasure in aesthetic form, color, or scent. What we mean in such cases by saying that the plant flourishes is that our interest in the plant, not its own, is thriving.

Whole Species

The topic of whole species, whether of plants or animals, can be treated in much the same way as that of individual plants. A whole collection, as such, cannot have beliefs, expectations, wants, or desires, and can flourish or languish only in the human interest-related sense in which individual plants thrive and decay. Individual elephants can have interests, but the species elephant cannot. Even where individual elephants are not granted rights, human beings may have an interest—economic, scientific, or sentimental—in keeping the species from dying out, and *that* interest may be protected in various ways by law. But that is quite another matter from recognizing a right to survival belonging to the species itself.

Still, the preservation of a whole species may quite properly seem to be a morally more important matter than the preservation of an individual animal. Individual animals can have rights but it is implausible to ascribe to them a right to life on the human model. Nor do we normally have duties to keep individual animals alive or even to abstain from killing them provided we do it humanely and nonwantonly in the promotion of legitimate human interests. On the other hand, we do have duties to protect threatened species, not duties to the species themselves as such, but rather duties to future human beings, duties derived from our housekeeping role as temporary inhabitants of this planet.

We commonly and very naturally speak of corporate entities, such as institutions, churches, and national states as having rights and duties, and an adequate analysis of the conditions for ownership of rights should account for that fact. A corporate entity, of course, is more than a mere collection of things that have some important traits in common. Unlike a biological species, an institution has a charter, or constitution, or bylaws, with rules defining offices and procedures, and it has human beings whose function it is to administer the rules and apply the procedures. When the institution has a duty to an outsider, there is always some determinant human being whose duty it is to do something for the outsider, and when the state, for example, has a right to collect taxes, there are always certain definite flesh and blood persons who have rights to demand tax money from other citizens.

We have no reluctance to use the language of corporate rights and duties because we know that in the last analysis these are rights or duties of individual persons, acting in their "official capacities." And when individuals act in their official roles in accordance with valid empowering rules, their acts are imputable to the organization itself and become "acts of state." Thus, there is no need to posit any individual superperson named by the expression "the State" (or for that matter, "the company," "the club," or "the church.") Nor is there any reason to take the rights of corporate entities to be exceptions to the interest principle. The United States is not a superperson with wants and beliefs of its own, but it is a corporate entity with corporate interests that are, in turn, analyzable into the interests of its numerous flesh and blood members.

Dead Persons

So far we have refined the interest principle but we have not had occasion to modify it. Applied to dead persons, however, it will have to be stretched to near the breaking point if it is to explain how our duty to honor commitments to the dead can be thought to be linked to the rights of the dead against us. The case against ascribing rights to dead men can be made very simply: a dead man is a mere corpse, a piece of decaying organic matter. Mere inanimate things can have no interests, and what is incapable of having interests is incapable of having rights. If, nevertheless, we grant dead men rights against us, we would seem to be treating the interests they had while alive as somehow surviving their deaths.

There is the sound of paradox in this way of talking, but it may be the least paradoxical way of describing our moral relations to our predecessors. And if the idea of an interest's surviving its possessor's death is a kind of fiction, it is a fiction that most living men have a real interest in preserving.

Most persons while still alive have certain desires about what is to happen to their bodies, their property, or their reputations after they are dead. For that reason, our legal system has developed procedures to enable persons while still alive to determine whether their bodies will be used for purposes of medical research or organic transplantation, and to whom their wealth is to be transferred. Living men also take out life insurance policies guaranteeing that the accumulated benefits be conferred upon beneficiaries of their own choice. They also make private agreements, both contractual and informal, in which they receive promises that certain things will be done after their deaths in exchange for some present service or consideration. In all these cases promises are made to living persons that their wishes will be honored after they are dead. Like all other valid promises, they impose duties on the promisor and confer correlative rights on the promisee.

How does the situation change after the promisee has died? Surely the duties of the promisor do not suddenly become null and void. If that were the case, and known to be the case there could be no confidence in promises regarding posthumous arrangements; no one would bother with wills or life insurance companies to pay benefits to survivors, which are, in a sense, only conditional duties before a man dies. They come into existence as categorical demands for immediate action only upon the promisee's death. So the view that death renders them null and void has the truth exactly upside down.

The survival of the promisor's duty after the promisee's death does not prove that the promisee retains a right even after death for we might prefer to conclude that there is one class of cases where duties to keep promises are not logically correlated with a promisee's right, namely, cases where the promisee has died. Still, a morally sensitive promisor is likely to think of his promised performance not only as a duty (i.e., a morally required action) but also as something owed to the deceased promisee as his due. Honoring such promises is a way of keeping faith with the dead.

To be sure, the promisor will not think of his duty as something to be done for the promisee's "good," since the promisee, being dead, has no "good" of his own. We can think of certain of the deceased's interests, however, (including especially those enshrined in wills and protected by contracts and promises) as surviving their owner's death, and constituting claims against us that persist beyond the life of the claimant. Such claims can be represented by proxies just like the claims of animals. This way of speaking, I believe, reflects more accurately than any other an important fact about the human condition: we have an interest while alive that other interests of ours will continue to be recognized and served after we are dead. The whole practice of honoring wills and testaments and the like, is thus for the sake of the living, just as a particular instance of it may be thought to be for the sake of one who is dead.

Conceptual sense, then, can be made of talk about dead men's rights; but it is still a wide open moral question whether dead men in fact have rights, and if so, what those rights are. In particular, commentators have disagreed over whether a man's interest in his reputation deserves to be protected from defamation even after his death. With only a few prominent exceptions, legal systems punish a libel on a dead man "only when its publication is in truth an attack upon the interests of living persons." A widow or a son may be wounded, or embarrassed, or even injured economically, by a defamatory attack on the memory of their dead husband or father. In Utah defamation of the dead is a misdemeanor and in Sweden a cause of action in tort. The law rarely presumes, however, that a dead man himself has any interests, representable by proxy, that can be injured by defamation, apparently because of the maxim that what a dead man doesn't know can't hurt him.

While it is true that a dead man cannot have his feelings hurt, it does not follow, therefore, that his claim to be thought of no worse than he deserves cannot survive his death. Almost every living person, I should think, would wish to have this interest protected after his death, at least during the lifetimes of those persons who were his contemporaries. We can hardly expect the law to protect Julius Caesar from defamation in the history books. This might hamper historical research and restrict socially valuable forms of expression. Even interests that survive their owner's death are not immortal. Anyone should be permitted to say anything he wishes about George Washington or Abraham Lincoln though perhaps not everything is morally permissible. Everyone ought to refrain from malicious lies even about Nero or King Tut, though not so much for those ancients' own sakes as for the sake of those who would now know the truth about the past. We owe it to the brothers Kennedy, however, as their due not to tell damaging lies about them to those who were once their contemporaries.

If the reader would deny that judgment, I can only urge him to ask himself whether he now wishes his own interest in reputation to be respected, along with his interest in determining the distribution of his wealth, after his death.

Human Vegetables

Mentally deficient and deranged human beings are hardly ever so handicapped intellectually that they do not compare favorably with even the highest of the lower animals, though they are commonly so incompetent that they cannot be assigned duties or be held responsible for what they do. Since animals can have rights, then, it follows that human idiots and madmen can too. It would make good sense, for example, to ascribe to them a right to be cured whenever effective therapy is available at reasonable cost, and even those incurables who have been consigned to a sanatorium for permanent "warehousing" can claim (through a proxy) their right to decent treatment.

Human beings suffering extreme cases of mental illness however, may be so utterly disoriented or insensitive as to compare quite unfavorably with the brightest cats and dogs. Those suffering from catatonic schizophrenia may be barely distinguishable in respect to those traits presupposed by the possession of interests from the lowliest vegetables. So long as we regard these patients as potentially curable, we may think of them as human beings with interests in their own restoration and treat them as possessors of rights. We may think of the patient as a genuine human person inside the vegetable casing struggling to get out, just as in the old fairy tales a pumpkin could be thought of as a beautiful maiden under a magic spell waiting only the proper words to be restored to her true self. Perhaps it is reasonable never to lose hope that a patient can be cured, and therefore to regard him always as a person "under a spell" with a permanent interest in his own recovery that is entitled to recognition and protection.

What if, nevertheless, we think of the catatonic schizophrenic and the vegetating patient with irreversible brain damage as absolutely incurable? Can we think of them at the same time as possessed of interests and rights too, or is this combination of traits a conceptual impossibility?

Shocking as it may at first seem, I am driven unavoidably to the latter view. If redwood trees and rosebushes cannot have rights, neither can incorrigible human vegetables. The trustees who are designated to administer funds for the care of these unfortunates are better understood as mere custodians than as representatives of their interests since these patients no longer have interests. It does not follow that they should not be kept alive as long as possible: that is an open moral question not foreclosed by conceptual analysis. Even if we have duties to keep human vegetables alive, however, they cannot be duties to them. We may be obliged to keep them alive to protect the sensibilities of others, or to foster humanitarian tendencies in ourselves, but we cannot keep them alive for their own good, for they are no longer capable of having a "good" of their own.

Without awareness, expectation, belief, desire, aim, and purpose, a being can have no interests; without interests, he cannot be benefited; without the capacity to be a beneficiary, he can have no rights. But there may nevertheless be a dozen other reasons to treat him as if he did.

Fetuses

If the interest principle is to permit us to ascribe rights to infants, fetuses, and generations yet unborn, it can only be on the grounds that interests can exert a claim upon us even before their possessors actually come into being, just the reverse of the situation respecting dead men where interests are respected even after their possessors have ceased to be.

Newly born infants are surely noisier than mere vegetables, but they are just barely brighter. They come into existence, as Aristotle said, with the capacity to acquire concepts and dispositions, but in the beginning we suppose that their consciousness of the world is a "blooming, buzzing confusion." They do have a capacity, no doubt from the very beginning, to feel pain, and this alone may be sufficient ground for ascribing both an interest and a right to them. Apart from that, however, during the first few hours of their lives, at least, they may well lack even the rudimentary intellectual equipment necessary to the possession of interests. Of course, this induces no moral reservations whatever in adults.

Children grow and mature almost visibly in the first few months so that those future interests that are so rapidly emerging from the unformed chaos of their earliest days seem unquestionably to be the basis of their present rights. Thus, we say of a newborn infant that he has a right now to live and grow into his adulthood, even though he lacks the conceptual equipment at this very moment to have this or any other desire.

A new infant, in short, lacks the traits necessary for the possession of interests, but he has the capacity to acquire those traits and his inherited potentialities are moving quickly toward actualization even as we watch him. Those proxies who make claims in behalf of infants, then, are more than mere custodians: they are (or can be) genuine representatives of the child's emerging interests, which may need protection even now if they are to be allowed to come into existence at all.

The same principle may be extended to "unborn persons." After all, the situation of fetuses one day before birth is not strikingly different from that a few hours after birth. The rights our law confers on the unborn child, both proprietary and personal, are for the most part, placeholders or reservations for the rights he shall inherit when he becomes a full-fledged interested being. The law protects a potential interest in these cases before it has even grown into actuality, as a garden fence protects newly seeded flower beds long before blooming flowers have emerged from them.

The unborn child's present right to property, for example, is a legal protection offered now to his future interest, contingent upon his birth, and instantly voidable if he dies before birth. Assuming that the child will be born, the law seems to say, various interests that he will come to have after birth must be protected from damage that they can incur even before birth. Thus prenatal injuries of a negligently inflicted kind can give the newly born child a right to sue for damages which he can exercise through a proxy-attorney and in his own name any time *after* he is born.

There are numerous other places, however, where our law seems to imply an unconditional 'right to be born,' and surprisingly no one seems ever to have found that idea conceptually absurd. One interesting example comes from an article given the following headline by the *New York Times*: "Unborn Child's Right Upheld over Religion." A hospital patient in her eighth month of pregnancy refused to take a blood transfusion even though warned by her physician that "she might die at any minute and take the life of her child as well." The ground of her refusal was that blood transfusions are repugnant to the principles of her religion (Jehovah's Witnesses). The Supreme Court of New Jersey expressed uncertainty over the constitutional question of whether a nonpregnant adult might refuse on religious grounds a blood transfusion pronounced necessary to her own survival, but the court nevertheless ordered the patient in the present case to receive the transfusion on the grounds that "the unborn child is entitled to the law's protection."

It is important to reemphasize here that the questions of whether fetuses do or ought to have rights are substantive questions of law and morals open to argument and decision. The prior question of whether fetuses are the kind of beings that can have rights, however, is a conceptual, not a moral, question, amenable only to what is called "logical analysis," and irrelevant to moral judgment.

The correct answer to the conceptual question, I believe, is that unborn children *are* among the sorts of beings of whom possession of rights can meaningfully be predicated, even though they are (temporarily) incapable of having interests, because their future interests can be protected now, and it does make sense to protect a potential interest even before it has grown into actuality. The interest principle, however, makes perplexing, at best, talk of an unconditional fetal right to be born; for fetuses, lacking actual wants and beliefs, have no actual interest in being born, and it is difficult to think of any other reason for ascribing any rights to them other than on the assumption that they will in fact be born.

Future Generations

We have it in our power now to make the world a much less pleasant place for our descendants than the world we inherited from our ancestors. We can continue to proliferate in ever greater numbers, using up fertile soil at an even greater rate, dumping our wastes into rivers, lakes, and oceans, cutting down our forests, and polluting the atmosphere with noxious gases.

All thoughtful people agree that we ought not to do these things. Most would say that we have a duty not to do these things, meaning not merely that conservation is morally required (as opposed to merely desirable) but also that it is something due our descendants, something to be done for their sakes. Surely we owe it to future generations to pass on a world that is not a used up garbage heap. Our remote descendants are not yet present to claim a livable world as their right, but there are plenty of proxies to speak now in their behalf. These spokesmen, far from being mere custodians, are genuine representatives of future interests.

Why then deny that the human beings of the future have rights which can be claimed against us now in their behalf? Some are inclined to deny them present rights out of a fear of falling into obscure metaphysics, by granting rights to remote and unidentifiable beings who are not yet even in existence. Our unborn great-great-grandchildren are in some sense "potential" persons, but they are far more remotely potential, it may seem, than fetuses. This, however, is not the real difficulty. Unborn generations are more remotely potential than fetuses in one sense, but not in another. A much greater period of time with a far greater number of causally necessary and important events must pass before their potentiality can be actualized, it is true; but our collective posterity is just as certain to come into existence "in the normal course of events" as is any given fetus now in its mother's womb. In that sense the existence of the distant human future is no more remotely potential than that of a particular child already on its way.

The real difficulty is not that we doubt whether our descendants will ever be actual, but rather that we don't know who they will be. It is not their temporal remoteness that troubles us so much as their indeterminacy—their present facelessness and namelessness. Five centuries from now men and women will be living where we live now. Any given one of them will have an interest in living space, fertile soil, fresh air, and the like, but that arbitrarily selected one has no other qualities we can presently envision very clearly. We don't even know who his parents, grandparents, or great-grandparents are, or even whether he is related to us.

Still, whoever these human beings may turn out to be, and whatever they might reasonably be expected to be like, they will have interests that we can affect, for better or worse, right now. That much we can and do know about them. The identity of the owners of these interests is now necessarily obscure, but the fact of their interest-ownership is crystal clear, and that is all that is necessary to certify the coherence of present talk about their rights. We can tell, sometimes, that shadowy forms in the spatial distance belong to human beings, though we know not who or how many they are; and this imposes a duty on us not to throw bombs for example, in their direction. In like manner, the vagueness of the human future does not weaken its claim on us in light of the nearly certain knowledge that it will, after all, be human.

Conclusion

For several centuries now human beings have run roughshod over the lands of our planet, just as if the animals who do live there and the generations of humans who will live there had no claims on them whatever. Philosophers have not helped matters by arguing that animals and future generations are not the kinds of beings who can have rights now, that they don't presently qualify for membership, even "auxiliary membership," in our moral community.

I have tried in this essay to dispel the conceptual confusions that make such conclusions possible. To acknowledge their rights is the very least we can do for members of endangered species (including our own). But that is something.

DO ROCKS HAVE RIGHTS?

RODERICK NASH (1977)

Thomas Jefferson stands out among the creators of the American political system in recognizing that an educated citizenry is prerequisite to an effective democracy. His advocacy of a hierarchical public education system was meant to insure that American yeomen were not just good farmers hut also intelligent voters.

In Jefferson's time, three-quarters of what would become the United States was wilderness. The only problems in man-environment relations concerned advancement of the former over the latter. Jimmy Carter's America, on the other hand, finds the relative position of man and environment reversed. Civilization dominates. It has often run roughshod over the natural processes and systems on which the social and biological future of mankind and other kinds depends.

Responsible citizenship today must include the capacity for dealing intelligently with the greatest long-term issues of our time. If the educated citizen was essential in Jefferson's era, the envirownentally educated, environmentally responsible citizen is vital in our own.

The idea of environmental education has some background in the American past. During Theodore Roosevelt's presidency, Liberty Hyde Bailey of Cornell University advanced the importance of nature study in the educational programs of an increasingly urbanized society. Conservation education, with a heavy slant toward the contour-plowing, tree-planting approach of the Civilian Conservation Corps, provided a rallying point in the 1930s. Following World War II, the growth of leisure and affluence gave rise to outdoor education with an emphasis on the development of recreational skills.

In the 1960s, environmental education came into vogue. Implicit was the idea that environmental quality (meaning such amenities as beauty, solitude, and the opportunity to observe wild animals) was just as important as environmental productivity. The emerging science of ecology, with its focus on interrelated systems of a total life community, also informed the new approach. Environmental educators tended to discredit the old confidence that a technological fix existed for every problem. They talked about mind pollution. They began to understand that the only sure, long-term solutions to environmental problems depended on changing people's attitudes and values. More specifically, the need was for personal and social restraint. Less, it was said, could be more. Small could be beautiful.

But the environmental and political leaders of the 1960s and 1970s who called upon Americans to subordinate immediate and individual advantage found the sledding rough. As Leo Marx has reminded us, in his 1970 *Science* article, "American

Institutions and Ecological Ideals," the ideal of long-term stability in man-environment relations ran directly against the growth-oriented American ethos. Conservation was nice when you could afford it; but the step from vague, general acceptance of this ideal to the tough, sacrificial decision needed to implement it was, for most persons, too great. What Garrett Hardin has called "the tragedy of the commons" worked to discourage environmental altruism. Why, after all, should the individual conserve energy, or limit his or her reproductive activity, or give a damn about whooping cranes and redwood trees?

The basic problem may be that in the midst of all the previous decade's clamor over conservation few paused to consider the need for a rationale. After all, most twentieth-century Americans are the beneficiaries of the good life which technological civilization made possible. They were the fortunate people chosen to reap the rewards of one hundred centuries of expert environmental exploitation. Certainly they were concerned about environmental problems crowding the headlines of the 1960s and 1970s.

But giving up their privileges—internalizing and personalizing the general concern about ecology—was not very appealing. Consequently, they professed an updated version of technological optimism: research and development would provide solutions. Or they blamed the problems of the world environment on teeming millions in other countries. Whenever environmental protection bills regarding air and water quality, or surface mining, or impact assessment became law, the first reaction of most Americans was to search the legislation for loopholes.

Reluctance to make personal sacrifices in life-style for the benefit of a healthy environment can be attributed in large part to the lack of a rationale. Old-style utilitarian conservation was not plagued by this problem. Man's material interests were indisputably paramount, and conservation served those ends. But the new style of conservation, labeled "environment" and "ecology," often involved compromising man's immediate material interests. There was an enormous difference between asking people to conserve forests so they could have an endless supply of timber and asking them to live in smaller houses. The new conservation frankly recognized that man was not the sole occupant of the planet. It tended to see *Homo sapiens* as a member, not the master, of a life community. And the new conservation attached greater importance to the welfare of the natural processes and systems that supported all life than it did to the prosperity of one precocious variety of life. Enlightened as were these sentiments, they offered a much poorer intellectual foundation for building public acceptance than did the old man-centered conservation.

It was at this juncture that environmental ethics, which imply that some kind of moral relationship does or should exist between people and nature, received increased attention as an ultimate justification for environmental responsibility. The utility of environmental ethics is readily apparent from an examination of social ethics. The latter, however imperfect, permit human society to exist just as the social-contract philosophers have explained. Social ethics and the laws arising from them, restrain the individual in his appetites. We refrain from raping and robbing other people because it is wrong.

But the earth is something else; it is beyond the limits of most Americans' ethical systems. Although a few prophets have tried to advance it, there is little general understanding that the concept of community and its attendant ethics might include nonhuman life and the nonliving earth. The rights of animals are dubious; the rights of rocks an absurdity. But some people are starting to realize that without such concepts, the whole rationale for conservation is laid upon a sandbar easily eroded by the tides of self-interest.

Energy and growth policies may come and go. Presidents may deliver impassioned messages. But real progress, many now feel, awaits substitution of ethical for economic criteria in calculating the impact of human action on the natural world. From this perspective, conservation is justified not because it is profitable or aesthetically pleasing, or even because it promotes a person's or race's survival. It is justified because, in the last analysis, it is right. The explosive force of this idea is only now beginning to be felt.

«««—»»»

Many exponents of the current gospel of ecology assume that environmental ethics originated in the 1960s. The fact is that an extended system of morality encompassing the land and its full complement of life has respectable intellectual roots. Granted, those roots are longer and stronger in Asian cultures, but some contemporary Western thinkers have made bold to venture against the prevailing grain of anthropocentrism and environmental exploitation.

St. Francis of Assisi, the twelfth century ascetic, offers a starting point for a brief look at the rise of environmental ethics in the West. His view that not only wolves and birds but fire, water and the sun were brothers of man led to the need for respect and fair treatment. St. Francis' ideas, however, proved far too great a challenge to the anthropocentrism inherent in medieval Christianity; he was dismissed as heretic at best, a lunatic at worst.

The rise of biological science opened new doorways to reverence for the earth. John Ray, the first of the great English botanist-philosophers, wrote a book in 1691 entitled *The Wisdom of God Manifested in the Works of Creation*. Ray saw nature, all of nature, as having the primary purpose of exhibiting evidence of God's glory. He attacked the prevailing assumption that there is "no other end of any creature, but some way or other to be serviceable to man." Animals, Ray explained, exist to enjoy themselves. Their value and right to life do not depend on their utilitarian function.

Alexander Pope later made the point in couplets:

> Has God, thou fool!, work'd solely for thy good,
> Thy Job, thy pastime, thy attire, thy food? ...
> Know, Nature's children all divide her care;
> The fur that warms a monarch, warm'd a bear.

A similar idea permeated the Lutheran minister John Bruckner's *A Philosophical Study of the Animal Creation* in 1768. What worried Bruckner was the tendency for one species on earth, his own, to threaten other species and what he called "the whole plan of Providence." Should man not respect a common life-force uniting all creatures? Did not other beings have a right to life?

It is a mistake to construe the importance of the evolutionary ideas of Charles Darwin gathered together in 1859 in *Origin of Species*, as documenting a total struggle for existence among self-interested biological units. True, Darwin wrote about competition. But the broader significance of Darwin's work, the American philosopher Edward Evans said in 1894, was to take the "conceit out of man." According to Evans, Darwin showed "that the flower blooms not for the purpose of giving him agreeable sensations, but for its own sake, and that it presumed to put forth sweet and beautiful blossoms long before he appeared on the earth."

Darwin gave every reason for man to see himself as part and product of biological processes. It was not a great intellectual leap from that to the idea of respect for other participants. Darwin himself made the step in 1871, in his book, *Descent of Man*. Arguing that moral sense was a product of evolution just like the eye or hand, Darwin hypothesized its expansion from the level of pure individual self-interest. Over time, man broadened his social or community instincts to include the family, tribe, and race. Eventually the moral sense evolved to the point of recognizing the rights of imbeciles, maimed persons, and, as Darwin put it, other useless members of society." Then he added the extraordinary idea that "sympathy beyond the confines of man...to the lower animals, seems to be one of the latest moral acquisitions." Ultimately, Darwin thought, all sentient beings could be included in man's ethical community.

After Darwin, a growing minority continued asking why the restraints people displayed in their interaction with other people were not extended to other forms of life and even to the earth itself. John Muir in his journals from the 1870s wonders "Why should man value himself as more than a small part of the one great unit of creation?" Every animal, plant, and, Muir added, "crystal" or rock, just by its existence, denies the proposition "that the world was made especially for the uses of man." Muir extolled the Buddhist concept of universal unity: "Every atom in creation may be said to be... married to every other."

It was two decades later that Edward Evans advanced to a recognition of the ethical consequences of universal unity. "Man," the sometime University of Michigan professor reasoned, "is as truly a part and product of nature as any other animal, and [the] attempt to set him up on an isolated point outside of it is philosophically false and morally pernicious." Evans applauded the gradual change in the law to punish cruelty to animals as an offense against the animal rather than the animal's owner.

The idea that animals had feelings and could suffer and that people should be kind to them led to the radical proposition that animals had rights. As early as 1891, Henry Salt, an English schoolmaster, used the concept as the basis for his Humanitarian League. "The basis of any real morality," said Salt, "must be in the sense of kinship between all living beings." Acting on his principles, Salt revolutionized his lifestyle, sought a retreat in the hills near Surrey, and lived a self-sufficient vegetarian existence.

Salt's major book, *Seventy Years Among Savages*, published in 1921, quoted with enthusiasm a remarkable statement by the English novelist Thomas Hardy:

> Few people seem to perceive that the most far-reaching consequences of the establishment of the common origin of species is ethical; that it logically involved a readjustment of altruistic morals, by enlarging, as a necessity of

rightness, the application of what has been called 'the Golden Rule' from the area of mere mankind to that of the whole animal kingdom.

Albert Schweitzer added his concept of "reverence for life" to the literature of environmental ethics in the early twentieth century. Schweitzer refused to prioritize life. "Life as such is sacred," he maintained. "A reasonable ethic demands constant consideration for all living things down to the lowliest manifestation of life." The point was "to extend to all life the respect which we have for our own,"

The Cornell horticulturist Liberty Hyde Bailey, went a step further in 1915 in his book *The Holy Earth*. The land itself, the hard rock of the earth, is divine, argued Bailey, "because man did not make it." There was a need, he concluded, to "put our dominion into the realm of morals. It is now in the realm of trade." Alfred North Whitehead agreed, in a general sense, in his contention that there was intrinsic value in everything in the universe down to the last atom. "Every stone," Whitehead declared, "has a past and future."

«««—»»»

While Salt and Bailey and Schweitzer experimented with an expanded ethic without significant influence on public attitudes, a young American forester was shaping a philosophy that would vitalize the American environmental movement.

Aldo Leopold learned about ecological communities in the wilderness of Arizona and New Mexico long before ecology emerged as a science in the United States. His formulation of what he called a land ethic began in seminal essays in 1933, 1938; and 1939. But not until the winter of 1947-48 did the busy founder of the American profession of wildlife management weave the various strands of his thinking together in the conclusion of a slender book, *A Sand County Almanac*. It was published in 1949, but Leopold could not celebrate. On April 21, 1948, he died while fighting a brush fire on a neighbor's land along the Wisconsin River.

The key to Leopold's ideas is the concept of sequential ethics. The diagram (following page) may help to explain both what he meant and what has been extrapolated from his philosophy.

This diagrammatic representation of the evolution of ethics applies to ideal, not necessarily actual, conduct. At particular times and in particular situations most people are mired in various parts of the lower ethical echelons. Human beings, after all, still kill each other; they even kill members of their own families. Although we fail as a society consistently to live up to our ethics, we do have the concept of right and wrong with respect to other people. It is the standard according to which we construct and enforce our laws which are nothing more than the institutional expression of the ethical conviction of the group. A husband might kill his wife, but because of the existence of a social ethic and its attendant laws, he is punished if apprehended.

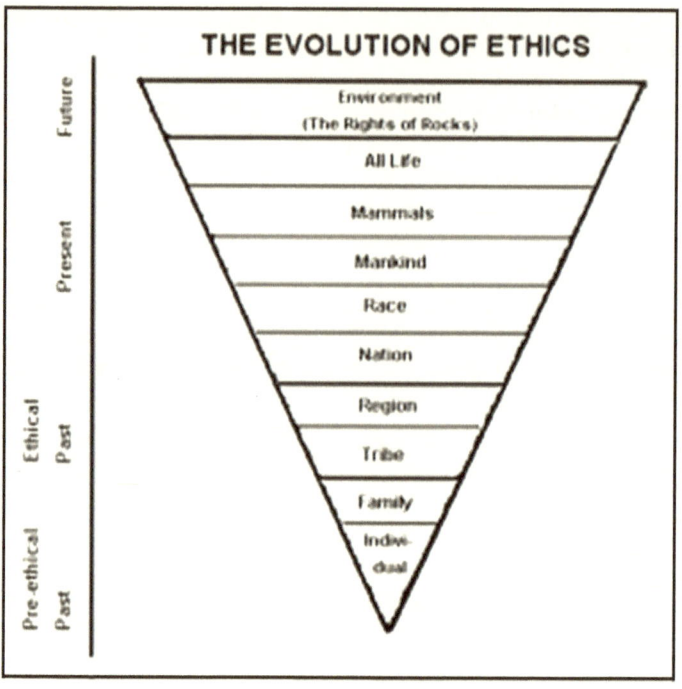

The central idea expressed in the diagram is that ethics have evolved over time to encompass increasingly larger communities. The timescale in the diagram expresses Leopold's assumption that at some point in the past ethics did not exist. The reason is simple: life existed before the mental capacity to think in terms of right and wrong. In what is labeled the "pre-ethical past" living things interacted on a strictly utilitarian, tooth-and-claw basis. The "ethical past" began when one form of life, man, evolved mentally to the point where it was possible to conceive of an action as being right or wrong on grounds other than those of utilitarianism. For eons, we can suppose, ethics applied only to the self and were, in fact, hardly an improvement on the pre-ethical world of isolated struggles for existence. Under pressure to survive, a person might cannibalize his mate or offspring without remorse or punishment at this rudimentary stage of ethical development.

The first expansion of ethics included families. Now a mate and offspring are encompassed in the envelope of ethical protection even though outside the family circle all was a dark tangle of unethical relationships. The extension may well have been prompted by the impulse to sustain one's kind. Ethics, then, were aids in the struggle for existence. They prompted the instinctively competitive individual to cooperate, according to Leopold, "in order that there may be a place to compete for." This realization sprang from the individual's recognition that he was "a member of a community of interdependent parts." As Leopold, the ecologist, saw it, all ethics stemmed from this recognition of community. In this sense the diagram traces the expanding definition of community or society as well as of ethics.

The extended family of aunts and cousins is a transition to the tribe. In this stage—which presumably prevailed for many thousands of years—the members of a tribe respect each other's rights. This means that they restrain their appetites and passions. They refuse to rape a fellow tribesman's daughter or to rob from the chief when his back is turned. From such primitive and unwritten roots social-contract theory originated. Restraint of the individual is the central concept. As Leopold put it, "an ethic, ecologically, is a limitation on freedom of action in the struggle for existence. An ethic, philosophically, is a differentiation of social from antisocial conduct." The two meanings converged in the tribe where Leopold noted a "tendency for interdependent individuals or groups to evolve modes of cooperation."

At the tribal stage morality ended abruptly after a short extension from the individual. It still does in the case of urban street gangs. There is honor among thieves, but outside the fraternity tooth-and-claw existence begins. To appreciate the force of ethics on human conduct, consider a chance meeting among members of the same tribe on a forest path far from the check of shame or punishment. The meeting involves no rape, robbery, enslavement, or murder. Now consider the same meeting between members of different tribes. Violence is almost certain, death a probability. Ethics explain the difference.

The tribes occupying the same region gradually discovered the benefits of mutual respect, and joined with other tribes in defining a more broadly based ethic. The roots of nations lie in such associations, as does the confidence that we can fly from New York or Arkansas to California without being raped, robbed, or killed. In time of war we see how powerful nation-based ethics are and how utterly unprotected is the enemy. International conventions that in theory support a system of ethics based on the dignity of all men have proven frail reeds in the face of the greed and hate generated by war.

A sense of racial identity is a transition between nation-based and species-based ethics in the same way that the extended family led the way to tribal allegiances. Most black people, regardless of nation, share a sense of community. So do white and red and yellow people. Ethics expand with this expansion of brotherhood.

Aldo Leopold took a particular interest in slavery. He described how the god-like Odysseus killed a dozen slave girls on his return from the Trojan Wars. It was not that Odysseus believed murder was right. Slaves simply did not fall into the ethical category that protected Odysseus' wife and fellow Greek citizens. The slaves were property and, as such beyond the ethical pale. Relations with them were strictly utilitarian, "a matter of expediency, not of right and wrong" in Leopold's words. For slaves the achievement of ethical identities awaited inclusion in the category "mankind." In the West such an extension of ethics did not come until the nineteenth century. In the United States, many historians feel, it required a civil war. But, as Leopold was quick to point out, "land, like Odysseus' slave girls, is still property." Land could be bought and sold, mistreated, even destroyed. Few laws ventured to penetrate the privacy of a person's relationship with *his* land.

«««—»»»

With the parallel between human and land slavery in mind, it is revealing to address for a moment the problem of how a land ethic would work to regulate man's use of the land. Could there be agriculture or forestry or mining if rocks had rights?

Leopold, who was, after all, a technician concerned with land productivity, clearly approved of such activities provided they were undertaken with respect for the land and knowledge of the natural processes that support its continuing health. Exploitation would end, just as it ended with the abolition of human slavery. In its place in the case of human labor came a wage system, labor unions, and recognition of the rights of working people. Work, some of it back-breaking, is still performed by one man for another. But the laborer is paid and his "person" respected.

Land, Leopold felt, might also be used but not abused, occupied but not owned absolutely. The expansion of ethics that made the enslavement of people wrong might continue until one day it abolished the enslavement of land. "We abuse land," Leopold concluded, "because we regard it as a commodity belonging to us. When we see land as a community to which we belong, we may begin to use it with love and respect."

Although he acknowledged imperfections in the system, Leopold accepted the fact that people include all human beings in their system of ethics. He understood religious concepts such as the Golden Rule as extending ethics to all mankind. The security with which most people travel throughout the world underscores the point. The presence of a species level ethic permits an Istanbul businessman to pass through Detroit without being captured and sold into slavery, just as it permits a Detroit secretary to visit Istanbul without fear of being pressed into concubinage.

What most concerned Leopold was the possibility of evolving beyond a definition of ethics that halted with *Homo sapiens*. The land ethic, he explained, "simply enlarges the boundaries of the community to include sods, waters, plants, and animals." The upper tiers of the diagram represent this enlargement. For most Americans today the first step is not too difficult. We are accustomed to including cute or loyal mammals in our ethical hierarchy. We literally love them and often treat them as fondly as children. Useful domestic animals also have a secure place in ethical constructs. For example, most people in the United States today would be shocked at the sight of someone killing a horse or a dog. They might even call the police or at least the Society for the Prevention of Cruelty to Animals. Somehow they feel killing a dog is wrong, that it is in the same moral category, if not yet on a legal parity with killing a person.

Despite these promising beginnings, ethical blindness begins soon after we pass Lassie and Snoopy or Smokey the Bear, on the way up the diagram. To extend the earlier example, few today would be offended at the sight of someone's trapping a gopher or spraying an insecticide on a column of ants. These forms of life are outside the ethics of most people. It is not that such people are unethical; they would probably protect their dog's life with their own. It is just that they have an ethical blind spot or cutoff. Dogs are inside the magic circle; snakes and worms and potato bugs are outside. Of course, there are variations. Everyone knows someone who keeps pet snakes. But what do the snake lovers think about the mice they drop into the cage as food?

Once the pet stage is passed, man's capacity for ethical relationships with other life forms declines rapidly. Only a few feel that plants of any kind deserve inclusion in the ethical fold; still fewer extend ethics to amoebae, bacteria, and similar primitive organisms. To do this is to affirm the value of life itself. Leopold did. His ecological perspective led him to see the role and importance in environmental processes of the most humble member of the life community. But he distinguished between importance and utility. The "biotic team," as he called it, did not work *for* man any more than it did for chipmunks or catfish.

The highest level of ethical evolution involves man's relations to parts of the environment not commonly regarded as alive such as air, water, and rocks. Leopold clearly had this extension in mind. He defines the "biotic team" as including inanimate matter like soil and water. Land, in fact, was Leopold's shorthand term for the entire environment—its living parts as well as those to which we commonly do not ascribe life.

In no relationship, then, was man excused from ethical responsibility. "A land ethic," Leopold explained, "changes the role of *Homo sapiens* from conqueror of the land-community to plain member and citizen of it. It implies respect for his fellow members, and also respect for the community as such." The "fellow members" are clearly other life forms, but Leopold is careful to recognize "the community as such," indicating his extension of ethics to habitat, system, process, and foundation—to the basic rock. Leopold, as an ecologist invariably thought holistically. He did not divide or prioritize the components of the environment. "A thing is right," he wrote, "when it tends to preserve the integrity, stability, and beauty of the biotic community. It is wrong when it tends otherwise."

The transition from the human level in the ethical pyramid to all life, and then the transition from life to non-life pose major philosophical problems. Person-to-person ethics is based on mutualism. I respect you and you respect me; the Golden Rule, *quid pro quo*. We can turn our backs on each other without fear. Mutualism is the basis of what philosophers call the "good reasons approach" to the explanation of the origin of moral behavior. There is a practical payoff to being moral, namely security. Under a social contract enlightened self-interest leads to the subordination of individual desires. Life then ceases to be, in Thomas Hobbes' words, "solitary, poor, nasty, brutish, and short."

Animals, plants, bacteria, and rocks do not have the capacity for moral mutualism with human beings. This is not to put them down. It only recognizes what is biologically obvious. The sensate components of the environment (and some would include plants as well as animals in that category) do have urges and appetites and, in that sense, *interests*. It is legitimate to speak of a dog's welfare. An animal can be harmed or benefited. It follows that cruelty to a dog is a violation of its interest and, in that sense, its rights. This is not to say that the dog is a genuine moral agent capable of entering into a social contract with people. Despite the anthropomorphic inclination of cartoons and motion, pictures, animals cannot be reasoned with or instructed in their moral duties. They cannot suppress passions or be blamed for actions.

Less highly evolved forms of life and nonliving objects lack even this form of interest. A rock has no sense of well-being. It cannot claim good treatment from people. What, after all, does a rock want? Using this logic, the philosopher Joel Feinberg, in his 1974 essay "The Rights of Animals and Unborn Generations," has concluded that "it is absurd to say that rocks can have rights… because rocks belong to a category of entities of whom rights cannot be meaningfully predicated." The point, Feinberg explains, is "that rocks themselves cannot validly claim good treatment from us."

This opens an obvious door to an acceptable meaning of the rights of rocks and of Leopold's land ethic. Rocks may not be moral beings, but moral beings can attribute rights to them, claim rights for them, and represent them in the quest for such rights. Right and wrong, after all, are human concepts and it is really the human interest that is being represented in the defense of the rights of an eagle or redwood or square mile of wilderness.

This is the crux of Christopher Stone's argument in *Should Trees Have Standing?*, published in 1975, and of Justice Douglas' decision in the Mineral King case of 1972. Since trees cannot speak for themselves, the people who care about them must. If and when these people succeed in formulating moral rules respecting nonhuman entities, it may be contended that these entities have rights. From this standpoint the meaning of the rights of rocks is that we should be ethical, not merely economic, in our treatment of rocks. To say that rocks have rights is not, then, to say that men have ethical relations with rocks.

This is not really a very unusual procedure. Countless times in history concerned people have stood up for what are called the rights of an inarticulate and oppressed group. Those who are oppressed often do not or cannot speak for themselves. Sometimes they take no active role in their benefaction. The ethical issue is solely the concern of the oppressors and the liberators. As previously noted, rocks and slaves have something in common here. There is a similar congruency between the environment and posterity. Future people do not exist, yet the rights of unborn generations (for instance, the right to a livable environment) are frequently used in rational discourse. In the case of posterity, just as in the case of environment, proxies define and represent the interests at stake.

There are several other ways of understanding the rights of nonhuman life and of the nonliving environment. One is to suppose that rocks, just like people, do have rights in and of themselves. It follows that it is the rock's interest, not the human interested in the rock, that is being protected. Some even go so far as to assume that rocks are alive. Such a belief is invariably mystical and more common among adherents to Zen and Shinto, or in primitive notions of animism, than among subscribers to the rational view of the West.

Leopold was too much the scientist to believe that rocks lived, but he did acknowledge a vital force in the ecosystem, the preservation of whose integrity and stability was the ultimate object of conservation. So Leopold could write about land health. His notion of a community included living and nonliving components. Leopold is also on the side of those who feel that rocks and oak trees and wolves are valuable in themselves, regardless of the human interest that might adhere to them. He explicitly rejects self-interest, however enlightened, as the proper rationale for conservation. Self-interest always prioritizes life and things according to their value to man and not according to their value to the ecosystem and themselves. Better, advised Leopold, to love the land—all of it— and to value it as you would a person whom you loved. Economics and self-interest do not figure in such a true love relationship.

Do Rocks Have Rights?

Whether this degree of altruism is possible is a moot point. Garrett Hardin believes only force (he calls it "mutual coercion mutually agreed upon") can temper man's inherent egocentricity. Many others agree that self-interest is here to stay and might as well be used as a motivation for environmental responsibility, at least until a higher one gains acceptance. Some, such as Joel Feinberg, dismiss the idea that rocks have rights but turn around and accept the idea as a convenient fiction. It appeals to Feinberg as a way of obtaining responsible behavior toward rocks and the environment. Pragmatically speaking, if it works to produce good results, why not believe it? This, in fact, is precisely the ground on which many have justified a belief in God. And that belief has had some consequences for ethical behavior.

Another alternative to comprehending the land ethic is to assume, as many environmentalists do, that man's abuse of nature will, in time, bring the entire life-support system, including man's, crashing down. From this point of view it is possible to salvage mutualism. If man abuses the environment, the environment will destroy man. This *quid pro quo* rationale is supported by the findings of ecological scientists who point to the delicately tuned interdependence of life and environment on spaceship earth. Aldo Leopold was keenly aware in the concluding pages of *A Sand County Almanac* that the price of not adhering to a land ethic was disruption of nature's capacity to support life.

It is intriguing to dwell on the possibility that the quest today for an environmental ethic is an effort to recover something that has been lost rather than to discover something new. Primitive man may well have possessed an ethic that extended well beyond his fellow men, one which embraced plants and animals, even mountains and rivers, all seen as members of his community and subject to ethical restraints. It is possible that, under the pressures of individualism, competition, technology, nationalism, and capitalism, mankind gradually lost this broad ethical perspective. Today, under the countervailing pressures of internationalism, exhaustion of resources, revision of priorities, and a growing understanding of ecological reality, we may be recovering—or rediscovering—something our ancestors instinctively grasped.

Environmental ethics, if socialized to the extent of human ethics, would have a revolutionary impact on current land use. Consider the problem of growth. The term refers, of course, to human growth, and a moment's reflection suggests that it cannot take place without infringing the rights of other forms of life to flourish or even to exist. Man's subdivisions expand at the expense of frogs' swamps. An environmental ethic would check such easy one-sided expansion just as the social ethics now extant normally check the desire of one person to grow at the expense, of another by robbing him. Ethics act as restraints on growth. We say we will not grow if growth entails destruction of our neighbor. What is needed, say advocates of environmental ethics, is a way of protecting life and the planet itself from the egocentric impulses of a single species.

Implicit here is the challenge of an ethical as opposed to an economic view of man-environment relations. The typical approach of the economist to environmental problems is to internalize externalities—to make polluters pay enough to clean up their mess. A land ethic would not condone the mess in the first place. It would deny the right to rape at any price. Most people can accept this principle in terms of human relations. Some things are just plain wrong and intolerable regardless of compensation.

Similarly Leopold explained that the value of land had to extend beyond economics to embrace things like "love, respect, and admiration." The essential attitude could be phrased quite succinctly: "Quit thinking about decent land use as solely an economic problem. Examine each question in terms of what is ethically and aesthetically right, as well as what is economically expedient." And then, coming as near as he ever did actually to defining the content of ethics, Leopold declared that "a thing is right when it tends to preserve the integrity, stability, and beauty of the biotic community. It is wrong when it tends otherwise." The cancerous growth of man's population and civilization can surely be condemned on these grounds alone.

The urgency of finding ethical rather than economic ways of ordering man's relationship to his habitat is increased by the probability that in the not-too-distant future man will have the technological power to take over the earth for his own purposes. The stakes would, of course, be higher just as they are with today's nuclear arms as opposed to the spear. For centuries man's appetites have been checked by his inabilities. But should technological advance make possible nearly complete exploitation of the environment, the need for restraints based on ethics will be more important than ever.

<<<—>>>

As he approached the end of his life in the mid 1940s, Aldo Leopold was not optimistic about the future of a land ethic. "No important change in ethics," he wrote, "was ever accomplished without an internal change in our intellectual emphases, loyalties, affections, and convictions. The proof that conservation has not yet touched these foundations of conduct lies in the fact that philosophy and religion have not yet heard of it." His next remark reflected his disgust at the economically motivated conservation efforts of the New Deal: "In our attempt to make conservation easy, we have made it trivial." As of the late 1940s, the American conservation movement "defines no right or wrong, assigns no obligations, calls for no change in the current philosophy of values."

Had he lived, Leopold would have been encouraged by the gradual penetration of environmental ethics into American thinking. There are still, of course, miles to go, but the ideal of man-environment relations based on ethics rather than economics has at least been stated and, in some important quarters, heard. In 1963, Secretary of the Interior Stewart L. Udall declared: "If asked to select a single volume, which contains a... plea for a new land ethic, most of us here at Interior would vote for Aldo Leopold's *A Sand County Almanac*."

Here and there in the 1960s, religious leaders began to understand that their responsibilities as moral leaders might not end with man-to-man relations. Many of their arguments about protecting the Creation differed little from John Ray's in 1691, but there was a new radical note. "A theology of the natural world," Allan R. Brockway maintained,

> declares that the nonhuman world has just as much right to its internal integrity as does the human world, that human beings transgress their divine authority when they destroy or fundamentally alter the rocks, the trees, the air,

the water, the soil, the animals—just as they do when they murder another human being.

Human beings spend nearly 20 years bringing up their young. A major part of that process is devoted to teaching them what is right and what is wrong in their relations with other people. Schools, churches and, if necessary, policemen and courts reinforce the lessons. The product is usually a person capable of participating as a responsible member of society. But, with the exception of not torturing dogs or pulling the tails of cats, responsibility ends at the person-to-person level. It is social, not ecological responsibility.

But consider if the same amount of time and effort were invested in instilling an environmental ethic as is now given over to building a personal one. Man-land responsibility, including the need for restraint and sacrifice on the part of the individual, would be within reach. The calls for protection would not blow away in the wind or be dismissed as good things for someone else to do.

The point is that protecting the environment cannot be a matter of dollars and cents (as it largely is today) any more than protecting one's family from being ravished and exploited is a matter of dollars and cents. One does not consider the price if someone threatens to rape one's daughter. With environmental ethics a reality, the same might be true of attempts to rape the land. The point is that the individual freedom we prize cannot connote freedom to abuse the earth any more than it does freedom to abuse other people. Ethics are restraints. They have helped order relations between people. Extended to include the relationship of people to the earth, ethics could be the guideline and, indeed, the key to environmental responsibility.

STRANGELY LIKE WAR

DERRICK JENSEN
(2003)

A Rigged System

It was the year 1985 when I finally understood how the U.S. political system works, and at the same time realized how irredeemable are that system and the culture at large. That was also the year many indigenous [American Indian] friends said to me, "What took you so long to figure that out?" They'd had plenty of experience opposing this system—five hundred and some years of resistance to this culture and its environmental and cultural degradation—and had long since apprehended the truth in Red Cloud's words: "They made us many promises, more than I can remember. But they never kept but one. They promised to take our land and they took it."

I was living in eastern Washington. I walked clearcuts there and in North Idaho that stretched for miles. No matter where I—or anyone—went, there they were. I saw streams scoured and essentially sterilized by "hundred-year" floods that came every few weeks in the spring. I saw migrating tundra swans dead, poisoned by lead from mine wastes flushed—sometimes to the tune of a million pounds per day—from the hills and into wetlands, rivers, and lakes by these floods. I saw politicians try to pretend nothing was happening as they scurried to protect the corporations that continued to cause the damage. (For years environmentalists at Forest Watch and the Inland Empire Public Lands Council in Spokane begged Tom Foley, their so-called representative and Speaker of the U.S. House of Representatives, to do something about the damage to the forests of his region. Finally, he deigned to say he'd take a look. The Public Lands Council arranged for a small airplane to take them all up. What happened next symbolizes much of what we're talking about in this book. Soon after the plane took off, Foley fell asleep. Two of the environmentalists kept waking him up and trying to get him to look at the clearcuts. He'd rouse himself long enough to yawn, rub his eyes, and glance outside before closing them again and returning to his dreams.)

I saw corporate journalists stumble blindly over themselves, eyes clamped shut to see nothing wrong, suggesting that there was no need for concern over lead pollution, for example, even though some of the highest blood-lead levels ever recorded in human beings were from children in the area, because "there are no human bodies lining the Spokane River." I saw populations of bull trout and Idaho cutthroat trout collapse. And through all of this the cutting continued.

There wasn't much we could do about cutting on lands controlled by corporations. Western culture—and this is an extraordinarily strange notion—values the "rights" of corporations—legal fictions, artificial constructs—above those of human, and especially nonhuman, life, and the landbase upon which all of this life depends. This value system meant we had only the most rudimentary tools available to us to slow the wholesale liquidation of forests on lands claimed by these legal fictions, lands to which, unsurprisingly, these corporations had for the most part gained title illegally from the public in the first place.

But we did have some tools to slow the deforestation on public lands. The U.S. Forest Service and Bureau of Land Management sell trees to timber corporations at grossly subsidized prices. The prices routinely don't cover even administrative costs, much less reach market value for the timber, much *much* less repay the immeasurable costs of destroying forests, even when government timber-sale planners cook their books to a degree that would make Arthur Anderson proud. These administrators also push for environmentally destructive and publicly subsidized cattle grazing on public lands, environmentally destructive and publicly subsidized mining on public lands, environmentally destructive and publicly subsidized oil and gas exploitation on public lands, environmentally destructive and publicly subsidized ski resorts on public lands, and so on. You get the picture. You also get the shaft.

One of the differences between corporate and public lands is that public lands administrators have to at least give lip service to following stricter laws (except under certain conditions, as we'll get to later). They must maintain the facade of serving the public good. Part of that facade consists of writing documents called environmental assessments (EA) and environmental impact statements (EIS).

The ostensible purpose of environmental assessments is, obviously, to assess the environmental damage that will be caused by any "action" the Forest Service proposes to carry out. Not surprisingly, the Forest Service almost always determines that *every* action will have "no significant impact." This is true for such minor actions as installing pit toilets in campgrounds or hand removal of exotic plant species (each of which might have an entirely uncontroversial one-page assessment), and it's true for massive timber sales involving thousands of acres of clearcuts (which have several-hundred-page assessments inevitably coming to the conclusion of "no significant impact").

The much larger, more comprehensive environmental impact statements are written when the damage caused by the project is so extreme that not even the Forest Service can pretend there will be "no significant impact." The document then describes (read: *understates*) the damage to be done.

By law, EAs and EISs are supposed to help the agency and the public make informed decisions about the "management" of the public's lands. As such, decision-makers within the agency are supposed to examine perhaps four or five alternative actions—which, in the case of a timber sale, may range from the "no action alternative" (no cutting) on one end, to clearcutting mile after square mile of forest and selling (below cost) tens of millions of board feet of timber on the other—and to choose among them the wisest course, based on the research that went into the document.

But the system is rigged. The Forest Service and the Bureau of Land Management (as well as other federal agencies) often fire, threaten to fire, or otherwise make life difficult for biologists and botanists who find that activities such as logging, mining, off-road vehicle use, and gas and oil extraction harm forests. Just as routinely, they fire, threaten to fire, or make life difficult for cultural specialists who determine that any of these activities harm archaeological sites or sites sacred to Native Americans. The same happens to hydrologists who disclose damage to aquifers, streams, and rivers, toxicologists who disclose the poisoning of people and the landscape, and so on.

Further, timber-sale planners and others are routinely moved to different forests every few years. This keeps honest planners from becoming attached to forests or communities, and guarantees dishonest ones a lack of accountability when their predictions of "no significant impact" are found to be false. The public does not even get the extremely hollow satisfaction of forcing the timber-sale planners to walk blasted streams. (Of course, if the planners were still there, they'd probably, like Tom Foley, simply close their eyes to the evidence anyway: After all, that's what they did through the planning process).

It will come as no surprise to anyone who has paid attention to American political processes—although I must admit at first it surprised me, naïve as I sometimes am—that EAs and EISs are a fact documents designed to help people make informed ions about *anything*, but instead attempts—often massive attempts—to justify decisions made long before, to satisfy back-deals cut between politicians and their corporate backers. To be truthful, the Forest Service doesn't make a serious effort to *pretend* EAs and EISs are actual decision-making documents: Out of the thousands of EAs and EISs from timber sales monitored and often opposed by groups with which I was associated, never once—*not even once*—did the Forest Service determine that the "no action alternative" was the best choice. The preferred alternative was *always* to deforest. Even a thousand chimpanzees typing on a thousand computers for a thousand years would eventually come up with an EA that determined it was in the best interests of the forest not to cut.

There are other ways the system is rigged, too, top to bottom. For example, general management of a particular national forest is at least ostensibly governed by what is called a Forest Plan. Often we would object to portions of the plans—primarily their emphasis on extractive industries—and would be told that our objections came at the wrong time: Instead we should appeal these points later on each specific EA or EIS. Then, when we followed their instructions and waited to raise the points on EAs and EISs, we were told again that our objections came at the wrong time: We should have appealed these points in the Forest Plan. Checkmate.

To appeal a timber-sale decision is a brain-busting process. The EAs and EISs are written in bureaucratese, which means it's almost impossible to figure out what the hell they're saying, if anything. The documents are intentionally deceptive—attempts to con an unsuspecting public into believing deforestation has "no significant impact." This makes the documents even more difficult to decipher. Terminology often changes. Each time we crack their old code for "clearcut," they come up with a new one, presumably in the hopes of sliding a bit more deforestation past us. Or maybe they enjoy destroying discourse as much as destroying forests.

We would read the documents, find the lies, determine the ways the Forest Service was violating such laws as the National Environmental Policy Act, the National Forest Management Act, the Endangered Species Act, the Clean Water Act, and so on. On one hand this was dead easy: the timber sales are glaringly illegal. On the other hand, the obfuscations made it tedious work to unravel. The work was made all the worse by the knowledge that those tying these words into rhetorical knots were pulling 30, 40, or 50 grand per year to confabulate the lies while most of us doing the unraveling weren't paid anything at all (a couple people on our side *were* getting paid, a whopping $16,000 per year). We were doing it for love, and because it was right. It is fun and fine and wonderful to do things for love, but it galled me no end that those destroying the natural world were getting paid for it while we had to try to stop their damage for free. If we had to describe the pathology of our culture in a nutshell, that might be it: our economic system rewards destructive behavior.

There is one night I'll never forget. It was winter. About 1:30 in the morning. Clear. Bright stars punctured the sky. The cold so sharp it pierced my cheekbones. I'd been tearing apart an EA since 6:00 that evening, and I knew I had to quit when I saw a chart on page 175 with a caption stating it was identical to one on page 43, "reproduced here only for readers' ease." But the charts were different. They were being used to make different points (the chart on page 43 was supposed to show how few cutthroat trout were in a stream, and that on page 175 was supposed to show the opposite). The authors had made up different charts—and different underlying data—to make their different points. I threw the EA across the room, put on my coat, and stalked into the cold.

I walked long through the night air, trying to unlock my brain, get it to stop spinning in fast tight circles that were making me ill and tired. I wanted to quit not just for the night but forever. I did not want to submit myself to this abuse.

But I knew I couldn't do that. That's what they wanted, to wear us down with their lies. And I wasn't going to let that happen.

We often received late-night calls from dissident Forest Service personnel. Someone might call from what sounded like a pay phone, not give a name, and say, "Look very carefully at page 57. Whatever you do, don't forget to notice the lack of analysis of the effects of this timber sale on both goshawks and Thompson's big-eared bats." Then the person would hang up.

We'd write the appeals, and send them, oddly enough, back to the same people who signed them in the first place. They would of course deny the appeal, and we would appeal their denial to their supervisor, who would of course then deny our appeal. We'd play this game all the way up the line, until someone finally granted the appeal or we took them to court. Sometimes we couldn't take them to court because we didn't have the money to throw at an attorney, but fortunately there were a fair number of attorneys willing to help us fight these battles, often for free or on the cheap.

But as is always the case when attempting to stop our culture from destroying some part of wild nature, all losses are permanent, all victories temporary. Winning a timber-sale appeal doesn't mean stopping a timber sale. It doesn't mean protecting a piece of ground. It means protecting a piece of ground for the year or two it takes the Forest Service to write up another EA, this time trying harder to bamboozle us. The score today is that less than 5 percent of the ancient forest in the United States remains.

Despite the fact that the whole system is rigged in favor of deforestation, a bunch of us were able to use the system's own rigged rules to stop, for a while, most of the illegal logging on the national forests of our region. Because nearly all commercial logging on public lands violates environmental protection laws, this means we stopped nearly all commercial logging on these forests. Activists across the country used similar tactics with similar success to try to enforce the law and protect the forests.

The response by our local Forest Service was to hire scores of new employees. Were these new hires biologists, botanists, hydrologists, and anthropologists, brought on in an attempt to better understand forests? No. They hired one timber-sale planner, and all the rest were technical writers directed to produce slicker documents.

The response nationally was rather more severe, and is what helped me learn how unwaveringly committed to the destruction of the planet our culture is. The timber industry, politicians, and the corporate media launched a massive propaganda campaign. This in itself is nothing new: It's what they all *do*. But they took the momentum we had gained in our descriptions of devastated forests and inverted it to declare: *The forests are suffering a major health crisis, so we need to move quickly to cut them down.*

Stop. Reread their declaration. Read it again. I've read that or similar lines too many times, and they still make no sense.

But that's one of the advantages of wielding the sort of totalitarian power held by the government/corporate interlock. While it's certainly more convenient for them to carry out their "preferred alternative" without too much public resistance, public assent to their goals is ultimately incidental. Any time the public finds a way to meaningfully participate in decisions concerning its own landbase—as we did with the appeals process—they simply change the rules. Almost any excuse will serve to allow them to sever public participation in the process. As we've seen time and again, on issue after issue, when the corporate press publishes absurdities often enough, the absurdities begin to seem palatable to some, confusing to others, and discouraging to still others. As long as it paralyzes the public, the corporations win. Ninety-five percent of the old growth is gone, and they're getting away with cutting the rest.

So in 1995 Congress passed, and [Democratic!] President Clinton signed, what became known as the Salvage Rider, which stated that the quickly worsening health of the forests demanded immediate action. Therefore, any timber sale that the Forest Service or Bureau of Land Management (BLM) declared necessary to improve "forest health" would be exempt from all environmental laws. The Salvage Rider contained something called "sufficiency language," a magical phrase meaning no appeals or other legal challenges are allowed. Public participation is explicitly prohibited. Of course.

Can you guess what happened? The Forest Service and BLM predictably declared nearly every timber sale to be necessary for forest health. It was a chainsaw massacre. Ancient forests fell everywhere. In my corner of the world, every one of the thousands upon thousands of acres I had worked to save—every goddamned acre, every fucking acre, every beautiful, vibrant, stunning, gracious, wise, living acre of ancient forest—was clearcut over the next two years. I did not have the courage to return to many of those places. I could not have borne to see them destroyed. Others I did go to see, and walked the moonscapes that until recently had been living, vibrant forests. It is not an experience I look forward to repeating, though of course it is an experience shared by all of us who love wild places and who are facing down the deforesters.

This is how our political system works. Choose your own equivalent example; they are myriad. This is why the system must go.

In one sense the whole salvage hoax was unbearably stupid. It doesn't take a genius to figure out that if any of the logging had been truly necessary to improve the health of the forest—health that was already being damaged by, you guessed it, logging—there would have been absolutely no reason to exempt it from environmental laws. In another sense the hoax was pretty clever, in that it took a genuine fear and turned the cause on its head. That's standard practice in propaganda. You don't try to make something out of nothing, because then your lies have no energy. Instead, you rechannel existing energy—fear, desire, anger, whatever—toward your own ends, your "preferred alternative." Those in the U.S. military-industrial complex twisted people's real desire for security into a military machine designed to achieve, according to the military's own Joint Vision 2020 statement of purpose, "full-spectrum domination." Those in the timber-political complex turned the energy from our efforts to halt deforestation back against us, or rather against the forests, with the "forest health" scam and subsequent Salvage Rider.

Now they're doing the same thing with forest fires, inflaming public fears as they did with forest health, using partial truths and often outright lies to turn some very real concerns to their own destructive ends. Fires are a normal part of forest ecology, especially for many of the forests of the arid west. In fact many species are fire-*dependent*. Lodgepole pines, for example, are shade-intolerant and need openings in the forest canopy such as those caused by fire to send up the new generation. To this end, lodgepole pinecones are tightly closed by resin that only fire can melt, and seeds can only germinate on exposed soil, where fire has removed leaf litter. Three-toed woodpeckers, also called black-backed woodpeckers, are colored to be camouflaged against the charred background of burned trunks. They exist only precariously where there is no fire, but arrive in droves to burned areas to eat bugs feeding inside blackened trunks.

Fires are a forest's way of renewing itself. In arid forests, fire, not bacteria or fungi, is the main agent for breaking down nutrients. Without fire, dead litter in these forests does not decay or rot, but simply piles up on the forest floor. Fires also redistribute these nutrients across space—in the form of windborn ash—much as salmon carry nutrients from ocean to forest. Fires mix things up: They're a tremendously creative force.

And for the most part, fires aren't all that dangerous. I know we've been raised on stories of sad Smokey the Bear clinging to a tree, his mother obviously murdered by the raging fires. He was saved (and imprisoned) by kind humans in green polyester pants. But who told us these stories? Those kind humans in green polyester pants themselves, the members of the Forest Service.

Would they lie to us?

Well, yes.

Most natural fires are pretty small—far less than 100 acres; even including larger fires the average is only about 240 acres—and they don't burn quickly or all that hot. They don't jump to the tops of big trees, but kill only their smaller cousins beneath. And there are a lot of these small fires: The Blue Mountains of Oregon got their name from the smoky haze of so many small wildfires. In their natural cycle most western forests burned every three to 20 years, with longer cycles in more moist forests. This means big trees in dry forests would experience perhaps 50 or 100 fires in their lives.

These small fires aren't terribly dangerous. Because the fires burn in patches, animals easily move to protected swales until the fire passes (or they climb trees and wait for mother to return, and hope she gets there before the bastards in the green polyester pants). The front usually advances at only a couple of miles per hour, meaning large mammals can easily amble in front of the flames, and birds can fly away. (Isn't it cool, by the way, how most birds raise young early in the year, which means fledglings are ready to fly before fire season?) Even small creatures are fairly safe from fires: Mammals head into their burrows, and insects just dig themselves into the soil, where a few inches below the surface the temperature remains remarkably constant.

The nature and danger of forest fires changed with the arrival of extractive forestry. Peshtigo, Wisconsin, October 8, 1871: only 20 years earlier the area had been part of a 200,000-square-mile unbroken native forest that covered much of Wisconsin, Michigan, and Minnesota. But the trees were cut, for lumber, for railroad ties, to clear land for agriculture. Fires escaped from logging slash piles and exploded into the logged-over forests, burning 1.25 million acres of pine trees, and killing 1,500 people. Hinkley, Minnesota, 1894. Metz, Michigan, 1908. Cloquet, Minnesota, 1918. These huge fires raged in the aftermath and as a result of extractive forestry.

As extractive forestry moved west, so did catastrophic fires. The Yacoult Fire of 1902 (actually a series of 110 fires), started by logger and settler fires, burned a million acres in Washington and Oregon and killed 30 people. Then came the Wallace Fire of 1910 in Idaho, sometimes called The Big Blowup. As usual, logging created conditions ripe for catastrophic fire—lots of slash piles, lots of trees killed by logging, lots of weak "dog-hair" trees coming up in dense even-age stands. By July of that year 3,000 fires—many started in slash piles—were burning in the forests of North Idaho. On August 20, "all hell broke loose," according to the District Forester: hot hurricane-force winds blew up from the southwest. They were strong enough to blow riders from their saddles, and strong enough to bring together the small fires into a conflagration that took out 3 million acres of white pine. Headlines from the region: "Wallace Fire Loss $1,000,000: 50 Dead—180 Missing in St. Joe Zone"; "Five Known Dead Near Newport"; "Terror-Stricken, 2000 Refugees Dash Through Flames to Safety"; "In Forest Fires 142 Dead, 185 Missing, Property Loss is $20,000,000"; "Fire Victims Number 185."

In response to the destruction caused by these logging-induced forest fires, the federal government decided to head right to the root of the problem and halt all industrial forestry, right? Well, no, not exactly. Instead administrators decided to eradicate not the disease but the symptom, and assumed what was called a "10 A.M. fire policy"—every fire must be out by ten o'clock the next morning. Inmate Smokey was conscripted into serving the propaganda effort on the part of the Forest Service to sell this policy to the people of the United States.

The net effect of this policy has been a further weakening of already stressed forests, as well as a dangerous buildup of those even-age stands so beloved of both foresters and fires. In other words, industrial forestry has combined with a misguided fire-suppression policy to create conditions ripe for disaster.

The federal government has, unsurprisingly, used this fear of conflagration to promote deforestation by greatly increasing logging and by suspending environmental laws and public participation on all timber sales determined to be necessary to "reduce fuel load." The Forest Service and the Bureau of Land Management have already put their old rubber stamps bearing "Necessary for Forest Health" into storage and replaced them with stamps bearing "Necessary to Reduce Fuel Load."

Expect another massacre. It doesn't really matter to the outcome that time after time the trees that are cut are the big old commercially valuable trees, not the dog-hair trees more prone to fire. A 1999 Government Accounting Office report stated that Forest Service managers "tend to (1) focus on areas with high-value commercial timber rather than on areas with high fire hazards or (2) include more large, commercially valuable trees in a timber sale than are necessary to reduce the accumulated fuels." Nor does it matter that a September 2000 report by the Department of the Interior and the Department of Agriculture stated, "The removal of large, merchantable trees from forests does not reduce fire risk and may, in fact, increase such risk." Nor does it matter that Forest Service fire specialist Denny Truesdale says, "The majority of the material that we need to take out is not commercial timber. It is up to three and four inches in diameter. We can't sell it."

Science doesn't matter. Logic doesn't matter. Public participation and democracy don't matter. Justice doesn't matter. Forests don't matter. Life doesn't matter.

Commercial logging removes large, fire-resistant trees and leaves behind flammable needles, limbs, and brush. What's more, removing the overstory reduces shade, drying and heating the materials below. Tree plantations are far more vulnerable to fire than natural forests, and there is a direct correlation between roads and fires. Add to this the fact that the overwhelming majority of forest fires—88 percent—are caused by humans, and that up to half of these are arson. There have already been many cases of people lighting fires *specifically* so they can benefit financially, whether through gaining employment as firefighters or through giving the Forest Service an excuse to offer up the dead trees as a timber sale, quite possibly to the arsonists themselves. The Forest Service's own fire laboratory found that the main factors determining whether buildings ignite are the materials used in the home and the amount of underbrush within 200 feet, *not* the merchantable timber within 200 miles. But to those in power who are deforesting the planet, it positively does not matter that study after study after study has shown that logging leads to catastrophic fires.

We'll tell you what does matter. Logging, under the guise of forest health, under the guise of reducing fuel loads, under any guise those in power claim, under no guise at all but just because those in power make the rules, serves the interests of the big timber corporations (which, not coincidentally, recently exercised "their first amendment right" to free speech to the tune of more than 3 million dollars in payola—sorry, campaign contributions—to the presidential campaign of George W. Bush).

This is how the U.S. political system works. This is why the system must go.

Globalization in the Real World

Which brings us, finally, to political mechanisms, webs of patron-client relationships that tie together the political, bureaucratic, military, and business elites within and between the producing and consuming nations. These webs include brainwashing that is euphemistically called public relations, phony public participation programs, underpaying civil servants to facilitate their corruption, repressing and eliminating resistance by peasant and native peoples, gunboat diplomacy, and engineering coups to install client regimes.

Corporations and governments routinely hire **public relations** firms to spin their atrocities into gold. Entire books have been written on this, notably *Toxic Sludge is Good for You*, by John Stauber and Sheldon Rampton. An example concerning forests is Chlopak, Leonard, Schechter & Associates, a PR firm that specializes in crisis management. It helps oil corporations fend off environmentalist and human rights groups opposing a 400-mile-long pipeline in Peru that will pass through indigenous homelands in the Amazon rainforest.

Public participation programs are replacements for genuine democracy. Public relations firms, government agencies, and consensus groups have developed sophisticated techniques for confusing, exhausting, and co-opting the concerned public. The fundamental understanding that guides this participation—and those in power are exquisitely aware of this understanding—is the impossibility of true negotiation between parties of grossly unequal power. For example, all through my years of filing timber-sale appeals, I participated in countless meetings with Forest Service officials who screwed encouraging looks to their faces and politely pretended to listen to our comments, which both we and they knew would be ignored. I also wrote out god-only-knows how many comments, which were duly noted, but also ignored. But I did participate in public process! Is this a great country, or what?

My experience is not unique. That *is* public participation in this country. We are "allowed" to "speak truth to power" all we want, but everyone knows that those in power will ignore these truths and go ahead and do whatever the hell they want. It's far more efficient to let the people have their meaningless say than it is to trundle them off to some distant gulag. This way we can all happily pretend the system works. Unfortunately, the system *does* work—in fact all too well—but never the way we were told.

Especially in the third world, **civil servants are routinely underpaid**. This facilitates their willingness to accept bribes to not prevent the theft of resources. (If Forest Service acquiescence in timber theft in the United States is any indication, American civil servants do not even need bribes to facilitate corruption.) A potent third-world example comes from Cameroon, where in a classic "structural adjustment" in 1992 and 1993, civil servant salaries were slashed 60 to 70 percent, making corruption of those servants an easier task. The result? Less than a third of Cameroon's timber is locally processed, a third of the cut is never even declared, and two-thirds of the timber taxes are never collected.

Central to the theft of resources are the **military and police repression** of peasant and native peoples, gunboat diplomacy, and coups to install client regimes [favorable to US interests]. This is, indeed, a primary function of the U.S. military. As former Secretary of Defense William Cohen said to a group of Fortune 500 leaders, "Business follows the flag.... We provide the security. You provide the investment." As shown, business doesn't even have to provide the investment: That's borne by the public.

The real-world results of these mechanisms are dispossession and poverty, forced labor, extraction of the commonwealth to produce raw materials and commodities, and the downward spiral of autonomous local markets into global economic production, consumption, depletion, and collapse. Collectively, these mechanisms are called 'globalization.'

The Failure of Solutions

We need to protect ecosystems—for their own sake most of all, but also for our own. More than 10,000 plant species are used as traditional medicines; most of them are gathered from the wild, from the forest. Around 80% of the people in non-industrialized nations depend upon them for their primary health care; 25% of modern drugs are also derived from these plants.

Restoration forestry restores ecological and genetic diversity and soil nutrients, structure, and biology. It can restore abused and fallow forest and agricultural lands. We can close roads to reduce erosion and prevent further entry by vehicles and other machinery. We know how to thin dog-hair stands to restore natural forest structures. We know enough to understand the need to control exotic pests and reintroduce the full natural diversity of trees and shrubs and fungi and animals and human forest-dwellers. We can restore streams to reduce erosion, restore anadromous fish, and so on. We know how to do all of this. So do forests.

Here is a definition of restoration forestry:

> Restoration forestry assists nature to heal degraded forests and bring them back to a state of biological productivity, biodiversity, ecological stability and resilience. Restoration forestry means increasing the area under forest cover and increasing the age classes, the standing volume and the diversity of forest ecosystems. It means careful harvesting [sic] methods that minimise disturbance of soil and plant communities. It means that many more people will have to be employed in the woods, not less; using smaller machines and more reliance on draft animals. It means smaller mills and more value-added processing close to the wood source. It means minimal waste, maximum recycling, and the development of non-tree paper pulp and alternative building materials. It means more people caring for the forest and researching its complex processes, so that we can ever refine our management/dance with the forest. Restoration forestry leads to a steady yield of high value timber. Clearcutting and/or short-rotation forestry leads to a periodic return of low-quality timber. Restoration forestry makes much better ecological sense and it makes better economic sense.

We need to distinguish restoration *forestry* from restoration *ecology*. Forestry is for producing a supply of wood. If you are an intelligent forester, you would restore tree stands (such as plantations) to a natural, optimal fiber-producing capacity. But you are still a forester, looking for wood fiber.

An ecologist would protect or restore fully-functioning forest ecosystems, and consider fiber production for human use to be completely subordinated to the full range of natural ecosystem functions.

Once again, what a concept.

We must move away from *industrial* forestry and toward *restoration* forestry. We must then move away from restoration *forestry* and toward restoration *ecology*.

We must also move away from globalization, toward community forestry:

Community forestry is a village-level forestry activity, decided on collectively and implemented on communal land, where local populations participate in the planning, establishing, and harvesting of forest crops, and so receive a major portion of the socio-economic and ecological benefits from the forest.

Successful community-forestry requires ... genuine popular participation in decision-making.... Experience has proven time and again that participation is more than a development cliché; it is an absolute necessity if goals are to be met. But working with people rather than policing them is a new role for many foresters.

Community forestry has the following characteristics: The local community controls a clearly and legally defined area of the forest; the local community is free from governmental outside pressure concerning the utilization of that forest; if the forestry involves commercial sale of timber or other products, then the community is free from economic exploitation of markets or other pressure from outside forces; the community has long-term security of tenure over the forest and sees its future as being tied to the forest.

Community forestry, social forestry and rural development forestry are more or less equivalent and reflect Abraham Lincoln's view of democracy—government of the people, by the people, for the people.

The political dimension of community forestry makes it a venue for people's struggle against domination and exploitation of the community's resources by 'outsiders.' Ecology, equity and social justice are part of this struggle.

Of course.

Rejecting Gilgamesh

"What we are doing to the forests of the world is but a mirror reflection of what we are doing to ourselves and to one another."
— Mahatma Gandhi

We have some declarations of our own. Immediately leave remaining frontier forests alone, and confine industrial forestry to existing plantations. Soon, once we have learned how, restore most and then all of the plantations to natural forests. This work could be done by restoration ecologists, who, like traditional forest-dwellers, are grounded in their specific local natural communities. Restoration ecology will be one step toward recovering indigenous knowledge and techniques, which is always specific to place. The purpose of restoration is not fiber production, even sustainable fiber production, but restoring ecosystems and their humans to their natural local patterns and processes.

Perhaps most important of all, relinquish control of land to those who belong to the land. Satellite data has shown that where indigenous people hold land title, there has been less forest destruction. Give back the land to the humans and nonhumans who live there, and who have lived there for a very long time, who belong to the land. Give it back to those from whom those in power stole it, and from whom they continue to steal it.

We can already hear the obvious objection: "That's absurd. It's not practical. Be real. Colonization has turned forest-dwellers into landless peasants working agricultural plantations, and industrialism has turned them into an urban working class for factories. This may have been regrettable, may have been unjust, but it happened. It's done (well, not exactly, since it's an ongoing process). Get over it. We've committed ourselves to industrial civilization, and we've got to see it through to the end. Do you think you can put trees back on stumps, unroll roads from forests, let peasants and factory workers become forest-dwellers again? What you are proposing is unrealistic, and in fact dangerous."

It is always odd to hear words like *realistic* and *dangerous* coming from the mouths of those who value money over life, who say things like "we must balance the needs of our economic system versus the environment" (which of course is a tacit and entirely accidental acknowledgment of what we all know: the needs of the economic system are in direct opposition to the needs of life).

>What is real?
>What do you love?
>What do you fear?
>What do you need?

The problems we face look far different, depending on who you are, on what you love, what you fear, what you need.

What are your actual and self-perceived relationships to forests, to power, to society?

Weyerhaeuser shareholders presumably perceive it in their best interest to maximize dividends by liquidating current assets: in other words, cut to the last stick. Shareholders do not relate to their actual assets (trees), much less to forests. They relate not to forests, nor trees, nor even to productive goods and services, but to wealth as dividends.

Most of us environmentalists—grassroots environmentalists, not the corporate environmentalists of the Sierra Club and Audubon national offices—are holding on by our fingernails, trying to save whatever scraps of forests we can, using whatever tools we can cobble together, putting our hearts and minds and time and sometimes bodies between the chainsaws and the forests we love. And we are praying, every moment of every day, for civilization to end. For this culture to run out of oil, to collapse in on itself. For this long and awful nightmare of deforestation and dispossession to end.

Some social justice activists see *inequality* as the root of the problem, and believe that if we just bring sufficient and equitable "development" to the poor, then the world's problems may be solved. In their hearts some hold hope for a great proletariat revolution that will bring justice to all. Does their "all" include those humans and nonhumans who live in forests?

What are the hopes and fears of Southern elites trapped between dispossessed countrymen and gringo bankers? Where do forests fit into their dreams, their nightmares? What do they want for and from these ancient trees? Or do they think of them at all?

And what is the perspective of the slum-dwellers in Brazil and other countries, dispossessed by five hundred years of colonial and neoliberal conquistadors? What do they want? What do they need? What do they fear? What can we—those of us who have been privileged enough to learn how to read books like this, printed on the flesh of trees torn from the soil where these people once lived—what can we do to help?

And what of the forest dwellers themselves? What of the indigenous? What do they want? What do they need? What are their relationships to the forests where they live? Can we help them, if only by leaving them to their own good and sufficient lives?

Tigers. Sumatran Rhinos. Orangutans. Hazel's forest frogs. What do they need? What do they want? How can we help?

And the trees. Redwoods. Lodgepole pines. Port Orford Cedars. American Chestnut. Lauan. Mahogany. Ipe. Greenheart. Purple-heart. Teak. What do they want? What do they need? What is your relationship with the trees and forests where you live?

It is our present course that is unrealistic, and doomed to a nightmare failure so complete that perhaps only those who are forced to live these horrors—the humans and nonhumans of the forests, and the forests themselves—are able to even partially comprehend it.

Plato observed, back when the soil of his home still bore recent memory of lions and forests and the people of the forests,

> What now remains compared with what then existed is like the skeleton of a sick man, all the fat and soft earth having wasted away, and only the bare framework of the land being left... There are some mountains which now have nothing but food for bees, but they had trees not very long ago.... There were many lofty trees of cultivated species and ... boundless pasturage for flocks. Moreover, it was enriched by the yearly rains from Zeus, which were not lost to it, as now, by flowing from the bare land into the sea; but the soil it had was deep, and therein it received the water, storing it up in the retentive loamy soil, and ... provided all the various districts with abundant supplies of spring-waters and streams, whereof the shrines still remain even now, at the spots where the fountains formerly existed.

Deforestation boils down to power. Those who deforest do so because they are supported by the full might of the state. It is ludicrous for anyone to suggest that those who stole these lands by force, and who maintain control by force, and who deforest at the point of a gun, will give the land back to its rightful human and nonhuman owners because it is the right thing to do, the sane thing to do, the human thing to do, the non-suicidal thing to do. No.

They will not leave the forests, and leave the forests alone, until either the forests are gone, or until those of us who love the land force them out of the forests.

We do not hope to stop deforestation with this book alone, any more than we can stop it by filing timber sales, compiling corporate profiles, voting, doing tree sits, or sending money to good organizations like Amazon Watch or Cultural Survival.

We do not know how to stop deforestation. We do not know how to get deforesters out of the forests. No one else—forest-dwellers or civilized—has figured that out either, or surely the deforesters would have been removed by now.

But we do know this. Once people see deforestation for the atrocity that it is, they will then stop those who continue to destroy. It is for this we wrote the book. It is to this we have dedicated our lives.

<<<—>>>

What is your relationship with the future?

There is nothing humans can do to maintain industrial wood and paper production, and maintain forests too. The crisis will resolve itself when civilized humans walk away from doing what they have been doing.

Those in power won't stop deliberately. Never forget Red Cloud's warning: "They made us many promises, more than I can remember. But they never kept but one. They promised to take our land and they took it."

What, then, can you do if you are of good heart? You can fight to keep this particular tree standing, this particular forest functioning. You can help open your friends' and coworkers' eyes to the wonder and intrinsic value and legitimate standing of forests and forest-dwellers.

We don't need to stop the forest crisis. Nature will stop it. As the global economy becomes more chaotic and the societies addicted to it become more impoverished, the best we can do is to keep some doors open, prevent those in power from causing those we love to go extinct. Defend what is important, undermine what is superfluous, and destroy what is destructive.

We can consume less. We can eat less meat, drink less coffee. We can eat locally grown foods. We can make our own food, clothing, and shelter, so as not to deny others the right and ability to provide for themselves. Those of us in the heart of empire can work to undermine the social and political basis for our inordinate power over others. We can work to implement radical equality.

We can spend time in forests. We can ask the trees—and forests—what they want. Early on, this book described a walk through an old-growth forest, and it ends on the same note, by inviting you to do the same. We humans came from forests, and to them we will return.

We have been the obedient servants of Gilgamesh for 5,000 years. We have cut a path of destruction, ignored the spreading deserts, disregarded the disappearing animals, the fouled air and water, the warming planet. We have destroyed most of the earth's natural forest cover, and we pretend we can live without it. The story we have been handed says that Gilgamesh defeated the forest protectors and that the forces of civilization won the battle for the forest, but it's not true. The epic is not over, and Enlil's curse will not be lifted until we reject the easy and false promises of Gilgamesh, and return with respect and humility to the forests.

ON BEING MORALLY CONSIDERABLE

KENNETH GOODPASTER (1978)

> "A thing is right when it tends to preserve the integrity, stability, and beauty of the biotic community. It is wrong when it tends otherwise."
> — Aldo Leopold

What follows is a preliminary inquiry into a question which needs more elaborate treatment than an essay can provide. The question can be and has been addressed in different rhetorical formats, but perhaps G. J. Warnock's formulation of it is the best to start with:

> Let us consider the question to whom principles of morality apply from, so to speak, the other end—from the standpoint not of the agent, but of the "patient." What, we may ask here, is the condition of moral relevance? What is the condition of having a claim to be considered, by rational agents to whom moral principles apply?

In the terminology of R. M. Hare (or even Kant), the same question might be put thus: In universalizing our putative moral maxims, what is the scope of the variable over which universalization is to range? A more legalistic idiom, employed recently by Christopher Stone,[1] might ask: What are the requirements for "having standing" in the moral sphere? However the question gets formulated, the thrust is in the direction of necessary and sufficient conditions on X in:

(1) For all A, X deserves moral consideration from A.

where A ranges over rational moral agents and moral 'consideration' is construed broadly to include the most basic forms of practical respect (and so is not restricted to "possession of rights" by X).

Section I

These developments emphasize the importance of clarity about the *framework* of moral consideration as much as about the *application* of that framework. We need to understand better, for example, the scope of moral respect, the sorts of entities that can and should receive moral attention, and the nature of the "good" which morality (since it at least *includes* beneficence) is supposed to promote. In addition, we need principles for weighing or adjudicating conflicting claims to moral consideration.

It seems to me that we should not only wonder about, but actually follow "the road not taken into the wood." Neither rationality nor the capacity to experience pleasure and pain seem to me necessary (even though they may be sufficient) conditions on moral considerability. And only our hedonistic and concentric forms of ethical reflection keep us from acknowledging this fact. Nothing short of the condition of *being alive* seems to me to be a plausible and non-arbitrary criterion. What is more, this criterion, if taken seriously, could admit of application to entities and systems of entities heretofore unimagined as claimants on our moral attention (such as the biosystem itself).

Section II

Warnock settles upon his own solution. The basis of moral claims, he says, may be put as follows:

> [J]ust as liability to be judged as a moral agent follows from one's general capability of alleviating, by moral action, the ills of the predicament, and is for that reason confined to rational beings, so the condition of being a proper "beneficiary" of moral action is the capability of *suffering* the ills of the predicament—and for that reason is not confined to rational beings, nor even to potential members of that class.

The criterion of moral considerability then, is located in the *capacity to suffer*:

> For all A, X deserves moral consideration from A if and only if X is capable of suffering pain (or experiencing enjoyment).

W. K. Frankena, in a recent paper, joins forces:

> Like Warnock, I believe that there are right and wrong ways to treat infants, animals, imbeciles, and idiots even if or even though (as the case may be) they are not persons or human beings—just because they are capable of pleasure and suffering, and not just because their lives happen to have some value to or for those who clearly are persons or human beings.

And Peter Singer writes:

> If a being is not capable of suffering, or of experiencing enjoyment or happiness, there is nothing to be taken into account. This is why the limit of sentience (using the term as a convenient, if not strictly accurate, shorthand for the capacity to suffer or experience enjoyment or happiness) is the only defensible boundary of concern for the interests of others.

I say that the mood is aggravated because, although I acknowledge and even applaud the conviction expressed by these philosophers that the capacity to suffer (or perhaps better, *sentience*) is sufficient for moral considerability, I fail to understand their reasons for thinking such a criterion necessary. To be sure, there are hints at reasons in each case. Warnock implies that non-sentient beings could not be proper "beneficiaries" of moral action. Singer seems to think that beyond sentience "there is nothing to take into account." And Frankena suggests that non-sentient beings simply do not provide us with moral reasons for respecting them unless it be potentiality for sentience.[2] Yet it is so clear that there *is* something to take into account, something that is not merely "potential sentience" and which surely does qualify beings as beneficiaries and capable of harm—namely, *life*—that the hints provided seem to me to fall short of good reasons.

Biologically, it appears that sentience is an adaptive characteristic of living organisms that provides them with a better capacity to anticipate, and so avoid, threats to life. This at least suggests, though of course it does not prove, that the capacities to suffer and to enjoy are ancillary to something more important rather than tickets to considerability in their own right. In the words of one perceptive scientific observer:

> If we view pleasure as rooted in our sensory physiology, it is not difficult to see that our neurophysiological equipment must have evolved via variation and selective retention in such a way as to record a positive signal to adaptationally satisfactory conditions and a negative signal to adaptationally unsatisfactory conditions . . . The pleasure signal is only an evolutionarily derived indicator, not the goal itself. It is the applause which signals a job well done, but not the actual completion of the job.

Nor is it absurd to imagine that evolution might have resulted (indeed might still result?) in beings whose capacities to maintain, protect, and advance their lives did not depend upon mechanisms of pain and pleasure at all.

So far, then, we can see that the search for a criterion of moral considerability takes one quickly and plausibly beyond humanism. But there is a tendency, exhibited in the remarks of Warnock, Frankena, and Singer, to draw up the wagons around the notion of sentience. I have suggested that there is reason to go further and not very much in the way of argument not to. But perhaps there is a stronger and more explicit case that can be made for sentience. I think there is, in a way, and I propose to discuss it in detail in the section that follows.

Section III

Joel Feinberg offers what may be the clearest and most explicit case for a restrictive criterion on moral considerability (restrictive with respect to life).

The central thesis defended by Feinberg is that a being cannot intelligibly be said to possess moral rights (read: deserve moral consideration) unless that being satisfies the "interest principle," and that only the subclass of humans and higher animals among living beings satisfies this principle:

> [T]he sorts of beings who can have rights are precisely those who have (or can have) interests. I have come to this tentative conclusion for two reasons: (1) because a right holder must be capable of being represented and it is impossible to represent a being that has no interests, and (2) because a right holder must be capable of being a beneficiary in his own person, and a being without interests is a being that is incapable of being harmed or benefited, having no good or "sake" of its own.

Implicit in this passage are the following two arguments, interpreted in terms of moral considerability:

(A1)   Only beings who can be *represented* can deserve moral consideration.
Only beings who have (or can have) *interests* can be represented.
———
Therefore, only beings who have (or can have) interests can deserve moral consideration.

(A2)   Only beings capable of being *beneficiaries* can deserve moral consideration.
Only beings who have (or can have) *interests* are capable of being beneficiaries.
———
Therefore, only beings who have (or can have) interests can deserve moral consideration.

I suspect that these two arguments are at work between the lines in Warnock, Frankena, and Singer, though of course one can never be sure. In any case, I propose to consider them as the best defense of the sentience criterion in recent literature.

I am prepared to grant, with some reservations, the first premises in each of these obviously valid arguments. The second premises, though, are *both* questionable. To claim that only beings who have (or can have) interests can be represented might mean that "mere things" cannot be represented because they have nothing to represent, no "interests" as opposed to "usefulness" to defend or protect. Similarly, to claim that only beings who have (or can have) interests are capable of being beneficiaries might mean that "mere things" are incapable of being benefited or harmed—they have no "well-being" to be sought or acknowledged by rational moral agents. So construed, Feinberg seems to be right; but he also seems to be committed to allowing any *living* thing the status of moral considerability. For as he himself admits, even plants

> are not "mere things"; they are vital objects with inherited biological propensities determining their natural growth. Moreover we do say that certain conditions are "good" or "bad" for plants, thereby suggesting that plants, unlike rocks, are capable of having a "good."

But Feinberg pretty clearly wants to draw the nets tighter than this—and he does so by interpreting the notion of "interests" in the two second premises more narrowly. The contrast term he favors is not 'mere things' but 'mindless creatures'. And he makes this move by insisting that "interests" logically presuppose *desires* or *wants* or *aims*, the equipment for which is not possessed by plants (nor, we might add, by many animals or even some humans?).

But why should we accept this shift in strength of the criterion? In doing so, we clearly abandon one sense in which living organisms like plants do have interests that can be represented. There is no absurdity in imagining the representation of the needs of a tree for sun and water in the face of a proposal to cut it down or pave its immediate radius for a parking lot. We might of course, on reflection, decide to go ahead and cut it down or do the paving, but there is hardly an intelligibility problem about representing the tree's interest in our deciding not to. In the face of their obvious tendencies to maintain and heal themselves, it is very difficult to reject the idea of interests on the part of trees (and plants generally) in remaining alive.

Nor will it do to suggest, as Feinberg does, that the needs (interests) of living things like trees are not really their own but implicitly *ours*: "Plants may need things in order to discharge their functions, but their functions are assigned by human interests, not their own." As if it were human interests that assigned to trees the tasks of growth or maintenance! The interests at stake are clearly those of the living things themselves, not simply those of the owners or users or other human persons involved. Indeed, there is a suggestion in this passage that, to be capable of being represented, an organism must *matter* to human beings somehow—a suggestion whose implications for human rights (disenfranchisement) let alone the rights of animals (inconsistently for Feinberg, I think)—are grim.

The truth seems to be that the "interests" that nonsentient beings share with sentient beings (over and against "mere things") are far more plausible as criteria of *considerability* than the "interests" that sentient beings share (over and against "mindless creatures"). This is not to say that interests construed in the latter way are morally irrelevant—for they may play a role as criteria of moral *significance*—but it is to say that psychological or hedonic capacities seem unnecessarily sophisticated when it comes to locating the minimal conditions for something's deserving to be valued for its own sake. Surprisingly, Feinberg's own reflections on "mere things" appear to support this very point:

> ...mere things have no conative life: no conscious wishes, desires, and hopes; or urges and impulses; or unconscious drives, aims, and goals; or latent tendencies, direction of growth, and natural fulfillments. Interests must be compounded somehow out of conations; hence mere things have no interests.

Together with the acknowledgment, quoted earlier, that plants, for example, are not "mere things," such observations seem to undermine the interest principle in its more restrictive form. I conclude, with appropriate caution, that the interest principle either grows to fit what we might call a "life principle" or requires an arbitrary stipulation of psychological capacities (for desires, wants, etc.) which are neither warranted by (A1) and (A2) nor independently plausible.

Section IV

Let us now turn to several objections that might be thought to render a "life principle" of moral considerability untenable quite independently of the adequacy or inadequacy of the 'sentience' or 'interest' principle.

(Objection #1) A principle of moral respect or consideration for life in all its forms is mere Schweitzerian romanticism, even if it does not involve, as it probably does, the projection of mental or psychological categories beyond their responsible boundaries into the realms of plants, insects, and microbes.

(Reply #1) This objection misses the central thrust of my discussion, which is not that the sentience criterion is necessary, but applicable to all life forms—rather the point is that the possession of sentience is not necessary for moral considerability. Schweitzer himself may have held the former view—and so have been "romantic"—but this is beside the point.

(Objection #2) To suggest seriously that moral considerability is coextensive with life is to suggest that conscious, feeling beings have no more central role in the moral life than vegetables, which is downright absurd—if not perverse.

(Reply #2) This objection misses the central thrust of my discussion as well, for a different reason. It is consistent with acknowledging the moral considerability of all life forms to go on to point out differences of moral significance among these life forms. And as far as perversion is concerned, history will perhaps be a better judge of our civilization's treatment of animals and the living environment on that score.

(Objection #3) Consideration of life can serve as a criterion only to the degree that life itself can be given a precise definition; and it can't.

(Reply #3) I fail to see why a criterion of moral considerability must be strictly decidable in order to be tenable. Surely rationality, potential rationality, sentience, and the capacity for or possession of interests fare no better here. Moreover, there do seem to be empirically respectable accounts of the nature of living beings available which are not intolerably vague or open-textured:

> The typifying mark of a living system ... appears to be its persistent state of low entropy, sustained by metabolic processes for accumulating energy, and maintained in equilibrium with its environment by homeostatic feedback processes.

Granting the need for certain further qualifications, a definition such as this strikes me as not only plausible in its own right, but ethically illuminating, since it suggests that the core of moral concern lies in respect for self-sustaining organization and integration in the face of pressures toward high entropy.

(Objection #4) If life, as understood in the previous response, is really taken as the key to moral considerability, then it is possible that larger systems besides our ordinarily understood "linear" extrapolations from human beings (e.g., animals, plants, etc.) might satisfy the conditions, such as the biosystem as a whole. This surely would be a *reductio ad absurdum* of the life principle.

(Reply #4) At best, it would be a reductio of the life principle in this form or without qualification. But it seems to me that such (perhaps surprising) implications, if true, should be taken seriously. There is some evidence that the biosystem as a whole exhibits behavior approximating to the definition sketched above,[3] and I see no reason to deny it moral considerability on that account. Why should the universe of moral considerability map neatly onto our medium-sized framework of organisms?

(Objection #5) There are severe epistemological problems about imputing interests, benefits, harms, etc. to nonsentient beings. What is it for a tree to have needs?

(Reply #5) 1 am not convinced that the epistemological problems are more severe in this context than they would be in numerous others which the objector would probably not find problematic. Christopher Stone has put this point nicely:

> I am sure I can judge with more certainty and meaningfulness whether and when my lawn wants (needs) water than the Attorney General can judge whether and when the United States wants (needs) to take an appeal from an adverse judgment by a lower court. The lawn tells me that it wants water by a certain dryness of the blades and soil—immediately obvious to the touch—the appearance of bald spots, yellowing, and a lack of springiness after being walked on; how does "the United States" communicate to the Attorney General?

We make decisions in the interests of others or on behalf of others every day—"others" whose wants are far less verifiable than those of most living creatures.

(Objection #6) Whatever the force of the previous objections, the clearest and most decisive refutation of the principle of respect for life is that one cannot *live* according to it, nor is there any indication in nature that we were intended to. We must eat, experiment to gain knowledge, protect ourselves from predation (macroscopic and microscopic), and in general deal with the overwhelming complexities of the moral life while remaining psychologically intact. To take seriously the criterion of considerability being defended, all these things must be seen as somehow morally wrong.

(Reply #6) This objection, if it is not met by implication in (R2), can be met, I think, by recalling the distinction made earlier between regulative and operative moral consideration. It seems to me that there clearly are limits to the operational character of respect for living things. We must eat, and usually this involves killing (though not always). We must have knowledge, and sometimes this involves experimentation with living things and killing (though not always). We must protect ourselves from predation and disease, and sometimes this involves killing (though not always). The regulative character of the moral consideration due to all living things asks, as far as I can see, for sensitivity and awareness, not for suicide (psychic or otherwise). But it is not vacuous, in that it does provide a *ceteris paribus* encouragement in the direction of nutritional, scientific, and medical practices of a genuinely life-respecting sort.

As for the implicit claim, in the objection, that since nature doesn't respect life, we needn't, there are two rejoinders. The first is that the premise is not so clearly true. Gratuitous killing in nature is rare indeed. The second, and more important, response is that the issue at hand has to do with the appropriate moral demands to be made on rational moral agents, not on beings who are not rational moral agents. Besides, this objection would tell equally against any criterion of moral considerability so far as I can see, if the suggestion is that nature is amoral.

«««—»»»

I have been discussing the necessary and sufficient conditions that should regulate moral consideration. As indicated earlier, however, numerous other questions are waiting in the wings. Central among them are questions dealing with how to balance competing claims to consideration in a world in which such competing claims seem pervasive. Related to these questions would be problems about the relevance of developing or declining status in life (the very young and the very old) and the relevance of the part-whole relation (leaves to a tree; species to an ecosystem). And there are many others.

Perhaps enough has been said, however, to clarify an important project for contemporary ethics, if not to defend a full-blown account of moral considerability and moral significance. Leopold's ethical vision and its implications for modern society in the form of an environmental ethic are important—so we should proceed with care in assessing it.

Notes

[1] *Should Trees Have Standing?* (Los Altos, Calif.: William Kaufmann, 1974); parenthetical page references to Stone will be to this book.

[2] "I can see no reason, from the moral point of view, why we should respect something that is alive but has no conscious sentiency and so can experience no pleasure or pain, joy or suffering, unless perhaps it is potentially a consciously sentient being, as in the case of a fetus. Why, if leaves and trees have no capacity to feel pleasure or to suffer, should I tear no leaf from a tree? Why should I respect its location any more than that of a stone in my driveway, if no benefit or harm comes to any person or sentient being by my moving it?" (Frankena, "Ethics and the Environment.")

[3] See J. Lovelock, "The Quest for Gaia;" *The New Scientist*, LXV, 935 (Feb. 6, 1975): 304-309.

THE MORAL STANDING OF NATURAL OBJECTS

ANDREW BRENNAN (1984)

Human beings are, as far as we know, the only animals to have moral concerns and to adopt moralities, but it would be a mistake to be misled by this fact into thinking that humans are also the only proper objects of moral consideration. I argue that we ought to allow even nonliving things a significant moral status, thus denying the conclusion of much contemporary moral thinking. First, I consider the possibility of giving moral consideration to nonliving things. Second, I put forward grounds which justify this extension of morality beyond its conventional boundaries. Third, I argue that natural objects have a status different from a special class of artifacts—works of art. Fourth, I discuss the notion of interest, and fifth I look briefly at the status of natural systems and at ways we might link the proposed extension of moral considerability with the rest of our moral thinking.

I. The Scope of Morality

There is considerable agreement among writers that if anything deserves moral consideration, then normal adult humans do, but given, in Waismann's phrase, the "open texture" of our language, we can easily imagine extending the language of rights, duty, respect, and obligation to children, the senile, the deranged, fetuses, the comatose, higher animals, human and animal corpses, and—perhaps less easily—also to other animals, trees, shrubs, vegetables, bacteria, cells, forests, valleys and even minerals. The length, and the ordering, of such a list is obviously a matter of considerable disagreement.

Following Warnock (*Object of Morality*) and Goodpaster ("On being morally considerable"), I take *moral considerability* as the core notion and consider extending it beyond our fellow humans to four progressively larger groups of things: (1) sentient beings whose psychological states are *models* of our own; (2) sentient beings of any kind; (3) living things; and (4) natural objects of any sort.

The notion of *model* in (1) is borrowed from Matthews who argues that there is a certain psychological unity within the animal kingdom. Human beings are not unique in forming plans and carrying them out, cooperatively if necessary. Lionesses on a hunt do the same. Cows weep when parted from their calves: do they not then feel the pain of separation? The point is so obviously true that it would be irritating for someone to defend it, as Hume noted long ago:

> Next to the ridicule of denying an evident truth is that of taking much pains to defend it; and no truth appears to me more evident, than that beasts are endow'd with thought and reason as well as man. The arguments are in this case so obvious that they never escape the most stupid and ignorant.

Of course, an appeal to our unity with other animals has its limits, for at some stage our psychological relatedness to other species becomes so attenuated as no longer to count for very much. Problems begin to arise when one tries to determine what the moral significance of this psychological unity is supposed to be.

An answer to this question may have something to do with the related question of *rights*. Passmore argues that legal obligations and rights can only be generated among beings who belong to one community of "mutual obligations" and "common interests," while others, like Feinberg, maintain that for something to be a potential rights holder it must have interests, for the holder of rights must be able to be represented (and what has no interests cannot be represented), and must be able to benefit in its own right (which again requires it to possess interests). It looks as if higher animals will certainly be candidates for moral consideration if Feinberg is right. And it can also be urged that humans and other animals do at least sometimes form communities of common interests.

We can think of the relationship between dolphins and those who study them—or if we include cases in which the participation of those involved is less than equal, the bond between people and pets. Even so, we can again ask: just what does the possession of interests, or the shared interests of a community, amount to?

Perhaps we can make sense of the appeal to interests, psychological models, and communities if we think of moral values as bound up with a framework of primarily human interests, needs, and purposes. The notion that a *moral* code provides a means of maximizing welfare within a society, for example, would be one way of accommodating this perspective, since considerations regarding welfare only seem to arise for beings who have interests. Alternatively, we can consider what set of principles it would be rational to choose for a society given both information and ignorance about one's place in that society. Or again, like Gewirth, we can seek to establish some fundamental moral principle on the ground that since we claim rights for ourselves in virtue of our having certain qualities, then others who possess these same qualities will also be able to claim similar rights.

What lies behind all these notions is a human- (or at least animal-) centered conception of ethics, a kind of ethical egoism once removed. Whereas the egoist interested in the welfare of one particular individual above all others, these more sophisticated views recognize that what it is *moral* to do may not always result in maximizing welfare or benefit to the agent, although a code based on these insights supposedly maximizes the welfare of a group, society, or community of appropriately characterized individuals. If my own access to certain benefits is through my membership in such groups, then I will be able to "identify" in some sense with the group and may come to associate my good with that of the group.

It is not my intention to undermine this strategy or to deny that something of moral interest can result from the strategy. Indeed, rather like Gewirth, I appeal to qualities common to humans and to some inanimate objects in order to make out a case for the moral considerability of the latter. Unlike Gewirth and most other theorists, however, the shared quality which I suggest is not anything like rationality, purposive agency, linguistic ability, or even sentience. This is not to deny that such qualities may be morally important. Perhaps a creature which is rational and talks has more of a moral claim on me than one which is rational but lacks language (assuming, for the moment, that rationality and linguistic ability can be separated). But if I am right, my argument at least challenges the notion that by the time we have reached sentience we are sure to have exhausted the fund of morally relevant features.

Significantly, then, I suggest that what it is moral to do may, on occasion, be something that does not benefit individual humans, communities of humans, or communities of humans and other beings with qualities like those of agency, rationality, or sentience. Does this mean that we, along with a wide variety of natural objects—perhaps all of them—form a community, the welfare of which is the proper object of morality? Perhaps, though as I show later this question may be more terminological than real. For the time being, it should be noted that I am not denying that for social life to be possible at all there have to be rules that take account of the often competing interests of those who live together in communities and that some of these will be moral rules. Nor am I dismissing the possibility of putting forward human-regarding arguments for the preservation of wildlife and wild places. On the contrary, such arguments seem to me to be very important and may themselves be—morally or otherwise—already decisive.

To pursue the hypothesis, should we not then think straightway about the extension of considerability to all sentient and living things? Pleasure and pain is something that is a central feature of human (and probably animal) experience, and interests, we might think, can still exist in the absence of sentience anyway. We need food, and it is a good thing for us, even if we lack the warm glow of contentment a full stomach sometimes brings. The defender of sentience may wonder why we should care for the goals of a being, albeit a *living* one, who is incapable of feeling frustration, fear, disappointment, hurt, or satisfaction. Now there is undoubtedly an *explanatory* route linking sentience with moral respect. If an item has feelings, this explains its possession of interests. And, as we have seen, its possession of interests can in turn explain why it is worthy of moral consideration. But what I suggest is another route to just this same destination—moral considerability. My route may not appear to be so obviously explanatory—this may be because it is not so well worn as the first one—but so long as the route I suggest is a possible one, then the dogma that moral respect is conceptually tied to sentience will be wide-open to challenge.

Suppose, then, that at least for the sake of the argument the possibility of moral consideration to our third group is allowed. Is there any good reason why we should pause there instead of sliding all the way down the slippery slope? Both works of art and natural objects like great deserts and mountains seem to command a certain respect for their own sakes. Is this a kind of moral respect? Or is it simply absurd to suggest so?

My strategy here is slightly devious. I start by arguing that it is at least not absurd to consider inanimate natural objects as worthy of moral consideration in their own right. Having thus established the possibility of a morality that gives nature its due, I then turn to the problem of what might motivate or justify such a moral stance. In the West, we are not used to taking seriously the idea that natural objects can have a moral claim on us. What seem to be clear moral intuitions, though, are quite often local to a time and a culture. Thus, in a culture strongly influenced by Buddhism, Jainism, or Shinto it would hardly have been necessary to argue as I have been doing for the considerability of living things.

II. Things and Their Functions

Supposing, at least for the sake of the argument, that there are possible principles which can be said to be moral principles and which allow consideration not only to living things but also to some nonliving natural objects, we might wonder if there are any other objects which might have a claim to moral status. Natural objects contrast with artifacts. Both sorts of object have structure of varying complexity, and both can have functions. The function of scissors is to cut, and good scissors cut well; the function of a heart is to pump blood, and good hearts pump well. But the function of an artifact is the result of design, and this design is intended to satisfy some end. By saying this, I mean to count beaver lodges as artifacts, but not coral reefs.

Now, a badly designed object may not fulfill its function well (or function instead as a different artifact), but the structure of complete natural objects is not the result of design, for they have no functions to fulfill. Parts of natural objects—like hearts, kidneys, leaves, and roots—do have functions, and these are determined by the contribution they make to the growth, maintenance, and survival of the complete, living thing of which they are parts. And, by extension, we may even count whole conglomerates of natural things—ecosystems—as containing whole objects within them which function to preserve the system as a whole. But we must be cautious with this extended use, for whole natural individuals, whether microbes or tigers, have no intrinsic functions at all.

It is important to be clear about this matter of intrinsic function. A cotoneaster shrub, let us suppose, functions to screen the compost heap in a garden. This is typical of the countless ways we—and other living things—use natural objects in the fulfillment of our schemes. Yet, it would be silly to try to define cotoneasters in terms of their contributions to gardens, or in terms of any other functions that we, or any other creature, might assign them. By contrast, to describe an item as a root, or a leaf, is to describe it in terms of its functions; an object that looked like a leaf, yet failed to promote growth by photosynthesis, and took no part in transpiration, would hardly be a genuine leaf. Thus, there seems to be an important distinction between whole natural objects and their functional parts.

It is not my intention here to contribute to the already large literature on function and teleology. Any reasonable account of function, nevertheless, will allow for the existence of defective or diseased things of a kind which fail to carry out the functions characteristic of that kind. Thus, we should no doubt want to distinguish false leaves (which do not function as leaves at all) from defective leaves (which would have functioned as normal leaves had not certain disturbing factors intervened). My notion of intrinsic function is rather like Enç's notion of function *simpliciter*. As he puts it:

What I am asserting here is that when we discover what the function of the heart, is, we also discover part of the identity conditions of a heart. Part of what it is to be a heart is to be capable of pumping blood under normal conditions...

It is no part of the identity conditions of cotoneasters that they screen eyesores. It follows that I can know that a certain bush screens my compost heap without knowing what kind of bush it is and a grasp of what a cotoneaster is involves no reference, to such overlaid (non-intrinsic) functions as that of screening other things.

Now for a problem case. Suppose we find an ecosystem in which stability is preserved in part by the appetite of a large predator. To the predator we assign the function within the system of keeping, say, the population of voles at a reasonable level. Moreover, the system which the predator helps to control may itself have determined a place in it for such a predator. In this case, it looks as if the predator is functionally adapted to the system.

Now there is a way in which we can try to take the sting out of this example and argue that the predator in fact has no function. The assignment of functions to individual predators, or to any other individual, risks a 'division fallacy.' Suppose our large predator is an eagle, and suppose further that eagles die out in the system under consideration. As they become extinct, their place is taken by some other species—by hawks of some kind. So long as the hawks control the voles to the same extent as the eagles did, our model of the system will not be substantially altered life claim that the eagle had this function prior to its extinction is not a claim about any individual bird. Rather it was a claim about a kind of animal, about the need for a group fulfilling the role in question to be represented in the ecosystem. But what is true of a group need not be true of any representative of that group. And the truth, if any there be, in talking about the function of a predator in a natural system is, at best, a truth about a group, not about any individual. One eagle dies, while another is hatched to replace it. Just as the heart cells do not function to pump blood (although hearts do) individual eagles do not function to control voles (although we may regard groups of them as doing so).[1]

My point, however, is more than the claim that nothing has a function *qua* individual. On the contrary, individual things may acquire this or that function in particular circumstances. And if we broaden the notion of non-intrinsic function to include roles—how well an individual discharges a given function (as mother, chairperson, or whatever) may itself be a matter of moral concern. The claim that nothing has function *qua* individual would, at best, be true only of intrinsic functions. And it is just such functions which individuals that are not physically parts of other objects are lacking.

As we have seen, this intrinsic functionlessness is coupled with a capacity to take on multifarious functions in different contexts. But what makes a factory worker more than a machine operator also makes an elm tree more than a windbreak; in each case we have an assigned function coupled with the potential for taking on many other functions—voluntarily or not—overlaid on an individual that is designed specifically neither for this nor for that, since the individual was not designed at all. And if we are to look for a quality by virtue of which all natural things may claim moral considerability, I tentatively suggest that we have come up with a candidate: their lack of intrinsic function.

III. Art and Autonomy

We celebrate the intrinsic lack of function of persons in various ways: they are not merely the means to others' ends, but have the potential for all sorts of different roles; within institutions they can acquire all sorts of functions, but none of this can undermine their fundamental autonomy. The thrust of my argument is that we do have some grounds, albeit slender ones, for recognizing a similar autonomy in other natural things.[2]

Few would deny that scissors, cars, and other products of human and animal invention lack this autonomy shared by natural objects. But there are some products of human labor which have seemed to, many to have a value beyond mere functional utility, and have instead appeared to have an intrinsic value for their own sakes. Works of art are perhaps the best examples of such products, and many modern writers have followed Hegel in ascribing a higher value to art than to nature.

We can see an attempt made to compare natural objects with artifacts. And if we are going to compare the claims of these two kinds of objects, it is interesting to know if the objects compete on the same basis. It may be that works of art are examples of the sort of objects whose existence we wondered about at the start of the preceding section: artifacts that have a claim to moral standing.

Some support for the idea that works of art are more than mere instruments of communication between artist, or composer, and audience is rendered by noting the affront people display when an important art work is vandalized, or one of a country's art treasures is threatened with export. To give a complete account of why art is viewed as something transcendent, and of value for its own sake, would take me too far from the central themes of this paper. Yet, I want to maintain that art works and natural objects do not compete for moral consideration on any similar basis. Unlike natural objects, art works do *not* seem to me to fall within the scope of morality.

Part of the "magic" of art is that masterpieces of music, literature, painting, and the rest are packed with symbolic richness. Not only is there no simple message conveyed by a great painting or sculpture, but rather a number of messages, allusions, and suggestions conveyed on many different levels. The symbolic content of such objects represents a great deal to a great many people. They are messages of great richness. This sheer expressive power that they represent enables us, I think, to account for their potency while staying within an account of art which treats it as a mode of communication between the creative agent and the audience.

If we do stay within such an account, then artworks are functional objects, and hence not on the same footing as complete natural objects. This is not to say that there is no room for talk of respect, duty, and obligation when we are dealing with art; rather, we need to be clear on the Kantian distinction between duties owed directly to objects, and duties we may have regarding an object. We owe no respect, no duties, to any of Leonardo's work, but we do have duties regarding it, duties which are owed to the many people for whom his work is of immense symbolic power. Likewise, a government contemplating a road building program owes no duty to a valley on the grounds that it is sacred to a particular local tribe; but the government does, of course, owe a duty to the tribe regarding the valley. If a road is built through the valley despite the protests of the tribe, it is the tribe, not the valley, that has been wronged.

The Moral Standing of Natural Objects

Yet, the valley is a natural object, and if what I have argued so far has any plausibility, it may be that we owe any valley, consecrated to ancestors or not, a certain moral respect which we do not owe any artifact. Subtract the expressive power and the fitness for its purposes from a painting and you are left with an artifact of no particular value: the canvas, the wood for the frame, even the frame itself and the pigments in the oils, might all have been put to better use. But subtract the functions assigned by people and animals to a valley and its river, take away the ski lifts, the beaver dams, and the scenic views and you are left with an object containing within it hundreds of self-regulating systems living in a kind of natural anarchy, an object that partly determines its own climate, serving no one's purpose, but still worthy of respect purely in its own right.

To argue in this way raises an interesting problem: could there be items of human or animal creation which, nonetheless, have a value purely for and in themselves, not merely one derived from their function? Gardens, parks, canals, and the like might seem to be of this type. And many animals may be thought, at first sight, to be artifacts themselves. As Callicott says, "Domestic animals are creations of man. They are living artifacts, but artifacts nevertheless.... It is literally meaningless to suggest that they be liberated." Certainly, intervention by unnatural selection, or by gardening, has allowed the production of living things and systems particularly suited to human ends and needs.

But we need to be wary about classifying such items. Suppose an alien biologist is puzzled to find a breed of (domestic) sheep particularly ill adapted to surviving in the wild. The biologist is enlightened by the discovery that the breed is the result of human intervention aimed at maximizing wool production and yielding a high proportion of edible flesh. Does the discovery tell the biologist more about the *nature* of the breed in question? Of course not: the puzzle was about the etiology of the breed, not about what kind of thing if was. It might be objected that one thing the biologist has found out is that the animals are of a certain kind, namely, the domestic kind. Little hangs on this point. The label "domestic" identifies no natural kind, and is dispensable from the taxonomist's point of view. It alerts us to the likelihood that the animal or plant in question is the result of selective breeding. Selective breeding yields "artifacts" in only an attenuated sense of that term.

Plants and rocks in a garden, however, represent a different case. They are incorporated as parts into a whole, which is the result of human design and that design is aimed at satisfying our own ends. Gardens, parks, and game reserves are thus artifacts in a perfectly literal sense. But their components are natural objects and our use of them within the artifact will more or less restrict their autonomy. A garden, then, has a double value. It has the sum of the values of the individual things within it; and additionally it has its value as an artifact—that is, value for those who use it and benefit from it.

IV. Interest

The position I have now reached has both benefits and drawbacks. From such a stance, we can see why the retention of certain areas in national parks, carefully stocked with selected species, seems to some people a poor attempt at giving nature her due, for such parks and game reserves become large artifacts, no different in kind from zoos and gardens. Of course, not all protected wilderness areas are managed in this way, and even if some are, the objects within them are, as I have argued, often pretty well autonomous. On the other side, much work remains to be done to show whether I am right in lumping together many different kinds of natural objects as all sharing the same autonomy.

And the details of how to distinguish parts of objects from whole objects have been conveniently skipped. Are *clouds* whole objects, or just parts of one object, the atmosphere? Are *human bodies* whole objects, or just temporary swarms of atoms? Ignoring these difficulties, nothing has been said to support the view that wilderness areas should be left alone, rare species protected and industrial pollution reduced—for the acknowledgement that natural objects are worthy of respect for themselves does not require in itself any prohibition on our use of them, although we might expect that taking their autonomy seriously would mean putting limits on our present somewhat selfish exploitation of them.

But before we take seriously talk about limits in this context, we have to consider how we might give weight to claims on behalf of natural objects at all. Do their interests compete with ours in any way? Does it even make sense to think of an inanimate thing having interests at all?

Much of the recent work on the question of respect—or rights—for natural objects has been stimulated by the case of the Mineral King Valley described in Stone's book *Should Trees Have Standing?* Stone's article of the same title was in part responsible for the Douglas dissent, in which an American Supreme Court judge argued for the extension of rights to natural objects. The trouble, though, with Stone's original position is that it seems to require us to recognize that such items as forests, rivers, and valleys have interests. Stone's arguments involve an appeal to the fact that we already accord recognition to the interests of such merely legal "persons" as countries, corporations, and so on, even though in the nineteenth-century jurists found such notions almost unintelligible. Thus, he writes:

> Perhaps injury to the Sierra Club was tenuous,... but the injury to Mineral King—the park itself—wasn't. If I could get the courts thinking about the park itself as a jural person—the way corporations are 'persons'—the notion of nature having rights would here make a significant operational difference....

As we have already seen, Feinberg argues that "the sorts of beings who *can* have rights are precisely those who have (or can have) interests," and so it is hardly surprising to find Stone taking the position he does.

Such a view, indeed, seems plausible when we focus on living things, or simple aggregates of living things, like forests. And let us suppose, perhaps implausibly, that the interests of a corporation can be identified by a reductionist strategy: we can appeal to the interests of employees, shareholders, customers, and so on. In a similar way, perhaps the interests of a forest can be identified in terms of the interests of its individual trees, the birds who nest in them, the fungi around their roots, and so forth.

Yet, even in this case there is an overwhelming difference. In the case of natural forest, there was no design, no purpose, no contracts, no statutes—in brief, none of the hallmarks of the artifacts which are corporations. Corporations have ends to serve, at least economically, but forests have none. But I have already argued that living things in general do have an interest in survival, growth, and freedom from disease. So perhaps we should include forests as special cases of living things. Alas, none of this comes close to establishing any sort of interest for mountains, the air, deserts, and rocky crests.

Another point about interests is that while we are expert as far as human interests are concerned (so we think), we can never be in a position to say just what the interests of other living or nonliving things might be. Perhaps rivers enjoy being dammed—how could we ever tell? Yet, if, in Tribe's words, we are to give "institutional expression to the perception that nature exists for itself," how could we do so while abandoning talk of interests? Aping Feinberg, we might suggest that a mountain has no interest unless we assign it a function within a scheme of human interests, and so a mountain *per se* could not be represented in any institutional legal process, especially in an adversarial system of law like our own. Seen in this way, Stone's appeal to corporations, municipalities, and the rest is not a very helpful precedent.

An opponent of species-centered morality might point out at this stage that our predicament merely confirms our alienation from nature. Since we are unable to determine the wants, needs, harms, injuries, and benefits of rivers and mountains, we are unable to let them figure in our institutional processes which are designed for handling just such matters.

The considerations I have advanced in this paper suggest that all natural objects share a certain functionlessness, unlike their parts, and that this may provide a basis for a fellow feeling, a respect, and a care for natural objects which is no less important for being outside the scope of social morality. My own view here is that to accept this way out, however attractive, is to restrict the scope of morality unduly. Although in my account we can talk of the harm caused to the fish and flora of a river by excessive fertilizer runoff, we can only talk of the harm to the river itself metaphorically. I admit that the river itself can have no interest, literally,[3] but to take this fact as showing that the river itself commands no moral respect is to fall back on a conception of morality that ties it to the social goals already mentioned. We already have notions that are at odds with such a conception. The pointless destruction of inanimate things is as much vandalism as the destruction in a similar spirit of living things.

The arguments in this paper might be thought to give some plausibility to an attempt to divorce an account of vandalism from simple reverence for life and to tie it instead to a recognition of the common predicament of all natural uncreated things. But I doubt whether, in the end, vandalism is the notion we should give our attention to. Artifacts are obvious victims of vandalism, and it seems dear that destruction for its own sake is not a necessary condition of a vandalistic act.

V. Individuals and Systems

So far I have been dealing with easy cases—with individuals, or simple aggregates (like forests) whose parts are individuals. Before inquiring further into the connections, if any, between the viewpoint I am urging and the accepted notions of what is of moral concern, it is necessary to take a look at one very distinctive view of environmental morality—Leopold's land ethic. This view can be neatly captured by the motto: "A thing is right when it tends to preserve the integrity, stability and beauty of the biotic community. It is wrong when it tends otherwise." It could be argued that the autonomous, intrinsically functionless individuals with which I have so far been concerned are themselves *parts* of certain larger wholes—ecosystems. Moreover, the good of such systems and the good of the individuals living within them are not wholly disconnected. As Stephen Clark puts it:

> Plants too, and every clod of earth, are animate: not mystically so, but in straightforward biological terms. The earth itself, the biosphere itself is made up of living things and their products in a single interconnected whole. We are all members one of another, and the lowliest organism may be as vital to the whole as any Nobel prize-winner. More so, indeed, for the very fact which can be immediately adduced to mark the difference between man and plants, or men and micro-organisms, reveals that the latter are strictly very much more important than anyone of us.

How can I, calling as I do for respect for rocky crests or great oceans, ignore the claims of individual ecosystems let alone those of that "multi-millionfold life-support system that is the terrestrial biosphere?"

One problem here is knowing just what the good of the biosphere is if it is something different from the sum of the goods of all the individuals living within it. Another, more technical, issue is whether we, or anything else are, literally, *parts* of ecosystems. It is certainly not right to think of our relationship to larger systems in the way that our components stand to us. At least, such an analogy is no more helpful than that which sees the relation of parts of a body to a whole body as similar to that of members of a family to the whole family, or citizens to the state.

To discuss this technical issue in detail here would not, I think, be rewarding. So let us stay neutral on the matter of parts and wholes, but bearing in mind that when I speak of the relation of members to a group I am in no way intending to suggest that this is at all the same as that of a component to a whole.

Anyone who is wary of facile reductionism would want to question the suggestion implicitly made at the start of the preceding paragraph that the good of the biosphere may be no more than the sum of the goods of its members.

Think of an analogy with *families*. The good of a family is not merely the sum of the goods of its members, at least not if saying this involves ignoring the fact that I may make a sacrifice for the good of the family (to which I belong). As I suggested in section one, I can come to identify with a group to which I belong, and cease to see a conflict between my good and its good. So my good (being identified with the good of the family) can involve sacrifices on my part. On the other hand, the good of the family is not something quite distinct from the good of its members. My sacrifices will benefit the family only because they benefit other members of it, and it is, no doubt, the fact that I care about their good that involves me in making the sacrifices I do.

Now is a family an intrinsically functionless thing? It is hardly an *individual* in the philosopher's sense, but it is a unitary entity of a sort. And even if we are troubled about agreeing that it is intrinsically functionless, there will be some intrinsically functionless groups in which I have some degree of membership. To be consistent, perhaps I ought to argue for the moral standing of such items, although such a claim would not be nearly so clear as one made on behalf of individuals, since the former depends on further clarifications of the status of such entities.

It should now be clear why I focused on individual natural things to begin with. This was no mere post-Renaissance individualism on my part, but rather a concern to work from the simpler cases. It is arguable that ecosystems fulfill the conditions for functionless objects and are therefore candidates for moral consideration every bit as worthy as trees, valleys, rivers and stones. If you take such a view, I have no objection to your taking my references to natural objects in this broad way. But I hope I have said enough to show that it is not a necessary corollary of this view that the good of such a large object will be distinct from, or even at odds with, the good of its members. Just as in the case of the family, the adoption of an appropriate environmental ethic may make it (morally) impossible for any opposition to arise between our good as humans and the good of the biosphere or of the planet.

But what is the focus of an appropriate environmental ethic? A question mark now hangs over notions of welfare or interest, for I am prepared to concede that rivers and deserts have, quite literally, no welfare or interests, and I would concede the point with regard to ecosystems as well. Of course, since the good of a system or group is, as I have admitted, not distinct from the good of its members, and since at least some members of every ecosystem have interests, we might be tempted by some reductionist account of the interests of such systems.

Indeed, we could no doubt try to make sense of acting charitably toward a river, or of being benevolent to a desert. The open texture of our language is perfectly hospitable to just such conceptual development, but it is not part of my aim to argue for it here. Nor am I urging any kind of reductionist ploy. So it may be that a utilitarian, for example, will need either to reinterpret what I say so that notions of welfare, benevolence, and interest can have some kind of application in such cases or else to dismiss my arguments as morally irrelevant.

One small hope I entertain is that reflection on the points I have tried to make may undermine the sympathetic reader's allegiance to a morality based exclusively on notions like those of welfare or interest. We are terribly tempted to simplify and systematize, to think that simple rules and formulas will work for much of our moral life. Suggestions like the ones made in this paper threaten the neat systematizations others have made, and raise problems that few have ever taken seriously. It is bad enough trying to count the interests of sentient things in our calculations: but how are we to proceed when we count in things that are not sentient and have no interests? We are inclined, at least if we take views like utilitarianism seriously, to dismiss this latter group of things simply because they cannot be *counted* or given weight in our *calculations* in any obvious way.

My response is to reject this kind of systematic approach to the problem. Let us give considerability to all intrinsically functionless natural things. The next step—not one I can take here—is to look at lots of cases, taking extended moral considerability seriously, and see how we can start to give due weight to the moral claims of the diverse items in the cases. I am pleased to see that others likewise distrust the appeal of systems in morality. Clark, for one, inveighs against moral systems which "present a sort of ghastly *reductio ad absurdum* of their own pretensions."

There are a couple of concepts that figure in our everyday moral thinking which do, I think, have application to the kinds of items for which I have been suggesting we take moral considerability seriously. The first is the idea of *freedom*, which seems to make little sense when applied to a functional component or to a merely functional artifact. For something to have an intrinsic function, its very existence as an item of the kind that it is depends upon its fulfilling whatever causal roles its function requires. An intrinsically functionless item, by contract, can change, develop, and organize itself subject to quite different constraints.

Of course, to be a flower of a certain sort is to have certain components organized in a certain structure—a structure determined in the end by the flower's microscopic genetic structure. But the same kind of flower will grow differently in different environments, play host to different sorts of insects, and fulfill all sorts of different imposed roles. We too have the freedom to adapt to various circumstances and environments, a freedom of which we ourselves are aware and a freedom that is far greater than that of a primula or a dandelion. But the difference between dandelions, primulas, and us is one of degree, not of kind.

What may come as a shock is not my notion that ecosystems may differ in degree rather than in kind from us, for after all, such systems are governed by internal principles which enable them to survive changes and crises almost as if they too were living things. Rather, the shock may come in the claim that deserts, rocks, and rivers are similar to us, too. The vagaries of human existence, our limited point of view, are no doubt important in explaining the difficulty we have in seeing such objects as self-organizing systems.

If millennia were but seconds to us, we would be immediately aware of the logic of the rock cycle, the growth of mountains, and the ebb and flow of deserts. In such a way we can perhaps start to make sense of Wiggins' remarks about a principle of activity. As it is, our knowledge of these things is only remote and indirect, but the claim that rivers, mountains, and wildernesses can be "tamed" is an implicit acknowledgement that they have, so to speak, their own wild, free way of existing.

If freedom is one notion that has a recognizable role in our moral thinking, another, I would suggest, is that of the *natural*. We can perhaps recognize that we ourselves are natural objects sharing the accident of existence with other autonomous natural objects This separateness and independence of all natural things gives rise to a kind of dignity noted even by the Romantic poets on the occasions when they were able to transcend their often self-indulgent enjoyment of nature. Iris Murdoch writes:

> A self-directed enjoyment of nature seems to me to be something forced. More naturally, as well as more properly, we take a self-forgetful pleasure in the sheer alien pointless independent existence of animals, birds, stones and trees.

In my account, the propriety of this self-forgetful pleasure is based on a certain common predicament that we and our fellow natural objects find ourselves in. That we, and other animals, can act purposively, set ourselves projects and strive intelligently to fulfill them should not lead us to forget the intrinsic functionlessness of uncreated things. We already have a concept of naturalness which leads us to protect and cherish the natural and mistrust the artificial. At its fashionable worst, respect for the natural is invoked in order to promote the sales of herbal shampoos and ginseng root, but such respect is also linked with our growing concern about factory farming, monoculture, deforestation, global pollution, genetic engineering, and loss of wilderness.

It may seem to some that what we are dealing with here might more properly be regarded as *aesthetic* rather than purely moral matters. But if this paper has set out mainly to challenge the notion that sentience, rationality, or even life itself exhaust the bases for moral concern, then a corollary would be a challenge to the view that respect for the natural can be dismissed as merely aesthetic. How, indeed, are we to separate the aesthetic and the moral? If we claim that morality, unlike aesthetics, deals with interest or welfare, than this would be merely question-begging. Perhaps our care for what is natural is both aesthetic and moral: the burden, I would argue, is on the objector to establish that such care is in some distinctive way nonmoral.

Notes

1. For readers who find the analogy with a physical thing of this sort inappropriate, a more convincing example may come from the "Ant Fugue" in D. R. Hofstadter's *Godel, Escher, Bach* (1979). Teams of ants form "signals," characterized by their function of conveying specialized ants to a part of a colony. But only the team, not the individual ants, have this function. The individual ants have the functions of nursing, cleaning, hunting, and so forth. Incidentally, I regard ant colonies as individuals, with ants as functional components: there is no more to the individual ant than its roles in the colony, whereas there is more to an eagle than its roles, say, as one of a nesting pair.

2. Murray MacBeath has impressed upon me that it can seem odd to hold mountains as autonomous, if by this we mean that they do things in a self-regulating way, getting on—as it were—with the business of being mountains. Interestingly, Wiggins (1980) writes of "geological terms like *river, lake, spring, sea, glacier,* or *volcano* [that] it will not be wildly inappropriate to speak of principles of activity."

3. However, granted the open texture of our language and the associated possibilities of conceptual development, we could probably work up a concept of interest that would apply to rivers.

PART IV:
ECO-PHILOSOPHY AND DEEP ECOLOGY

STEPS TO AN ECOLOGY OF MIND

GREGORY BATESON (1968-70)

Conscious Purpose versus Nature

Our civilization, which is on the block here for investigation and evaluation, has its roots in three main ancient civilizations: the Roman, the Hebrew and the Greek; and it would seem that many of our problems are related to the fact that we have an imperialist civilization leavened or yeasted by a downtrodden, exploited colony in Palestine. In this conference, we are again going to be fighting out the conflict between the Romans and the Palestinians.

You will remember that St. Paul boasted, "I was born free." What he meant was that he was born Roman, and that this had certain legal advantages.

We can engage in that old battle either by backing the downtrodden or by backing the imperialists. If you are going to fight that battle, you have to take sides in it. It's that simple.

On the other hand, of course, St. Paul's ambition, and the ambition of the downtrodden, is always to get on the side of the imperialists—to become middle-class imperialists themselves—and it is doubtful whether creating more members of the civilization which we are here criticizing is a solution to the problem.

There is, therefore, another more abstract problem. We need to understand the pathologies and peculiarities of the whole Romano-Palestinian system. It is this that I am interested in talking about. I do not care, here, about defending the Romans or defending the Palestinians—the upper dogs or the underdogs. I want to consider the dynamics of the whole traditional pathology in which we are caught, and in which we shall remain as long as we continue to struggle within that old conflict. We just go round and round in terms of the old premises.

Fortunately our civilization has a third root—in Greece. Of course Greece got caught up in a rather similar mess, but still there was a lot of clean, cool thinking of a quite surprising kind which was different.

Let me approach the bigger problem historically. From St. Thomas Aquinas to the eighteenth century in Catholic countries, and to the Reformation among Protestants (because we threw out a lot of Greek sophistication with the Reformation), the structure of our religion was Greek. In mid-eighteenth century the biological world looked like this: there was a supreme mind at the top of the ladder, which was the basic explanation of everything downwards from that—the supreme mind being, in Christianity, God; and having various attributes at various philosophic stages. The ladder of explanation went downwards deductively from the Supreme to man to the apes, and so on, down to the infusoria.

This hierarchy was a set of deductive steps from the most perfect to the most crude or simple. And it was rigid. It was assumed that every species was unchanging.

Lamarck, probably the greatest biologist in history, turned that ladder of explanation upside down. He was the man who said it starts with the infusoria and that there were changes leading up to man. His turning the taxonomy upside down is one of the most astonishing feats that has ever occurred. It was the equivalent in biology of the Copernican revolution in astronomy.

The logical outcome of turning the taxonomy upside down was that the study of evolution might provide an explanation of *mind*.

Up to Lamarck, mind was the explanation of the biological world. But, hey presto, the question now arose: Is the biological world the explanation of mind? That which was the explanation now became that which was to be explained. About three quarters of Lamarck's *Philosophie Zoologique* (1809) is an attempt, very crude, to build a comparative psychology. He achieved and formulated a number of very modern ideas: that you cannot attribute to any creature psychological capacities for which it has no organs; that mental process must always have physical representation; and that the complexity of the nervous system is related to the complexity of mind.

There the matter rested for 150 years, mainly because evolutionary theory was taken over, not by a Catholic heresy but by a Protestant heresy, in the mid-nineteenth century. Darwin's opponents, you may remember, were not Aristotle and Aquinas, who had some sophistication, but fundamentalist Christians whose sophistication stopped with the first chapter of Genesis. The question of the nature of mind was something which the nineteenth-century evolutionists tried to exclude from their theories, and the matter did not come up again for serious consideration until after World War II. (I am doing some injustice to some heretics along the road, notably to Samuel Butler—and others.)

In World War II it was discovered what sort of complexity entails mind. And, since that discovery, we know that: wherever in the Universe we encounter that sort of complexity, we are dealing with mental phenomena. It's as materialistic as that.

Let me try to describe for you that order of complexity, which is in some degree a technical matter. Russel Wallace sent a famous essay to Darwin from Indonesia. In it he announced his discovery of natural selection, which coincided with Darwin's. Part of his description of the struggle for existence is interesting:

> The action of this principle [the struggle for existence] is exactly like that of the steam engine, which checks and corrects any irregularities almost before they become evident; and in like manner no unbalanced deficiency in the animal kingdom can ever reach any conspicuous magnitude, because it would make itself felt at the very first step, by rendering existence difficult and extinction almost sure to follow.

The steam engine with a governor is simply a circular train of causal events, with somewhere a link in that chain such that the more of something, the less of the next thing in the circuit. The *wider* the balls of the governor diverge, the *less* the fuel supply. If causal chains with that general characteristic are provided with energy, the result will be (if you are lucky and things balance out) a self-corrective system.

Wallace, in fact, proposed the first cybernetic model.

Nowadays cybernetics deals with more complex systems of this general kind; and we know that when we talk about the processes of civilization, or evaluate human behavior, human organization, or any biological system, we are concerned with self-corrective systems. Basically these systems are always *conservative* of something. As in the engine with a governor, the fuel supply is changed to conserve to keep constant—the speed of the flywheel, so always in such systems changes occur to conserve the truth of some descriptive statement, some component of the *status quo*. Wallace saw the matter correctly, and natural selection acts primarily to keep the species unvarying; but it may act at higher levels to keep constant that complex variable which we call "survival."

Dr. Laing noted that the obvious can be very difficult for people to see. That is because people are self-corrective systems. They are self-corrective against disturbance, and if the obvious is not of a kind that they can easily assimilate without internal disturbance, their self-corrective mechanisms work to sidetrack it, to hide it, even to the extent of shutting the eyes if necessary, or shutting off various parts of the process of perception. Disturbing information can be framed like a pearl so that it doesn't make a nuisance of itself; and this will be done, according to the understanding of the system itself of what would be a nuisance. This too—the premise regarding what would cause disturbance is something which is learned and then becomes perpetuated or conserved.

At this conference, fundamentally, we deal with three of these enormously complex systems or arrangements of conservative loops. One is the human individual. Its physiology and neurology conserve body temperature, blood chemistry, the length and size and shape of organs during growth and embryology, and all the rest of the body's characteristics. This is a system which conserves descriptive statements about the human being, body or soul. For the same is true of the psychology of the individual, where learning occurs to conserve the opinions and components of the *status quo*.

Second, we deal with the society in which that individual lives—and that society is again a system of the same general kind.

And third, we deal with the ecosystem, the natural biological surroundings of these human animals.

Let me start from the natural ecosystems around man. An English oak wood, or a tropical forest, or a piece of desert, is a community of creatures. In the oak wood perhaps 1000 species, perhaps more; in the tropical forest perhaps ten times that number of species live together.

I may say that very few of you here have ever seen such an undisturbed system; there are not many of them left; they've mostly been messed up by *Homo sapiens* who either exterminated some species or introduced others which became weeds and pests, or altered the water supply, etc., etc. We are rapidly, of course, destroying all the natural systems in the world, the balanced natural systems. We simply make them unbalanced—but still natural.

Be that as it may, those creatures and plants live together in a combination of competition and mutual dependency, and it is that combination that is the important thing to consider. Every species has a primary Malthusian capacity. Any species that does not, potentially, produce more young than the number of the population of the parental generation is out. They're doomed. It is absolutely necessary for every species and for every such system that its components have a potential positive gain in the population curve. But, if every species has potential gain, it is then quite a trick to achieve equilibrium. All sorts of interactive balances and dependencies come into play, and it is these processes that have the sort of circuit structure that I have mentioned.

The Malthusian curve is exponential. It is the curve of population growth and it is not inappropriate to call this the population *explosion*.

You may regret that organisms have this explosive characteristic, but you may as well settle for it. The creatures that don't are out.

On the other hand, in a balanced ecological system whose underpinnings are of this nature, it is very clear that any monkeying with the system is likely to disrupt the equilibrium. Then the exponential curves will start to appear. Some plant will become a weed, some creatures will be exterminated, and the system as a *balanced* system is likely to fall to pieces.

What is true of the species that live together in a wood is also true of the groupings and sorts of people in a society, who are similarly in an uneasy balance of dependency and competition. And the same truth holds right inside you, where there is an uneasy physiological competition and mutual dependency among the organs, tissues, cells, and so on. Without this competition and dependency you would not be, because you cannot do without any of the competing organs and parts. If any of the parts did not have the expansive characteristics they would go out, and you would go out, too. So that even in the body you have a liability. With improper disturbance of the system, the exponential curves appear.

In a society, the same is true.

I think you have to assume that all important physiological or social change is in some degree a slipping of the system at some point along an exponential curve. The slippage may not go far, or it may go to disaster. But in principle if, say, you kill off the thrushes in a wood, certain components of the balance will run along exponential curves to a new stopping place.

In such slippage there is always danger—the possibility that some variable, *e.g.*, population density, may reach such a value that further slippage is controlled by factors which are inherently harmful. If, for example, population is finally controlled by available food supply, the surviving individuals will be half starved and the food supply overgrazed, usually to a point of no return.

Pathologies of Epistemology

[I]n the last twenty years, [we have developed a new] broad conception of the world in which we live—a new way of thinking about what a *mind* is. Let me list what seem to me to be those essential minimal characteristics of a system, which I will accept as characteristics of mind:

(1) The system shall operate with and upon *differences*.

(2) The system shall consist of closed loops or networks of pathways along which differences and transforms of differences shall be transmitted. (What is transmitted on a neuron is not an impulse, it is news of a difference.)

(3) Many events within the system shall be energized by the respondent part rather than by impact from the triggering part.

(4) The system shall show self-correctiveness in the direction of homeostasis and/or in the direction of runaway. Self-correctiveness implies trial and error.

Now, these minimal characteristics of mind are generated whenever and wherever the appropriate circuit structure of causal loops exists. Mind is a necessary, an inevitable function of the appropriate complexity, wherever that complexity occurs.

But that complexity occurs in a great many other places besides the inside of my head and yours. We'll come later to the question of whether a man or a computer has a mind. For the moment, let me say that a redwood forest or a coral reef with its *aggregate* of organisms interlocking in their relationships has the necessary general structure. The energy for the responses of every organism is supplied from its metabolism, and the total system acts self-correctively in various ways. A human society is like this with closed loops of causation. Every human organization shows both the self-corrective characteristic and has the potentiality for runaway.

Now, let us consider for a moment the question of whether a computer thinks. I would state that it does not. What "thinks" and engages in "trial and error" is the man *plus* the computer *plus* the environment. And the lines between man, computer, and environment are purely artificial, fictitious lines. They are lines *across* the pathways along which information or difference is transmitted. They are not boundaries of the thinking system. What thinks is the total system which engages in trial and error, which is man plus environment.

But if you accept self-correctiveness as the criterion of thought or mental process, then obviously there is "thought" going on inside the man at the autonomic level to maintain various internal variables. And similarly, the computer, if it controls its internal temperature, is doing some simple thinking within itself.

Now we begin to see some of the epistemological fallacies of Occidental civilization. In accordance with the general climate of thinking in mid-nineteenth-century England, Darwin proposed a theory of natural selection and evolution in which the unit of survival was either the family line or the species or subspecies or something of the sort. But today it is quite obvious that this is not the unit of survival in the real biological world. The unit of survival is *organism* plus *environment*. We are learning by bitter experience that the organism which destroys its environment destroys itself.

If, now, we correct the Darwinian unit of survival to include the environment and the interaction between organism and environment, a very strange and surprising identity emerges: *the unit of evolutionary survival turns out to be identical with the unit of mind.*

Formerly we thought of a hierarchy of taxa—individual, family line, subspecies, species, etc.—as units of survival. We now see a different hierarchy of units—gene-in-organism, organism-in-environment, ecosystem, etc. Ecology, in the widest sense, turns out to be the study of the interaction and survival of ideas and programs (*i.e.*, differences, complexes of differences, etc.) in circuits.

Let us now consider what happens when you make the epistemological error of choosing the wrong unit: you end up with the species versus the other species around it or versus the environment in which it operates. Man against nature. You end up, in fact, with Kaneohe Bay polluted, Lake Erie a slimy green mess, and "Let's build bigger atom bombs to kill off the next-door neighbors." There is an ecology of bad ideas, just as there is an ecology of weeds, and it is characteristic of the system that basic error propagates itself. It branches out like a rooted parasite through the tissues of life, and everything gets into a rather peculiar mess. When you narrow down your epistemology and act on the premise "What interests me is me, or my organization, or my species," you chop off consideration of other loops of the loop structure. You decide that you want to get rid of the by-products of human life and that Lake Erie will be a good place to put them. You forget that the eco-mental system called Lake Erie is a part of *your* wider eco-mental system—and that if Lake Erie is driven insane, its insanity is incorporated in the larger system of *your* thought and experience.

You and I are so deeply acculturated to the idea of "self" and organization and species that it is hard to believe that man might view his relations with the environment in any other way than the way which I have rather unfairly blamed upon the nineteenth-century evolutionists. So I must say a few words about the history of all this.

Anthropologically, it would seem from what we know of the early material, that man in society took clues from the natural world around him and applied those clues in a sort of metaphoric way to the society in which he lived. That is, he identified with or empathized with the natural world around him and took that empathy as a guide for his own social organization and his own theories of his own psychology. This was what is called "totemism."

In a way, it was all nonsense, but it made more sense than most of what we do today, because the natural world around us really has this general systemic structure and therefore is an appropriate source of metaphor to enable man to understand himself in his social organization.

The next step, seemingly, was to reverse the process and to take clues from himself and apply these to the natural world around him. This was "animism," extending the notion of personality or mind to mountains, rivers, forests, and such things. This was still not a bad idea in many ways. But the next step was to separate the notion of mind from the natural world, and then you get the notion of gods.

But when you separate mind from the structure in which it is immanent, such as human relationship, the human society, or the ecosystem, you thereby embark, I believe, on fundamental error, which in the end will surely hurt you.

Struggle may be good for your soul up to the moment when to win the battle is easy. When you have an effective enough technology so that you can really act upon your epistemological errors and can create havoc in the world in which you live, then the error is lethal. Epistemological error is all right, it's fine, up to the point at which you create around yourself a universe in which that error becomes immanent in monstrous changes of the universe that you have created and now try to live in.

You see, we're not talking about the dear old Supreme Mind of Aristotle, St. Thomas Aquinas, and so on down through ages—the Supreme Mind which was incapable of error and incapable of insanity. We're talking about immanent mind, which is only too capable of insanity, as you all professionally know. This is precisely why you're here. These circuits and balances of nature can only too easily get out of kilter, and they inevitably get out of kilter when certain basic errors of our thought become reinforced by thousands of cultural details.

I don't know how many people today really believe that there is an overall mind separate from the body, separate from the society, and separate from nature. But for those of you who would say that that is all "superstition," I am prepared to wager that I can demonstrate with them in a few minutes that the habits and ways of thinking that went with those superstitions are still in their heads and still determine a large part of their thoughts. The idea that *you can see me* still governs your thought and action in spite of the fact that you may know intellectually that it is not so. In the same way we are most of us governed by epistemologies that we know to be wrong.

Form, Substance, and Difference

Having stated [the] relationship between biological part and whole, I can now go on to the question of what is *a* mind.

What do I mean by "my" mind?

I suggest that the delimitation of an individual mind must always depend upon what phenomena we wish to understand or explain. Obviously there are lots of message pathways outside the skin, and these and the messages which they carry must be included as part of the mental system whenever they are relevant.

Consider a tree and a man and an axe. We observe that the axe flies through the air and makes certain sorts of gashes in a pre-existing cut in the side of the tree. If now we want to explain this set of phenomena, we shall be concerned with differences in the cut face of the tree, differences in the retina of the man, differences in his central nervous system, differences in his efferent neural messages, differences in the behavior of his muscles, differences in how the axe flies, to the differences which the axe then makes on the face of the tree. Our explanation (for certain purposes) will go round and round that circuit. In principle, if you want to explain or understand anything in human behavior, you are always dealing with total circuits, completed circuits. This is the elementary cybernetic thought.

The elementary cybernetic system with its messages in circuit is, in fact, the simplest unit of mind; and the transform of a difference traveling in a circuit is the elementary idea. More complicated systems are perhaps more worthy to be called mental systems, but essentially this is what we are talking about. The unit which shows the characteristic of trial and error will be legitimately called a mental system.

But what about "me"? Suppose I am a blind man, and I use a stick. I go tap, tap, tap. Where do *I* start? Is my mental system bounded at the handle of the stick? Is it bounded by my skin? Does it start halfway up the stick? Does it start at the tip of the stick? But these are nonsense questions. The stick is a pathway along which transforms of difference are being transmitted. The way to delineate the system is to draw the limiting line in such a way that you do not cut any of these pathways in ways which leave things inexplicable. If what you are trying to explain is a given piece of behavior, such as the locomotion of the blind man, then, for this purpose, you will need the street, the stick, the man; the street, the stick, and so on, round and round.

But when the blind man sits down to eat his lunch, his stick and its messages will no longer be relevant—if it is his eating that you want to understand.

And in addition to what I have said to define the individual mind, I think it necessary to include the relevant parts of memory and data "banks." After all, the simplest cybernetic circuit can be said to have memory of a dynamic kind—not based upon static storage but upon the travel of information around the circuit. The behavior of the governor of a steam engine at Time 2 is partly determined by what it did at Time 1—where the interval between Time 1 and Time 2 is that time necessary for the information to complete the circuit.

We get a picture, then, of mind as synonymous with cybernetic system—the relevant total information-processing, trial-and-error completing unit. And we know that within Mind in the widest sense there will be a hierarchy of subsystems, any one of which we can call an individual mind.

But this picture is precisely the same as the picture which I arrived at in discussing the *unit of evolution*. I believe that this identity is the most important generalization which I have to offer you tonight.

In considering units of evolution, I argued that you have at each step to include the completed pathways outside the protoplasmic aggregate, be it DNA-in-the-cell, or cell-in-the-body, or body-in-the-environment. The hierarchic structure is not new. Formerly we talked about the breeding individual or the family line or the taxon, and so on. Now each step of the hierarchy is to be thought of as a *system*, instead of a chunk cut off and visualized as *against* the surrounding matrix.

This identity between the unit of mind and the unit of evolutionary survival is of very great importance, not only theoretical, but also ethical.

It means, you see, that I now localize something which I am calling "Mind" immanent in the large biological system—the ecosystem. Or, if I draw the system boundaries at a different level, then mind is immanent in the total evolutionary structure. If this identity between mental and evolutionary units is broadly right, then we face a number of shifts in our thinking.

First, let us consider ecology. Ecology has currently two faces to it: the face which is called bioenergetics—the economics of energy and materials within a coral reef, a redwood forest, or a city—and, second, an economics of information, of entropy, negentropy, etc. These two do not fit together very well precisely because the units are differently bounded in the two sorts of ecology. In bioenergetics it is natural and appropriate to think of units bounded at the cell membrane, or at the skin; or of units composed of sets of nonspecific individuals. These boundaries are then the frontiers at which measurements can be made to determine the additive-subtractive budget of energy for the given unit. In contrast, informational or entropic ecology deals with the budgeting of pathways and of probability. The resulting budgets are fractionating (not subtractive). The boundaries must enclose, not cut, the relevant pathways.

Moreover, the very meaning of "survival" becomes different when we stop talking about the survival of something bounded by the skin and start to think of the survival of the system of ideas in circuit. The contents of the skin are randomized at death and the pathways within the skin are randomized. But the ideas, under further transformation, may go on out in the world in books or works of art. Socrates as a bioenergetic individual is dead. But much of him still lives as a component in the contemporary ecology of ideas.

It is also clear that theology becomes changed and perhaps renewed. The Mediterranean religions for 5,000 years have swung to and fro between immanence and transcendence. In Babylon the gods were transcendent on the tops of hills; in Egypt, there was god immanent in Pharaoh; and Christianity is a complex combination of these two beliefs.

The cybernetic epistemology which I have offered you would suggest a new approach. The individual mind is immanent but not only in the body. It is immanent also in pathways and messages outside the body; and there is a larger Mind of which the individual mind is only a subsystem. This larger Mind is comparable to God and is perhaps what some people mean by "God," but it is still immanent in the total interconnected social system and planetary ecology.

Freudian psychology expanded the concept of mind inwards to include the whole communication system within the body—the autonomic, the habitual, and the vast range of unconscious process. What I am saying expands mind outwards. And both of these changes reduce the scope of the conscious self. A certain humility becomes appropriate, tempered by the dignity or joy of being part of something much bigger. A part—if you will—of God.

If you put God outside and set him *vis-a-vis* his creation and if you have the idea that you are created in his image, you will logically and naturally see yourself as outside and against the things around you. And as you arrogate all mind to yourself, you will see the world around you as mindless and therefore not entitled to moral or ethical consideration. The environment will seem to be yours to exploit. Your survival unit will be you and your folks or conspecifics against the environment of other social units, other races and the brutes and vegetables.

If this is your estimate of your relation to nature *and you have an advanced technology*, your likelihood of survival will be that of a snowball in hell. You will die either of the toxic by-products of your own hate, or, simply, of overpopulation and overgrazing. The raw materials of the world are finite.

If I am right, the whole of our thinking about what we are and what other people are has got to be restructured. This is not funny, and I do not know how long we have to do it in. If we continue to operate on the premises that were fashionable in the pre-cybernetic era, and which were especially underlined and strengthened during the Industrial Revolution, which seemed to validate the Darwinian unit of survival, we may have twenty or thirty years before the logical *reductio ad absurdum* of our old positions destroys us. Nobody knows how long we have, under the present system, before some disaster strikes us, more serious than the destruction of any group of nations. The most important task today is, perhaps, to learn to think in the new way. Let me say that *I* don't know how to think that way. Intellectually, I can stand here and I can give you a reasoned exposition of this matter; but if I am cutting down a tree, I still think "Gregory Bateson" is cutting down the tree. I am cutting down the tree. "Myself" is to me still an excessively concrete object, different from the rest of what I have been calling "mind."

The step to realizing—to making habitual—the other way of thinking—so that one naturally thinks that way when one reaches out for a glass of water or cuts down a tree—that step is not an easy one.

THE SHALLOW AND THE DEEP, LONG-RANGE ECOLOGY MOVEMENT: A SUMMARY

ARNE NAESS (1973)

The emergence of ecologists from their former relative obscurity marks a turning-point in our scientific communities. But their message is twisted and misused. A shallow, but presently rather powerful movement, and a deep, but less influential movement, compete for our attention. I shall make an effort to characterize the two.

1. *The Shallow Ecology movement*:

Fight against pollution and resource depletion. Central objective: the health and affluence of people in the developed countries.

2. *The Deep Ecology movement*:

(1) Rejection of the man-in-environment image in favour of *the relational, total-field image*. Organisms as knots in the biospherical net or field of intrinsic relations. An intrinsic relation between two things *A* and *B* is such that the relation belongs to the definitions or basic constitutions of *A* and *B*, so that without the relation, *A* and *B* are no longer the same things. The total-field model dissolves not only the man-in-environment concept, but every compact thing-in-milieu concept—except when talking at a superficial or preliminary level of communication.

(2) *Biospherical egalitarianism*—in principle. The 'in principle' clause is inserted because any realistic praxis necessitates some killing, exploitation, and suppression. The ecological field-worker acquires a deep-seated respect, or even veneration, for ways and forms of life. He reaches an understanding from within, a kind of understanding that others reserve for fellow men and for a narrow section of ways and forms of life. To the ecological field-worker, *the equal right to live and blossom* is an intuitively clear and obvious value axiom. Its restriction to humans is an anthropocentrism with detrimental effects upon the life quality of humans themselves. This quality depends in part upon the deep pleasure and satisfaction we receive from close partnership with other forms of life. The attempt to ignore our dependence and to establish a master-slave role has contributed to the alienation of man from himself.

Ecological egalitarianism implies the reinterpretation of the future-research variable, 'level of crowding', so that *general* mammalian crowding and loss of life-equality is taken seriously, not only human crowding. (Research on the high requirements of free space of certain mammals has, incidentally, suggested that theorists of human urbanism have largely underestimated human life-space requirements. Behavioural crowding symptoms [neuroses, aggressiveness, loss of traditions...] are largely the same among mammals.)

(3) *Principles of diversity and of symbiosis.* Diversity enhances the potentialities of survival, the chances of new modes of life, the richness of forms. And the so-called struggle of life, and survival of the fittest, should be interpreted in the sense of ability to coexist and cooperate in complex relationships, rather than ability to kill, exploit, and suppress. 'Live and let live' is a more powerful ecological principle than 'Either you or me.'

The latter tends to reduce the multiplicity of kinds of forms of life, and also to create destruction within the communities of the same species. Ecologically inspired attitudes therefore favour diversity of human ways of life, of cultures, of occupations, of economies. They support the fight against economic and cultural, as much as military, invasion and domination, and they are opposed to the annihilation of seals and whales as much as to that of human tribes or cultures.

(4) *Anti-class posture.* Diversity of human ways of life is in part due to (intended or unintended) exploitation and suppression on the part of certain groups. The exploiter lives differently from the exploited, but both are adversely affected in their potentialities of self-realization. The principle of diversity does not cover differences due merely to certain attitudes or behaviours forcibly blocked or restrained. The principles of ecological egalitarianism and of symbiosis support the same anti-class posture. The ecological attitude favours the extension of all three principles to any group conflicts, including those of today between developing and developed nations. The three principles also favour extreme caution towards any over-all plans for the future, except those consistent with wide and widening classless diversity.

(5) *Fight against pollution and resource depletion.* In this fight ecologists have found powerful supporters, but sometimes to the detriment of their total stand. This happens when attention is focused on pollution and resource depletion rather than on the other points, or when projects are implemented which reduce pollution but increase evils of the other kinds. Thus, if prices of life necessities increase because of the installation of anti-pollution devices, class differences increase too. An ethics of responsibility implies that ecologists do not serve the shallow, but the deep ecological movement. That is, not only point (5), but all seven points must be considered together.

Ecologists are irreplaceable informants in any society, whatever their political colour. If well organized, they have the power to reject jobs in which they submit themselves to institutions or to planners with limited ecological perspectives. As it is now, ecologists sometimes serve masters who deliberately ignore the wider perspectives.

(6) *Complexity, not complication.* The theory of ecosystems contains an important distinction between what is complicated without any Gestalt or unifying principles—we

may think of finding our way through a chaotic city—and what is complex. A multiplicity of more or less lawful, interacting factors may operate together to form a unity, a system. We make a shoe or use a map or integrate a variety of activities into a workaday pattern. Organisms, ways of life, and interactions in the biosphere in general, exhibit complexity of such an astoundingly high level as to colour the general outlook of ecologists. Such complexity makes thinking in terms of vast systems inevitable. It also makes for a keen, steady perception of the profound *human ignorance* of biospherical relationships and therefore of the effect of disturbances.

Applied to humans, the complexity-not-complication principle favours division of labour, *not fragmentation of labour*. It favours integrated actions in which the whole person is active, not mere reactions. It favours complex economies, an integrated variety of means of living. (Combinations of industrial and agricultural activity, of intellectual and manual work, of specialized and non-specialized occupations, of urban and non-urban activity, of work in city and recreation in nature with recreation in city and work in nature...)

It favours soft technique and 'soft future-research,' less prognosis, more clarification of possibilities. More sensitivity towards continuity and live traditions, and—most importantly—towards our state of ignorance.

The implementation of ecologically responsible policies requires in this century an exponential growth of technical skill and invention—but in new directions, directions which today are not consistently and liberally supported by the research policy organs of our nation-states.

(7) *Local autonomy and decentralization.* The vulnerability of a form of life is roughly proportional to the weight of influences from afar, from outside the local region in which that form has obtained an ecological equilibrium. This lends support to our efforts to strengthen local self-government and material and mental self-sufficiency. But these efforts presuppose an impetus towards decentralization. Pollution problems, including those of thermal pollution and recirculation of materials, also lead us in this direction, because increased local autonomy, if we are able to keep other factors constant, reduces energy consumption. (Compare an approximately self-sufficient locality with one requiring the importation of foodstuff, materials for house construction, fuel and skilled labour from other continents. The former may use only five per cent of the energy used by the latter.)

Local autonomy is strengthened by a reduction in the number of links in the hierarchical chains of decision. (For example a chain consisting of local board, municipal council, highest sub-national decision-maker, a state-wide institution in a state federation, a federal national government institution, a coalition of nations, and of institutions, e.g. E.E.C. top levels, and a global institution, can be reduced to one made up of local board, nation-wide institution, and global institution.) Even if a decision follows majority rules at each step, many local interests may be dropped along the line, if it is too long.

«««—»»»

Summing up, then, it should, first of all, be borne in mind that the norms and tendencies of the Deep Ecology movement are not derived from ecology by logic or induction. Ecological knowledge and the life-style of the ecological field-worker have *suggested, inspired, and fortified* the perspectives of the Deep Ecology movement. Many of the formulations in the above seven-point survey are rather vague generalizations, only tenable if made more precise in certain directions. But all over the world the inspiration from ecology has shown remarkable convergencies. The survey does not pretend to be more than one of the possible condensed codifications of these convergencies.

Secondly, it should be fully appreciated that the significant tenets of the Deep Ecology movement are clearly and forcefully *normative*. They express a value priority system only in part based on results (or lack of results) of scientific research. Today, ecologists try to influence policy-making bodies largely through threats, through predictions concerning pollutants and resource depletion, knowing that policy-makers accept at least certain minimum norms concerning health and just distribution. But it is clear that there is a vast number of people in all countries, and even a considerable number of people in power, who accept as valid the wider norms and values characteristic of the Deep Ecology movement. There are political potentials in this movement which should not be overlooked and which have little to do with pollution and resource depletion. In plotting possible futures, the norms should be freely used and elaborated.

Thirdly, in so far as ecology movements deserve our attention, they are *ecophilosophical* rather than ecological. Ecology is a *limited* science which makes use of scientific methods. Philosophy is the most general forum of debate on fundamentals, descriptive as well as prescriptive, and political philosophy is one of its subsections. By an *ecosophy* I mean a philosophy of ecological harmony or equilibrium. A philosophy as a kind of *sofia* wisdom, is openly normative, it contains *both* norms, rules, postulates, value priority announcements and hypotheses concerning the state of affairs in our universe. Wisdom is policy wisdom, prescription, not only scientific description and prediction.

The details of an ecosophy will show many variations due to significant differences concerning not only 'facts' of pollution, resources, population, etc., but also value priorities. Today, however, the seven points listed provide one unified framework for ecosophical systems.

DEEP ECOLOGY: A NEW PHILOSOPHY OF OUR TIME?

WARWICK FOX (1984)

The Australian philosopher William Godfrey-Smith has remarked that

> deep ecology... has an unfortunate tendency to discuss everything at once. Thus a social critique of deep ecology may be backed by such disparate authorities as Ginsberg, Castenada, Thoreau, Spinoza, Buddhist visionaries, and Taoist physics. With a cast of prima donnas like this on stage it is very hard to follow the script.

In this paper, I shall try not to "discuss everything at once" by confining my attention mainly to what I take to be the central intuition of deep ecology, and to some considerations related to that intuition. Even so, I shall still be making reference to "Buddhist visionaries and Taoist physics" for at least one compelling reason: not to refer to the parallels between deep ecology, the mystical traditions, and the so-called "new physics (i.e. post 1920s physics) might well indicate that one had *misused* the central intuition of deep ecology since, fundamentally, each of these fields of understanding subscribes to a similar structure of reality, a similar cosmology. Deep ecology's "disparate authorities" turn out to be not as disparate as they at first appear. Moreover, comparison with these other fields can, I believe, be fruitful in clarifying some of deep ecology's vaguer or more contradictory aspects.

The distinction between 'shallow' and 'deep' ecology was made in 1972 (and published the following year) by the distinguished Norwegian philosopher Arne Naess, and has subsequently been developed by a number of thinkers (most notably, Bill Devall and George Sessions) to the point where we may now reasonably refer to an intellectual 'deep ecology movement.' The shallow/deep ecology distinction has generated so much discussion that it has become difficult to distil to any simple essence but, for the sake of brevity, it could be characterized by the following three points.

First, shallow ecology views humans as separate from their environment. Figure/ground boundaries are sharply drawn such that humans are perceived as the significant figure against a ground that only assumes significance in so far as it enhances humans' images of themselves *qua* important figures. Shallow ecology thus views humans as the source of all value and ascribes only instrumental (or use) value to the nonhuman worlds it is, in short, anthropocentric, representing that attitude to conservation that says: "We ought to preserve the environment (i.e., what lies outside the boundary) not for its own sake but because of its value to us (i.e., what lies inside the boundary)." Deep ecology, on the other hand, rejects "the (human)-in-environment image in favour of the relational, total-field image." Organisms are then viewed rather "as knots in the biospherical net or field of intrinsic relations." Figure/ground boundaries are replaced by a holistic or gestalt view where, in Devall's words, "the person is not above or outside of nature... (but)... is part of creation on-going."

This 'total-field' conception dissolves not only the notion of humans as separate from their environment but the vent notion of the world as composed of discrete, compact, separate 'things'. When we do talk about the world as if it were a collection of discrete, isolable 'things' we are, in Naess's view, "*talking at a superficial or preliminary level of communication.*" Deep ecology thus strives to be non-anthropocentric by viewing humans as just one constituency among others in the biotic community, just one particular strand in the web of life, just one kind of knot in the biospherical net. The intrinsic value of the nonhuman members of the biotic community is recognized and the right of these members to pursue their own evolutionary destinies is taken as "an intuitively clear and obvious value axiom." In contrast, the idea that humans are the source or ground of all value ('the measure of all things') is viewed as the arrogant conceit of those who dwell in the moral equivalent of a Ptolemaic universe. Deep ecologists are concerned to move heaven and earth in this universe in order to effect a 'paradigm shift' of comparable significance to that associated with Copernicus.

Second (and directly related to the above), in its acceptance of what Sessions refers to as 'discrete entity metaphysics,' shallow ecology accepts by default or positively endorses the dominant metaphysics of mechanistic materialism. Viewing knowledge, too, as amenable to discrete compartmentalization, the shallow approach considers ethics in isolation from metaphysics with the consequence that the dominant metaphysics is usually implicitly assumed. Deep ecology, however, is concerned to criticize mechanistic materialism and to replace it with a better 'code for reading nature.' This code can be generally described as one of 'unity in process.' By this is indicated both the idea that all things are fundamentally (i.e., internally) related and the idea that these interrelationships are in constant flux (i.e., they are characterized by process/dynamism/instability/novelty/creativity, etc). This conception of the world lends itself far more readily to organismic rather than mechanical metaphors, and thus to panpsychic or pantheistic rather than inert, dead-matter conceptions of the nonhuman world.

Among Western philosophers, Spinoza, Whitehead and Heidegger are most invoked for the purposes of articulating this vision of the world or, particularly in the case of Heidegger, for the purposes of articulating the 'letting be' mode of being most appropriate to such a deep ecological understanding of the world. Deep ecology also has an enormous respect for many non-Western views since 'unity in process' and panpsychic conceptions of the world have received sophisticated elaboration in Eastern spiritual traditions and in the mythological systems of other non-Western peoples. This respect also extends to the entire sensibility or mode of being-in-the-world of some of these traditions since this often accords with the non-power-seeking sensibility of deep ecology. In stressing the interconnection between ethics and metaphysics, deep ecology recognizes that an ecologically effective ethics can only arise within the context of a more persuasive and more enchanting cosmology than that of mechanistic materialism.

Deep Ecology: A New Philosophy of Our Time

Third, in terms of its social, political and economic project, shallow ecology tends to accept by default or positively endorse the ideology of economic growth which characterizes industrial and developing societies of all political complexions. It is thus often referred to as the 'Resource Management' or 'Resource Conservation and Development' approach. As such, it is content to operate in a reformist fashion within the dominant social paradigms and, often, to accept the economic reduction (i.e., the reduction of all values to economic terms) for the purposes of decision making. Deep-ecology on the other hand, is concerned to address existing social, political and economic arrangements and to replace the ideology of economic growth with the ideology of ecological sustainability. It is insisted that economics (etymologically: 'management of the household') must be seen as subsidiary to ecology ('study of the household'), and the economic reduction of values is thus firmly resisted. Key ideas in deep ecology's social, political and economic project include those of a just and sustainable society, carrying capacity, frugality (or 'voluntary simplicity'), dwelling in place, cultural and biological diversity, local autonomy and decentralization, soft energy paths, appropriate technology, reinhabitation, and bioregionalism.

These last two perhaps require some elaboration. *Reinhabitation* refers to the process of relearning how to live in place, how to establish a 'sense of place', how to dwell in and care for a place. Some people are attempting to cultivate, consciously this sense, under the most difficult of circumstances, by moving into areas that have been degraded by industrial 'development' and participating in the re-establishment of a rich and diverse ecosystem. *Bioregions* refer to areas possessing common characteristics of soils, watersheds, plants and animals (e.g., the Amazon jungle). It is argued that bioregions should replace nation-states as the fundamental geographical unit in terms of which humans think and live. The human carrying capacity for each bioregion should be determined in terms of the number of humans that can be supported living at a level of resource use that is adequate for their needs but minimally intrusive on their environment. Here, of course, lie a multitude of difficult questions for the political agenda of deep ecology. However, these questions have, in various forms, been addressed by numerous societies in the past (including a minority tradition in Western society) and are now being taken up by increasing numbers of thinkers in highly industrialized societies.

It should be clear from this summary that many writers whose work falls within the ambit of deep ecology do not necessarily describe themselves as 'deep ecologists.' A good example is Theodore Roszak who, in his 1972 book *Where the Wasteland Ends*, pointed to the same kind of distinction as Naess:

> Ecology stands at a critical cross-roads. Is it, too, to become another anthropocentric technique of efficient manipulation, a matter of enlightened self-interest and expert, long-range resource budgeting? Or will it meet the nature mystics on their own terms and so recognize that we are to embrace nature as if indeed it were a beloved person in whom, as in ourselves, something sacred dwells?... The question remains open: which will ecology be, the last of the old sciences or the first of the new?

However, despite this and other attempts by philosophers, historians and sociologists to distinguish between various streams of environmentalism, Naess' 12 year old shallow/deep ecology terminology seems to have stuck as the most economical and striking way of referring to the major division within contemporary environmental thought. The conceptualization of this division dearly constitutes a powerful organizing idea in terms of providing a focal point from which to view the relationships between a number of otherwise very diffuse strands of ecologically oriented thought.

The intuition of Deep Ecology

It should be clear from my brief outline of the shallow/deep ecology distinction that many of the views held by deep ecologists go well beyond the data of ecology conceived as an empiric-analytic science. As Arne Naess said when introducing the shallow/deep ecology distinction:

> [T]he norm and tendencies of the Deep Ecology movement are not derived from ecology by logic or induction. Ecological knowledge and the life-style of the ecological field-worker have *suggested, inspired, and fortified* the perspectives of the Deep Ecology movement.

Deep ecologists have, therefore, taken the point made by Donald Worster in his study of the history of ecological ideas from the eighteenth century to the early 1970s:

> In the case of the ecological ethic... one might say that its proponents picked out their values first and only afterward came to science for its stamp of approval. It might have been the better part of honesty if they had come out and announced that, for some reason or by some personal standard of value, they were constrained to promote a deeper sense of integration between (humans) and nature, a more-than-economic relatedness—and to let all the appended scientific arguments go. 'Ought' might then be its own justification, its own defence, its own persuasion, regardless of what 'is.'
>
> That more straightforward stance has now and again been adopted by a few intuitionists, mystics, and transcendentalists. Most people, however, have not been so willing to trust their inner voices, perhaps due to lack of self-confidence or out of fear that such wholly individual exercise of choice will lead to the general disintegration of the moral community.

Deep ecologists *are* 'willing to trust their inner voices' in the hope that the dominant social paradigm (within which the moral community is situated) *will* disintegrate—although in a creative rather than a destructive manner. Again, Arne Naess is quite explicit on these points in a recent interview in *The Ten Directions*, a magazine published by the Zen Centre of Los Angeles:

Ten Directions: This brings us back to the question of information versus intuition. Your feeling is that we can't expect to have an ideal amount of information but must somehow act on what we know?

Naess: Yes. It's easier for deep ecologists than for others because we have certain fundamental values, a fundamental view of what's meaningful in life, what's worth maintaining, which makes it completely clear that we are opposed to further development for the sake of increased domination and an increased standard of living. The material standard of living should be drastically reduced and the quality of life, in the sense of basic satisfaction in the depths of one's heart or soul, should be maintained or increased. This view is intuitive, as are all important views, in the sense that it can't be proven. As Aristotle said, it shows a lack of education to try to prove everything because you have to have a starting point. You can't prove the methodology of science, you can't prove logic, because logic presupposes fundamental premises.

However, the central intuition of deep ecology, the one from which Naess' views on practice flow, is the first point I made in my summary of the shallow/deep ecology distinction. This is the idea that there is no firm ontological divide in the field of existence. In other words, the world simply is not divided up into independently existing subjects and objects, nor is there any bifurcation in reality between the human and non-human realms. Rather all entities are constituted by their relationships. To the extent that we perceive boundaries, we fall short of a deep ecological consciousness. In Devall's words: "Deep ecology begins with unity rather than dualism which has been the dominant theme of Western philosophy."

DEEP ECOLOGY

BILL DEVALL AND GEORGE SESSIONS (1985)

The term *deep ecology* was coined by Arne Naess in his 1973 article, "The Shallow and the Deep, Long Range Ecology Movements." Naess was attempting to describe the deeper, more spiritual approach to nature exemplified in the writings of Aldo Leopold and Rachel Carson. He thought that this deeper approach resulted from a more sensitive openness to ourselves and nonhuman life around us. The essence of deep ecology is to keep asking more searching questions about human life, society, and Nature as in the Western philosophical tradition of Socrates. As examples of this deep questioning, Naess points out

> that we ask why and how, where others do not. For instance, ecology as a science does not ask what kind of a society would be the best for maintaining a particular ecosystem—that is considered a question for value theory, for politics, for ethics.

Thus deep ecology goes beyond the so-called factual scientific level to the level of self and Earth wisdom.

Deep ecology goes beyond a limited piecemeal shallow approach to environmental problems and attempts to articulate a comprehensive religious and philosophical worldview. The foundations of deep ecology are the basic intuitions and experiencing of ourselves and Nature which comprise ecological consciousness. Certain outlooks on politics and public policy flow naturally from this consciousness. And in the context of this book, we discuss the minority tradition as the type of community most conducive both to cultivating ecological consciousness and to asking the basic questions of values and ethics addressed in these pages.

Many of these questions are perennial philosophical and religious questions faced by humans in all cultures over the ages. What does it mean to be a unique human individual? How can the individual self maintain and increase its uniqueness while also being an inseparable aspect of the whole system wherein there are no sharp breaks between self and the *other*? An ecological perspective, in this deeper sense, results in what Theodore Roszak calls "an awakening of wholes greater than the sum of their parts. In spirit, the discipline is contemplative and therapeutic."

Ecological consciousness and deep ecology are in sharp contrast with the dominant worldview of technocratic-industrial societies which regards humans as belated and fundamentally separate from the rest of Nature, as superior to, and in charge of, the rest of creation. But the view of humans as separate and superior to the rest of Nature is only part of larger cultural patterns. For thousands of years, Western culture has become increasingly obsessed with the idea of *dominance*: with dominance of humans over nonhuman Nature, masculine over the feminine, wealthy and powerful over the poor, with the dominance of the West over non-Western cultures. Deep ecological consciousness allows us to see through these erroneous and dangerous illusions.

For deep ecology, the study of our place in the Earth household includes the study of ourselves as part of the organic whole. Going beyond a narrowly materialist scientific understanding of reality, the spiritual and the material aspects of reality fuse together. While the leading intellectuals of the dominant worldview have tended to view religion as "just superstition," and have looked upon ancient spiritual practice and enlightenment, such as found in Zen Buddhism, as essentially subjective, the search for deep ecological consciousness is the search for a more objective consciousness and state of being through an active deep questioning and meditative process and way of life.

Many people have asked these deeper questions and cultivated ecological consciousness within the context of different spiritual traditions— Christianity, Taoism, Buddhism, and Native American rituals, for example. While differing greatly in other regards, many in these traditions agree with the basic principles of deep ecology.

Warwick Fox, an Australian philosopher, has succinctly expressed the central intuition of deep ecology:

> It is the idea that we can make no firm ontological divide in the field of existence: That there is no bifurcation in reality between the human and the non-human realms... to the extent that we perceive boundaries, we fall short of deep ecological consciousness.

From this most basic insight or characteristic of deep ecological consciousness, Arne Naess has developed two ultimate norms or intuitions which are themselves not derivable from other principles or intuitions. They are arrived at by the deep questioning process and reveal the importance of moving to the philosophical and religious level of wisdom. They cannot be validated, of course, by the methodology of modern science based on its usual mechanistic assumptions and its very narrow definition of data. These ultimate norms are *self-realization* and *biocentric equality*.

I. Self-Realization

In keeping with the spiritual traditions of many of the world's religions, the deep ecology norm of self-realization goes beyond the modern Western self which is defined as an isolated ego striving primarily for hedonistic gratification or for a narrow sense of individual salvation in this life or the next. This socially programmed sense of the narrow self or social self dislocates us, and leaves us prey to whatever fad or fashion is prevalent in our society or social reference group. We are thus robbed of beginning the search for our unique spiritual/biological personhood. Spiritual growth, or unfolding, begins when we cease to understand or see ourselves as isolated and narrow competing egos and begin to identify with other humans from our family and friends to, eventually, our species. But the deep ecology sense of self requires a further maturity and growth, an identification which goes beyond humanity to include the nonhuman world. We must see beyond our narrow contemporary cultural assumptions and values, and the conventional wisdom of our time and place, and this is best achieved by the meditative deep questioning process. Only in this way can we hope to attain full mature personhood and uniqueness.

A nurturing non-dominating society can help in the "real work" of becoming a whole person. The "real work" can be summarized symbolically as the realization of "self-in-Self" where 'Self' stands for organic wholeness. This process of the full unfolding of the self can also be summarized by the phrase, "No one is saved until we are all saved," where the phrase 'one' includes not only me, an individual human, but all humans, whales, grizzly bears, whole rain forest ecosystems, mountains and rivers, the tiniest microbes in the soil, and so on.

II. Biocentric Equality

The intuition of biocentric equality is that all things in the biosphere have an equal right to live and blossom and to reach their own individual forms of unfolding and self-realization within the larger Self-realization. This basic intuition is that all organisms and entities in the ecosphere, as parts of the interrelated whole, are equal in intrinsic worth. Naess suggests that biocentric equality as an intuition is true in principle, although in the process of living, all species use each other as food, shelter, etc. Mutual predation is a biological fact of life, and many of the world's religions have struggled with the spiritual implications of this. Some animal liberationists who attempt to side-step this problem by advocating vegetarianism are forced to say that the entire plant kingdom including rain forests have no right to their own existence. This evasion flies in the face of the basic intuition of equality. Aldo Leopold expressed this intuition when he said humans are "plain citizens" of the biotic community, not lord and master over all other species.

Biocentric equality is intimately related to the all-inclusive Self-realization in the sense that if we harm the rest of Nature then we are harming ourselves. There are no boundaries and everything is interrelated. But insofar as we perceive things as individual organisms or entities, the insight draws us to respect all human and non-human individuals in their own right as parts of the whole without feeling the need to set up hierarchies of species with humans at the top.

The practical implications of this intuition or norm suggest that we should live with minimum rather than maximum impact on other species and on the Earth in general. Thus we see another aspect of our guiding principle: "simple in means, rich in ends."

A fuller discussion of the biocentric norm as it unfolds itself in practice begins with the realization that we, as individual humans, and as communities of humans, have vital needs which go beyond such basics as food, water, and shelter to include love, play, creative expression, intimate relationships with a particular landscape (or Nature taken in its entirety) as well as intimate relationships with other humans, and the vital need for spiritual growth, for becoming a mature human being.

Our vital material needs are probably more simple than many realize. In technocratic-industrial societies there is an overwhelming propaganda and advertising which encourages false needs and destructive desires designed to foster increased production and consumption of goods. Most of this actually diverts us from facing reality in an objective way and from beginning the "real work" of spiritual growth and maturity.

Many people who do not see themselves as supporters of deep ecology nevertheless recognize an overriding vital human need for a healthy and high-quality natural environment for humans, if not for all life, with minimum intrusion of toxic waste, nuclear radiation from human enterprises, minimum acid rain and smog, and enough free flowing wilderness so humans can get in touch with their sources, the natural rhythms and the flow of time and place.

Drawing from the minority tradition and from the wisdom of many who have offered the insight of interconnectedness, we recognize that deep ecologists can offer suggestions for gritting maturity and encouraging the processes of harmony with nature, but that there is no grand solution which is guaranteed to save us from ourselves.

The ultimate norms of deep ecology suggest a view of the nature of reality and our place as an individual (many in the one) in the larger scheme of things. They cannot be fully grasped intellectually but are ultimately experiential.

III. Basic Principles of Deep Ecology

In April 1984, during the advent of spring and John Muir's birthday, George Sessions and Arne Naess summarized 15 years of thinking on the principles of deep ecology while camping in Death Valley, California. In this great and special place, they articulated these principles in a literal, somewhat neutral way hoping that they would be understood and accepted by persons coming from different philosophical and religious positions.

Readers are encouraged to elaborate their own versions of deep ecology, clarify key concepts and think through the consequences of acting from these principles.

Basic Principles

1. The well-being and flourishing of human and nonhuman life on earth have value in themselves (synonyms: intrinsic value, inherent value). These values are independent of the usefulness of the non-human world for human purposes.

2. Richness and diversity of life forms contribute to the realization of these values and are also values in themselves.

3. Humans have no right to reduce this richness and diversity except to satisfy *vital* needs.

4. The flourishing of human life and cultures is compatible with a substantial decrease of the human population. The flourishing of nonhuman life requires such a decrease.

5. Present human interference with the nonhuman world is excessive, and the situation is rapidly worsening.

6. Policies must therefore be changed. These policies affect basic economic, technological, and ideological structures. The resulting state of affairs will be deeply different from the present.

7. The ideological change is mainly that of appreciating *life quality* (dwelling in situations of inherent value) rather than adhering to an increasingly higher standard of living. There will be a profound awareness of the difference between big and great.

8. Those who subscribe to the foregoing points have an obligation directly or indirectly to try to implement the necessary changes.

Naess and Sessions Provide Comments on the Basic Principles

RE (1). This formulation refers to the biosphere, or more accurately to the ecosphere as a whole. This includes individuals, species, populations, habitat, as well as human and nonhuman cultures. From our current knowledge of all-pervasive intimate relationships, this implies a fundamental deep concern and respect. Ecological processes of the planet should, on the whole, remain intact. "The world environment should remain 'natural'" (Gary Snyder).

The term "life" is used here in a more comprehensive nontechnical way to refer also to what biologists classify as "nonliving": rivers (watersheds), landscapes, ecosystems. For supporters of deep ecology slogans such as "Let the river live" illustrate this broader usage so common in most cultures.

Inherent value as used in (1) is common in deep ecology literature. ("The presence of inherent value in a natural object is independent of any awareness, interest, or appreciation of it by a conscious being.")

RE (2). More technically this is a formulation concerning diversity and complexity. From an ecological standpoint, complexity and symbiosis are conditions for maximizing diversity. So-called simple, lower, or primitive species of plants and animals contribute essentially to the richness and diversity of life. They have value in themselves and are not merely steps toward the so-called higher or rational life forms. The second principle presupposes that life itself, as a process over evolutionary time, implies an increase of diversity and richness. The refusal to acknowledge that some life forms have greater or lesser intrinsic value than others (see points 1 and 2) runs counter to the formulations of some ecological philosophers and New Age writers.

Complexity, as referred to here, is different from complication. Urban life may be more complicated than life in a natural setting without being more complex in the sense of multifaceted quality.

RE (3). The term "vital needs" is left deliberately vague to allow for considerable latitude in judgment. Differences in climate and related factors, together with differences in the structures of societies as they now exist, need to be considered (for some Eskimos, snow-mobiles are necessary today to satisfy vital needs).

People in the materially richest countries cannot be expected to reduce their excessive interference with the nonhuman world to a moderate level overnight. The stabilization and reduction of the human population will take time. Interim strategies need to be developed. But this in no way excuses the present complacency—the extreme seriousness of our current situation must first be realized. But the longer we wait the more drastic will be the measures needed. Until deep changes are made, substantial decreases in richness and diversity are liable to occur: the rate of extinction of species will be ten to one hundred times greater than any other period of earth history.

RE (4). The United Nations Fund for Population Activities in their *State of World Population Report* (1984) said that high human population growth rates (over 2.0 percent annum) in many developing countries "were diminishing the quality of life for many millions of people." During the decade 1974-1984, the world population grew to nearly 800 million—more than the size of India. "And we will be adding about one Bangladesh (population 93 million) per annum between now and the year 2000."

The report noted that "The growth rate of the human population has declined for the first time in human history. But at the same time, the number of people being added to the human population is bigger than at any time in history because the population base is larger."

Most of the nations in the developing world (including India and China) have as their official government policy the goal of reducing the rate of human population increase, but there are debates over the types of measures to take (contraception, abortion, etc.) consistent with human rights and feasibility.

The report concludes that if all governments set specific population targets as public policy to help alleviate poverty and advance the quality of life, the current situation could be improved.

As many ecologists have pointed out, it is also absolutely crucial to curb population growth in the so-called developed (i.e., overdeveloped) industrial societies. Given the tremendous rate of consumption and waste production of individuals in these societies, they represent a much greater threat and impact on the biosphere per capita than individuals in Second and Third World countries.

RE (5). This formulation is mild. For a realistic assessment of the situation, see the unabbreviated version of the IUCN's *World Conservation Strategy*. There are other works to be highly recommended, such as Gerald Barney's *Global 2000 Report to the President the United States*.

The slogan of "noninterference" does not imply that humans should not modify some ecosystems as do other species. Humans have modified the earth and will probably continue to do so. At issue is the nature and extent of such interference.

The fight to preserve and extend areas of wilderness or near-wilderness should continue and should focus on the general ecological functions of these areas (one such function: large wilderness areas are required in the biosphere to allow for continued evolutionary speciation of animals and plants). Most present designated wilderness areas and game preserves are not large enough to allow for such speciation.

RE (6). Economic growth as conceived and implemented today by the industrial states is incompatible with (1)-(5). There is only a faint resemblance between ideal sustainable forms of economic growth and present policies of the industrial societies. And "sustainable" still means "sustainable in relation to humanity."

Present ideology tends to value things because they are scarce and because they have a commodity value. There is prestige in vast consumption and waste (to mention only several relevant factors).

Whereas "self-determination," "local community," and "think globally, act locally," will remain key terms in the ecology of human societies, nevertheless the implementation of deep changes requires increasingly global action—action across borders.

Governments in Third World countries (with the exception of Costa Rica and a few others) are uninterested in deep ecological issues. When the governments of industrial societies try to promote ecological measures through Third World governments, practically nothing is accomplished (e.g., with problems of desertification). Given this situation, support for global action through nongovernmental international organizations becomes increasingly important. Many of these organizations are able to act globally "from grassroots to grassroots," thus avoiding negative governmental interference.

Cultural diversity today requires advanced technology that is, techniques that advance the basic goals of each culture. So-called soft, intermediate, and alternative technologies are steps in this direction.

RE (7). Some economists criticize the term 'quality of life' because it is supposed to be vague. But on closer inspection, what they consider to be vague is actually the non-quantitative nature of the term. One cannot quantify adequately what is important for the quality of life as discussed here, and there is no need to do so.

RE (8). There is ample room for different opinions about priorities: what should be done first, what next? What is most urgent? What is clearly necessary as opposed to what is highly desirable but not absolutely pressing?

ECO-PHILOSOPHY AND DEEP ECOLOGY

HENRYK SKOLIMOWSKI (1988)

Philosophy is an unending process of articulating the world around us. Deep Ecology is an attempt to articulate the structure of the world as we have inherited it in the second part of the 20th century. *The Ecologist* has done service to us by publishing three pieces on Deep Ecology. However the process of articulation awaiting us is of such a magnitude that it will take dozens of minds to determine "What is going on?", "Where we are?" and "Where should we be going?" We are only beginning to articulate the new post-industrial worldview, which is much inspired by ecology.

Since I am partial to this newly emerging world view, having published a book on the subject, *Eco-Philosophy: Designing New Tactics for Living*, let me address the issues. It has struck me that the ideas of many scholars have been too hurriedly subsumed under the umbrella of Deep Ecology. This umbrella is too vast, and it is leaking. If we wish to move forward, we had better create a smaller but a more enduring umbrella, for Deep Ecology claims too much and delivers too little.

Any movement which attempts to replace today's vast scientific-empiricist worldview is obliged to propose and articulate its own cosmology, its own ethics, and its own eschatology. In addition it must demonstrate that the three fit coherently into one structure, as they do in traditional worldviews where cosmology and ethics remain in a feedback relationship.

Ethics follows from the general conception about how things 'are' out there: in heaven and on earth. Ethics, in turn, supports the order presupposed by cosmology. Furthermore, eschatology (or the doctrine concerning the *ultimate ends,* or *ultimate meaning or purpose*) is related to both ethics and cosmology and often defined by them, if only indirectly. The relationship is thus triangular.

Now if we examine carefully the tenets of Deep Ecology, particularly as propounded by its most vocal exponents Devall and Sessions in their book *Deep Ecology: Living as if Nature Mattered*, then we find that the cosmology of Deep Ecology is not sufficiently articulated to be a real challenge to today's mechanistic cosmology. Neither are the ethics of Deep Ecology Sufficiently developed to be a guide in our daily life. As for an eschatology, it hardly exists within Deep Ecology.

Eschatology

Let me start with eschatology. One of the underlying principles of Deep Ecology is *to live in harmony with the biotic community*. This is wonderful. But it does not go far enough, deep enough. It does not answer the supreme questions: What is our destiny? What are our ultimate ends? What we are here for? Without answering these questions, our quest for meaning is going to be frustrated. And if there is no foundation to the meaning of our life, we are adrift. One of the agonizing dilemmas of our times is the death of meaning. The relentless march of the empiricist worldview has denuded us of meaning. We all know the causes and the consequences. The tremendous push for material progress has made our psyche numb and our heart cold. Alienation is one consequence. The value-vacuum is another.

Any large scale movement which attempts to replace empirics must find an antidote to the gospel of material progress must be capable of creating a new foundation for meaning. When we look deeper into the question we realize that unless deeper questions of human destiny are considered and answered, our quest for meaning cannot be truly satisfied.

In traditional religious worldviews, Christianity especially, all human strings are ultimately redeemed by the promise of eternal salvation. The idea of Eternal Salvation shines back on us, and infuses meaning into all our actions; redeems our quest for meaning: and it does so even if life is found unsatisfactory in earthly terms. Thus, in religious worldviews, the eschatology of transcendent heavens pervades the sense of human life, pervades human values, and pervades human meaning.

In the materialist-scientific worldview, by contrast, there is no transcendent eschatology. We would be mistaken however to think that there is no eschatology at all in the empiricist world view. True enough, the universe does not have any intrinsic meaning—nor, indeed, does human life. Thus, in this scheme of things, questions about *ultimate* human destiny are considered misconceived. So often, we are told by the prophets of the materialist gospel (including Jean Paul Sartre), there are no further horizons beyond those which our eyes immediately see. Material gratification is all that matters. Material fulfillment is the only form of fulfillment. The meaning of life is to be conceived in terms of material fulfillment.

It is important to realise that there is *fit* between cosmology, values and eschatology within the empiricist worldview. We may not be inspired by its values—indeed, we are not—and for this reason we invariably ask ourselves; Is it all there is to human life? Should we not, must we not, demand more? Where is the outlet for our higher needs, higher aspirations and more sublime ends? In evolving higher needs, and more sublime ends, we are *ipso facto* postulating an eschatology which goes beyond the merely material; we are subconsciously gravitating toward a transcendent realm, toward spiritual values.

How does Deep Ecology respond to these deeper questions? It appears to me that it does not respond at all. My hypothesis is that, at heart, deep ecologists are secular humanists. They avoid the discussion of eschatology, perhaps because they do not have much to offer; but also because deep down they think that eschatology is to be limited to the life here on earth "in decent terms", "in being in harmony with the biotic community." This is in many ways admirable, but not deep enough.

Eco-Philosophy and Deep Ecology

Deep Ecology does not seem to wish to go beyond the earth. And why? Is not the living earth—Gaia—part of the living universe? If so, is not the *process* which has brought about the living earth and the living universe (namely, evolution) not to be cherished and recognized? It has struck me over and again that Deep Ecology is limited to the here and NOW. But in order to know where we are *now*, we must know where we have been; we must be able to answer at least tentatively the ultimate question—"Why are we here?" We are back to eschatological questions.

In contrast to the shallowness of Deep Ecology (as far as eschatology is concerned) Eco-philosophy, as I have developed it, does not avoid spiritual questions, and attempts to provide the rudiment of a new eschatology. As I see it, we are a part of the evolutionary unfolding, and in realizing evolution, we are actualizing our own potential. This perspective does not deny the rights of others. On the contrary, it is precisely because of the level of our consciousness that we have evolved moral codes, as well as the idea of our obligations towards others. We have tempered our selfishness by the awareness that other forms of life have the right to live as well as ourselves. This awareness is a part of our higher consciousness. The principle of the "Great Compassion," particularly emphasized by Tibetan Buddhists, is a supreme crystallization of human consciousness. This principle tells us that because no life wants to suffer, (and because we are fully aware of this fact) we must try to help all sentient beings. The principle of compassion is a great *evolutionary* attainment.

Eschatological questions are bound, sooner or later, to lead us to the realm of theology. A far reaching ecological conception of the world is incomplete without some form of eco-theology. As Rene Dubos puts it: "A truly ecological view of the world has religious overtones." Equally aware of the gravity of the problem was E.F. Schumacher who postulated that the most important task of our times is to provide a metaphysical and a religious reconstruction. Any thorough-going metaphysical reconstruction must find some answers to the deepest problems that have always fascinated and troubled the human mind—and these are the problems of human destiny, a dilemma which is ultimately religious in nature. For this reason my notion of Eco-Philosophy has been extended in recent years and has begotten Eco-Theology. In 1985, I published a booklet on the subject *(Eco-theology: Toward Religion for Our Times)*. To outline a new religion is a gigantic task. No one would claim that we can articulate fully an ecological religion fitting at our times in our first attempt. The most we can do is to attempt to examine ultimate eschatological questions within an ecological framework. This is what my Eco-Theology has tried to do.

Evolution

One of the structural weaknesses of Deep Ecology is its inherently ambiguous attitude toward evolution. Deep Ecology does not want to deny evolution, nor does it not want to affirm it. There is a fear of the idea of evolution which pervades the ranks of deep ecologists. Like every fear, this one is partly justified; but only partly.

If evolution is conceived within the straitjacket of Social Darwinism, then it is to be avoided, for, as such, it is only a form of ideology, justifying inequities and injustices, under the banner of the survival of the fittest. Secondly, if evolution means the glorification of one species at the expense of other species, if it becomes the basis of narrow anthropocentrism (with the attendant short-changing of other species) then, again, it is to be avoided.

The philosophy of Teilhard de Chardin (1881-1955) is routinely rejected by deep ecologists because he is supposedly an arch anthropocentrist. For this reason, his entire interpretation of evolution is rejected. This is throwing out the baby with the bath water. Teilhard was limited in many ways, but what thinker is not? His adulation of the human species, and within the human species his denigration of the yellow species, are serious shortcomings. We have to see Teilhard's blind spots. But we also have to see the magnificence of Telhard's opus—and there is much that is magnificent in Teilhard! I have a deep suspicion that many who reject him out of hand have never read him carefully.

Teilhard transcended the dreary Darwinian view of evolution. "Evolution is a light illuminating all facts, a curve that all lines must follow." He clarified and unified our world view. He wove one huge homogeneous tapestry in which the prehistory of life; life; the phenomenon of man; and life beyond man are parts of one unbroken, unfolding glory. He explained the rise of life and its incessant self-perfectibility through one single law: complexification / consciousness—the increasing complexity of the inner organization of organisms being seen as the key to their increasing performance, and to their status on the evolutionary ladder. He introduced the idea of the *noosphere*—that is, the sphere of the mind or of thought as another natural envelope of life at large—and showed that all life has been groping to articulate itself in the shape of noosphere. He broadened our conception of evolution, and with it our conception of *seeing*, so that it becomes a vision of one continuous homogeneous unfolding. He also enlarged our conception of science and of ourselves, introducing the notion of 'Omega Point' or the point of ultimate conversions, in terms of which alone we can make sense of all previous stages and strivings of life.

All these points are of *some* importance to a new ecological view of the world. In general it seems foolish to me to think that we can propose and articulate a new cosmological *Weltanschaung* while bypassing or ignoring evolution. The attributes of *Gaia*—the earth which is alive, the universe which is alive, the mind which is alive, and the capacity of compassion for and solidarity with all forms of being—are products of evolution: they are the stages of evolution unfolding. If we do not perceive at least that much, we lock ourselves into a vision which is so restricted that we actually doom ourselves to conceiving the universe as being as small as our immediate gaze... or we must return to older conceptions of the universe in which God has created all, and is controlling all.

Evolution must be taken seriously because only then can we take ourselves seriously, as evolving creatures, limited in our capacities, yet capable of taking the responsibility for all there is, including future generations and the future shape of the universe.

We need to be creative and evolving in our views of evolution. To think of evolution in Darwinian terms alone is lamentably backward. After all, over 125 years have passed since the publication of Darwin's *magnum opus*. Henri Bergson was actually born in 1859, the year Darwin's *Origin of the Species* was published. By the time

Bergson achieved maturity, the Darwinian story of evolution was not only absorbed, but could be creatively transcended. This is what Bergson did in *Creative Evolution*. Bergson does not deny the idea of evolution, he only gives it wings and a creative potency. For Darwin and Neo-Darwinians, evolution is an almost dreary process of chance and necessity (Jacques Monod's *Chance and Necessity* is a prime example); for Bergson, by contrasts evolution is an exquisitely creative process. This was the first step in liberating evolution from the dreariness of the semi-deterministic and, at the same time, semi-incomprehensible, framework of Darwinism.

Teilhard made another step, as he showed creative evolution to be all-pervading and leading from matter to spirit. Teilhard not only considered evolution creative but also spiritual in character. This contribution was to demonstrate that there is no inconsistency in considering evolution to be both scientific and spiritual in character, thus obeying the laws of science and the laws of the spirit. And for a good reason: if evolution embraces all, it lends itself to scientific and spiritual interpretations. Cosmogenesis is both a material (physical) and a spiritual process: matter is transformed into matter, but also matter is transformed into spirit. Evolution must be taken seriously, if we are to take ourselves (and other species) seriously.

Cosmology

Because evolution is not taken seriously by leading proponents of Deep Ecology, its cosmology and ethics do not have a solid foundation. To say that the fundamental intuition of Deep Ecology is that "everything does indeed hang together" is to say close to nothing. Every movement and every school of thought which has rebelled against the crippling narrowness of the modern mechanistic worldview embraces this notion of 'holism'—an admirable doctrine to assert, but not in itself sufficient as the foundation for a new cosmology.

Such notations as 'realistic praxis,' 'egalitarianism in principle,' and 'anti-anthropocentrism,' point to a new metaphysics. But these notions (which seem to be so important for the distinctiveness of Deep Ecology) are not coherently woven together into one structure. Warwick Fox is right, I think, when he says that:

> In pursuing their central intuition of unity (i.e. of no boundaries in the biospherical field), deep ecologists have possibly lost sight of the significance of the 'in process' aspect of their 'unity in process' metaphysics.

But then, Fox does not seem to perceive that the very notion of the "significance of processes" implies the recognition of the process of evolution. Without the notion of evolution (of things evolving, 'getting better', in one sense or other of the term 'getting better'), the idea of processes and particularly the idea of 'significant processes'—and, above all, the idea of new states of consciousness and new values—is lost or becomes groundless.

Finally, let us be aware that a new cosmology requires an over-arching metaphor. For the mechanistic cosmology, this metaphor is a clock-like mechanism. Within the Eco-Cosmology that I have developed, the main metaphor of the universe is that of the sanctuary: we are its guardians and its dwellers; also its stewards, in the best sense of the term 'steward'. We are the guardians and stewards of the cosmic sanctuary within the matrix of unfolding evolution, which gives the *raison d'etre* for our responsibility; for our care for our brothers and sisters, within the human family and within the biotic community; for our interactions with the universe at large (we are evolution conscious of itself, helping the cosmos to evolve further); for our valves, one of which is frugality, which means grace without waste; and for our ultimate strivings—in helping ourselves and evolution to arrive at Omega Point, or whatever name we use for the point of ultimate perfection by which we are somehow bound.

My central point is that the three constituents: cosmology, eschatology and value (or ethics) must be coherently connected together, must support each other, and must co-define each other. May I be presumptuous enough to notice that they are so connected in my Eco-philosophy? May I also point out that they are not so connected within Deep Ecology?

Conclusion

So, in conclusion, I shall observe that as admirable as the *intentions* of Deep Ecology are, its foundations are not deep enough, its assertions constantly beg questions, its cosmology leaves too much to be desired, and its spirituality is completely lacking. The umbrella Deep Ecology provides is definitely leaky.

Without spirituality, there is no deeper justification of our eschatology—if, that is, we aim at an eschatology capable of transcending the consumer eschatology. Without assuming the significance of evolution, there is no meaningful way of ascribing significance to 'processes'. Yet, without processes, the idea of the seamless web of organic unity does not make sense. A new cosmology cannot be established by mere critique of old cosmologies.

Against the triviality, and constantly trivializing influence, of the old mechanistic worldview, we have to have the courage to ask what is the meaning of the universe, what it takes delight in and what it abhors. The universe does not delight in just 'being'. It delights in life. The universe does not delight in life. It delights in consciousness. The universe does not delight in consciousness. It delights in love. The universe does not delight in love. It delights in us reaching the orbit of God. When the primordial explosion of light becomes New Light in the shape of God, then the universe truly delights.

PART V:
APPLIED ECO-ETHICS

THE AGE OF HEALING

JOHN SEYMOUR (1995)

The Age of Plunder is nearly at an end.

The Age of Healing is ready to be born. And whether it arrives or not depends upon two people: you and me.

The Age of Plunder was the natural successor to the so-called Age of Reason: the Age in which humankind decided that it knew better than God. For 200 years now the greedy and ruthless have been plundering the planet but their time will soon be up. The whole thing is going to come crashing down.

It could not have gone on much longer anyway—because soon there will be nothing left to plunder. The forests have almost gone from the Earth, the fish of the sea are all but exhausted, the air surrounding us and the waters of the Earth will soon be able to take no more poisonous wastes and, most serious of all, the soil is going. For we soil organisms, this could be terminal. As long as the oil reserves last, agribusiness will be able to produce the agrichemicals needed to keep some sort of production of vitiated food going from the eroded soil, but the oil deposits—that Pandora's Box of evil things—will soon be exhausted and then the final account, long deferred, will come up for payment. The bailiffs who present it will have strange names, like Famine, Pestilence and War.

But, thank God, maybe the old Earth will not have to wait for this to happen. The whole great edifice of international trade and finance—the whole mighty plunder-machine—is quite likely to burst like a balloon that has grown too big. The whole thing is becoming unsustainable: it has grown too huge to manage.

«««—»»»

Owing to the incorrigible tendency towards cannibalism by the huge industrial corporations—the tendency of the bigger ones to swallow up the smaller ones—these Molochs are becoming too large for humans to control or the planet to support. Ten years ago no economist would have predicted the complete collapse of the mighty Soviet machine that had engulfed half the Earth. International capitalism will follow.

It is in the nature of a limited company that it can have no responsibility either to the environment around it or to the people who work for it. It is no use blaming the directors—if they do anything that might reduce profits for the shareholders they will quickly be replaced. And the shareholders not only have no liability for debts incurred by the company—but they take no responsibility for the world of nature around them. If the directors can secure bigger profits by dumping poisons into the nearest river— they have to do this. If they do not, they will very quickly be replaced. If they can make more profit by halving the work force—they will have to do so or again they will be replaced. If both shareholders and directors suffer from that most uncapitalist thing—a conscience—to the extent that it interferes with profits—that company will be swallowed up by another giant that has no such inconvenient scruples.

One of the most dramatic effects of the Age of Plunder has been to drive most of the world's population into vast conurbations. These huge assemblies of uprooted people, called cities, are not only ugly but also *dangerous*. The billions who live in them can only be kept alive by an enormous system of transport which brings water, food, power, fuel and all the necessities of life, often great distances. Any breakdown in the supply of all this would be disastrous. And the great plundering Molochs of companies which run it all get fewer and fewer, and bigger and bigger, and more and more people find themselves out of work, not needed, redundant and disempowered.

«««—»»»

If we open our eyes, we will realize that all this is bound to come crashing down in the end. Then, in the ashes of the Age of Plunder, a new age could arise. The *real* New Age: the *Age of Healing*!

We will set about it, just you and me, to heal the ravaged Earth. If we do not—if we fail—then there will not be an Age of Healing: there will be an Age of Chaos and it will not be nice.

And we do not have to wait for the end of the Age of Plunder to start the work. We must start *now*.

And how can we—just the two of us, you and me, who are so few and disempowered—start this great work by ourselves?

Firstly, say to yourself, and I promise I will do the same, the following resolution: "I am only one. I can only do what one can do. But what one can do, I *will* do!" Then consider what you can do:

- Refuse to work for the plunderers. Refuse to buy their shoddy goods. Give up the ambition of living like a Texan millionaire.

- Refuse to shop in the plunderers' "supermarkets."

- Work, always, for a decentralist economy. Support local traders and producers—try to get what you need from as near your home as you can.

- Take part in your local politics—boycott the politics of the huge scale, the remote and far away.

- Work for an economy in which land and property are fairly shared out among the people so that "everybody has enough and nobody has too much."

- We must withhold our work, our custom, and our inventions from plundering industry. This may cause us "financial hardship"; then we must endure "financial hardship."

- Road transport is the most destructive thing of all. If you live in a city, you do not need a car. If you live in the country, you may need one—use it as little as possible.

- Boycott most goods brought from far away. Take some trouble to find locally produced goods and buy them. Heavy road transport is enormously polluting.

- Oppose new road building. Building new roads never relieves traffic congestion—it simply generates more traffic. The only way of solving the traffic problem is to *have less traffic.*

- If you possibly can, do not work for huge organizations. If we withhold our labour from them, they will wither away. (Do not be afraid that this will lose "jobs." It will create more jobs—a multitude of small firms create more "jobs" than a few big ones).

- Support local cultural activities. Boycott mass "culture" coming from countries far away.

- Encourage, support, and initiate, local credit and finance organizations.

- Buy, if you cannot grow, organically produced food. Thus you will help destroy the polluting chemical industry—and you will be healthier. Boycott, absolutely consistently, all products that have involved cruelty to animals.

- Support the local and the small-scale.

- I will do the same as I ask you to do.

The tiny amount you and I can do is hardly likely to bring the huge worldwide Moloch of plundering industry down? Well, if you and I don't do it, it will not be done, and the Age of Plunder will terminate in the Age of Chaos. We have to do it—just the two of us—just you and me. There is no "them"—there is nobody else. Just you and me. On our infirm shoulders we must take up this heavy burden now—the task of restoring the health, the wholeness, the beauty and the integrity of our planet. We must start the Age of Healing now! Tomorrow will be too late.

ECO-PSYCHOLOGY SINCE 1992

THEODORE ROSZAK (2002)

As far as I am aware, the term 'ecopsychology' was coined in the pages of my book *The Voice of the Earth* in 1992. That was the year of the Earth Summit in Rio when the air was filled with debate about the future of the environmental movement. The *Voice of the Earth* offered the concept of ecopsychology as an appeal to environmentalists and psychologists for a dialogue that would enrich both fields and play a significant role in public policy. The catch phrase that encapsulated the proposal was "ecology needs psychology, psychology needs ecology." At the time, there were various efforts around the fringes of professional psychotherapy to achieve that goal. They bore names like "green psychology," "nature-based therapy," or "ecotherapy." Each was some one therapist's idea about how to include the more-than-human world in their work with clients whose problems seemed to transcend the social context that delimits conventional psychology. There was also the well-developed field called "environmental psychology," but that has to do with the harmonious design of rooms, buildings, and landscape—the architectural environment of urban life, which is more the problem than the solution when it comes to our alienation from Nature.

It is hardly unusual for fields of study to work out the sort of alliance ecopsychology seeks. All interdisciplinary efforts arise from the fact that the demarcations dividing specialists are wholly artificial and may at some point limit our understanding. For example, where does one sensibly draw a hard and fast line between economics and political science, or between geography and geology? Or consider sociobiology, a much-publicized effort to bring sociology, evolutionary biology, and psychology together in support of some highly controversial conclusions about human nature. In much the same spirit of intellectual adventure, ecopsychology suggests that what psychologists have learned about human behavior may have much to tell us about our bad habits toward the Earth. Since conservationists seek to change those habits, would it not be helpful for them to draw on what psychologists can tell them? This would seem to be especially important where the human behavior in question is wholly irrational, even to the point of self-destruction.

I began to wonder about this possibility several years before I wrote *The Voice of the Earth*. I was struck by how often people characterize the behavior of our species as "crazy." It is "crazy" to destroy the ozone layer in order to enjoy the convenience of spray cans. It is "crazy" to wipe out magnificent wilderness areas to build shopping malls and parking lots. It is "crazy" to keep filling the atmosphere with automobile exhaust in order to drive around in sport utility vehicles. In all these cases, people have been given the facts of the matter, but most of them continue doing irreparable damage to the planetary ecology as if they can't help themselves. Environmentalists scold them, but that does no more good than scolding a pyromaniac for setting fires.

Many environmentalists believe they have an adequate answer to the question of irrational environmental conduct. They believe there are profiteers at work acting against the public interest. There are real estate interests out to make money at the expense of polluting rivers; there are conscienceless marketers whose bottom line depends on selling things that waste resources. True enough. But that only removes the problem by another step. At some point activists have to recognize that the relentless pursuit of money is among the most widespread kinds of craziness in our world. There are fabulously wealthy CEOs who are literally killing themselves on the job to make another million—and taking down whole rainforests with them. Had there been some greater ecological awareness in their time, would Freud or Jung, Sullivan or Homey agree that behavior like this is "sane" because it leads to greater profits for Exxon or Monsanto?

Like everybody who speaks to the world about the environmental crisis, I was once in the habit of scolding people about the stupidly destructive things we do to the planetary ecology. I would, for example, show them a plastic six-pack holder and tell them with blood in my eye how these silly objects find their way out of the landfill where we bury them into the lakes and oceans where they have been known to strangle waterfowl. Or I would call attention to the styrofoam cups they had brought to the lecture, then bawl them out for adding to the CFCs that are eating away the ozone. I was good at that kind of tongue-lashing. I had a hundred examples of thoughtlessly harmful behavior to unload on my audience. It made me feel virtuous to stand before them predicting the cataclysm our way of life would soon bring down on us. But I also recognized that presentations like this were making less and less of a difference, and indeed I was growing weary with spreading gloom. The public that responded to scare tactics and guilt trips had been used up, and it was not the vast majority. Too many others were either not paying attention or just did not care.

And then I began doing something unusual for anybody in the environmental movement. I stopped scolding and began listening. I asked people why they did the ecologically destructive things they did and gave them a chance to talk. The answers were jarring. They had nothing to do with ignorance, greed, or indifference. There were few people I met who were not aware of our troubled relations with the planet. Some confessed to having dreams about the failing state of the world, dreams about forests and rivers and animals that made them sad. They spoke of times and places, a favorite tree or a lovely landscape they recalled from their childhood that was now gone. Deep inside some were grieving about the natural beauties they had seen vanish in their lifetime. No psychologist had ever asked them about those dreams, but they were having them just the same. I was reminded of the opening scene in the movie *Sex, lies, and videotape*. The woman tells her shrink that she is seriously anxious about all the garbage that is piling up in the world. She wishes she could do something about it. Her therapist responds, "Tell me more about your marriage."

I discovered that, far from being under-informed, people are often overwhelmed by the magnitude of the environmental crisis. The situation seems so far gone that they assume there is nothing they can do. Every day they see reports of disaster in the news; every day they receive mail from groups announcing the imminent death of another species, another dire prediction of global famine or draught. Which are they to save first, the whale or the tiger, the rivers or the valleys? What can they do to stop the devastation of an old-growth forest they were told ten years ago could not survive another decade? Hasn't time run out? At last they withdraw with a sense of helplessness. But ironically, their despair is the direct result of bad psychology on the part of the very people who want to enlist them in the cause of protecting Nature. The environmental movement would seem to have invented a problem so big that there is no way to solve it.

Another common response I elicited was the sense of being trapped. People inherit a way of life; everything about that way of life is interconnected. Tell them that they have to throw out the whole social order by next Monday morning, and they cannot help but be stunned. If they stop using their automobile, they will lose their jobs...and their homes. If everything on sale in the supermarket is toxic or environmentally incorrect, what will they eat? Even if the situation is that bad, it is fruitless to ask people to change too much, too fast, and worse than useless to blame them for global catastrophe.

In some cases I discovered such accusations make people both angry and stubborn. They respond by reviling the grieving greenies and stop listening.

I learned that people are especially interested in talking about their consumption habits—as good a place as any to begin. At the 1992 Rio Earth Summit, President George Bush, attending with great reluctance, made a speech in which he announced that he had not come to Rio to undermine the American way of life—by which he meant getting and spending without limit. So I asked people to tell me about how and why they consume. I don't know if I expected them to confess to swinish greed, but what they did tell me was as pathetic as it was illuminating. "When I feel really depressed, I go shopping." Scores of people gave me that answer. "I like to be where there are lots of happy people. So I go to the mall...and I end up buying something I don't need." "Every time I break up with a guy, I throw out all my clothes and jewelry and use up my credit card buying a new wardrobe." Several women admitted to that. Other people said they enjoyed the experience of power they gained by deciding which product to buy; it made them feel they had some control over their lives.

Or consider another remarkable finding. When asked why they continued to commute one-to-a-car when they knew that car pooling makes more sense, some people confessed that the hour or two they spent in their car was the only chance they found in the course of the day to be on their own and reflect on their lives. So here we have two bad environmental habits, one that turns out to be a flight from depression, the other a search for solitude. At least to me, it made a difference to see those habits as something more than blind ignorance or selfish acquisitiveness.

And finally, most revealing of all, there were many who admitted that they experienced shopping as a form of "addiction." They felt ashamed to admit it, but they simply could not control themselves. Going out and buying something—*anything*—relieved some terrible agony within.

That became a major insight for me. Addiction is, after all, an irresistible compulsion to do something that one knows is harmful, demeaning, or destructive. I talked that over with some psychologist friends who were quick to tell me that the worst thing to do with addicts is to shame them. Shame is what brought them into therapy in the first place; they don't need more of it. Making them feel guiltier may only make things worse. As one therapist put it, "If you shame them more, you lose them."

I found myself asking how many of our ecologically destructive habits stem from compulsive behavior that people do not understand and cannot stop. In short, crazy behavior, but crazy behavior by now so well rationalized that it passes for realistic public policy and practical economics. If that is so, then reason and logic on their own cannot solve our dilemma. Some greater force within us, some instinctive loyalty to the living planet, will have to be invoked.

Thinking along these lines, I soon found myself dealing with deeper and darker questions than the shopping habits of the modern world. I eventually had to agree with the environmental philosopher Paul Shepard that our total orientation toward Nature in the modern world is a form of madness. Shepard was the first ecopsychologist, the first thinker in the conservation movement to apply psychological categories to our treatment of the planet. "Why do men persist in destroying their environment?" he asked at the beginning of his classic work *Nature and Madness*. And he did mean "men," for his answer was that men are "ontogenetically crippled" by childish fantasies of power:

> The West is a vast testimony to childhood botched to serve its own purposes, where history, masquerading as myth, authorizes men of action to alter the world to match their regressive moods of omnipotence and insecurity.

Working along much the same lines, I have also come to believe that, at its deepest level, the environmental crisis traces to the twisted dynamics of male gender identity.

When we speak of costs and benefits, we are using an economic category; when we speak of resource depletion, we invoke an ecological category. But "crazy" is a psychological category. Ecologists and economists are not at home dealing with craziness. Psychologists are. They try to understand the crazy things people do. They have developed a rich fund of ideas about irrational conduct. I began *The Voice of the Earth* with a question. If abusing the living Earth has become the psychopathology of everyday life in our time, might psychologists not have something of value to offer environmentalists who are seeking to change people's behavior? I naively assumed that both psychologists and environmentalists would find such a dialogue worthwhile.

I was wrong.

I discovered that few psychologists have any interest in relationships that reach beyond couples, families, and maybe the workplace. The fact that all these relationships are contained and sustained by the natural environment goes totally unrecognized, something not worth mentioning. The guiding light of the profession, the *Diagnostic and Statistical Manual* (DSM), mentions Nature in only one respect: seasonal major depressive episodes, feeling blue when the weather turns rainy. The DSM offers scores of refined categories for sexual disorders, substance abuse, and antisocial behavior. It never asks about the quality of people's relationship with the natural world in which our species spent 99% of its evolutionary history.

Eco-Psychology Since 1992

Ecopsychology could go a long way toward correcting the self-defeating public relations of the conservation movement. But there is a great deal more the field has to offer. Indeed, in the century ahead as the science of ecology matures, psychologists may come to see that our sympathetic bond with the natural world—the "ecological unconscious," as I call it—is a defining feature of human nature, the one aspect of the psyche that has been most cruelly repressed by urban industrial culture. It may assume the place that sexuality holds in Freudian psychology, religious archetypes hold in Jung's psychology, and family relations hold in several more recent schools.

At a conference dealing with ecopsychology in 1994, I was approached by the psychology editor of the *New York Times*, a reasonably well-informed authority. He had heard about ecopsychology, but he was skeptical. (After all, I was from California.) He was curious about this idea that human beings have some kind of emotional rapport with Nature that might be worth serious psychological attention. Were there any "hard data" for that?

Hard data? What could he possibly mean? Might Wordsworth and Shelley qualify as hard data? Would generations of landscape painting qualify? Would Taoism and other forms of Nature mysticism qualify? What about the myth, folklore, and fairy tales of countless centuries past to which every child still seems to respond with spontaneous fascination? My principal interest in *The Voice of the Earth* had been material of that kind. Would that qualify? No. The editor wanted quantification. After all, psychology is a science. And science assumes that numbers are more real than experience. I did find numbers for him, and he then did a report on this odd new direction in psychology.

I found the numbers by logging on to *Psychological Abstracts* and searching for descriptors like "nature," "wilderness," "mental health," "trees," "animals," "therapy," "experience," etc. I stopped when I had printed out 80 single-spaced pages of titles and abstracts. The titles were all rather like this: "The Effects of a Wilderness Therapy Program on Changes in Self-Esteem and Teacher-Rated Behavior of Youth at Risk," "The Effects of Wilderness Camping and Hiking on the Self-Concept and Environmental Attitudes and Knowledge of Twelfth Graders," "The Impact of a Wilderness Experience on the Social Interactions and Social Expectations of Behaviorally Disordered Adolescents."

As for the abstracts, they read something like this: "This study provides empirical confirmation of the limited research that reports positive effects of wilderness therapy on changes in self and behavior of youth at risk." "Results indicated that participating adolescents showed a significant increase in cooperative behaviors and that direct observation procedures were more sensitive to behavior changes than were standardized measures." It was only after I submitted the results of my search that the *Times* editor felt secure enough to run a story on ecopsychology.

I remain bewildered that so large a body of research has had so little influence among professional psychologists. I am just as bewildered that conservationists have made nothing of this evidence for the healing value of wilderness. I assume this body of work has simply been ignored in favor of more important matters. Almost everything psychologists say about money, sex, or eating gets attention. If a therapist delivers a paper at a professional conference dealing with the anxieties that result from making a killing on the stock market or ending a love affair, it is almost certain to be reported in the media.

It was not only the quantity of published research on the psychological benefits of Nature I found impressive, but even more so the uniformity of the findings. Take a group of battered wives, abused kids, cocaine addicts, terminal cancer patients, convicts, depressed junior executives, or suicidal adolescents for a walk in the woods, a canoeing trip, a seashore retreat a hike in the desert...and they feel better. As every Romantic poet once knew, viewed against the background of an alpine landscape, a stormy sea, or a lovely sunset, personal problems take on a distinctly lesser scale. When it comes to getting out of one's own, self-obsessed world of money worries, broken love affairs, or office politics, there is no tranquilizer more effective than standing under a starry sky at night and breathing in the wonder. There were even hard data on these matters, statistics that read something like: "After climbing a mountain, alcoholic housewives achieved an 87% improvement in self-image as measured by the XYZ index; this effect degraded by 15% over the next twenty-two weeks." As far as I could tell by reviewing all the testing and all the numbers, nobody came back from any kind of exposure to open space and grand vistas feeling worse. Some felt they had come close to God.

And yet, the environmental crisis remains of little interest to practicing psychologists. I suspect things will remain that way until ecological craziness is given a numbered heading in the *Diagnostic and Statistical Manual*. Until that happens, no therapist will be able to bill for his or her services. A major barrier. Even more threatening may be the fact that resorting to the healing powers of Nature—getting away from it all as we often seek to do when we take a vacation, going into deep retreat, standing in the presence of natural magnificence—requires little intervention from professionals. Again, a financial loss to the profession.

Beyond these purely mercenary considerations, there is a more formidable problem. If our culture is profoundly invested in an anti-environmental ethos, then psychologists may find challenging that ethos is simply too much to take on. After all, they too are residents of our urban industrial society, well-embedded in its values and assumptions. They earn from urban angst. Most therapists I know are content to tinker, adjust, and above all prescribe; it is all their clients seem to expect. Going deeper takes longer and hurts more. As long as there is Prozac, who needs environmental sanity? The courage with which Freud faced the radical madness of modern life in *Civilization and its Discontents* is rare. He was prepared to psychoanalyze our entire culture. Few have followed in his footsteps.

Nevertheless, it is my conviction that ecopsychology has a promising role to play in public policy. One of its more well-defined initiatives impinges upon environmental law. Suppose the *Diagnostic and Statistical Manual* contained an ecologically oriented definition of mental health, something with an impressively clinical name like "dysfunctional environmental relations syndrome." It might then be possible for lawyers to bring cases based on the damage done to the mental health of a community by destruction to the natural world. That would be even more feasible if the Wilderness Act were amended to more directly include the psychological benefits people gain from untamed Nature.

The environmental lawyer Christopher Stone has written a classic essay on environmental law titled "Should Trees Have Standing?" by which he means, should a forest, a pristine wilderness area, or a species have rights at law? Stone believes they should. But he admits this would require a "shift of consciousness." It would require people to overcome the "sense of separateness" that makes them believe Nature is the "dominion" of humankind. Obviously few people, especially in government and business, are ready for such a change. For better or worse, in the modem world, transformations of consciousness have been staked out by professional psychologists as their province. What, then, does ecopsychology ask of them? That they offer us an environmentally based criterion of mental health that reconnects us with the living planet that mothered the troubled human psyche into existence.

THE ROOTS OF ECOLOGICAL CRISIS

GREGORY BATESON (1970)

Other testimony has been presented regarding bills to deal with particular problems of pollution and end environmental degradation. It is hoped that the proposed Office of Environmental Quality Control will go beyond this *ad hoc* approach and will study the more basic causes of the current rash of environmental troubles.

The present testimony argues that these basic causes lie in the *combined* action of (a) technological advance; (b) population increase; and (c) conventional (but wrong) ideas about the nature of man and his relation to the environment.

It is concluded that the next five to ten years will be a period like the Federalist period in United States history, in which the whole philosophy of government, education, and technology must be debated.

We submit:

(1) That all *ad hoc* measures leave uncorrected the deeper causes of the trouble and, worse, usually permit those causes to grow stronger and become compounded. In medicine, to relieve the symptoms without curing the disease is wise and sufficient *if and only if* either the disease is surely terminal *or* will cure itself.

The history of DDT illustrates the fundamental fallacy of *ad hoc* measures. When it was invented and first put to use, it was itself an *ad hoc* measure. It was discovered in 1939 that the stuff was an insecticide (and the discoverer got a Nobel Prize). Insecticides were "needed" (a) to increase agricultural products; and (b) to save people, especially troops overseas, from malaria. In other words, DDT was a symptomatic cure for troubles connected with the increase of population.

By 1950, it was known to scientists that DDT was seriously toxic to many other animals (Rachel Carson's popular book *Silent Spring* was published in 1962).

But in the meanwhile, (a) there was a vast industrial commitment to DDT manufacture; (b) the insects at which DDT was directed were becoming immune; (c) the animals which normally ate those insects were being exterminated; (d) the population of the world was permitted by DDT, to increase.

In other words, the world became *addicted* to what once an *ad hoc* measure and is now known to be a major danger. Finally in 1970, we begin to prohibit or control this danger. And we still do not know, for example, whether the human species on its present diet can surely survivor the DDT which is already circulating in the world and will be there for the next twenty years even if its use is immediately and totally discontinued.

It is now reasonably certain (since the discovery of significant amounts of DDT in the penguins of Antarctica) that *all* the fish-eating birds as well as the land-going carnivorous birds and those which formerly ate insect pests are doomed. It is probable that all the carnivorous fish will soon contain too much DDT for human consumption and may themselves become extinct. It is possible that the earthworms, at least in forests and other sprayed areas, will vanish—with what effect upon the forests is anybody's guess. The plankton of the high seas (upon which the entire planetary ecology depends) it is believed to be still unaffected.

That is the story of one blind application of an *ad hoc* measure; and the story can be repeated for a dozen other *inventions*.

(2) That the proposed combination of agencies in State Government and in the University should address itself to diagnosing, understanding and, if possible, suggesting remedies for the wider processes of social and environmental degradation in the world and should attempt to define policy in view of these processes.

(3) That *all* of the many current threats to man's survival are traceable to three root causes:
    (a) technological progress.
    (b) population increase.
    (c) certain errors in the thinking and attitudes of western culture. Our "values" are wrong.

We believe that all three of these fundamental factors are necessary conditions for the destruction of our world. In other words, we optimistically believe that the correction of any one of them would save us.

(4) That these fundamental factors certainly interact. The increase of population spurs technological progress and creates that anxiety which sets us against our environment as an enemy; while technology both facilitates increase of population and reinforces our arrogance, or "Hubris," vis-à-vis natural environment.

The attached diagram (Figure 1) illustrates the interconnections. It will be noted that in this diagram each corner is clockwise denoting that each is by itself a self-promoting (or, as scientists say, "autocatalytic") phenomenon: the bigger the population, the faster it grows; the more technology we have the faster the rate of new invention; and the more we believe in our "powers" over an enemy environment, the more "power" we seem to have and the more spiteful the environment seems to be.

Similarly the pairs of corners are clockwise connected to make three self-promoting subsystems.

The problem facing the world is simply how to introduce some anti-clockwise processes into this system.

It appears, at present, that the only possible entry point for reversal of the process is the conventional attitudes toward the environment.

The Roots of Ecological Crisis

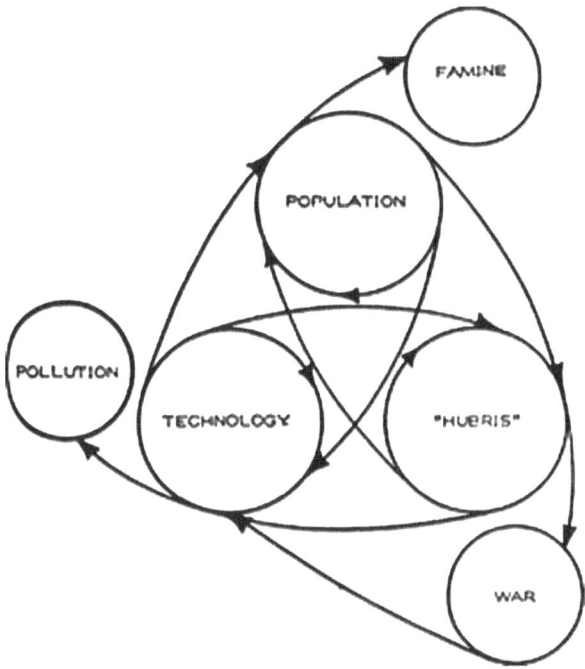

(5) That further technological progress cannot now be prevented, but that it can possibly be steered in appropriate directions, to be explored by the proposed offices.

(6) That the population explosion is the single most important problem facing the world today. As long as population continues to increase, we must expect the continuous creation of new threats to survival perhaps at a rate of one per year, until we reach the ultimate condition of famine. We offer no solution here to the population explosion, but we note that every solution which we can imagine is made difficult or impossible by the thinking and attitudes of western culture.

(7) That the very first requirement for ecological stability is a balance between the rates of birth and death. For better or for worse, we have tampered with the death rate especially by controlling the major epidemic diseases and the death of infants. Always, in any living (*i.e.*, ecological) system, every increasing imbalance will generate its own limiting factors as side effects of the increasing imbalance. In the present instance, we begin to know some of Nature's ways of correcting the imbalance—smog, pollution, DDT poisoning, industrial wastes, famine, atomic fallout, and war. *But the imbalance has gone so far that we cannot trust Nature not to overcorrect.*

(8) That the ideas which dominate our civilization at present time date in their most virulent form from the Industrial Revolution. They may be summarized as:

221

(a) It's us against the environment.
(b) It's us against other men.
(c) It's the individual (or the individual company, or the individual nation) that matters.
(d) We can have unilateral control over the environment and must strive for that control.
(e) We live within an infinitely expanding "frontier."
(f) Economic determinism is common sense.
(g) Technology will do it for us.

We submit that these ideas are simply proved *false* by the great but ultimately destructive achievements of our technology in the last 150 years. Likewise they appear to be false under modern ecological theory. *The creature that wins against its environment destroys itself.*

(9) That other attitudes and premises—other systems of human "values"—have governed man's relation to his environment and his fellow man in other civilizations and at other times. Our modern way is not the only possible human way. *It is conceivably changeable.*

(10) That change in our thinking has already begun—among scientists and philosophers, and among young people. But it is not only long-haired professors and long-haired youth who are changing their ways of thought. There are also many thousands of businessmen and even legislators who *wish* they could change but feel that it would be unsafe or not "common sense" to do so. The changes will continue as inevitably as technological progress.

(11) That these changes in thought will impact upon ours government, economic structure, educational philosophy, and military stance because the old premises are deeply built into all these sides of our society.

(12) That nobody can predict what new patterns will emerge from these drastic changes. We hope that the period of change may be characterized by wisdom rather than by either violence or the fear of violence. Indeed, the ultimate goal of this bill is to make such a transition possible.

(13) We conclude that the next five to ten years will be a period comparable to the Federalist period in United States history. New philosophies of government, education, and technology must be debated both inside the government and in the public press, and especially among leading citizens.

CRITIQUE:
OF COMMONER'S *THE CLOSING CIRCLE*

PAUL EHRLICH AND JOHN HOLDREN (1972)

In his recent book *The Closing Circle* (1971), Barry Commoner presents his views of the origins of man's environmental predicament. Commoner has gained great prominence as a spokesman on the environment, and has made extensive contributions to debates on issues ranging from the dangers of atomic fallout to the ecological consequences of man's intervention in the nitrogen cycle. His book contains much interesting material on the misuse of technology by industrialized societies, and it is written in a powerful and appealing style. Certainly he summarizes the dilemma beautifully when he states:

> We come, then, to a fundamental paradox of man's life on earth: that human civilization involves a series of cyclically interdependent processes, most of which have a built-in tendency to grow, except one—the natural, irreplaceable, absolutely essential resources represented by the earth's minerals and the ecosphere. (p. 122)

It is especially unfortunate, then, that so prominent and articulate an advocate for the environment should have written a book as inexplicably inconsistent and dangerously misleading as *The Closing Circle* proves to be. The book's principle defects are three: First, Commoner implicitly assumes that environmental deterioration consists only of pollution; this oversimplification leads him to discuss the environmental crisis as if it had begun only in the 1940s. Second, in his zeal to place the blame for pollution on faulty technology alone, he resorts to biased selection of data, unconventional definitions, numerical sleight of hand, and bad ecology; only thus can he explain away the contributions of population growth and increased affluence. Finally, his misconceptions concerning certain aspect of demography lead him to draw erroneous conclusion about the "self-regulation" of human populations and viable strategies for population limitation.

[...]

Commoner admits that the factors contributing to environmental impact are multiplicative rather than additive; he offers (in a footnote) the equation

Pollution = (population) x (production / capita) x (pollution emission / production)

Here the second factor on the right, "production per capita," is in some sense a measure of affluence, and the last factor, "pollution per unit of production," is a measure of the relative environmental impact of the technology that provides the affluence. For compactness, let us rewrite this equation

$$I = P \times A \times T$$

Here, I is for *impact* (a better word than 'pollution'), P is for *population*, A is for *affluence*, and T for *technology*.

FACT SHEETS

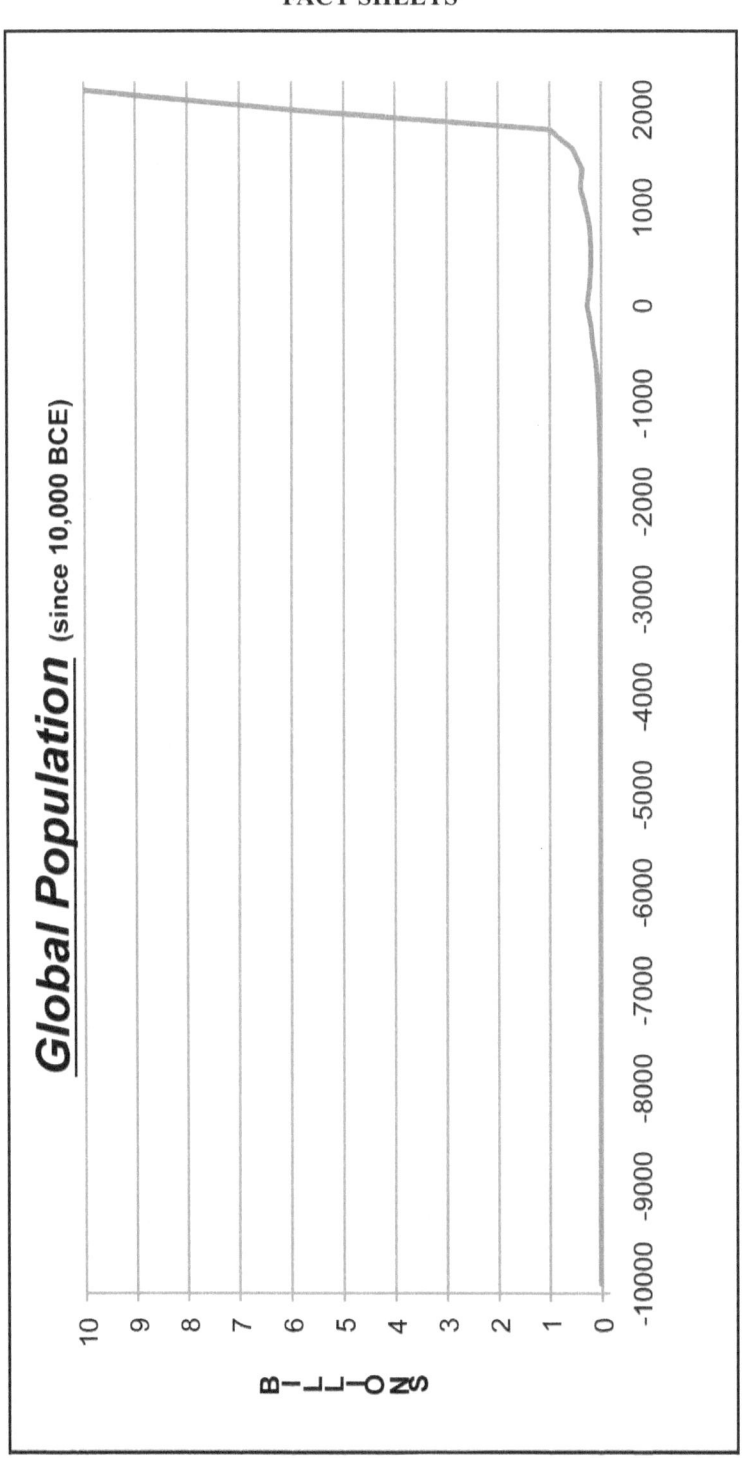

FACT SHEETS

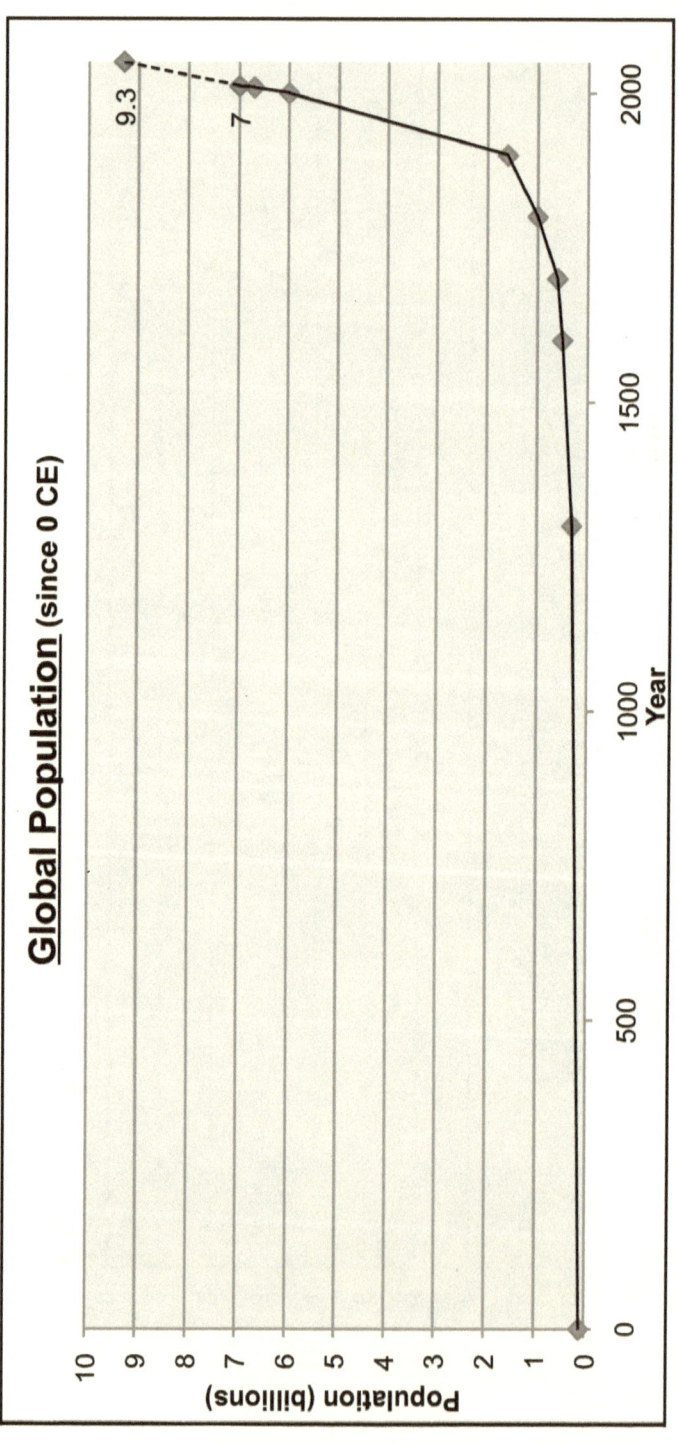

FACT SHEETS

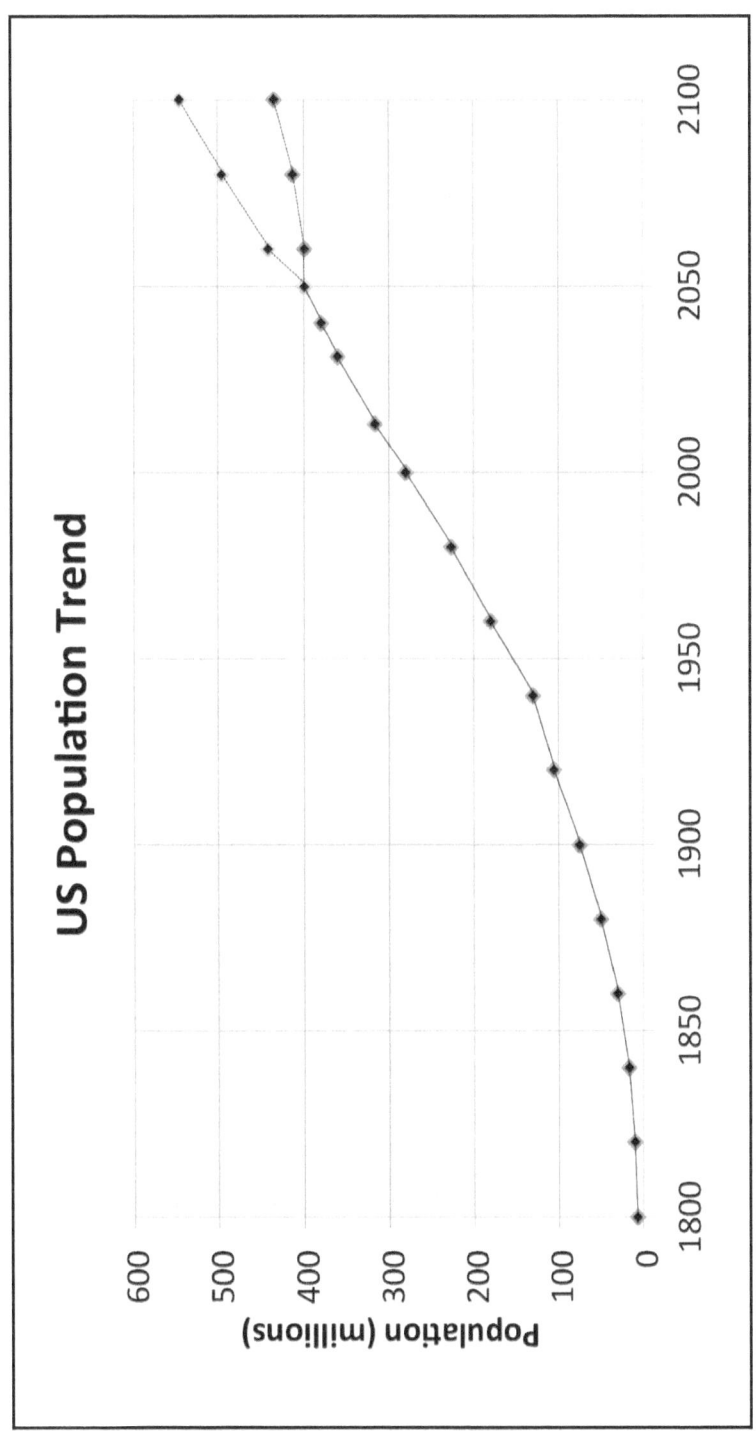

GOODBYE CRUEL WORLD

THE GUARDIAN - U.K. (2 OCT, 2003)

Collectively, the householders of the world could be about to put the cat out. African lion numbers have fallen by 90% in the past 20 years, according to a recent report. There are only about 23,000 alive today. That's the number of seats at Barnsley football club stadium.

The tiger is also an endangered species. At the highest estimate, there are fewer than 8,000 left. To put that number in perspective, about that many people work on Ministry of Defence sites in Wales. There are probably only 15,000 or so cheetahs in the whole of Africa. The Iberian lynx is down to about 600.

And it's not just the cats that we're putting out. The Cross River gorilla sub species, for example, which lives on the border between Nigeria and Cameroon, is down to about 200 at the most. That is fewer than the number of British men who each year develop breast cancer. There are fewer than 50 Chinese alligators surviving in China. Most books give an estimate for sperm whales of 1 to 2 million, but a paper published last year gave an estimate of 360,000. The most recent estimate for southern hemisphere minke whales is about half the total estimate of 760,000 derived from surveys in the late 1980s.

Lions, cheetahs and lynxes share certain characteristics with many other threatened creatures: they are large, they are carnivores, they are fussy about where they live, they need a large range, they have small litters and a long gestation period, and they are hunted.

This makes them natural candidates for extinction in a world in which human numbers have soared from 2.5 billion to more than 6 billion in 50 years. The planet's population grows by more than 80 million every year. There are roughly 240,000 extra mouths to feed every day.

Each of these humans has a personal ecological footprint: that is, each appropriates an average of 2.1 hectares (5.2 acres) to provide water, food, energy, housing, transport, commerce and somewhere to tip the waste. (Americans on average take up almost 10 hectares—about 25 acres—each.) Even though the rate of growth in human numbers is beginning to decline, the wild things are being pushed towards oblivion at an ever faster rate. That is because the numbers of individual households—empty nesters, yuppies, singletons and one-parent families—is exploding, even in those countries with low population growth. That means yet more pressure on the wild to provide timber, gravel and lime, plant fibres, food and water.

Survivors in an increasingly human world need a different set of characteristics. They must be small herbivores that produce large numbers of offspring very swiftly, adapt happily to concrete, tarmac and fossil-fuel pollution and are prepared to live anywhere. So the typical wild animals of the 21st century, as one American biologist predicted more than 30 years ago, "will be the house sparrow, the grey squirrel, the Virginia opossum and the Norway rat". The lion, denied the lion's share, could slope off into the eternal night.

The big animals are merely the most visible of endangered species. One eighth of all bird species are at serious risk of extinction. At least 13% of the world's flowering plants could be about to perish. One-fourth of all mammals are to some extent endangered and around 30 species are down to their last thousand members. There are 19 critically endangered primates, and 16 species of albatross could be about to fly away forever. These are sober estimates from the International Union for the Conservation of Nature about animals that are already well studied. But biologists simply do not know how many species there are on the planet. The big ones are easy to spot, the smaller ones are literally beyond counting. About 1.8 million little birds, beasts and beetles have been named, but there could be seven million or even 70 million.

Five years ago, John Lawton, a population biologist and now the chief of Britain's Natural Environment Research Council, tried to take the measure of biodiversity in the Cameroon. He and colleagues marked out a few plots of forest and started trying to count the species in eight taxonomic groups. They spent 10,000 hours on the research and then abandoned it: the job would have kept 1,200 taxonomists busy for years.

> We surveyed birds, butterflies, ants and then all the way down to itsy-bitsy nematode worms. The percentage of species we found that were actually known and described by taxonomists was inversely related to their body size. In other words, we didn't discover any new birds. We found a new subspecies of butterfly. And 90% of all the nematode worms had never been seen by a scientist before. It was just a huge effort: the number of scientist days it took to identify the things was again inversely related to their body size, the smaller the critters were the longer and longer and longer it took to sort them out.

The Earth's most heart-rending problem comes with a catch-all title, biodiversity. These six clumsy syllables sum up the totality of life on Earth, from subterranean fungi to wind-borne spores, from cloud-forest beetles to Arctic bears, from ocean algae to tubeworms in the abyss. Many of these creatures quietly underwrite human economic growth: they oxygenate the atmosphere, cleanse drinking water, fix nitrogen, recycle waste and pollinate crops. A team at the University of Maryland once calculated that nature delivered goods and services worth $33 trillion to the global economy every year. The gross national product of the whole world at the time was only about $18 trillion.

One school of thought argues that if the big, beautiful beasts—the charismatic mega-vertebrates—are going, then thousands of small, nondescript creatures could go with them, with unpredictable consequences. There are almost apocalyptic predictions about rates of extinction. Edward O. Wilson, one of America's most distinguished biologists, once calculated that 27,000 species of creature went extinct every year in the tropical forests alone. A few years later, a team of biologists at Stanford University suggested that populations of plants and animals were being wiped out at the rate of 1,800 an hour. These may be wild overestimates, but even the most conservative biologists tell a bleak story: this, they say, is the sixth great extinction of life in the history of the planet. The first five extinctions, recorded in the ancient rocks, were all natural: from volcanic catastrophe, climate change, asteroid impact, or even deadly radiation from an exploding star. But this one, they all agree, is the unwitting work of humankind.

Robert May—Lord May of Oxford, president of the Royal Society, a former government chief scientific adviser and once a research partner of Wilson—reckons that at the very least, the rate of extinction is now 1,000 times faster than the "background" rate of extinction over hundreds of millions of years, recorded in fossils from Cretaceous, Jurassic and Triassic rocks. Should people care? Most conservation action by bodies such as the WWF concentrates entirely on the charismatic big vertebrates, such as the panda and tiger, rhino and lion. Could we live without them? "Maybe we can, but if people aren't going to care about them disappearing, who is going to give a stuff about the insects and fungi until the consequences emerge?" May says. "A stronger argument is that we are not sure how much we can simplify the world and still have it deliver all the services we depend on."

Lions won't be extinguished, he says. "They will be kept in reserves and zoos. But the question is, whether you are keeping a lion or whether you are keeping a Latin binomial, *Felis leo*, and that is a question that is awkward to ask."

The lion, according to Georgina Mace, director of science at the Zoological Society of London, was the one animal conservationists had not been worried about. Until recently, it had been widespread in Africa, though it had all but disappeared from Asia. There are two ways of alarming conservationists, she says.

> One is that you are incredibly rare and you just sit on a remote island, being a species that is found nowhere else and there are just 50 of you, but you could have been rare for ever and ever: that is the nature of the life you have. The other way of being of conservation concern is to decline very quickly, and we have been much better at spotting the former rather than the latter. But the latter is probably the one that is going to affect most species. If you are just sitting there being very rare, people are usually protecting you.

The lion, as she sees it, is not an isolated case. The population of bluefin tuna had crashed by 95% before anybody noticed. The passenger pigeon once existed in tens of millions, but was wiped out. The American buffalo almost disappeared. There would once have been lions by the million.

> Carnivore numbers fluctuate. If you are looking in one place, you'd see them come and go. Actually, what they are doing is moving large scale across the landscape, occupying areas where there is abundant prey and then moving somewhere else; they are quite hard to monitor. You think, oh, they are rare here—and then you suddenly realise that actually, they are rare everywhere.

The bitterest irony is that animal populations are dwindling and extinctions accelerating despite a 30-year campaign to establish parks and wildlife reserves in all the great wilderness areas of the world: the rainforests, savannahs, estuaries, deserts, mountains, grasslands, wetlands and so on. These wildernesses cover 46% of the land surface, but hold just 2.4% of the population. More than 10% of these places are now protected by national and international edict. Yet ultimately they cannot protect the wild things. Poachers look to make a killing in both senses of the word. Big animals stray and become a menace to small farmers, who drive them off or kill them. And the tourists turn up, bringing even more of mankind and its expensive ways into the wilderness. A study of the Wolong Reserve in China—opened decades ago to protect the giant panda—revealed that the panda was still in decline and that more humans had moved in, cutting back the bamboo forest for roads, homes and tourist services. The lions in Africa—and all the creatures in Africa's national parks—are still being hunted, hounded or harassed by humans.

There are some who argue that some species will only be saved in zoos (indeed, London Zoo played a big part in saving the almost-extinct Arabian oryx and restoring it to its native wild). But Mark Collins of the UN world conservation monitoring centre in Cambridge says he cannot accept the idea that the lion might survive only in safari parks, or that zoos could be the last resort as the saviours of species. The big wilderness reserves exist, and they could be made to work.

> I feel we have sufficient knowledge of how to manage these key habitats. It is just a matter of political will. I do not accept that the doors are closed. We have parks, and even outside parks, we have the technology and the knowledge to manage most of these habitats like forests and so on, properly. It's just that we are not actually doing it.

Life's richest places are also those where humans are poorest. Africans are already struggling against hunger, poverty, Aids, malaria, cattle diseases and—in many cases—civil war. Nobody knows how this one is going to end. "It is all very well for you and me, but if I was some poor, oppressed farmer in Africa I am not so sure I would look kindly on the elephants that trample my crops," says May. Nor have Europeans and Americans held up much of an example. When western governments began pressing African and Asian nations about the fate of the elephant, developing nations retaliated by suggesting that the Atlantic cod, too, should be protected. The point is well made. Developed nations with sophisticated fishing technology have knowingly put cod and tuna at risk, and had begun to wipe out the barn door skate and great white shark as their nets swept through the seas. "There is a real irony," says Mace.

The lions of Africa—and the wild creatures further down the food chain—can only be saved by money and political will from both national and international communities. The developing nations do have an incentive to protect their biodiversity. It represents potential wealth, one way or the other. Some extinctions of already rare creatures are inevitable. But spend on the lions, says Lawton, and you could save a lot more besides. Committed spending saved the black and white rhino—targets of poachers as well as victims of human pressure—but the sums of money invested were critical.

If you create big, effective reserves for these charismatic guys at the top of the food chain, huge numbers of other creatures we don't even know exist could just slip through to the end of the century on the coat-tails of the lions. So it is a matter of putting enough resources in. In a world which is prepared to spend an extra $100 billion on a war in Iraq, we are talking about peanuts.

EARTH ALIVE

ECOLOGICAL FOOTPRINT

<u>**US (48 states)**</u> has about <u>2 billion</u> acres of land.

Per the World Wildlife Fund, the average American uses an equivalent of <u>25 acres</u> of land, per person (for energy, food, housing, roads, forests/wood, wastes, water, etc), on an on-going basis. This is our *"ecological footprint."*

Therefore, 320 million Americans use:

320m x 25 = <u>8 billion acres total</u>. (more than we have!)

«««—»»»

If we were to live on our available land, then we need fewer people. Our 2 billion acres, at 25 per person, can only support:

2 billion acres / 25 = <u>80 million people</u>!

However, to be ecologically sustainable, we need a large portion – perhaps 50% – reserved as *pure wilderness*. So, sustainably, that leaves only 1 billion acres of usable land:

1 billion acres / 25 = <u>40 million people</u>!!

And yet we are <u>320 million</u> today, heading toward <u>600 million people</u> by the year 2100 – problem?

<u>Michigan</u>:

Total land area = 36 million acres.

Current population = 10 million.

Total footprint: 10m x 25 = <u>250m acres</u> (7 times our land area)

To live sustainably, we can use only half our area, or 18 m acres:

18 million acres / 25 = <u>700,000 people</u>!

LIFEBOAT ETHICS: THE CASE AGAINST HELPING THE POOR

GARRETT HARDIN (1974)

Environmentalists use the metaphor of the earth as a "spaceship" in trying to persuade countries, industries and people to stop wasting and polluting our natural resources. Since we all share life on this planet, they argue, no single person or institution has the right to destroy, waste, or use more than a fair share of its resources.

But does everyone on earth have an equal right to an equal share of its resources? The spaceship metaphor can be dangerous when used by misguided idealists to justify suicidal policies for sharing our resources through uncontrolled immigration and foreign aid, in their enthusiastic but unrealistic generosity, they confuse the ethics of a spaceship with those of a lifeboat.

A true spaceship would have to be under the control of a captain, since no ship could possibly survive if its course were determined by committee. Spaceship Earth certainly has no captain: the United Nations is merely a toothless tiger, with little power to enforce any policy upon its bickering members.

If we divide the world crudely into rich nationals and poor nations, two thirds of them are desperately poor, and only one third comparatively rich, with the United States the wealthiest of all. Metaphorically each rich nation can be seen as a lifeboat full of comparatively rich people. In the ocean outside each lifeboat swim the poor of the world, who would like to get in, or at least to share some of the wealth. What should the lifeboat passengers do?

First, we must recognize the limited capacity of any lifeboat. For example, a nation's land has a limited capacity to support a population and as the current energy crisis has shown us, in some ways we have already exceeded the carrying capacity of our land.

Adrift In a Moral Sea

So here we sit, say 50 people in our lifeboat. To be generous, let us assume it has room for 10 more, making a total capacity of 60. Suppose the 50 of us in the lifeboat see 100 others swimming in the water outside, begging for admission to our boat or for handouts. We have several options: we may be tempted to try to live by the Christian ideal of being "our brother's keeper," or by the Marxist ideal of "to each according to his needs." Since the needs of all in the water are the same, and since they can all be seen as "our brothers," we could take them all into our boat, making a total of 150 in a boat designed for 60. The boat swamps, everyone drowns. Complete justice, complete catastrophe.

Since the boat has an unused excess capacity of 10 more passengers, we could admit just 10 more to it. But which 10 do we let in? How do we choose? Do we pick the best 10, the neediest 10, "first come, first served"? And what do we say to the 90 we exclude? If we do let an extra 10 into our lifeboat, we will have lost our "safety factor," an engineering principle of critical importance. For example, if we don't leave room for excess capacity as a safety factor in our country's agriculture, a new plant disease or a bad change in the weather could have disastrous consequences.

Suppose we decide to preserve our small safety factor and admit no more to the lifeboat. Our survival is then possible, although we shall have to be constantly on guard against boarding parties.

While this last solution clearly offers the only means of our survival, it is morally abhorrent to many people. Some say they feel guilty about their good luck. My reply is simple: "Get out and yield your place to others." This may solve the problem of the guilt-ridden person's conscience, but it does not change the ethics of the lifeboat. The needy person to whom the guilt-ridden person yields his place will not himself feel guilty about his good luck. If he did, he would not climb aboard. The net result of conscience-stricken people giving up their unjustly held seats is the elimination of that sort of conscience from the lifeboat.

This is the basic metaphor within which we must work out our solutions. Let us now enrich the image, step by step, with substantive additions from the real world, a world that must solve real and pressing problems of overpopulation and hunger.

The harsh ethics of the lifeboat become even harsher when we consider the reproductive differences between the rich nations and the poor nations. The people inside the lifeboats are doubling in numbers every 87 years; those swimming around outside are doubling, on the average, every 35 years, more than twice as fast as the rich. And since the world's resources are dwindling, the difference in prosperity between the rich and the poor can only increase.

As of 1973, the U.S. had a population of 210 million people [today, 320 million], who were increasing by 0.8 percent per year [now, 1.0% per year]. Outside our lifeboat, let us imagine another 210 million people, (say the combined populations of Colombia, Ecuador, Venezuela, Morocco, Pakistan, Thailand and the Philippines) who are increasing at a rate of 3.3 percent per year. Put differently, the doubling time for this aggregate population is 21 years, compared to 87 years for the U.S.

Multiplying the Rich and the Poor

Now suppose the U.S. agreed to pool its resources with those seven countries, with everyone receiving an equal share. Initially the ratio of Americans to non-Americans in this model would be one to one. But consider what the ratio would be after 87 years, by which time the Americans would have doubled to a population of 420 million. By then, doubling every 21 years, the other group would have swollen to 354 billion. Each American would have to share the available resources with more than eight people.

But one could argue, this discussion assumes that current population trends will continue, and they may not. Quite so. Most likely the rate of population increase will decline much faster in the U.S. than it will in the other countries, and there does not seem to be much we can do about it. In sharing with "each according to his needs," we must recognize that needs are determined by population size, which is determined

LIFE BOAT ETHICS: THE CASE AGAINST HELPING THE POOR

by the rate of reproduction, which at present is regarded as a sovereign right of every nation, poor or not. This being so, the philanthropic load created by the sharing ethic of the spaceship can only increase.

The Tragedy of the Commons

The fundamental error of spaceship ethics, and the sharing it requires, is that it leads to what I call "the tragedy of the commons." Under a system of private property, the men who own property recognize their responsibility to care for it, for if they don't they will eventually suffer. A farmer, for instance, will allow no more cattle in a pasture than its carrying capacity justifies. If he overloads it, erosion sets in, weeds take over, and he loses the use of the pasture.

If a pasture becomes a commons open to all, the right of each to use it may not be matched by a corresponding responsibility to protect it. Asking everyone to use it with discretion will hardly do, for the considerate herdsman who refrains from overloading the commons suffers more than a selfish one who says his needs are greater. If everyone would restrain himself, all would be well; but it takes only one less than everyone to ruin a system of voluntary restraint. In a crowded world of less than perfect human beings, mutual ruin is inevitable if there are no controls. This is the tragedy of the commons.

One of the major tasks of education today should be the creation of such an acute awareness of the dangers of the commons that people will recognize its many varieties. For example, the air and water have become polluted because they are treated as commons. Further growth in the population or per-capita conversion of natural resources into pollutants will only make the problem worse. The same holds true for the fish of the oceans. Fishing fleets have nearly disappeared in many parts of the world, technological improvements in the art of fishing are hastening the day of complete ruin. Only the replacement of the system of the commons with a responsible system of control will save the land, air, water and oceanic fisheries.

The World Food Bank

In recent years there has been a push to create a new commons called a World Food Bank, an international depository of food reserves to which nations would contribute according to their abilities and from which they would draw according to their needs. This humanitarian proposal has received support from many liberal international groups, and from such prominent citizens as Margaret Mead, U.N. Secretary General Kurt Waldheim, and Senators Edward Kennedy and George McGovern.

A world food bank appeals powerfully to our humanitarian impulses. But before we rush ahead with such a plan, let us recognize where the greatest political push comes from, lest we be disillusioned later. Our experience with the "Food for Peace Program," or Public Law 480, gives us the answer. This program moved billions of dollars worth of U.S. surplus grain to food-short, population-long countries during the past two decades. But when P.L. 480 first became law, a headline in the business magazine *Forbes* revealed the real power behind it. "Feeding the World's Hungry Millions: How it Will Mean Billions for U.S. Business."

And indeed it did. In the years 1960 to 1970, U.S. taxpayers spent a total of $7.9 billion on the Food for Peace program. Between 1948 and 1970, they also paid an additional $50 billion for other economic-aid programs, some of which went for food and food-producing machinery and technology. Though all U.S. taxpayers were forced to contribute to the cost of P.L. 480, certain special interest groups gained handsomely under the program. Farmers did not have to contribute the grain; the Government, or rather the taxpayers, bought it from them at full market prices. The increased demand raised prices of farm products generally. The manufacturers of farm machinery, fertilizers and pesticides benefited by the farmers' extra efforts to grow more food. Grain elevators profited from storing the surplus until it could be shipped. Railroads made money hauling it to ports, and shipping lines profited from carrying it overseas. The implementation of P.L. 480 required the creation of a vast Government bureaucracy, which then acquired its own vested interest in continuing the program, regardless of its merits.

Extracting Dollars

Those who proposed and defended the Food for Peace program in public rarely mentioned its importance to any of these special interests. The public emphasis was always on its humanitarian effects. The combination of silent selfish interests and highly vocal humanitarian apologists made a powerful and successful lobby for extracting money from taxpayers. We can expect the same lobby to push now for the creation of a World Food Bank.

However great the potential benefit to selfish interests, it should not be a decisive argument against a truly humanitarian program. We must ask if such a program would actually do more good than harm, not only momentarily but also in the long run. Those who propose the food bank usually refer to a current "emergency" or "crisis" in terms of world food supply. But what is an emergency? Although they may be infrequent and sudden, everyone knows that emergencies will occur from time to time. A well-run family, company, organization or country prepares for the likelihood of accidents and emergencies. It expects them, it budgets for them, it saves for them.

Learning the Hard Way

What happens if some organizations or countries budget for accidents and others do not? If each country is solely responsible for its own well-being, poorly managed ones will suffer. But they can learn from experience. They may mend their ways, and learn to budget for infrequent but certain emergencies. For example, the weather varies from year to year, and periodic crop failures are certain. A wise and competent government saves out of the production of the good years in anticipation of bad years to come. Joseph taught this policy to Pharaoh in Egypt more than 2,000 years ago. Yet the great majority of the governments in the world today do not follow such a policy. They lack either the wisdom or the competence, or both. Should those nations that do manage to put something aside be forced to come to the rescue each time an emergency occurs among the poor nations?

"But it isn't their fault!" Some kindhearted liberals argue. "How can we blame the poor people who are caught in an emergency? Why must they suffer for the sins of their governments?" The concept of blame is simply not relevant here. The real question is, what are the operational consequences of establishing a world food bank? If it is open to every country every time a need develops, slovenly rulers will not be motivated to take Joseph's advice. Someone will always come to their aid. Some countries will deposit food in the world food bank, and others will withdraw it. There will be almost no overlap. As a result of such solutions to food shortage emergencies, the poor countries will not learn to mend their ways, and will suffer progressively greater emergencies as their populations grow.

Population Control the Crude Way

On the average, poor countries undergo a 2.5 percent increase in population each year, rich countries, about 0.8 percent. Only rich countries have anything in the way of food reserves set aside, and even they do not have as much as they should. Poor countries have none. If poor countries received no food from the outside, the rate of their population growth would be periodically checked by crop failures and famines. But if they can always draw on a world food bank in time of need, their population can continue to grow unchecked, and so will their "need" for aid. In the short run, a world food bank may diminish that need, but in the long run it actually increases the need without limit.

Without some system of worldwide food sharing, the proportion of people in the rich and poor nations might eventually stabilize. The overpopulated poor countries would decrease in numbers, which the rich countries that had room for more people would increase. But with a well-meaning system of sharing, such as a world food bank, the growth differential between the rich and the poor countries will not only persist, it will increase. Because of the higher rate of population growth in the poor countries of the word, 88 percent of today's children are born poor, and only 12 percent rich. Year by year the ratio becomes worse, as the fast-reproducing poor outnumber the slow-reproducing rich.

A world food bank is thus a commons in disguise. People will have more motivation to draw from it than to add to any common store. The less provident and less able will multiply at the expense of the abler and more provident, bringing eventual ruin upon all who share in the commons. Besides, any system of "sharing" that amounts to foreign aid from the rich nations to the poor nations will carry the taint of charity, which will contribute little to the world peach so devoutly desired by those who support the idea of a world food bank.

As past U.S. foreign-aid programs have amply and depressingly demonstrated, international charity frequently inspires mistrust and antagonism rather than gratitude on the part of the recipient nation.

Chinese Fish and Miracle Rice

The modern approach to foreign aid stresses the export of technology and advice, rather than money and food. As an ancient Chinese proverb goes: "Give a man a fish and he will eat for a day; teach him how to fish and he will eat for the rest of his days." Acting on this advice, the Rockefeller and Ford Foundations have financed a number of programs for improving agriculture in the hungry nations. Known as the "Green Revolution," these programs have led to the development of "miracle rice" and "miracle wheat," new strains that offer bigger harvests and greater resistance to crop damage. Norman Borlaug, the Nobel Prize winning agronomist who, supported by the Rockefeller Foundation, developed "miracle wheat," is one of the most prominent advocates of a world food bank.

Whether or not the Green Revolution can increase food production as much as its champions claim is a debatable but possibly irrelevant point. Those who support this well-intended humanitarian effort should first consider some of the fundamentals of human ecology, ironically, one man who did was the late Alas Gregg, a vice president of the Rockefeller Foundation. Two decades ago he expressed strong doubts about the wisdom of such attempts to increase food production. He likened the growth and spread of humanity over the surface of the earth to the spread of cancer in the human body, remarking that "cancerous growths demand food: but, as far as I know, they have never been cured by getting it."

Overloading the Environment

Every human born constitutes a draft on all aspects of the environment: food, air, water, forests, beaches, wildlife, scenery and solitude. Food can, perhaps, be significantly increased to meet a growing demand. But what about clean beaches, unspoiled forests, and solitude? If we satisfy a growing population's need for food, we necessarily decrease its per capita supply of the other resources needed by men.

India, for example, now has a population of 600 million [in 1974], which increases by 15 million each year [now, increasing by 25 million each year]. This population already puts a huge load on a relatively impoverished environment. The country's forests are now only a small fraction of what they were three centuries ago, and floods and erosion continually destroy the insufficient farmland that remains. Every one of the 15 million new lives added to India's population puts an additional burden on the environment and increases the economic and social costs of crowding. However humanitarian our intent, every Indian life saved through medical or nutritional assistance from abroad diminishes the quality of life for those who remain, and for subsequent generations, if rich countries make it possible, through foreign aid, for 600 million Indians to swell to 1.2 billion in a mere 28 years [actually it was 'only' 1.02 billion in 2002; but India will be at 1.6 billion by 2050], as their current growth rate threatens, will future generations of Indians thank us for hastening the destruction of their environment? Will our good intentions be sufficient excuse for the consequences of our actions?

My final example of a commons in action is one for which the public has the least desire for rational discussion—*immigration*. Anyone who publicly questions the wisdom of current U.S. immigration policy is promptly charged with bigotry, prejudice, ethnocentrism, chauvinism, isolationism or selfishness. Rather than encounter such accusations, one would rather talk about other matters, leaving immigration policy to wallow in the crosscurrents of special interests that take no account of the good of the whole, or the interests of posterity.

Perhaps we still feel guilty about things we said in the past. Two generations ago the popular press frequently referred to Dagos, Wops, Polacks, Chinks and Krauts, in articles about how America was being "overrun" by foreigners of supposedly inferior genetic stock. But because the implied inferiority of foreigners was used then as justification for keeping them out, people now assume that restrictive policies could only be based on such misguided notions. There are other grounds.

A Nation of Immigrants

Just consider the numbers involved. Our government acknowledges a net inflow of 400,000 immigrants a year. While we have no hard data on the extent of illegal entries, educated guesses put the figure at about 600,000 a year. Since the natural increase (excess of births over deaths) of the resident population now runs about 1.7 million per year, the yearly gain from immigration amounts to at least 19 percent of the total annual increase, and may be as much as 37 percent if we include the estimate for illegal immigrants. Considering the growing use of birth control devices, the potential effect of educational campaigns by such organizations as Planned Parenthood Federation of America and Zero Population Growth, and the influence of inflation and the housing shortage, the fertility rate of American women may decline so much that immigration could account for *all* the yearly increase in population. Should we not at least ask if that is what we want?

For the sake of those who worry about whether the "quality" of the average immigrant compares favorably, with the quality of the average resident, let us assume that immigrants and native born citizens are of exactly equal quality, however one defines that term. We will focus here only on quantity; and since our conclusions will depend on nothing else, all charges of bigotry and chauvinism become irrelevant.

Immigration vs. Food Supply

World food banks move food to the people, hastening the exhaustion of the environment of the poor countries. Unrestricted immigration, on the other hand, moves people to the food, thus speeding up the destruction of the environment of the rich countries. We can easily understand why poor people should want to make this latter transfer, but why should rich hosts encourage it?

As in the case of foreign-aid programs, immigration receives support from selfish interests and humanitarian impulses. The primary selfish interest in unimpeded immigration is the desire of employers for cheap labor, particularly in industries and trades that offer degrading work. In the past, one wave of foreigners after another was brought into the U.S. to work at wretched jobs for wretched wages. In recent years the Cubans, Puerto Ricans and Mexicans have had this dubious honor. The interests of the employers of cheap labor mesh well with the guilty silence of the country's liberal intelligentsia. White Anglo-Saxon Protestants are particularly reluctant to call for a closing of the doors to immigration for fear of being called bigots.

But not all countries have such reluctant leadership. Most educated Hawaiians, for example, are keenly aware of the limits of their environment, particularly in terms of population growth. There is only so much room on the islands, and the islanders know it. To Hawaiians, immigrants from the other 49 states present as great a threat as those from other nations. At a recent meeting of Hawaiian government officials in Honolulu, I had the ironic delight of hearing a speaker, who like most of his audience was of Japanese ancestry, ask how the country might practically and constitutionally close its doors to further immigration. One member of the audience countered: "How can we shut the doors now? We have many friends and relatives in Japan that we'd like to bring here some day so that they can enjoy Hawaii too." The Japanese-American speaker smiled sympathetically and answered: "Yes, but we have children now, and someday we'll have grandchildren too. We can bring more people here from Japan only by giving away some of the land that we hope to pass on to our grandchildren some day. What right do we have to do that?"

At this point, I can hear U.S. liberals asking: "How can you justify slamming the door once you're inside? You say that immigrants should be kept out. But aren't we all immigrants, or the descendants of immigrants? If we insist on staying, must we not admit all others?" Our craving for intellectual order leads us to seek and prefer symmetrical rules and morals: a single rule for me and everybody else; the same rule yesterday, today and tomorrow. Justice, we feel, should not change with time and place.

We Americans of non-Indian ancestry can look upon ourselves as the descendants of thieves who are guilty morally, if not legally, of stealing this land from its Indian owners. Should we then give back the land to the now living America descendants of those Indians? However morally or logically sound this proposal may be, I, for one, am unwilling to live by it and I know no one else who is. Besides, the logical consequence would be absurd. Suppose that, intoxicated with a sense of pure justice, we should decide to turn our land over to the Indians. Since all our other wealth has also been derived from the land, wouldn't we be morally obliged to give that back to the Indians too?

Pure Justice vs. Reality

Clearly, the concept of pure justice produces an infinite regression to absurdity. Centuries ago, wise men invented statutes of limitations to justify the rejection of such pure justice, in the interest of preventing continual disorder. The law zealously defends property rights, but only relatively recent property rights. Drawing a line after an arbitrary time has elapsed may be unjust, but the alternatives are worse.

We are all the descendants of thieves, and the world's resources are inequitably distributed. But we must begin the journey to tomorrow from the point where we are today. We cannot remake the past. We cannot safely divide the wealth equitably among all peoples so long as people reproduce at different rates. To do so would guarantee that our grandchildren, and everyone else's grandchildren, would have only a ruined world to inhabit.

To be generous with one's own possessions is quite different from being generous with those of posterity. We should call this point to the attention of those who, from a commendable love of justice and equality, would institute a system of the commons, either in the form of a world food bank, or of unrestricted immigration. We must convince them if we wish to save at least some parts of the world from environmental ruin.

Without a true world government to control reproduction and the use of available resources, the sharing ethic of the spaceship is impossible. For the foreseeable future, our survival demands that we govern our actions by the ethics of a lifeboat, harsh though they may be. Posterity will be satisfied with nothing less.

US Population Growth

	2000	Net Births		Immigration		Total	2060
White	198	0.30%	+	0.08%	=	0.38%	230
Hispanic	37	1.70%	+	1.80%	=	3.50%	171
Black	41	0.58%	+	0.10%	=	0.68%	55
Asian	14	0.71%	+	3.43%	=	4.14%	87
Other	5	1.20%	+	1.20%	=	2.40%	16
TOTAL	**295**						**559**

FACT SHEETS ON LAND USE

US Land Area (48 States)

Total land area = 1900 million acres.

1) <u>Ownership</u>: Fed gov   408 Mac (21%)
                  State/private 1483 Mac (79%)

2) <u>Usage</u>:
   - **Non-Agriculture**   <u>715 Mac</u> (38%)
     - Forests   412 Mac (22%)
     - Rec and wildlife   95 Mac (5%)
     - Residential   80 Mac (4%)
   - **Agriculture**   <u>1179 Mac</u> (62%)
     - Pasture/range   645 Mac (34%)]
     - Grazed forest   140 Mac (7%)] **Total dedicated to animals**
     - Animal crops   158 Mac (8%)] (= 943 Mac, <u>50% of total US</u>)
     - People crops   159 Mac (8%)
     - Other misc ag.   77 Mac (4%)

USDA Data.

LIVESTOCK

Land Use in the US

Lower 48S

    million
1900 ac.   **total land area**
      98 mac 5% developed/urban
      1802 mac 95% rural/undeveloped/wilderness

      170 mac 9% state/local gov
      1322 mac 70% private land
      408 mac 21% fed land
          360 mac   mining/foresting/grazing/military
          48 mac   **"wilderness"**   (= **2.5%** of total land area of 1900 mac)

      But, EF! argues that <u>only 20%</u> of "wilderness" is truly roadless, wild land:
          10 mac true wilderness   (= **0.5%** of total land area of 1900 mac)
          38 mac false wilderness

Michigan

        total land
36 mac **area**

      32.1 mac 89% state/local/private land (5.5 mac state land)
      3.9 mac 11% fed land

    32.1 mac **Non-fed land**
      28.6 mac 89% undeveloped (rural/agriculture/forest)
      3.5 mac 11% developed   (= **10%** of total land area of 36 mac)

    3.9 mac **Fed land**
      3.65 mac   mining/foresting/grazing/military
      0.25 mac   **"wilderness"**   (= **0.7%** of total land area of 36 mac)
          (Half of this is Isle Royale, other half = 13 small areas, 12 in UP)
        0.05 mac true wilderness   (= **0.1%** of total land area of 36 mac)
          0.2 mac false wilderness

Michigan loses **<u>10 acres of open space per hour</u>** (= 240 / day, = 87,000 / year).

LIVESTOCK A MAJOR THREAT TO ENVIRONMENT

REMEDIES URGENTLY NEEDED

FAO Newsroom (Nov. 29, 2006)

Which causes more greenhouse gas emissions, rearing cattle or driving cars? Surprise!

According to a new report published by the United Nations Food and Agriculture Organization, the livestock sector generates more greenhouse gas emissions as measured in CO2 equivalent – 18 percent – than transport. It is also a major source of land and water degradation.

Says Henning Steinfeld, Chief of FAO's Livestock Information and Policy Branch and senior author of the report: "Livestock are one of the most significant contributors to today's most serious environmental problems. Urgent action is required to remedy the situation."

With increased prosperity, people are consuming more meat and dairy products every year. Global meat production is projected to more than double from 229 million tons in 1999/2001 to 465 million tons in 2050, while milk output is set to climb from 580 to 1043 million tons.

Long shadow

The global livestock sector is growing faster than any other agricultural sub-sector. It provides livelihoods to about 1.3 billion people and contributes about 40 percent to global agricultural output. For many poor farmers in developing countries livestock are also a source of renewable energy for draft and an essential source of organic fertilizer for their crops.

But such rapid growth exacts a steep environmental price, according to the FAO report, *Livestock's Long Shadow–Environmental Issues and Options*. "The environmental costs per unit of livestock production must be cut by one half, just to avoid the level of damage worsening beyond its present level," it warns.

When emissions from land use and land use change are included, the livestock sector accounts for 9 percent of CO2 deriving from human-related activities, but produces a much larger share of even more harmful greenhouse gases. It generates 65 percent of human-related nitrous oxide, which has 296 times the Global Warming Potential (GWP) of CO2. Most of this comes from manure.

And it accounts for respectively 37 percent of all human-induced methane (23 times as warming as CO2), which is largely produced by the digestive system of ruminants, and 64 percent of ammonia, which contributes significantly to acid rain.

Livestock now use 30 percent of the earth's entire land surface, mostly permanent pasture but also including 33 percent of the global arable land, used to producing feed for livestock, the report notes. As forests are cleared to create new pastures, it is a major driver of deforestation, especially in Latin America where, for example, some 70 percent of former forests in the Amazon have been turned over to grazing.

Land and water

At the same time herds cause wide-scale land degradation, with about 20 percent of pastures considered as degraded through overgrazing, compaction and erosion. This figure is even higher in the drylands where inappropriate policies and inadequate livestock management contribute to advancing desertification.

The livestock business is among the most damaging sectors to the earth's increasingly scarce water resources, contributing among other things to water pollution, euthropication and the degeneration of coral reefs. The major polluting agents are animal wastes, antibiotics and hormones, chemicals from tanneries, fertilizers and the pesticides used to spray feed crops. Widespread overgrazing disturbs water cycles, reducing replenishment of above and below ground water resources. Significant amounts of water are withdrawn for the production of feed.

Livestock are estimated to be the main inland source of phosphorous and nitrogen contamination of the South China Sea, contributing to biodiversity loss in marine ecosystems.

Meat and dairy animals now account for about 20 percent of all terrestrial animal biomass. Livestock's presence in vast tracts of land and its demand for feed crops also contribute to biodiversity loss; 15 out of 24 important ecosystem services are assessed as in decline, with livestock identified as a culprit.

Remedies

The report, which was produced with the support of the multi-institutional Livestock, Environment and Development (LEAD) Initiative, proposes explicitly to consider these environmental costs and suggests a number of ways of remedying the situation, including:

Land degradation–controlling access and removing obstacles to mobility on common pastures. Use of soil conservation methods and silvopastoralism, together with controlled livestock exclusion from sensitive areas; payment schemes for environmental services in livestock-based land use to help reduce and reverse land degradation.

Atmosphere and climate–increasing the efficiency of livestock production and feed crop agriculture. Improving animals' diets to reduce enteric fermentation and consequent methane emissions, and setting up biogas plant initiatives to recycle manure.

Water–improving the efficiency of irrigation systems. Introducing full-cost pricing for water together with taxes to discourage large-scale livestock concentration close to cities.

These and related questions are the focus of discussions between FAO and its partners meeting to chart the way forward for livestock production at global consultations in Bangkok this week. These discussions also include the substantial public health risks related to the rapid livestock sector growth as, increasingly, animal diseases also affect humans; rapid livestock sector growth can also lead to the exclusion of smallholders from growing markets.

A New Global Warming Strategy

How Environmentalists are Overlooking Vegetarianism as the Most Effective Tool Against Climate Change in Our Lifetimes

by Noam Mohr

Global warming poses one of the most serious threats to the global environment ever faced in human history. Yet by focusing entirely on carbon dioxide emissions, major environmental organizations have failed to account for published data showing that other gases are the main culprits behind the global warming we see today. As a result, they are neglecting what might be the most effective strategy for reducing global warming in our lifetimes: advocating a vegetarian diet.

Global Warming and Carbon Dioxide

The environmental community rightly recognizes global warming as one of the gravest threats to the planet. Global temperatures are already higher than they've ever been in at least the past millennium, and the increase is accelerating even faster than scientists had predicted. The expected consequences include coastal flooding, increases in extreme weather, spreading disease, and mass extinctions.

Unfortunately, the environmental community has focused its efforts almost exclusively on abating carbon dioxide (CO_2) emissions. Domestic legislative efforts concentrate on raising fuel economy standards, capping CO_2 emissions from power plants, and investing in alternative energy sources. Recommendations to consumers also focus on CO_2: buy fuel-efficient cars and appliances, and minimize their use.

This is a serious miscalculation. Data published by Dr. James Hansen and others show that CO_2 emissions are not the main cause of observed atmospheric warming. Though this may sound like the work of global warming skeptics, it isn't: Hansen is Director of NASA's Goddard Institute for Space Studies who has been called "a grandfather of the global warming theory." He is a longtime supporter of action against global warming, cited by Al Gore and often quoted by environmental organizations, who has argued against skeptics for subverting the scientific process. His results are generally accepted by global warming experts, including bigwigs like Dr. James McCarthy, co-chair of the International Panel on Climate Change's Working Group II.

The focus solely on CO_2 is fueled in part by misconceptions. It's true that human activity produces vastly more CO_2 than all other greenhouse gases put together. However, this does not mean it is responsible for most of the earth's warming. Many other greenhouse gases trap heat far more powerfully than CO_2, some of them tens of thousands of times more powerfully. When taking into account various gases' global warming potential—defined as the amount of actual warming a gas will produce over the next one hundred years—it turns out that gases other than CO2 make up most of the global warming problem.

Even this overstates the effect of CO2, because the primary sources of these emissions—cars and power plants—also produce aerosols. Aerosols actually have a cooling effect on global temperatures, and the magnitude of this cooling approximately cancels out the warming effect of CO2. The surprising result is that sources of CO2 emissions are having roughly zero effect on global temperatures in the near-term!

This result is not widely known in the environmental community, due to a fear that polluting industries will use it to excuse their greenhouse gas emissions. For example, the Union of Concerned Scientists had the data reviewed by other climate experts, who affirmed Hansen's conclusions. However, the organization also cited climate contrarians' misuse of the data to argue against curbs in CO2. This contrarian spin cannot be justified.

While CO2 may have little influence in the near-term, reductions remains critical for containing climate change in the long run. Aerosols are short-lived, settling out of the air after a few months, while CO2 continues to heat the atmosphere for decades to centuries. Moreover, we cannot assume that aerosol emissions will keep pace with increases in CO2 emissions. If we fail start dealing with CO2 today, it will be too late down the road when the emissions catch up with us.

Nevertheless, the fact remains that sources of non-CO2 greenhouse gases are responsible for virtually all the global warming we're seeing, and all the global warming we are going to see for the next fifty years. If we wish to curb global warming over the coming half century, we must look at strategies to address non-CO2 emissions. The strategy with the most impact is vegetarianism.

Methane and Vegetarianism

By far the most important non-CO2 greenhouse gas is *methane*, and the number one source of methane worldwide is animal agriculture.

Methane is responsible for nearly as much global warming as all other non-CO2 greenhouse gases put together. Methane is 21 times more powerful a greenhouse gas than CO2. While atmospheric concentrations of CO2 have risen by about 31% since pre-industrial times, methane concentrations have more than doubled. Whereas human sources of CO2 amount to just 3% of natural emissions, human sources produce one and a half times as much methane as all natural sources. In fact, the effect of our methane emissions may be compounded as methane-induced warming in turn stimulates microbial decay of organic matter in wetlands—the primary natural source of methane.

With methane emissions causing nearly half of the planet's human-induced warming, methane reduction must be a priority. Methane is produced by a number of sources, including coal mining and landfills—but the number one source worldwide is animal agriculture. Animal agriculture produces more than 100 million tons of methane a year. And this source is on the rise: global meat consumption has increased fivefold in the past fifty years, and shows little sign of abating. About 85% of this methane is produced in the digestive processes of livestock, and while a single cow releases a relatively small amount of methane, the collective effect on the environment of the hundreds of millions of livestock animals worldwide is enormous. An additional 15% of animal agricultural methane emissions are released from the massive "lagoons" used to store untreated farm animal waste, and already a target of environmentalists' for their role as the number one source of water pollution in the U.S.

The conclusion is simple: arguably the best way to reduce global warming in our lifetimes is to reduce or eliminate our consumption of animal products. Simply by going vegetarian (or, strictly speaking, vegan), we can eliminate one of the major sources of emissions of methane, the greenhouse gas responsible for almost half of the global warming impacting the planet today.

Advantages of Vegetarianism over CO2 Reduction

In addition to having the advantage of immediately reducing global warming, a shift away from methane-emitting food sources is much easier than cutting carbon dioxide.

First, there is no limit to reductions in this source of greenhouse gas that can be achieved through vegetarian diet. In principle, even 100% reduction could be achieved with little negative impact. In contrast, similar cuts in carbon dioxide are impossible without devastating effects on the economy. Even the most ambitious carbon dioxide reduction strategies fall short of cutting emissions by half.

Second, shifts in diet lower greenhouse gas emissions much more quickly than shifts away from the fossil fuel burning technologies that emit carbon dioxide. The turnover rate for most ruminant farm animals is one or two years, so that decreases in meat consumption would result in almost immediate drops in methane emissions. The turnover rate for cars and power plants, on the other hand, can be decades. Even if cheap, zero-emission fuel sources were available today, they would take many years to build and slowly replace the massive infrastructure our economy depends upon today.

Similarly, unlike carbon dioxide which can remain in the air for more than a century, methane cycles out of the atmosphere in just eight years, so that lower methane emissions quickly translate to cooling of the earth.

Third, efforts to cut carbon dioxide involve fighting powerful and wealthy business interests like the auto and oil industries. Environmental groups have been lobbying for years to make fuel-efficient SUVs available or phase out power plants that don't meet modern environmental standards without success. At the same time, vegetarian foods are readily available, and cuts in agricultural methane emissions are achievable at every meal.

Also, polls show that concern about global warming is widespread, and environmental activists often feel helpless to do anything about it. Unless they happen to be buying a car or major appliance, most people wanting to make a difference are given little to do aside from writing their legislators and turning off their lights. Reducing or eliminating meat consumption is something concerned citizens can do every day to help the planet.

Finally, it is worth noting that reductions in this source of greenhouse gas have many beneficial side effects for the environment. Less methane results in less tropospheric ozone, a pollutant damaging to human health and agriculture. Moreover, the same factory farms responsible for these methane emissions also use up most of the country's water supply, and denude most of its wilderness for rangeland and growing feed. Creating rangeland to feed western nations' growing appetite for meat has been a major source of deforestation and desertification in third world countries. Factory farm waste lagoons are a leading source of water pollution in the U.S. Indeed, because of animal agriculture's high demand for fossil fuels, the average American diet is far more CO_2-polluting than a plant-based one.

WHAT'S IN THE MEAT?

ERIC SCHLOSSER (2001)

Much like the human immunodeficiency virus (HIV) responsible tor causing AIDS, the E. coli 0157:H7 bacterium is a newly emerged pathogen whose spread has been facilitated by recent social and technological changes. E. coli was first isolated in 1982; HIV was discovered the following year. People who are infected with HIV can appear healthy for years, while cattle infected with E. coli show few signs of illness. Although cases of AIDS date back at least to the late 1950s, the disease did not reach epidemic proportions in the United States until increased air travel and sexual promiscuity helped transmit the virus far and wide. E. coli was most likely responsible for some human illnesses thirty or forty years ago. But the rise of huge feedlots, slaughterhouses, and hamburger grinders seems to have provided the means for this pathogen to become widely dispersed in the nation's food supply. American meat production has never before been so centralized: thirteen large packinghouses now slaughter most of the beef consumed in the United States. The meatpacking system that arose to supply the nation's fast food chains — an industry molded to serve their needs, to provide massive amounts of uniform ground beef so that all of McDonald's hamburgers would taste the same — has proved to be an extremely efficient system for spreading disease.

Although E. coli has received a good deal of public attention, over the past two decades scientists have discovered more than a dozen other new food-borne pathogens, including *Campylobacter jejuni, Cryptosporidium parvum, Cyclospora cayetanensis, Listeria monocytogenes*, and Norwalk-like viruses. The CDC estimates that more than three-quarters of the food-related illnesses and deaths in the United States are caused by infectious agents that have not yet been identified. While medical researchers have gained important insights into the links between modern food processing and the spread of dangerous diseases, the nation's leading agribusiness firms have resolutely opposed any further regulation of their food safety practices. For years the large meatpacking companies have managed to avoid the sort of liability routinely imposed on the manufacturers of most consumer products. Today the U.S. government can demand the nationwide recall of defective softball bats, sneakers, stuffed animals, and foam-rubber toy cows. But it cannot order a meatpacking company to remove contaminated, potentially lethal ground beef from fast food kitchens and supermarket shelves. The unusual power of the large meatpacking firms has been sustained by their close ties and sizable donations to Republican members of Congress. It has also been made possible by a widespread lack of awareness about how many Americans suffer from food poisoning every year and how these illnesses actually spread.

The newly recognized food-borne pathogens tend to be carried and shed by apparently healthy animals. Food tainted by these organisms has most likely come in contact with an infected animal's stomach contents or manure, during slaughter or subsequent processing. A nationwide study published by the USDA in 1996 found that 7.5 percent of the ground beef samples taken at processing plants were contaminated with Salmonella, 11.7 percent were contaminated with *Listeria monocytogenes*, 30 percent were contaminated with *Staphylococcus aureus*, and 53.3 percent were contaminated with *Clostridium perfringens*. All of these pathogens can make people sick; food poisoning caused by Listeria generally requires hospitalization and proves fatal in about one out of every five cases. In the USDA study 78.6 percent of the ground beef contained microbes that are spread primarily by fecal material. The medical literature on the causes of food poisoning is full of euphemisms and dry scientific terms: coliform levels, aerobic plate counts, sorbitol, MacConkey agar, and so on. Behind them lies a simple explanation for why eating a hamburger can now make you seriously ill: There is shit in the meat.

In the early years of the twentieth century, hamburgers had a bad reputation. According to the historian David Gerard Hogan, the hamburger was considered "a food for the poor," tainted and unsafe to eat. Restaurants rarely served hamburgers; they were sold at lunch carts parked near factories, at circuses, carnivals, and state fairs. Ground beef, it was widely believed, was made from old, putrid meat heavily laced with chemical preservatives. "The hamburger habit is just about as safe," one food critic warned, "as getting your meat out of a garbage can." White Castle, the nation's first hamburger chain, worked hard in the 1920s to dispel the hamburger's tawdry image. As Hogan notes in his history of the chain, *Selling 'Em by the Sack* (1997), the founders of White Castle placed their grills in direct view of customers, claimed that fresh ground beef was delivered twice a day, chose a name with connotations of purity, and even sponsored an experiment at the University of Minnesota in which a medical student lived for thirteen weeks on "nothing but White Castle hamburgers and water."

The success of White Castle in the East and the Midwest helped to popularize hamburgers and to remove much of their social stigma. The chain did not attract a broad range of people, however. Most of White Castle's customers were urban, working class, and male. During the 1950s, the rise of drive-ins and fast food restaurants in southern California helped turn the once lowly hamburger into America's national dish. Ray Kroc's decision to promote McDonald's as a restaurant chain for families had a profound impact on the nation's eating habits. Hamburgers seemed an ideal food for small children — convenient, inexpensive, hand-held, and easy to chew.

Before World War II, pork had been the most popular meat in the United States. Rising incomes, falling cattle prices, the growth of the fast food industry, and the mass appeal of the hamburger later pushed American consumption of beef higher than that of pork. By the early 1990s, beef production was responsible for almost half of the employment in American agriculture, and the annual revenues generated by beef were higher than those of any other agricultural commodity in the United States. The average American ate three hamburgers a week. More than two-thirds of those hamburgers were bought at fast food restaurants. And children between the ages of seven and thirteen ate more hamburgers than anyone else.

In January of 1993, doctors at a hospital in Seattle, Washington, noticed that an unusual number of children were being admitted with bloody diarrhea. Some were suffering from hemolytic uremic syndrome, a previously rare disorder that causes kidney damage. Health officials soon traced the outbreak of food poisoning to undercooked hamburgers served at local Jack in the Box restaurants. Tests of the hamburger patties disclosed the presence of E. coli. Jack in the Box issued an immediate recall of the contaminated ground beef, which had been supplied by the Vons Companies, Inc., in Arcadia, California. Nevertheless, more than seven hundred people in at least four states were sickened by Jack in the Box hamburgers, more than two hundred people were hospitalized, and four died. Most of the victims were children. One of the first to become ill, Lauren Beth Rudolph, ate a hamburger at a San Diego Jack in the Box a week before Christmas. She was admitted to the hospital on Christmas Eve, suffered terrible pain, had three heart attacks, and died in her mother's arms on December 28, 1992. She was six years old.

The Jack in the Box outbreak received a great deal of attention from the media, alerting the public to the dangers of E. coli. The Jack in the Box chain almost went out of business amid all the bad publicity. But this was not the first outbreak of E. coli linked to fast food hamburgers. In 1982 dozens of children were sickened by contaminated hamburgers sold at McDonald's restaurants in Oregon and Michigan. McDonald's quietly cooperated with investigators from the CDC, providing ground beef samples that were tainted with E. coli — samples that for the first time linked the pathogen to serious illnesses. In public, however, the McDonald's Corporation denied that its hamburgers had made anyone sick. A spokesman for the chain acknowledged only "the possibility of a statistical association between a small number of diarrhea cases in two small towns and our restaurants."

In the eight years since the Jack in the Box outbreak, approximately half a million Americans, the majority of them children, have been made ill by E. coli. Thousands have been hospitalized, and hundreds have died.

E. coli is a mutated version of a bacterium found abundantly in the human digestive system. Most E. coli bacteria help us digest food, synthesize vitamins, and guard against dangerous organisms. E. coli, on the other hand, can release a powerful toxin — called a "verotoxin" or a "Shiga toxin" — that attacks the lining of the intestine. Some people who are infected with E. coli do not become ill. Others suffer mild diarrhea. In most cases, severe abdominal cramps are followed by watery, then bloody, diarrhea that subsides within a week or so. Sometimes the diarrhea is accompanied by vomiting and a low-grade fever.

In about 4 percent of reported E. coli cases, the Shiga toxins enter the bloodstream, causing hemolytic uremic syndrome (HUS), which can lead to kidney failure, anemia, internal bleeding, and the destruction of vital organs. The Shiga toxins can cause seizures, neurological damage, and strokes. About 5 percent of the children who develop HUS are killed by it. Those who survive are often left with permanent disabilities, such as blindness or brain damage.

Children under the age of five, the elderly, and people with impaired immune systems are the most likely to suffer from illnesses caused by E. coli. The pathogen is now the leading cause of kidney failure among children in the United States. Nancy Donley, the president of Safe Tables Our Priority (STOP), an organization devoted to food safety, says it is hard to convey the suffering that E. coli causes children. Her six-year-old son, Alex, was infected with the bug in July of 1993 after eating a tainted hamburger. His illness began with abdominal cramps that seemed as severe as labor pains. It progressed to diarrhea that filled a hospital toilet with blood. Doctors frantically tried to save Alex's life, drilling holes in his skull to relieve pressure, inserting tubes in his chest to keep, him breathing, as the Shiga toxins destroyed internal organs. "I would have done anything to save my son's life," Donley says. "I would have run in front of a bus to save Alex." Instead, she stood and watched helplessly as he called out for her, terrified and in pain. He became ill on a Tuesday night, the night after his mother's birthday, and was dead by Sunday afternoon. Toward the end, Alex suffered hallucinations and dementia, no longer recognizing his mother or father. Portions of his brain had been liquefied. "The sheer brutality of his death was horrifying," Donley says.

As Lee Harding learned, adults in perfect health can be stricken by the pathogen, too. Six months after seemingly recovering from his bout of E. coli food poisoning, Harding began to urinate blood. He was diagnosed as having a kidney infection, one that he believes was facilitated by residual tissue damage from the Shiga toxins. Although the infection soon passed, Harding still experiences occasional pain three years after eating a Hudson Beef hamburger. Nevertheless, he considers himself lucky.

Antibiotics have proven ineffective in treating illnesses caused by E. coli. Indeed the use of antibiotics may make such illnesses worse by killing off the pathogen and prompting a sudden release of its Shiga toxins. At the moment, little can be done for people with life-threatening E. coli infections, aside from giving them fluids, blood transfusions, and dialysis.

Efforts to eradicate E. coli have been complicated by the fact that it is an extraordinarily hearty microbe that is easy to transmit. E. coli is resistant to acid, salt, and chlorine. It can live in fresh water or seawater. It can live on kitchen countertops for days and in moist environments for weeks. It can withstand freezing. It can survive heat up to 160 degrees Fahrenheit. To be infected by most food-borne pathogens, such as Salmonella, you have to consume a fairly large dose — at least a million organisms. An infection with E. coli can be caused by as few as five organisms. A tiny uncooked particle of hamburger meat can contain enough of the pathogen to kill you.

The heartiness and minute infectious dose of E. coli allow the pathogen to be spread in many ways. People have been infected by drinking contaminated water, by swimming in a contaminated lake, by playing at a contaminated water park, by crawling on a contaminated carpet. The most common cause of food-borne outbreaks has been the consumption of undercooked ground beef. But E. coli outbreaks have also been caused by contaminated bean sprouts, salad greens, cantaloupe, salami, raw milk, and unpasteurized apple cider. All of those foods most likely had come in contact with cattle manure, though the pathogen may also be spread by the feces of deer, dogs, horses, and flies.

Person-to-person transmission has been responsible for a significant proportion of E. coli illnesses. Roughly 10 percent of the people sickened during the Jack in the Box outbreak did not eat a contaminated burger, but were infected by someone who did. E. coli is shed in the stool, and people infected with the bug, even those showing no outward sign of illness, can easily spread it through poor hygiene. Person-to-person transmission is most likely to occur among family members, at day care centers, and at senior citizen homes. On average, an infected person remains contagious for about two weeks, though in some cases E. coli has been found in stool samples two to four months after an initial illness.

Some herds of American cattle may have been infected with E. coli decades ago. But the recent changes in how cattle are raised, slaughtered, and processed have created an ideal means for the pathogen to spread. The problem begins in today's vast feedlots. A government health official, who prefers not to be named, compared the sanitary conditions in a modern feedlot to those in a crowded European city during the Middle Ages, when people dumped their chamber pots out the window, raw sewage ran in the streets, and epidemics raged. The cattle now packed into feedlots get little exercise and live amid pools of manure. "You shouldn't eat dirty food and dirty water," the official told me. "But we still think we can give animals dirty food and dirty water." Feedlots have become an extremely efficient mechanism for "recirculating the manure," which is unfortunate, since E. coli can replicate in cattle troughs and survive in manure for up to 90 days.

Far from their natural habitat, the cattle in feedlots become more prone to all sorts of illnesses. And what they are being fed often contributes to the spread of disease. The rise in grain prices has encouraged the feeding of less expensive materials to cattle, especially substances with a high protein content that accelerate growth. About 75 percent of the cattle in the United States were routinely fed livestock wastes — the rendered remains of dead sheep and dead cattle — until August of 1997. They were also fed millions of dead cats and dead dogs every year, purchased from animal shelters. The FDA banned such practices after evidence from Great Britain suggested that they were responsible for a widespread outbreak of bovine spongiform encephalopathy (BSE), also known as "mad cow disease." Nevertheless, current FDA regulations allow dead pigs and dead horses to be rendered into cattle feed, along with dead poultry. The regulations not only allow cattle to be fed dead poultry, they allow poultry to be fed dead cattle. Americans who spent more than six months in the United Kingdom during the 1980s are now forbidden to donate blood, in order to prevent the spread of BSE's human variant, Creutzfeldt-Jakob disease. But cattle blood is still put into the feed given to American cattle. Steven P. Bjerklie, a former editor of the trade journal *Meat & Poultry*, is appalled by what goes into cattle feed these days. "Goddamn it, these cattle are ruminants," Bjerklie says. "They're designed to eat grass and, maybe, grain. I mean, they have four stomachs for a reason — to eat products that have a high cellulose content. They are not designed to eat other animals."

The waste products from poultry plants, including the sawdust and old newspapers used as litter, are also being fed to cattle. A study published a few years ago in *Preventive Medicine* notes that in Arkansas alone, about 3 million pounds of chicken manure were fed to cattle in 1994. According to Dr. Neal D. Bernard, who heads the

Physicians Committee for Responsible Medicine, chicken manure may contain dangerous bacteria such as Salmonella and Campylobacter, parasites such as tapeworms and *Giardia lamblia*, antibiotic residues, arsenic, and heavy metals.

The pathogens from infected cattle are spread not only in feedlots, but also at slaughterhouses and hamburger grinders. The slaughterhouse tasks most likely to contaminate meat are the removal of an animal's hide and the removal of its digestive system. The hides are now pulled off by machine; if a hide has been inadequately cleaned, chunks of dirt and manure may fall from it onto the meat. Stomachs and intestines are still pulled out of cattle by hand; if the job is not performed carefully, the contents of the digestive system may spill everywhere. The increased speed of today's production lines makes the task much more difficult. A single worker at a "gut table" may eviscerate sixty cattle an hour. Performing the job properly takes a fair amount of skill. A former IBP "gutter" told me that it took him six months to learn how to pull out the stomach and tie off the intestines without spillage. At best, he could gut two hundred consecutive cattle without spilling anything. Inexperienced gutters spill manure, far more often. At the IBP slaughterhouse in Lexington, Nebraska, the hourly spillage rate at the gut table has run as high as 20 percent, with stomach contents splattering one out of five carcasses.

The consequences of a single error are quickly multiplied as hundreds of carcasses quickly move down the line. Knives are supposed to be cleaned and disinfected every few minutes, something that workers in a hurry tend to forget. A contaminated knife spreads germs to everything it touches. The overworked, often illiterate workers in the nation's slaughterhouses do not always understand the importance of good hygiene. They sometimes forget that this meat will eventually be eaten. They drop meat on the floor and then place it right back on the conveyer belt. They cook bite-sized pieces of meat in their sterilizers, as snacks, thereby rendering the sterilizers ineffective. They are directly exposed to a wide variety of pathogens in the meat, become infected, and inadvertently spread disease.

A recent USDA study found that during the winter about 1 percent of the cattle at feedlots carry E. coli in their gut. The proportion rises to as much as 50 percent during the summer. Even if you assume that only 1 percent are infected, that means three or four cattle bearing the microbe are eviscerated at a large slaughterhouse every hour. The odds of widespread contamination are raised exponentially when the meat is processed into ground beef. A generation ago, local butchers and wholesalers made hamburger meat out of leftover scraps. Ground beef was distributed locally, and was often made from cattle slaughtered locally. Today large slaughterhouses and grinders dominate the nationwide production of ground beef. A modern processing plant can produce 800,000 pounds of hamburger a day, meat that will be shipped throughout the United States. A single animal infected with E. coli can contaminate 32,000 pounds of that ground beef.

To make matters worse, the animals used to make about one-quarter of the nation's ground beef— worn-out dairy cattle—are the animals most likely to be diseased and riddled with antibiotic residues. The stresses of industrial milk production make them even more unhealthy than cattle in a large feedlot. Dairy cattle can live as long as forty years, but are often slaughtered at the age of four, when their milk output starts to decline. McDonald's relies heavily on dairy cattle for its hamburger supplies, since the animals are relatively inexpensive, yield low-fat meat, and enable the chain to boast that all its beef is raised in the United States. The days when hamburger meat was ground in the back of a butcher shop, out of scraps from one or two sides of beef, are long gone. Like the multiple sex partners that helped spread the AIDS epidemic, the huge admixture of animals in most American ground beef plants has played a crucial role in spreading E. coli. A single fast food hamburger now contains meat from dozens or even hundreds of different cattle.

The Clinton administration's efforts to implement a tough, science-based food inspection system received an enormous setback when the Republican Party gained control of Congress in November of 1994. Both the meatpacking industry and the fast food industry have been major financial supporters of the Republican Party's right wing. Speaker of the House Newt Gingrich's 'Contract With America,' stressing government deregulation and opposition to an increased minimum wage, fit perfectly with the legislative agenda of the large meatpackers and fast food chains. A study of campaign contributions between 1987 and 1996, conducted by the Center for Public Integrity, found that Gingrich received more money from the restaurant industry than any other congressman. Among the top 25 House recipients of restaurant industry funds, only four were Democrats. The meatpacking industry also directed most of its campaign contributions to conservative Republicans, providing strong support in the Senate to Mitch McConnell of Kentucky, Jesse Helms of South Carolina, and Orrin Hatch of Utah. Between 1987 and 1996, Phil. Gramm, a Republican from Texas, received more money from the meatpacking industry than any other U.S. senator. Gramm is a member of the Senate Agriculture Committee, and his wife, Wendy Lee, sits on the board of IBP.

The meatpacking industry's allies in Congress worked hard in the 1990s to thwart modernization of the nation's meat inspection system. A great deal of effort was spent denying the federal government any authority to recall contaminated meat or impose civil fines on firms that knowingly ship contaminated products. Under current law, the USDA cannot demand a recall. It can only consult with a company that has shipped bad meat and suggest that it withdraw the meat from interstate commerce. In extreme cases, the USDA can remove its inspectors from a slaughterhouse or processing plant, for all intents and purposes shutting down the facility. That step is rarely taken, however — and can be challenged by a meatpacker in federal court. In most cases, the USDA conducts negotiations with a meatpacking company over the timing and the scale of a proposed recall. The company has a strong economic interest in withdrawing as little meat as possible from the market (especially if the meat is difficult to trace) and in limiting publicity about the recall. And every day the USDA and the company spend discussing the subject is one more day in which Americans risk eating contaminated meat.

The Hudson Foods outbreak revealed many of the flaws in the current USDA policies on recall. Officials at Hudson Foods were informed late in July of 1997 that its frozen hamburger patties had infected Lee Harding with E. coli. Because Harding had saved the box, Hudson Foods knew the exact lot number and production code of the tainted meat. The company made no effort to warn the public or to recall the frozen patties for another three weeks, until the USDA found a second box of Hudson Foods patties contaminated with E. coli. On August 12 the company announced that it was *voluntarily* recalling 20,000 pounds of ground beef, an amount determined through negotiations with the USDA. The recall seemed surprisingly small, considering that the Hudson Foods plant in Columbus, Nebraska, could produce as much as 400,000 pounds of ground beef in a single shift — and that tainted patties had been manufactured, according to the product codes on their boxes, on at least three separate days in June. As food safety advocates and reporters began to question the size of the recall, it started to expand, reaching 40,000 pounds on August 13, 1.5 million pounds on August 15, and 25 million pounds on August 21. The recall eventually extended to 35 million pounds of ground beef, most of which had already been eaten.

The USDA had not only been forced to negotiate the Hudson Foods recall, it had to rely on company officials for information about how much meat needed to be recalled. Two of those officials suggested that just a few small lots of ground beef might have been contaminated. In reality, Hudson Foods had for months been using "rework" — ground beef left over from the previous day of production — as part of its routine processing supply. It had shipped hamburger meat potentially contaminated with the same strain of E. coli from at least May of 1997 until the third week of August, when the company voluntarily agreed to shut the plant. Brent Wolke, the manager of the Hudson Foods plant in Columbus, and Michael Gregory, the company director of customer relations and quality control, were indicted in December of 1998. Federal prosecutors claimed that the pair had deliberately misled USDA inspectors and had falsified company documents to minimize the scale of the recall. Both men were later found innocent.

Once a company has decided voluntarily to pull contaminated meat from the market, it is under no legal obligation to inform the public — or even state health officials — that a recall is taking place. During the Jack in the Box outbreak, health officials in Nevada did not learn from the company that contaminated hamburger patties had been shipped there; they got the news when people noticed trucks pulling up to Jack in the Box restaurants in Las Vegas and removing the meat. Once the investigators realized that tainted ground beef had reached Nevada, a number of cases of severe food poisoning that might otherwise have been wrongly diagnosed were linked to E. coli. In 1994, Wendy's tried to recall about 250,000 pounds of ground beef without officially notifying state health officials, the USDA, or the public. The meat had been shipped to Wendy's restaurants in Illinois, Michigan, Minnesota, Missouri, and Wisconsin. When news of the recall leaked, Wendy's issued a press release claiming that only 8,000 pounds was being withdrawn, because it "had not been fully tested." The press release failed to mention that some ground beef from the same lot had indeed been tested—and had tested positive for E. coli.

A subsequent investigation by Cox News Service reporters Elliot Jaspin and Scott Montgomery found that the USDA does not inform the public when contaminated meat is recalled from fast food restaurants. "We live in a very litigious society," Jacque Knight, a USDA spokesman explained; if every meat recall was publicly announced, companies would face problems from "everybody with a stomachache."

What's in the Meat?

Between 1996 and 1999, the USDA didn't tell the public about more than one-third of the Class I recalls, cases in which consumers faced a serious and potentially lethal threat. The USDA now informs the public about every Class I recall, but will not reveal exactly where contaminated meat is being sold (unless it is being distributed under a brand name at a retail store). State health officials have attacked the USDA policy, arguing that it makes outbreaks much more difficult to trace and puts victims of food poisoning at much greater risk. Someone infected with E. coli, unsure about what has caused his or her symptoms and unaware of a local outbreak, may take over-the-counter medications that make the illness much worse.

Both the USDA and the meatpacking industry argue that details about where a company has distributed its meat must not be revealed in order to protect the firm's "trade secrets." In February of 1999, when IBP recalled 10,000 pounds of ground beef laced with small pieces of glass, the company would disclose only that the meat had been shipped to stores in Florida, Indiana, Michigan, and Ohio. Neither IBP, nor the USDA, would provide the names of those stores. "It's very frustrating for us," an Indiana health official told a reporter, explaining why the beef containing broken glass could not easily be removed from supermarket shelves. "If they don't give [the information] to us, there's not much we can do."

In addition to letting meatpacking executives determine when to recall ground beef, how much needs to be recalled, and who should be told about it, for years the USDA allowed these companies to help write the agency's own press releases about the recalls. After the Hudson Foods outbreak, Secretary of Agriculture Dan Glickman ended the policy of submitting USDA recall announcements to meatpacking companies for prior approval. Two years later, however, USDA officials proposed that the agency stop issuing any press releases about meat recalls, leaving that task entirely to the meatpacking industry. That proposal was never adopted. In January of 2000, the USDA decided to announce every meat recall with an official press release; the recalls are also noted on the agency's Web site. The new policy, however, has not made it any easier to learn where contaminated meat has been sold. "Press releases will not identify the specific recipients of product," the USDA directive says, "unless the supplier chooses to release the information to the public."

A recent IBP press release, announcing the recall of more than a quarter of a million pounds of ground beef possibly tainted with E. coli, suggests that the industry's needs and those of consumers are not always the same. "In an abundance of caution, IBP is conducting this voluntary recall," the release said on June 23, 2000, implying that the move had been prompted mainly by a spirit of corporate generosity and good will. Hamburger meat potentially contaminated with the lethal pathogen had been shipped to wholesalers, distributors, and grocery stores in twenty-five states. At times, the press release reads more like an advertisement for IBP than an urgent health warning. It devotes more space to a description of the company's food safety program — with its "Triple Clean" slaughterhouse system and its "approved and accredited laboratories" — than to the details of how IBP managed to distribute nationwide enough suspect meat to make at least a million life-threatening hamburgers. Nowhere does the press release mention, for example, that the E. coli in IBP's ground beef was first detected not by one of the firm's own accredited laboratories, not by employees at the Geneseo, Illinois, IBP plant where the meat was produced, not by USDA inspectors — but by investigators from the Arkansas Department of Health, who found the pathogen in a package of IBP ground beef at Tiger Harry's restaurant in El Dorado, Arkansas. Thirty-six people who'd recently eaten at Tiger Harry's had been sickened by E. coli. Despite the discovery of tainted ground beef in the restaurant freezer, the Arkansas Department of Health could not conclusively link IBP meat to the El Dorado E. coli outbreak. "There have been no illnesses associated with this product," the company's press release brashly asserted. IBP's voluntary recall was issued about six weeks after the ground beef's production date. By then, almost all of the questionable meat had been eaten.

In the aftermath of the Jack in the Box outbreak, the Clinton administration backed legislation to provide the USDA with the authority to demand meat recalls and impose civil fines on meatpackers. Republicans in Congress failed to enact not only that bill, but also similar legislation introduced in 1996, 1997, 1998, and 1999. The inability of the USDA to seek monetary damages from the meatpacking industry is highly unusual, given the federal government's power to use fines as a means of regulatory enforcement in the airline, automobile, mining, steel, and toy industries. "We can fine circuses for mistreating elephants," Secretary of Agriculture Dan Glickman complained in 1997, "but we can't fine companies that violate food-safety standards."

Surrounded by parents whose children had died after eating hamburgers tainted with E. coli, President Clinton announced in July of 1996 that the USDA would finally adopt a science-based meat inspection system. Under the new regulations, every slaughterhouse and processing plant in the United States would by the end of the decade have to implement a government-approved HACCP plan and submit meat to the USDA for microbial testing. Clinton's announcement depicted the changes as the most sweeping reform of the federal government's food safety policies since the days of Theodore Roosevelt. The USDA plan, however, had been significantly watered down during negotiations with the meatpacking industry and Republican members of Congress. The new system would shift many food safety tasks to company employees. The records compiled by those employees — unlike the reports traditionally written by federal inspectors — would not be available to the public through the Freedom of Information Act. And meatpacking plants would not be required to test for E. coli, a pathogen whose discovery might lead to immediate condemnation of their meat. Instead, they could test for other bacteria as a broad measure of fecal contamination levels; the results of those tests would not have to be revealed to the government; and meat containing whatever organisms the tests found could still be sold to the public.

Many federal meat inspectors opposed the Clinton administration's new system, arguing that it greatly diminished their authority to detect and remove contaminated meat. Today the USDA's Food Safety and Inspection Service is demoralized and understaffed. In 1978, before the first known outbreak of E. coli, the USDA had 12,000 meat inspectors; now it has about 7,500. The federal inspectors I interviewed felt under enormous pressure from their USDA superiors not to slow down the line speeds at slaughterhouses. "A lot of us are feeling beaten down," one inspector told me. Job openings at the service are going unfilled for months. Federal inspectors warn that the new HACCP plans are only as good as the people running them—and that in the wrong hands HACCP stands for Have a Cup of Coffee and Pray. The Hudson Foods plant in Columbus, Nebraska, was operating under a HACCP plan in 1997 when it shipped 35 million pounds of potentially tainted meat.

"We give no serious validity to company-generated records," a longtime federal inspector told me. "There's a lot of falsification going on." His view was confirmed by other inspectors, and by former meatpacking workers who were in charge of quality control. According to Judy, a former "QC" at one of IBP's largest slaughterhouses, the HACCP plan at her plant was terrific on paper but much less impressive in real life: senior management cared much more about production than food safety. The quality control department was severely understaffed. A single QC had to keep an eye on two production lines simultaneously. "I had to check the sterilizer temperature, I had to check the Cryovac temperature, I had to look at packaging, I had to note the vats — did they have foreign objects in them or not? — I had to keep an eye on workers, so they wouldn't cheat," Judy said. "I was overwhelmed with work, it was just impossible to keep up with it all." She routinely falsified her checklist, as did the other QCs. The HACCP plan would have been "fantastic" if three people had been employed doing her job. There was no way that one person could get all the tasks on the list properly done.

Though the meatpacking industry has fought almost every federal effort to mandate food safety, it has also invested millions of dollars in new equipment to halt the spread of dangerous pathogens. IBP, for example, has installed expensive steam pasteurization cabinets at all of its beef slaughterhouses. Sides of beef enter the new contraption, which blow-dries them, bathes them in 220-degree steam for eight seconds, and then sprays them with cold water. When used properly, steam pasteurization cabinets can kill off most of the E. coli and reduce the amount of bacteria on the meat's surface by as much as 90 percent. But an IBP internal corporate memo from 1997 suggests that the company's large investment in such technologies has been motivated less by a genuine concern for the health and well-being of American consumers than by other considerations.

"We have been informed that carcasses in your plant are occasionally being delayed for extended periods of time on the USDA out-rail for final disposition (up to 6 hours)," the IBP memo began. It was sent by the company's vice president for quality control and food safety to the plant manager at the Lexington, Nebraska, slaughterhouse. It warned that the longer a carcass remains on the out-rail, the harder it is to clean. With every passing minute, bacteria grows more firmly attached and difficult to kill. "This delayed carcass deposition," the memo emphasized, "is of concern and is cause for extraordinary actions regarding such affected carcasses." When carcasses sat for half an hour on the out-rail, supervisors were instructed to find the cause for the delay. When carcasses sat for an hour, supervisors were told to spray the meat with a special acid wash. Carcasses that sat for longer than two hours, that were at highest risk for bacterial contamination, were not to be destroyed, or sent to rendering, or set aside for processing into precooked meats. "Such carcasses," IBP's top food safety executive advised, "are to be designated for outside (non-IBP) carcass sale." The dirtiest meat was to be shipped out and sold for public consumption — but not with an IBP label on it.

Instead of focusing on the primary causes of meat contamination—the feed being given to cattle, the overcrowding at feedlots, the poor sanitation at slaughterhouses, excessive line speeds, poorly trained workers, the lack of stringent government oversight—the meatpacking industry and the USDA are now advocating an exotic technological solution to the problem of food-borne pathogens. They want to irradiate the nation's meat. Irradiation is a form of bacterial birth control, pioneered in the 1960s by the U.S. Army and by NASA. When microorganisms are zapped with low levels of gamma rays or x-rays, they are not killed, but their DNA is disrupted, and they cannot reproduce. Irradiation has been used for years on some imported spices and domestic poultry. Most irradiating facilities have concrete walls that are six feet thick, employing cobalt 60 or cesium 137 (a waste product from nuclear weapons plants and nuclear power plants) to create highly charged, radioactive beams. A new technique, developed by the Titan Corporation, uses conventional electricity and an electronic accelerator instead of radioactive isotopes. Titan devised its SureBeam irradiation technology during the 1980s, while conducting research for the Star Wars antimissile program.

The American Medical Association and the World Health Organization have declared that irradiated foods are safe to eat. Widespread introduction of the process has thus far been impeded, however, by a reluctance among consumers to eat things that have been exposed to radiation. According to current USDA regulations, irradiated meat must be identified with a special label and with a 'radura' (the internationally recognized symbol of radiation). The Beef Industry Food Safety Council — whose members include the meatpacking and fast food giants — has asked the USDA to change its rules and make the labeling of irradiated meat completely voluntary. The meatpacking industry is also working hard to get rid of the word "irradiation," much preferring the phrase "cold pasteurization."

One slaughterhouse engineer that I interviewed—who has helped to invent some of the most sophisticated food safety equipment now being used—told me that from a purely scientific point of view, irradiation is safe and effective. But he is concerned about the introduction of highly complex electromagnetic and nuclear technology into slaughterhouses with a largely illiterate, non-English-speaking workforce. "These are not the type of people you want working on that level of equipment," he says. He also worries that the widespread use of irradiation might encourage meatpackers "to speed up the kill floor and spray shit everywhere." Steven Bjerklie, the former editor of *Meat & Poultry*, opposes irradiation on similar grounds. He thinks it will reduce pressure on the meatpacking industry to make fundamental and necessary changes in their production methods, allowing unsanitary practices to continue. "I don't want to be served irradiated feces along with my meat," Bjerklie says.

For years some of the most questionable ground beef in the United States was purchased by the USDA— and then distributed to school cafeterias throughout the country. Throughout the 1980s and 1990s, the USDA chose meat suppliers for its National School Lunch Program on the basis of the lowest price, without imposing additional food safety requirements. The cheapest ground beef was not only the most likely to be contaminated with pathogens, but also the most likely to contain pieces of spinal cord, bone, and gristle left behind by Automated Meat Recovery Systems (contraptions that squeeze the last shreds of meat off bones). A 1983 investigation by NBC News said that the Cattle King Packing Company—at the time, the USDA's largest supplier of ground beef for school lunches and a supplier to Wendy's—routinely processed cattle that were already dead before arriving at its plant, hid diseased cattle from inspectors, and mixed rotten meat that had been returned by customers into packages of hamburger meat. Cattle King's facilities were infested with rats and cockroaches. Rudy "Butch" Stanko, the owner of the company, was later tried and convicted for selling tainted meat to the federal government, He had been convicted just two years earlier on similar charges. That earlier felony conviction had not prevented him from supplying one-quarter of the ground beef served in the USDA school lunch program.

More recently, an eleven-year-old boy became seriously ill in April of 1998 after eating a hamburger at his elementary school in Danielsville, Georgia. Tests of the ground beef, which had been processed by the Bauer Meat Company, confirmed the presence of E. coli. Bauer Meat's processing plant in Ocala, Florida, was so filthy that on August 12, 1998, the USDA withdrew its inspectors, a highly unusual move. Frank Bauer, the company's owner, committed suicide the next day. The USDA later declared Bauer's meat products "unfit for human consumption," ordering that roughly 6 million pounds be detained. Nearly a third of the meat had already been shipped to school districts in North Carolina and Georgia, U.S. military bases, and prisons. Around the same time, a dozen children in Finley, Washington, were sickened by E. coli. Eleven of them had eaten undercooked beef tacos at their school cafeteria; the twelfth, a two-year-old, was most likely infected by one of the other children. The company that had supplied the USDA with the taco meat—Northern States Beef, a subsidiary of ConAgra—had in the previous 18 months been cited for 171 "critical" food safety violations at its facilities. A critical violation is one likely to cause serious contamination and to harm consumers. Northern States Beef was also linked to a 1994 outbreak of E. coli in Nebraska that sickened 18 people. Nevertheless, the USDA continued to do business with the ConAgra subsidiary, buying about 20 million pounds of its meat for use in American schools.

In the summer and fall of 1999, a ground beef plant in Dallas, Texas, owned by Supreme Beef Processors failed a series of USDA tests for Salmonella. The tests showed that as much as 47 percent of the company's ground beef contained Salmonella—a proportion five times higher than what USDA regulations allow. Every year in the United States food tainted with Salmonella causes about 1.4 million illnesses and 500 deaths. Moreover, high levels of Salmonella in ground beef indicate high levels of fecal contamination. Despite the alarming test results, the USDA continued to purchase thousands of tons of meat from Supreme Beef for distribution in schools. Indeed, Supreme Beef Processors was one of the nation's largest suppliers to the school meals program, annually providing as much as 45 percent of its ground beef. On November 30, 1999, the USDA finally took action, suspending purchases from Supreme Beef and removing inspectors from the company's plant, effectively shutting it down.

Supreme Beef responded the next day by suing the USDA in federal court, claiming that Salmonella was a natural organism, not an adulterant. With backing from the National Meat Association, Supreme Beef challenged the legality of the

USDA's science-based testing system and contended that the government had no right to remove inspectors from the plant. A. Joe Fish, a federal judge in Texas, heard Supreme Beef's arguments and immediately ordered USDA inspectors back into the plant, pending final resolution of the lawsuit. The plant shutdown — the first ever attempted under the USDA's new science-based system — lasted less than one day. A few weeks later, USDA inspectors detected E. coli in a sample of meat from the Supreme Beef plant, and the company voluntarily recalled 180,000 pounds of ground beef that had been shipped to eight states. Nevertheless, just six weeks after that recall, the USDA resumed its purchases from Supreme Beef, once again allowing the company to supply ground beef for the nation's schools.

On May 25, 2000, Judge Fish issued a decision in the Supreme Beef case, ruling that the presence of high levels of Salmonella in the plant's ground beef was not proof that conditions there were "unsanitary." Fish endorsed one of Supreme Beef's central arguments: a ground beef processor should not be held responsible for the bacterial levels of meat that could easily have been tainted with Salmonella at a slaughterhouse. The ruling cast doubt on the USDA's ability to withdraw inspectors from a plant where tests revealed excessive levels of fecal contamination. Although Supreme Beef portrayed itself in the case as an innocent victim of forces beyond its control, much of the beef used at the plant had come from its own slaughterhouse in Ladonia, Texas. That slaughterhouse had repeatedly failed USDA tests for Salmonella.

Not long after the ruling, Supreme Beef failed another Salmonella test. The USDA moved to terminate its contract with the company and announced tough new rules for processors hoping to supply ground beef to the school lunch program. The rules sought to impose the same sort of food safety requirements that fast food chains demand from their suppliers. Beginning with the 2000-2001 school year, ground beef intended for distribution to schools would be tested for pathogens; meat that failed the tests would be rejected; and "downers"— cattle too old or too sick to walk into a slaughterhouse — could no longer be processed into the ground beef that the USDA buys for children. The meatpacking industry immediately opposed the new rules.

SPRAWL CITY

"BUT WHAT ABOUT DETROIT?"

In the fall of 1999, environmentalists had gathered in San Francisco to strategize against sprawl, and Richard Schneider was trying to add something to the agenda. A leader in the Bay Area Chapter of the Sierra Club, Schneider rose to complain that all the plans to combat sprawl were neglecting a key cause of sprawl—population growth.

But his concerns were dismissed with the cry of "What about Detroit?"

That basically stopped any more discussion of population growth at the meeting. Indeed, simply saying, "What about Detroit?" has been one of the most effective tactics around the country in keeping the population factor off the anti-sprawl agenda.

"What about Detroit?" refers to the fact that the Detroit Urbanized Area's population actually declined by 7% from 1970 to 1990, yet its land area grew by 28%. Indeed, what about Pittsburgh, Milwaukee, Cleveland, New York City, Buffalo, and Dayton? Each of these Urbanized Areas, and several others, also lost population between 1970 and 1990. And all but one had sprawl—lots of sprawl, in several cases.

Obviously, based on those examples, sprawl can be caused by something other than just population growth. In Detroit, 100% of the sprawl was caused by non-population factors. The entire cause of Detroit's sprawl was a complex of factors that led to an increase in urban land consumption per person (in other words, that led to declining density).

The fact that Detroit's sprawl is unrelated to population growth sometimes is taken to mean that the sprawl of other cities is also unrelated to population growth. But it may simply mean that population growth is not the only factor in sprawl.

To understand what the Detroit model can teach us about sprawl, we must ask: Do Urbanized Areas with population growth experience sprawl in significantly higher amounts than Urbanized Areas with population decline? The answer from Census Bureau data on the 100 largest Urbanized Areas is a clear "yes." On average, the more population growth of an Urbanized Area, the worse the sprawl. While Detroit with its population decline sprawled by 28%, the 89 cities which *had* population growth experienced an average sprawl of 75%.

Those 89 cities with population growth sprawled by nearly three times as much as the 11 cities with population decline, which averaged 26% sprawl.

Our literature search found that many anti-sprawl advocates and planners fail to make that comparison. Thus, they tend to draw the wrong conclusion about what cities like Detroit teach us.

They are correct in pointing to Detroit as an example that shows us that even when there is no population growth, there still tends to be a substantial "background rate" of sprawl brought about by many factors.

Census Bureau data on the 100 largest U.S. Urbanized Areas show that about half the sprawl in the country is related to land use and consumption factors that increase the amount of urban land per resident. In a few Urbanized Areas like Detroit those factors are related to all of the sprawl. Such facts are stark reminders that any anti-sprawl campaign that ignores land use and consumption factors is doomed to failure—because stabilizing population is not by itself enough to stop sprawl.

But Detroit does not prove that population growth is irrelevant to sprawl. Rather, it provides a comparison that proves the opposite. Yes, Detroit had extensive sprawl even though it lost population. If, however, Detroit's population had actually grown at the rate of the average Urbanized Area in America, the sprawl likely would have been far worse—based on the experience of the rest of the country. In comparison with the experience of other cities, Detroit had minor sprawl.

The citizens and decision-makers of Detroit need to hear about the population growth aspect of sprawl even though population growth may not be occurring in their area. Such education not only will help them understand why their sprawl problems are not as bad as the average city but also may keep them from becoming careless about adopting city policies designed to increase their population.

So, what about Detroit? Well, because it had no population growth, it apparently had a lot less sprawl than most other cities.

"DON'T PANIC, BUT..."

CIA EXPERT SAYS ENVIRONMENTAL TERRORISTS THREATEN ALL HUMANITY

Ann Arbor News (J. Tilove)

In a tabloid the headline might be: "MAD SCIENTISTS PLOT END OF MANKIND! Small But Dedicated Band Driven by Love of Planet."

It's a strange story. According to the CIA's former chief of counter-terrorism there are a few "highly educated scientists" who, in the name of saving the Earth from the destructive habits of the people who inhabit it, are working to develop a virus that could wipe out humankind while leaving the rest of the animal kingdom undisturbed.

"It may seem ultimately self-defeating, but there are small organized clandestine cells working on the development of technologies to diminish or even eliminate the race of man from Earth."

So says Vincent M. Cannistraro, a calm and amiable man who retired from the CIA last fall and now analyzes terrorism as a senior fellow at the National Strategy Information Center, which describes itself as the only conservative think tank specializing in intelligence.

Cannistraro's concern focuses on the extreme fringe of the environmental movement. He fears its adherents may eventually act on the belief that people are the enemy of the planet and must be stopped before it's too late.

Radical environmentalists do not believe there are those among them preparing to actually wipe out humanity, and suspect such talk may be a government effort to smear their movement. Still, some will allow that as a purely theoretical notion, Cannistraro's nightmare isn't a half-bad idea.

"The human race is a failed species that isn't going to be around for very long," says Robert F. Mueller of Staunton, Va., who says he would be among those plotting man's demise if he were a biologist and not a geologist.

Mueller is not alone in wanting to see an America reduced to 10 million hunter-gatherers, sort of the way it was before white men arrived. He is active in Earth First!, a group dedicated to saving the planet from what they view as mankind's ruinous growth and meddling. The FBI has investigated the involvement of people associated with Earth First! in "monkeywrenching"—such tactics as driving spikes into trees in order to shatter the saw blades of timbermen.

The philosophy at work here is something called *deep ecology*. Among its basic principles is species equality, which holds that all forms of life—human beings, mosquitoes, dandelions and malaria protozoa—have the same intrinsic value.

Another basic principle is that there are too many humans on the planet. But it is a long way from advocating population control to plotting the destruction of the species.

"Every radical movement has a more radical fringe." Says Doug Bandow, who has examined 'eco-terrorism' for the conservative Heritage foundation. But Bandow, a fellow with the Cato Institute, says it's a "big jump" from wanting a world with fewer people to doing something violent about it. "It's hard to imagine any of these people would countenance mass murder."

Rik Scarce, the author of *Eco-Warriors: Understanding the Radical Environmental Movement*, says the most extreme anti-human talk "is really hyperbole" designed to provoke debate and thought.

Hyperbole or not, there are those who, at least anonymously, talk about saving the world by killing people.

About a year ago, according to John Lilburn, an Earth First!er in Montana, the organization's contact people throughout the country received an unsigned flyer suggesting the time had come to eliminate the human race. Lilburn says he has heard nothing of it since.

The *Earth First! Journal* is a rich repository of provocative misanthropy. An excerpt from an anonymous letter of Nov. 1, 1984:

> The only way to stop all the destruction of our home is to decrease the birth rate or increase the death rate.... It does no good to kill a few selected folks. That is a retail operation. What we need is a wholesale operation.... The simple expedient: biological warfare! Think about it. It fits. It's species-specific. Bacteria are, and viruses tend to be, deadly to only one species. Only a very few of human pathogens are shared by other partners on our planet. Biological warfare will have no impact in other creatures, big or small, if we design it carefully.

In the May 1987 journal, a pseudonymous Miss Ann Thropy suggests that "as radical environmentalists, we can see AIDS not as a problem, but a necessary solution." (Miss Ann Thropy was identified by others in the movement as Christopher Manes, the author of *Green Rage: Radical Environmentalism and the Unmaking of Civilization*. Manes was not available for an interview, according to his agent, unless it was about his book.)

The most recent journal includes a contribution from the Voluntary Human Extinction Movement (VHEMT, pronounced "vehement") in Portland, Ore., but its only weapon is wit—its slogan is "Live Long and Die out!"—and its purpose is to encourage people not to have children.

More seriously, Earth First! co-founder Dave Foreman in his book, *Confessions of an Eco-warrior*, declares, "We humans have become a disease—the Humanpox." Foreman considers himself part of a "new race of Neanderthals, humans who love the wild, whose primary loyalty is to Earth and not to Homo sapiens," who will act as "antibodies to the Humanpox."

"Antibodies need no justification," Foreman writes. "Their job is merely to fight and destroy that which would destroy the greater body of which they are a part, for which they form the warrior society."

Foreman is due to go on trial next month on federal charges of conspiracy to blow up power lines to nuclear plants in three western states. Lilburn's house has been raided by the FBI. Earth First!ers consider it likely that their phones are tapped and that a comrade may be an FBI infiltrator.

Last year, when a bomb exploded in the car of Judi Bari, an Earth First! organizer in northern California, she and her companion found themselves the authorities' top suspects. No charges were filed, but Bari, who says it is ludicrous to think she accidentally blew herself up, worries about Cannistraro's conspiracy talk.

"They could use these alleged mad scientists off in the hills to come and try to kill me," she says.

Cannistraro denies any nefarious intent. He says he is an avid, if non-violent, environmentalist.

He dropped his bombshell last month without fanfare, almost as an afterthought, at a inaugural gathering of a group of experts he calls the Counterterrorism Study Group. At the end of a paper detailing all the many terrorist threats on the globe, from the IRA to the PLO, Cannistraro quickly mentioned these scientists bent on destroying mankind as "potentially the most lethal of all terrorist movements."

Cannistraro, who has done stints with the Defense Department and National Security Council, acknowledges its surface implausibility. "It sounds exactly like the movie version."

"We don't want to make too much of it," he says. "I think what we've identified is a potential source of terrorism rather than a current source. I can't give you any judgment about how serious and how extensive it is. I suspect it's very small and very confidential, but that there are a few people thinking like this and seeking wherewithal to pursue their vision."

The FBI is obliged to say "no comment," but seems unaware of any such diabolical plot and unable to fathom it.

After all, Special Agent Barbara Madden wonders, "What would the Earth be for if man is not here?"

DEFENDING THE EARTH

DAVE FOREMAN (1991)

Like everything else, I think that we have to defend the Earth in a lot of different ways. I am not telling people to do only one thing, to use only one tactic or approach. In one sense, I don't care how people choose to defend the Earth—whether they write letters to the editor, recycle newspapers, canvass for an environmental candidate, blockade nuclear power plants with a few thousand other people, or spike trees and sabotage bulldozers alone in wild areas.

I do care, however, that people get off their butts in front of the TV set and do something. You have got to take responsibility for your life and the world. You have got to do something to pay your rent for the privilege of inhabiting this beautiful, blue-green, living Earth. If more people would simply get off their butts and do something, we would have a far better chance of survival and defending the Earth and its many species.

However, I don't think that the goals and strategies that we choose are all equally valuable or effective. Besides getting off our butts, we have got to think hard and figure out what goals and strategies best defend the Earth. I certainly have more questions than answers about this, but a few things seem clear to me. For one thing, I think the moderate and so-called pragmatic approach is limited and frequently counter-productive.

I would be the last one to say that electoral politics, court challenges, and lobbying for good legislation have no place in the tactics of our movement. I think such tactics can be effective and should not be rejected out of out of hand. As I said before, I used to work at The Wilderness Society as their lobbying coordinator in Washington, D.C. I was also the New Mexico Chair of Conservationists for Carter in 1976. Even though Jimmy Carter's public lands policies led to the formation of Earth First!, he did some good things while in office. That can't be denied. I have also spent many hours negotiating with the U.S. Forest Service and taking part in the public hearings that have been a part of their planning process. Out of this experience, however, I have become convinced that these tactics, by themselves, are simply not effective or practical enough to defend the existing roadless areas that are in such danger today.

At a minimum you would think that the public lands conservation movement would aim, as one of its most important goals, at keeping industrial "civilization" out of the few wild places that remain. Yet, the mainstream movement has become so loyal a courtier in the dominant industrial order that it cannot even effectively defend this limited goal. You can see the pattern of their current strategy as early as 1956, when conservationists accepted a compromise on the Colorado River Storage Act which cancelled a huge dam on the Green and Yampa Rivers in Dinosaur National Monument by agreeing to one on the Colorado River at Glen Canyon. Today the conservation movement's strategy is to bargain away huge portions of the wild world in order to protect a dwindling core of "untouchable" wilderness areas. This gets us nowhere.

Sure, the mainstream conservation movement's efforts at electoral politics, lobbying, and court battles slow the encroachment process down, but they do not ultimately halt it, let alone reverse it. Let's face it, our representative democracy has broken down. Our government primarily represents the big money boys and stacks the deck against reform movements. Playing only by the system's rules limits you. That is why the reformist conservation movement doesn't even think it is realistic to try to defend all of the remaining wilderness in the United States, let alone expand wilderness areas through ecological restoration. Trying to fit in, to not seem radical or extreme, to always seek compromise obviously keeps you pretty damn manageable. It is no wonder that the mainstream conservation movement has been outmaneuvered over the last fifteen years because of its timid vision and tactics.

For example, in the early summer of 1977, the U.S. Forest Service began an 18-month-long inventory and evaluation of the remaining roadless and undeveloped areas in the national forests which are eligible by law for congressional consideration as protected wilderness preserves. All in all, there were some 80 million acres in the national forests retaining a significant degree of natural diversity and wildness. Along with the national parks and monuments, national wildlife refuges, existing wilderness areas and some state lands, these roadless areas represent the remaining wilderness in the United States. These are the places that hold North America together, that contain the genetic information of life, that represent natural sanity in a whirlwind of industrial madness.

Now you need to remember that from its very beginning the U.S. Forest Service has viewed the national forests as an arena for industrial logging, grazing, mineral and energy development, road-building, and motorized recreation. It should not come as a surprise, then, that in January of 1979 the Forest Service announced the following results of its wilderness assessment: out of the 80 million remaining acres of undeveloped lands in the national forests, only 15 million acres were recommended for protection against logging, road building, and other "developments."

In the big-tree state of Oregon, for example, only 370,000 acres were proposed for wilderness protection out of the remaining 4.5 million acres of roadless, uncut forest lands. Of the areas nationally slated for protection, most areas were too high, too dry, too cold, too steep to offer much in the way of "resources" to the loggers, miners, and grazers. Those roadless areas with critical old-growth forest values were allocated for the sawmill. Important grizzly bear habitat in the northern Rockies was tossed to the oil industry and the loggers. Off-road-vehicle fanatics and the landed gentry of the livestock industry won out in the Southwest and Great Basin.

Unfortunately, the response of the conservation movement was not to call for the preservation of the last remaining wilderness lands in their entirety or to use every legitimate tactic at their disposal to protect these lands and resist government and corporate encroachment on wild public lands. Instead, the conservation movement sought to be realistic and compromise, trading most of the wilderness away, in exchange for a marginal increase in the amount of proposed acreage to be legally protected. Because of the very limited nature of their goals, these tactics were ultimately effective in achieving this objective, though even this was a big struggle. But it should be remembered that this achievement was hardly a significant victory for wilderness.

Furthermore, the Forest Service has since come up with a plan that will effectively block any future conventional efforts at expanding the acreage of protected wilderness in the national forests. Generally only roadless areas are considered for wilderness protection within the national forests. During the 1980's, the Forest Service developed and began implementing a 15-year plan to get rid of the remaining roadless areas by building over 75,000 miles of new road within the national forests. This immense road network (enough to encircle the planet three times) will cost the American taxpayer over three billion dollars to provide large timber corporations access to a mere 500 million dollars worth of timber. More importantly, it will cause a considerable decline in the biological integrity of this country's remaining wilderness areas and destroy these areas' ability to support a huge variety of plant and animal species.

It would appear that the U.S. Forest Service folks consciously and deliberately sat down and asked themselves, "How can we keep from being plagued by conservationists and their damned wilderness proposals?" Their plans seem to be working out quite well. The Forest Service today is systematically destroying unprotected roadless areas through a massive road-building campaign. The result is that the effectiveness of conventional political lobbying and electoral work to protect wild lands is evaporating and in half a decade the saw, the bulldozer, and the drill will devastate most of what is now wild but legally unprotected. The battle for wilderness by conventional means will soon be over. Perhaps 3% of the United States will be more or less protected and it will be open season on the rest.

Ironically, the conventional political tactics that Linda calls our strongest, most pragmatic, most effective weapons for making reforms in the here and now cannot even protect what little natural landscape we have left in this country, a very minimal goal from my perspective. This is why I believe that a truly effective, wilderness preservation strategy needs to include a large dose of *uncompromising, nonviolent direct action and resistance*. I think electoral politics, legislation, those mainstream approaches can still play a crucial part, but nonviolent direct action also has to be an important means of defending the wilderness. I say let's approach the problem by looking for the weaknesses in the system, the places where we can throw the wooden shoe in the gears of the machinery, or where we can put the handcuffs on an agency and take power away from them. We need a campaign of resistance whenever and wherever the dying industrial empire tries to invade the remaining wilderness. We need to delay, resist, and thwart the current system using *all* the tools available to us. Sure, this includes filing appeals and lawsuits as well as encouraging legislation that ties the hands of corporations and agencies like the U.S. Forest Service.

However, to truly get the job done, we will also need to demonstrate, engage in mass nonviolent civil disobedience, and, frankly, illegally monkeywrench and sabotage wilderness-destroying projects. It is now time for women and men, individually, in small groups, and in large public movements to develop a widely-dispersed, strategic movement of nonviolent resistance against wilderness destruction all across the land.

I believe that such a campaign of resistance can be effective in stopping timber cutting, road-building, overgrazing, oil and gas exploration, mining, dam building, powerline construction, off-road-vehicle use, trapping, ski area development and other forms of destruction of the wilderness as well as cancerous suburban sprawl. I believe such campaigns can be effective because such campaigns hit the rape-the-land artists where they live—in their pocket books.

Many of the projects that are encroaching on roadless wilderness areas are economically marginal. The profit margins on such activities are real but they are very vulnerable to cost overruns. It is very costly for the Forest Service, timber companies, oil companies, mining companies and others to scratch out the "resources" in these last wild areas. A broad resistance strategy can make it even more costly, perhaps prohibitively expensive. The rising cost of repairs, the hassle, the delay, the down-time caused by "on-the-ground" wilderness resistance activities as well as the loss of public support and the rise of consumer boycotts, strikes, and other forms of community resistance could protect millions of acres of wilderness far more effectively than any congressional act.

Such "extreme" and "uncompromising" actions are not pointlessly "utopian." They are strategically sound. They are pragmatic. Such tactics do, however, require a greater degree of personal involvement and risk than working within normal channels. It takes courage to put your body between the machine and the wilderness, to stand before the chainsaw or the bulldozer or the FBI. More of us need to stand before the mad machine as Valerie Wade did in climbing 80 feet high into an ancient Douglas Fir to keep it from being cut down, or as Howie Wolke did in pulling up survey stakes along a proposed gas exploration road in prime elk habitat.

Sure, both of these Earth First! activists put their lives in jeopardy and both went to jail. Yet I am reminded of the famous story about Henry David Thoreau being sent to jail for refusing to pay his poll tax to protest the U.S. war against Mexico. When Ralph Waldo Emerson came to bail him out, Emerson called through an open window and said, "Henry, what are you doing in there?" Thoreau quietly replied, "Ralph, what are you doing out there?" We need that kind of courage and spirit in our movement today.

Conventional efforts at reform are certainly safer and they are, in some ways, better rewarded. By staying within normal channels you can usually avoid serious political repression. You are also validated rather than vilified. The effect of this validation, however, is to dampen the effectiveness of a movement. I suspect that it is basic human nature to want to be accepted by the social milieu in which you find yourself. It hurts to be dismissed by the official arbiters of opinion as "nuts," "terrorists," "wackos," or "extremists." I think much of the desire to be "moderate" and "pragmatic" grows out of the understandable desire to gain credibility or legitimacy with the media and the political and economic leaders currently running our society.

The American political system is very effective at co-opting and moderating dissidents by giving them attention and then encouraging them to be "reasonable" so their ideas will be taken "more seriously." Appearing on the evening news, testifying before congressional hearings, or getting a job with some government agency are just some of the methods used by the establishment to entice one to share key assumptions of the dominant worldview and to enter the negotiating room to compromise with madmen who are destroying everything pure and beautiful. Take a look at much of the mainstream conservation movement today. The political vision of most of these reformers includes, at a minimum, a global population of 10 to 12 billion human beings, nation-states, multinational corporations, the private automobile, and people in business suits on every continent. Such a limited vision is not going to spark or lead a movement for the creation of a wilderness-loving and egalitarian society.

Indeed, such a limited vision has little or no future. Modern society is a driverless hot rod without brakes going 90 miles an hour down a dead-end alley with a brick wall at the end. We do not live in a stable society. We're in the most volatile society that has ever existed on this planet. I think the shit is going to hit the fan in my lifetime; that the greed, the insanity, the domination of nature and human beings, this whole madness is going to come to a head. I think that terrible things will happen in the not-so-distant future that will make the current social and ecological crisis seem like the good old days. To seek only "realistic" reforms, to use only conventional means of social change at this point in time, really means giving up the fight. Reforms that are realistic within the current distribution of institutional power simply cannot take us from here to where we need to be.

In many ways, Earth First! represents a fundamentalist revival within the wilderness/wildlife preservation movement, a return to basics and a reaction against reformist co-optation and compromise. Over the last several decades, as the conservation movement has grown in prominence, Aldo Leopold's now famous "Land Ethic" has been replaced with "political pragmatism." It has dramatically limited its political vision. It now views the entire question of wilderness preservation and species diversity as purely a question of pragmatically balancing competing special interest groups and working out compromises between giant economic interests and public recreation enthusiasts. Earth First! takes the stand that wilderness preservation is an ethical question, a moral question. It can't be simply reduced to the conventional political currency of self-interest, or even the more humanistic concern for human sustainability.

As Ed Abbey frequently said, human beings have a right to be here, but not everywhere, not all at once, not all in the same place. Human society has stepped beyond the bounds; we are destroying the very processes of life. Wilderness is more than puny little backpacking parks in areas with little or no "development" potential. Wilderness areas are the arena for natural evolution, and must be large enough so natural forces can have free rein. There must be vast areas in every bioregion that are off-limits to human habitation and economic activity. These areas must simply be left alone to carry on the important work of spontaneous natural evolution.

This is a radical vision to be sure, one which calls many of our social assumptions into question. Yet, any reasonable policy, given the level of wilderness destruction to date, requires much more than the containment of the current encroachments of "civilization" onto existing public wilderness reserves. It is our job, as defenders of the Earth, to reclaim much of the now asphalted land, the barren fields, ripped forests and silent mountains. One of the centerpieces of every ecology group's platform should be to protect or create a big core wilderness preserve in every region. Other wilderness preserves, both large and small, should also be established and protected throughout each region as well as wilderness corridors to allow for the free flow of genetic material between them and the wilderness preserves in other bioregions.

Of course, we will need human management and intervention to help nature restore a suitably large area in each region, at least a million acres, to wildness. If certain native animals have been extirpated, they must be reintroduced. If possible, grizzly, wolf, cougar, jaguar, bison, elk, moose, otter, wolverine all must find a home in our public lands again. If salmon streams must be repaired, clearcuts rehabilitated, prairies replanted, roads removed—then that becomes one of the key tasks of ecological restoration.

This is a truly revolutionary ecological vision. Any genuinely effective movement to respond to the ecology crisis will require us to mount widespread nonviolent resistance campaigns, including strategic monkeywrenching, to protect as much wilderness as possible from destruction. It will also require us to challenge the government, the corporations, and the people as a whole with an ethical vision of Big Wilderness. Yet, frankly, even this is not enough. The radical ecology movement also needs to do the important work of organizing the new ecological society that will emerge out of the ashes of the old industrial empire.

Some of this work may not even seem radical or revolutionary at first glance, but it is. For example, I think the people who are developing cheap and simple low-tech gizmos like solar cookers are doing some of the best work on the planet. These people are saving trees in the Third World by decreasing the demand for wood as fuel. I think their work is profoundly revolutionary because it is also saying that big is not necessarily better, that we don't need big corporate / government techno-solutions, and that people can solve some of their problems on their own. We owe much to the alternative technology movement which has been experimenting over many years with composting toilets, organic gardens, handicrafts, recycling, solar collectors, wind generators, and solar cookers.

Yet these people, like me, are just one piece of the puzzle. If high-tech techno-fixes aren't going to get to the root of the problem, low-tech techno-fixes aren't going to do the job by themselves either. We must also directly challenge current social institutions on a political and economic level. For instance, we need to make sure that the so-called developed world stops treating Third World people and land as mere resources to be exploited.

We in the United States clearly have a responsibility to resist the efforts of multinational corporations and First World governments to force Third World societies to produce export cash crops for consumption in the First World instead of producing subsistence crops for their own people. This is not just a matter of elemental social justice, it is a key requirement in overcoming the global ecological crisis. Plantation style, single-crop, export agriculture is far more damaging to the natural world than small-scale, diversified, subsistence agriculture for local and regional consumption. This is but one example of how we need to fundamentally reorganize how we make a life on the portion of the planet that we do inhabit.

Besides the emergence of Earth First!, I think the most encouraging development in North America of late has been the *bioregional movement*. Bioregionalism is fundamentally concerned with reinhabiting the land in decentralized, egalitarian, and ecologically sound ways. It is a concept far removed from the way of life currently common in almost all suburbs, cities, and farms on this continent. Reinhabitation stresses creatively adapting human communities to the natural region they inhabit instead of single-mindedly adapting the place to an exploitative human society. It means self-consciously and respectfully becoming part of the food chain, the water cycle, the environment of a particular natural region, instead of imposing an exclusively human-centered, global industrial order on the same area.

So while I work very hard to try to prevent the mad thrashing of the dying industrial Storm Trooper from destroying everything beautiful on this earth, I'm glad there are people like Murray in the greens, in the bioregional movement, in projects like the Green City Program in San Francisco, who are trying to create the new society that will come after us. That's their job. It's as important as my job is. My job is more limited. I'm trying to protect as much as possible from the dollar, from destruction in the last days of industrial society. I think Murray and others, in turn, are laying out the concepts and working out the practicalities of a sustainable ecological society that can come after it.

In closing, let me just say, I very much agree with Murray that this society is rotten to its core. I think it's so fundamentally destructive that it's ultimately unreformable in any conventional sense. I simply can't get from here to where I want to be through the strategic approach outlined by Linda. Indeed, it may not take us far enough to even ensure the continued existence of most of the Earth's species, including human beings. A genuinely radical vision and strategy may not succeed either, but I am convinced that it is the best shot that we have got.

Second Thoughts of an Eco-Warrior

As an activist, my chosen task is to argue the case of non-human nature. I resolutely stand with John Muir on the side of the bears in the war industrial society has declared against the Earth. Yet this does not mean that I hate human beings. It does not follow that I am unmoved by human suffering, economic injustice, imperialism, or abuses of human rights. While it is true that I don't identify myself as a leftist, for all the reasons I have mentioned, I do agree with much of the libertarian, democratic left on a large number of social concerns. I certainly recognize the need for increasing the connections between the left's social concerns and my heartfelt and longtime ecological concerns.

I have learned much from Murray Bookchin's criticisms and I acknowledge failings on my part in the past. I have often left unstated, and sometimes unexamined, the social components of problems like overpopulation, poverty, and famine while trying to discuss their biological nature. I have also not always made it clear that I abhor the human misery involved in such problems. I have been insensitive, albeit unintentionally, and for that I humbly apologize.

Let me give just two examples. In 1986, Professor Bill Devall, co-author of *Deep Ecology*, interviewed me for the Australian magazine *Simple Living*. In that interview I made two statements I now regret, one on famine in Ethiopia and the other on Latin

American immigration to the United States. In the first example, I said, as part of a much longer discussion of famine and overpopulation, that "the worst thing we could do in Ethiopia is to give aid—the best thing would be to just let nature seek its own balance, to let the people there just starve... the alternative is that you go in and save these half-dead children who never will live a whole life. Their development will be stunted. And what's going to happen in ten years' time is that twice as many people will suffer and die."

On the question of immigration, I commented that "letting the USA be an overflow valve for problems in Latin America is not solving a thing. It's just putting more pressure on the resources we have in the USA."

While I think it is unfortunate that these two passing comments have been used to deny the validity of everything I have to say and to paint me as a racist and fascist clone of David Duke, I do agree that these comments were both insensitive and simplistic. Taken out of the context of my larger concerns and writings, I can see how those remarks suggest a callous Fortress America chauvinism on my part. However, in the first case, I did not clearly say what I really meant and, in the second, I now reject some of what I did mean at the time.

Indeed, after listening carefully to the criticism I've received, I have rethought and modified my opinion on illegal immigration. While I still believe that massive and unlimited immigration into any country is a serious problem, I do not support beefing up the Border Patrol and the other agencies that try to keep Latin Americans out of this country. I do not think that this is a realistic or ethical response to the underlying problem.

As I said earlier, I have long been in deep sympathy with the sanctuary movement. I have also always opposed the Reagan-Bush effort to support the home-grown *caballero juntas* to the south and to overthrow progressive reform governments like the Sandinistas in Nicaragua. Indeed, I have long supported the U.S. solidarity movements attempt to aid and abet reform and revolutionary movements in Central America. I think we need to disband the CIA and prohibit other U.S. government agencies from covert or overt military intervention in the Third World. I am convinced that there will be no land reform, no democracy, and no end to repression and death squads without the Latin American middle class, rural *campesinos,* and urban intellectuals uniting in disgust and effecting true reform through revolutions such as that which toppled Somoza in Nicaragua.

Nonetheless, I still have honest questions about whether, by sticking to the liberal dogma about unlimited immigration, we might actually be postponing revolutions or effective democratic reform movements in Latin America. This is one of the potential costs of having our nation serve as an overflow valve for Latin America's unruly, angry, economically dispossessed, and politically active citizens, to say nothing of the ecological impact. While Ed Abbey's proposal to send every illegal refugee that is caught home with a rifle and a thousand rounds of ammunition may be considered flippant and impractical, its underlying spirit has some merit that liberals and far too many leftists ignore.

So while I apologize for how my views on illegal immigration may have been stated in the *Simple Living* interview, I cannot rid myself of my nagging questions about unlimited immigration. Despite all my sympathies and affections for the oppressed people of Mexico and Central America, despite my distaste for artificial national borders, despite my antipathy for the Border Patrol, I cannot convince myself that unlimited immigration from Latin America, or from anywhere else for that matter, will fundamentally solve problems either here or there. A little troll in the back of my brain keeps whispering nagging questions. Who is really being helped by unlimited immigration? Is it sustainable? Does it actually exacerbate social and ecological problems here and in Latin America? What are effective and humane solutions for the real and underlying problems in this tragic situation?

Similarly, I have serious doubts and nagging questions about conventional "humanitarian" foreign aid responses to the increasing problem of famine in the Third World. That is what I was trying to get at in my comments on famine in Ethiopia. In my oft-quoted remark about famine in Ethiopia, however, I failed to clearly make this point. Indeed, I implied through my sloppy, off-the-cuff remark that famine was *purely* a biological question of too many people and too few resources, completely unrelated to social organization, economic exploitation, or international relations. I also implied that the best possible social response was for us to do nothing, offer no assistance of any kind, and to just let the hungry starve. I very much regret the way I phrased these comments. Standing by themselves, out of context, they sound truly cold hearted.

The point I was trying to make, and which I think is made when the rest of the interview is taken into account, is that oftentimes a feel-good humanitarian response from the United States or Western Europe may not have the result we hope and may even have the opposite result. The problem of famine has a number of important causes which can and should be addressed by insightful, creative actions on the part of social movements in the United States and by the rest of the First World. There is undoubtedly a positive role that we can play even though the answers are not often clear to me and the problem is very complex and entrenched.

I still have honest questions about the much-admired relief effort during the Ethiopian famine of the mid-1980s. I think these questions desperately need to be explored. Did shipping food to Ethiopia actually alleviate suffering? Does such aid, at its best, ever do more than stave off abject starvation for a short time, while leaving the underlying problems untouched? What is the lot of those poor wretches kept alive by the food shipments in 1985-86? Did most survive with their bodies and minds intact or are they permanently disabled or handicapped? If the latter, will these unfortunates be an impossible burden preventing Ethiopia from dealing with its problems? These are terrible and hard questions I know, but I think we have to at least consider them given that another famine lurks on the horizon of that increasingly desert-like land.

We need to carefully analyze the on-the-ground results of this very sincere—and sometimes heroic—relief effort. From what I have read, it appears that very little was accomplished and that the Ethiopian military junta used the food supplies as a political weapon to favor those who supported the central government and to punish those who supported the rebels in the civil war. Is it implausible then to argue that the principal beneficiaries of the Ethiopian relief effort (besides the military junta) were the contributors to it in the West, who derived liberal, do-gooder satisfaction without having to confront the massive inequities between the First and Third Worlds or question the economic imperialism of transnational corporations and financial institutions like the World Bank or change their own excessively consumptive lifestyles?

I think it can be persuasively argued that such uncritical, one-shot relief efforts actually inhibit a well thought out, long-term aid program to help native agriculturalists get back on their feet with tools and crops suitable for their particular ecological conditions and social needs. Indeed, it has to be asked, and I admit it is a terrible question, if such last-minute relief efforts actually allow a human population stretched beyond the land's carrying capacity to eke out existence for a few more years and, in the process, cause even greater deterioration of the land's capacity to support humans and other species. There is that little troll in the back of my brain again. Do such liberal, humanitarian relief efforts do more harm than good in terms of both human beings and the land?

Certainly, a growing number of radical social activists are aware of many of the problems I raise here. Unfortunately, however, many leftists (and rightists) still posit simplistic reasons for the tragedy in places like Ethiopia due to their desire to make the strongest possible case for the particular institutional demon highlighted by their particular social ideology. They also frequently discount the ecological or biological factors that often underlie problems of famine.

Please, let's be realistic and admit that there are several different and interrelated demons at work fostering famine conditions and that overpopulation is one of them and has to be vigorously addressed. While I agree that the population question can be approached in narrow, racist, and fascistic ways, I strenuously reject the idea that any and all ecologically-grounded concerns about human overpopulation are racist and fascist. Is it racist and fascist, for example, to propose making birth control methods and devices, including the French abortion pill and sterilization, freely available to any woman or man in the world who desires them?

I am unwilling to silence the heretical troll in my brain in order to be certified "politically correct" by conventional leftists. Yet I do see the problem of overpopulation more clearly now than I did back in 1986. I have come to understand through Murray that those of us who worry about the results of the population bomb need to make our case as carefully as possible. We need to acknowledge the many social, cultural, and economic causes of population growth as well as the biological, and we need to campaign for economic justice and an end to maldistribution of land, food, and other necessities of life as well as for the humane and long-term reduction of the human population. That's my position on population. If anyone has a bone to pick with it, fine, but please criticize it and not some five-year-old, off-the-cuff, out-of-context statement that does not accurately represent my considered opinion.

Unfortunately, I doubt that these careful clarifications and apologies will satisfy all of my critics. There seems to be a dogmatic, blind rage among many of my critics that renders them incapable of entering into a reasoned dialogue with me to explore our various positions and political differences together. Murray is an appreciated exception. Sadly, those who shout me down at speaking engagements, loudly chanting "racist" or "fascist" at me, or who make the same vocal charges over and over again in the press, have made a straw man out of me that resembles their fantasies and fears far more than it resembles me or my positions. Even more sadly, I believe these angry and uninformed hecklers are playing into the hands of FBI provocateurs. The FBI has clearly targeted me and hopes to shut me up—not just through harassment with a phony felony indictment but by using their talents at movement disruption (honed during the COINTELPRO era against the Black Panthers, Martin Luther King, Jr., and the American Indian Movement) to exploit this straw man and label me a racist.

I have frequently been written off completely by people whose sole knowledge of my political perspective is gleaned from these two short quotes of mine taken out of context from the vast amount I have said or written. I have also routinely been misquoted. And, perhaps most maddening of all, I have been smeared by "guilt by association." Unfortunately, it is commonly assumed by many of my critics that, because I admired Ed Abbey and was a longtime friend of his, I agree with every one of his opinions on every single topic that he ever chose to talk or write about. I have also been held responsible for every statement made in Earth First! while I was its editor. Personally, I would like to meet any editor of a movement publication who has always agreed with every word of every article that he or she has ever agreed to publish. This kind of guilt by association is simply absurd.

I am aware, however, that my personal brand of deep ecology politics does represent a real heresy from some of the orthodoxies embedded within most liberal and left opinion today. The little troll in the back of my mind frequently troubles me, too. Why shouldn't the difficult questions it raises trouble others? Perhaps one of my biggest differences with Murray is that I am significantly more pessimistic about the future than he. I am not sure we really have enough time to turn things around before most of the world is overtaken by famine, genocide, war, totalitarianism, plagues, and economic collapse. When I look into the future, it is rare that I see pretty scenes of protected wilderness, prosperous farms, soft-technology abundance, and smiling children. I hope for this. I work for it, but it usually seems like a long shot to me.

I value my heretical little troll, however, because if we do have any real hope to turn things around it will depend on squarely facing our predicament. There is no realistic hope until enough of us have the courage to correctly identify the root problems of the ecological crisis. These root problems most certainly include social, political, and economic aspects but they also include ecological and biological realities as well. We need to rethink and rebuild our social ethics and politics along ecological lines. That's where my little troll comes in handy. Facing up to the ecological roots of our predicament means, in large part, asking difficult and troubling questions about the limited carrying capacity of the Earth's biosphere.

This line of questioning is hard for people who have embraced the cornucopian myths of modern industrialism and the unending historic march of material progress. It is particularly hard for liberals and leftists, many of whom believe that the only way to successfully overcome poverty and injustice is to exponentially expand the available economic surplus until we create a super-abundant, post-scarcity society where there is little need to fight over the size of everybody's slice of the economic pie because the pie itself is so huge. The very concept of ecological scarcity and carrying capacity limits calls this whole "utopian" project into question.

Interestingly, the basic ecological notion of carrying capacity is accepted when applied to cattle or elephants by all except the most beef-witted rancher or the most starry-eyed animal lover. Yet, we are loath to admit that we humans are animals, too, and that carrying capacity thus applies to us in some very real ways. My repeated statements about the reality of ecological scarcity may be the most heretical thing I have to say. It may indeed be the great divide between my view and that of most of my critics on the left (and the right). Any such suggestion is immediately called Malthusian and dismissed as long discredited, pseudo-scientific hog wash at best, and racist and imperialist propaganda at worst.

Thomas Malthus is, of course, an easy target for dismissal. His dire warnings of economic collapse and global famine in the early 10th century did not materialize as predicted. His argument that human population naturally grows at an exponential rate while food production only grows arithmetically was also simplistic. To his credit, however, Malthus was right about his general argument that human societies exist within an ecological context that presents real natural limits that human beings must either adapt to or ultimately suffer some form of social and ecological crash. The nature of our ecosystem provides many opportunities for the human species but it also presents human societies with serious biological constraints that are not of our own choosing and which can only temporarily be ignored.

Unfortunately, to deny this ecological reality leaves completely unchallenged the very social trends that are pushing our society to catastrophically overshoot the Earth's limited carrying capacity. Such ostrich-like ignorance will lead most likely, along with other social forces, to a hellish future fraught everywhere with famine, plagues, economic collapse, devastating war, genocide, and totalitarianism. To the extent that the social justice movement ignores the whole question of our overshooting the Earth's carrying capacity, it inadvertently contributes to the likelihood of this future for everyone.

Indeed, Malthus might be considered an optimist by the standards of the late 20th century, for he only focused on the constraints that limited food supplies posed for human population growth and economic development. As ecologically-minded political scientist William Ophuls points out,

> Instead of simple Malthusian overpopulation and famine, we must now also worry about shortages of the vast array of energy and mineral resources necessary to keep the engines of industrial production running, about pollution and other limits of tolerance in natural systems, about such physical constraints as the laws of thermodynamics, about complex problems of planning and administration, and about a host of other factors Malthus never dreamed of.

I strongly recommend that every environmental and social justice activist read and grapple with William Catton's *Overshoot: The Ecological Basis of Revolutionary Change*. In his book, Catton provides the best and most informed discussion yet published on the relationship of carrying capacity to human societies. He restates Malthus' dictum in ecological terms as "The biotic potential of any species exceeds the carrying capacity of its habitat." Human beings are included here just as are elephants or lemmings. This book might well change how you think about the world. I agree with Native American scholar Vine Deloria, Jr. who, on the back cover of Catton's book, describes it as "one of the most important books I have read in my lifetime."

By itself, however, Catton's instrumental evaluation of how to live successfully within the carrying capacity limits of the biosphere is not sufficient. There are several possible ways of life that do not, on a global level, overshoot the Earth's carrying capacity. Some of these ways are moral and benefit the entire community and others do not. A barely sustainable "resource-fascism" is more than a speculative possibility for the future. It may well be the path of least resistance. We thus need a strong ethical foundation in order to choose what kind of ecologically sustainable society we should work toward. We need, ultimately, to get clear on more than just the ecological carrying capacity constraints on our behavior. We also need to explore the ethical limitations we should adopt, in Aldo Leopold's words, on our "freedom of action in the struggle for existence."

The libertarian left has some very good things to say about the ethical limitations on our behavior when it comes to the social relationships between members of the human community. Humanist social ethics foster a vision of society that is equitable, democratic, and respectful to all members of the human community. I myself subscribe to much of this ethical vision—as far as it goes. However, it is very limited. Unfortunately, the vast majority of the left, even the environmentally oriented left, has next to nothing to say about environmental ethics beyond an ultimately anthropocentric commitment to provide a sustainable, non-toxic, and aesthetically pleasing environment for all human beings.

To me, this leftist anthropocentrism represents a huge failure of moral imagination and will ultimately lead, if successful, to a world where Big Wilderness and a significant degree of biodiversity are lost forever. Everything inside me rebels against this callous, morally impoverished view. I believe a grizzly bear snuffling along Pelican Creek in Yellowstone National Park with her two cubs has just as much natural right to her life as any human has to his or hers. All living things have intrinsic value, inherent worth. Their value is not determined by what they will rug up on the cash register of the GNP, nor by whether or not they are aesthetically pleasing to human beings. They just are. They have traveled that same three-and-a-half-billion-year evolutionary course we have. They live for themselves, for their own sakes, regardless of any real or imagined value to human civilization. They should never be considered mere means to our ends for they are, like us, also ends in themselves.

If I were to suggest only one book for people to read on environmental ethics, it would be Aldo Leopold's *A Sand County Almanac*. Aldo Leopold perhaps thought harder about nature and our relationship to it than anyone else in 20th century America. Forest supervisor, game manager, pioneer ecologist, and university professor, Leopold was always on the cutting edge of conservation. His posthumously published *Almanac* ranks among the finest discussions of environmental ethics ever written. In fact, for my money, it is the most important, the loveliest, the wisest book ever penned. He has made thousands of people into heretics and frankly the times call for a generous dose of radical ecological heresy.

I believe that the intrinsic value of living things demands direct moral consideration in how we organize our societies. I reject anthropocentrism completely and argue that besides our social commitments we also need to honor direct moral duties to the larger ecological community to which we belong. We have a moral obligation to preserve wilderness and biodiversity, to develop a respectful and symbiotic relationship with that portion of the biosphere that we do inhabit, and to cause no unnecessary harm to non-human life. Furthermore, I believe that these moral obligations frequently supersede the self-interests of humanity. Human well-being is vitally important to me, but it is not the ultimate ethical value. I agree with Aldo Leopold that ultimately "a thing is right when it tends to enhance the integrity, stability, and beauty of the biotic community." For social ethics to be ecologically grounded they must become consistent with this larger ecological moral imperative. That is why I am for Earth first.

Such an ecological sensibility is surely radical but it is far from new. It has been, in one form or another, a common feature of the philosophical outlook of most primal peoples throughout history. It has, however, just begun to gain significant ground among citizens of the industrialized nations. For many, it is a shocking departure from what they were brought up to believe. Right now, the whole field of environmental ethics is exploding as more and more people try to flesh out an almost intuitive non-anthropocentric orientation into a well-reasoned, usable ethic to guide human interaction with the rest of the natural world.

I dub my tentative attempts *biocentrism*, others like Warwick Fox describe their approach as *ecocentrism*. Murray Bookchin describes his approach as "the ethics of complementarity." There is, of course, much overlap between these various non-anthropocentric perspectives. There are also some serious disagreements about what constitutes a morally appropriate relationship between humanity and the rest of the natural world that deserve further discussion. Indeed, there are significant differences even among those who call themselves biocentrics. Philosopher Paul Taylor, for example, has written an elaborate treatise on the biocentric outlook on nature and, while I appreciate his effort, I take exception to much of his approach. Biocentrism is hardly a monolithic perspective. Clearly, the search for Earth wisdom has just begun for most of us.

Arne Naess has noted that there are three fairly distinct tendencies within the deep, long-range, ecology movement: the "naturals," the "spirituals," and the "socials." I am by temperament a "natural." My primary concern is conservation biology and the defense of the wild. However, politically, I have been drawn over time into an increasing appreciation of the "socials" who focus primarily on fundamentally reconstructing human society along socially and ecologically non-hierarchical lines. Such an approach is surely needed if we are to resolve the overarching ecological crisis which is shaking our planet. On my best days, I seek a creative synthesis of all of these approaches into an integrated and coherent perspective which can guide our movement even as radical ecology activists continue to specialize in their particular areas of interest. That is why I am proud to have taken part in this dialogue with Murray Bookchin, one of the pioneers of social ecology.

My fear, however, is that this synthesis will not ultimately take firm root and that one of these three tendencies will simply become so dominant that the vital contributions of the other perspectives will be minimized or lost. This concerns me because I believe it would weaken the larger movement even more than our current fractured condition, where all of the limited approaches are at least alive and well. I thus think that the most responsible stance for anyone in any of these tendencies is to assume that their approach is both valid and limited.

We need to be open to the criticisms of others in order to sharpen our own perspectives. We also need to be willing to sharpen the perspective of other wings of the movement through adding our own constructive criticisms to the ongoing dialogue and debate. And we must be tolerant and respectful of individuals with whom we may differ in this discussion. How can we create a human society that is tolerant and respectful of individuals if we cannot create a movement in which we are tolerant and respectful of individuals with whom we disagree?

My biggest worry about the limited perspective of a socially-oriented ecology is that it can all too easily become overwhelmingly social and insufficiently ecological. I see this tendency among many social ecologists when they argue that we should "work to reharmonize humanity with nature by reharmonizing the social relationships between human and human." This strategic axiom appears to emphasize the traditional social concerns of the libertarian left over direct day-to-day struggles to defend wilderness, foster an ecological sensibility, or reconstruct our society's interaction with the rest of the natural world here and now. The view here seems to be that, once the social relationships between human beings are all resolved, an ecological sensibility will automatically flower, and appropriate ecological changes in our society's relationship to nature will be made.

Certainly, not all social ecologists are under this illusion that our ecological problems can all wait to be resolved until after a libertarian, democratic social revolution is successful. Many, if not most, clearly realize that we don't have this luxury even if we want it. To his credit, Murray has explicitly and repeatedly expressed the need for organizing around both social and ecological questions in the here and now. Yet the way this social ecology slogan is formulated and frequently repeated by a variety of social ecology groups does suggest a subtle tendency among many socially-oriented ecologists to devalue the validity of the important (though admittedly limited) activities of the "naturals." Indeed, I suspect it represents a holdover from the anthropocentric perspective that is still so common among leftists and social justice activists.

Ironically, such a tendency can even be seen today within Earth First!, once a stronghold of non-anthropocentric "naturals." I have become increasingly uncomfortable with the influx of new people into Earth First! who seem more adapted to a traditional social and economic justice worldview than to a radical ecological one. These new activists seem to be drawn to the organization primarily because of its media exposure and our reputation for confrontational, kick-ass direct action. Frankly, I worry that rather than reflecting a process of creative synthesis, this evolution represents a subtle but increasing disregard for the valid insights of the early "naturals" who originally built Earth First!.

Mind you, these differences between the "old" and "new guard" in Earth First! are, for the most part, honest differences between decent people who respect one another. Furthermore, I feel that much vital and important work remains to be done by the most recent incarnation of Earth First!. Yet, given my perspective as an uncompromising, wilderness-loving "natural," I feel the need to work within a new organization explicitly committed to biocentrism and doggedly focused on ecological wilderness identification, preservation, and restoration.

For this reason, I've left Earth First! and begun to explore with others the possibilities of starting a new organization along these lines. Hopefully, this new organization will complement the work of the many and varied groups in the conservation movement as well as provide a continuing clear voice for the "naturals" within the larger radical ecology movement as we all labor together to find a common, integrated perspective that overcomes the limitations of each radical ecological tendency while maintaining the vital insights of each.

«««—»»»

THE REWILDING INSTITUTE (rewilding.org)

Current scientific research and theory, and conservation experience tell us that:

- To do serious conservation in North America, we must do conservation on the scale of North America.
- Furthermore, history, policy analysis, and conservation experience tell us that:
- To be effective in conservation work of all kinds, we must be guided by vision, strategy, and hope.
- Based on these understandings, The Rewilding Institute Mission is:
- To develop and promote the ideas and strategies to advance continental-scale conservation in North America, particularly the need for large carnivores and a permeable landscape for their movement, and to offer a bold, scientifically credible, practically achievable, and hopeful vision for the future of wild Nature and human civilization in North America.

To carry out this mission, The Rewilding Institute (TRI) has three broad goals:

1) To effectively integrate conservation biology and wildlands and wildlife conservation.
2) To provide a long-term, hopeful vision for conservation in North America.
3) To create a North American Wildlands Network Vision and a strategy to implement it.

Rewilding Institute projects are guided by these goals.

The Rewilding Institute first serves wild Nature. But to serve wild Nature, we serve North America's wonderful grassroots conservation community. We do not compete with other conservation groups, and we strive to share credit. Our projects are geared to provide that support. Rewilding Institute Projects are summarized below; more information is available or forthcoming on other pages on this website.

Education and Outreach

The Rewilding Institute works to bring the science of conservation biology into both the big-picture and the day-to-day work of the wildlands and wildlife conservation movement, whether grassroots, professional, or agency. Through public presentations, educational materials, and a website, The Rewilding Institute explains the need for rewilding on a continental-scale. Executive Director Dave Foreman gives dozens of presentations to a variety of audiences every year.

Fellows Dave Parsons, Bob Howard, and Don Waller give PowerPoint presentations on The Rewilding Institute and the science behind it. Fellow Oscar Moctezuma is available to give presentations in the U.S. and Canada on jaguar protection efforts in northern Mexico. Other Fellows give many presentations on different aspects of continental-scale rewilding. The Rewilding Institute website lists upcoming talks and appearances by Rewilding Institute Fellows and is a source for scheduling future appearances. Go to the Fellows Page to schedule talks.

The Rewilding Institute is producing educational materials on the need for rewilding: the recovery of top predators and their wild habitats. Dave Foreman's book, Rewilding North America, covers rewilding and continental-scale conservation in detail and is available on TRI's website. (Foreman is currently at work on two new books—The Myth(s) of the Environmental Movement and The War on Nature.) Papers by Fellows and others on the ecological concepts behind rewilding can be downloaded from TRI's website. Books by Fellows are available for purchase through the website.

EcoWild

The Rewilding Institute is developing guidelines for using ecological criteria to select and design Wilderness Areas and other protected areas so that they better protect wild habitat and wildlife movement permeability. TRI has also drafted priority reforms for public land management that would help rewilding and continental-scale conservation. Conservation Fellows are developing strategies on how to get conservation groups to embrace these approaches and how to implement them on the ground. Having such a program already developed will give conservationists a jump-start in working with a conservation-friendly administration, congress, or parliament when they are finally elected. Rewilding Institute Fellows met this summer in Albuquerque to form a working group on this project.

Rewilding Institute Fellows will soon meet with other land scientists, conservationists, and agency managers to discuss the issue of appropriate ecological protection and restoration in Wilderness Areas. How do we return wounded landscapes in protected areas to robust good health? How do we restore extirpated species, particularly large carnivores, beavers, and prairie dogs? How do we restore natural fire and flooding? How should invasive exotic species be fought in Wilderness? Out of this workshop and working group, The Rewilding Institute will prepare guidelines and other materials.

North America Jaguar

Recent fossils and current field research show that jaguars are not only tropical and subtropical cats, but lived in temperate habitats throughout much of what is now the United States. Today's northernmost breeding population of jaguars (about 120 total animals) is in Sonora, Mexico, little more than 100 miles south of the Arizona border. This population is the source for the jaguars that have been photographed in Arizona and New Mexico recently. Led by Mexican biologists and the Mexican conservation group Naturalia, the Northern Jaguar Coalition is raising money to buy ranches in the core of the jaguar range so the big cats will be safe from poaching. One 15,000-acre ranch has been purchased and is under management by Naturalia. Additional ranches for purchase have been identified. If this jaguar population can be protected, it will expand, and more young jaguars will head off to good, safe habitat in the southwestern United States, which will then have a breeding population. The Rewilding Institute is helping to raise funds from zoos and other sources to buy more ranches and manage them.

The Denver Zookeepers association just collected $3000 for the project and sent it to The Rewilding Institute for transfer to the ranch purchase fund; we are working with Margo McKnight of the Wildlands Project to raise additional money from zoos. Dave Foreman and other Fellows helped with a major fundraising event in Santa Fe this fall for the Northern Jaguar Project. The Rewilding Institute is spreading the word about this remarkable opportunity by helping to bring Naturalia's director and Rewilding Institute Fellow, Oscar Moctezuma, to the United States for public talks, such as one this fall in Albuquerque.

Wildlife Recovery and Protection Visions

For the last several decades, conservation groups, agencies, and academic biologists have worked to restore wild species to their native habitat. The return of the gray wolf to Yellowstone National Park is perhaps the best-known success. However, these recovery efforts have been scattered, piecemeal, and largely uncoordinated. They have, in short, lacked a vision. Rewilding Institute Fellows and other experts are developing comprehensive visions for the recovery and protection of highly interactive species in North America. Wolf and mountain lion (cougar) visions have been prepared and appear on TRI's website. Other visions are in development for species ranging from jaguar to prairie dog to grizzly bear. The Rewilding Institute, its Fellows, and cooperating groups work to promote these visions as guidelines for full recovery. At the Carnivores 2004 Conference in Santa Fe this fall, wolf protection groups in the greater Southwest endorsed TRI's Wolf Vision. Plans are being made to further promote it and use it as the overarching wolf recovery strategy in temperate North America. See the Wildlife Vision Page.

MegaLinkages

MegaLinkages are the centerpiece of a continental conservation vision. The Rewilding Institute and the Wildlands Project are working together with other groups to design and implement a North American Wildlands Network made up of core wild areas and wildlife linkages. The Rewilding Institute emphasizes the big picture of the continental network along Four Continental MegaLinkages (Pacific, Spine of the Continent, Atlantic, and Arctic-Boreal), while the Wildlands Project works on the design and implementation of detailed regional wildlands networks, which will make up the continental network. TRI will convene meetings at appropriate zoos to draft MegaLinkage maps. The MegaLinkages will identify large core wild complexes and areas of landscape permeability connecting them that are suitable for recovered populations of large carnivores.

Barrier Modification

Highways, other barriers, and fracture zones for wildlife movement fragment even the wildest regions of North America. The Rewilding Institute encourages the identification of the most serious barriers and building wildlife overpasses or underpasses across them. Recent efforts have shown how this is possible. For example: The South Coast Wildlands Project worked with other conservation groups, government agencies, and Caltrans (the California transportation department) to identify priority barriers for mountain lions in southern California. Caltrans has removed an on-off ramp on the Riverside Freeway and converted it to a mountain lion underpass to link up habitat cut by the freeway. The Cascade Partnership in Washington has raised tens of millions of dollars to buy tens of thousands of acres in Snoqualmie Pass along I-90 to restore linkages for wolverine, lynx, and other species.

In the summer of 2003, the New Mexico Department of Fish and Game, other state and federal agencies, The Rewilding Institute, other conservationists, and the NM State Highway Department held a workshop to identify the most troublesome barriers to wildlife on the state highway system and to set priorities for modifications. An active local citizens group with participation by The Rewilding Institute, the Wildlands Project, and state and federal agencies is now working to include wildlife undercrossings or overpasses on reconstruction of I-40 in Tijeras Canyon east of Albuquerque. Rewilding Institute Fellow and Executive Director of the Southern Rockies Ecosystem Project, Monique DiGiorgio, has organized workshops throughout Colorado with the highway department and others to identify highway barriers and solutions. Similar programs are underway in California, Washington, Oregon, and other states.

earth liberation front .com

updated 08:30 June 17th, 2004

- NEWS
- LIBRARY
- PRISONERS
- DIARY OF ACTIONS
- MEDIA INFO
- ABOUT THE ELF

Get your **NEWS** via email!

Now receive important email news items and updates from earthliberationfront.com and animalliberation.net.

Subscribe to Frontline-News mailing list

Resource Links:

animalliberation.net

activist computer security

directaction.info

Press Release: ELF Torches Lumberyard in West Jordan, $1.5 Million in Damages

June 17, 2004 - The ELF Press Office has been informed of a claim of responsibility in a fire in West Jordan, Utah on June 14th, 2004. The fire targeted Stock Building Supply and caused $1.5 million in damages.

Press Release: ELF Likely Responsible For Development Fires in Snohomish Washington; Causes $1 Million in Damages

April 22, 2004 - Through media reports, the ELF Press Office has been made aware of Earth Liberation Front actions against urban sprawl April 20th and 21st. Although the ELF Press Office has received no communications about these actions from the persons responsible, a note found at the site of one of the fires was signed "ELF" and reportedly contained statements condemning suburban developments. In the absence of other information, this note does indicate a claim of responsibility for the fires and fire attempts by ELF activists.

Article: Rethinking the ELF and the War on Terror

On June 1, 2001, fires were set at the Schoppert Logging Company in Eagle Creek, Oregon. Schoppert was due to begin logging on US Forest Service land. One whole logging truck, valued $50,000 was destroyed and two others damaged. This was terrorism, the FBI's Joint Terrorism Task Force said. If convicted, defendants could receive up to $1 million in fines or up to 80 years in prison, more than twelve times the average sentence for rape, a class one felony. (from infoshop.org)

Press Release: ELF Damages Construction Equipment

ELF In the News:

Teen gets prison sentence for environmental sabotage
04/13/04

Exclusive interview with Caltech's 'accused terrorist'
04/13/04

Extreme environmentalists target vehicles, buildings
04/11/04

Calif. Student Charged in Anti-SUV Arson & Denied Bail
03/18/04

more

Frequently Asked Questions about the E.L.F.

"The ELF realizes the profit motive caused and reinforced by the capitalist society is destroying all life on this planet. The only way, at this point in time, to stop that continued destruction of life is to by any means necessary take the profit motive out of killing."

> **at Charlottesville Site**
> February 9, 2004 - The Earth Liberation Front has taken credit for its second known action of 2004 with an attack on equipment at a building site in Charlottesville, Virginia.
>
> **Special Report: Underground Direct Actions Totals for 2003**
> January 13, 2004 - There were 75 illegal direct actions taken in North America in 2003, an increase of 8% over claimed illegal direct actions taken in 2002. Animal liberation actions comprised just under 50%, or 37 actions, while 38 actions were committed for a combination of earth liberation, anti-GMO, anti-SUV, anti-development, anti-war and other reasons.
>
> **Press Release: Three Plead Guilty to ELF Actions - Richmond, Virginia**
> January 12, 2004 - The ELF Press Office has learned that three self-identified members of the Earth Liberation Front have plead guilty to charges of conspiracy to destroy by fire vehicles and property used in interstate commerce as a result of ELF-claimed actions that took place in and around Richmond, Virginia in 2002. Adam Blackwell, Aaron Linas, and John Wade plead guilty to the charges separately on December 18, January 7, and January 12th.

EARTH LIBERATION FRONT (ELF)
Meet the E.L.F.

The Earth Liberation Front is an international underground movement consisting of autonomous groups of people who carry out direct action according to the E.L.F. guidelines. Since 1997, E.L.F. cells have carried out dozens of actions resulting in close to $100 million in damages.

Modeled after the Animal Liberation Front, the E.L.F. is structured in such a way as to maximize effectiveness. By operating in cells (small groups that consist of one to several people), the security of group members is maintained. Each cell is anonymous not only to the public but also to one another. This decentralized structure helps keep activists out of jail and free to continue conducting actions.

As the E.L.F. structure is non-hierarchical, individuals involved control their own activities. There is no a centralized organization or leadership tying the anonymous cells together. Likewise, there is no official "membership". Individuals who choose to do actions under the banner of the E.L.F are driven only by their personal conscience or decisions taken by their cell while adhering to the stated guidelines.

Who are the people carrying out these activities? Because involved individuals are anonymous, they could be anyone from any community. Parents, teachers, church volunteers, your neighbor, or even your partner could be involved. The exploitation and destruction of the environment affects all of us—some people enough to take direct action in defense of the earth.

Any direct action to halt the destruction of the environment and adhering to the strict nonviolence guidelines, listed below, can be considered an E.L.F. action. Economic sabotage and property destruction fall within these guidelines.

Earth Liberation Front Guidelines:

- To inflict economic damage on those profiting from the destruction and exploitation of the natural environment.
- To reveal and educate the public on the atrocities committed against the earth and all species that populate it.
- To take all necessary precautions against harming any animal, human and non-human.

There is no way to contact the E.L.F. in your area. It is up to each committed person to take responsibility for stopping the exploitation of the natural world. No longer can it be assumed that someone else is going to do it. If not you, who? If not now, when?

Philosophy of the ELF

1) The current system of production and consumption is unsustainable. It is destroying the Earth, and hence it must end.

2) The sooner it ends, the better.

3) The system is too entrenched, and cannot be reformed in time.

4) Therefore, direct action against the system is morally necessary.

5) Direct action is described as attacks against the physical and financial infrastructure of the system. These attacks do not aim to harm any living being, and hence are non-violent.

6) Every direct action inflicts financial damage on the system, and thus hastens its end.

7) Every action, no matter how small, has an effect.

8) By defending the Earth, the ELF is defending the dignity of nature, and ultimately the dignity of humanity.

Earth Alive

ELF Communiqué:

At 5:30AM on January 1, 2003, the Earth Liberation Front attacked several SUV's at Bob Ferrando Ford Lincoln Mercury in Erie, Pennsylvania. At least four vehicles were entirely destroyed and several others sustained heavy damage, costing an estimated $90,000.

Despite decades of popular environmental activism, the mainstream environmental movement, which began arguably in the early 1960s, has failed in its attempts to bring about the protection needed to stop the destruction of life on this planet. In many ways, it has served only to accelerate this destruction. Its occasional "victories", reforms or small concessions, have fostered hope in a means of social change that has proven unable to produce tangible protection of life, time after time.

By focusing its energy on temporary "solutions", they have altogether ignored the roots of the problem at hand. Western civilization, with its throw away conveniences, its status symbols, and its unfathomable hoards of financial wealth, is unsustainable, and comes at a price. Its pathological decadence, fueled by brutality and oceans of bloodshed, is quickly devouring all life and undermining the very life support systems we all need to survive. The quality of our air, water, and soil continues to decrease as more and more life forms on the planet suffer and die as a result. We are in the midst of a global environmental crisis that adversely affects and directly threatens every human, every animal, every plant, and every other life form on the face of the Earth.

There is absolutely no excuse for any one of us, out of greed, to knowingly allow this to continue. There is a direct relationship between our irresponsible over-consumption and lust for luxury products, and the poverty and destruction of other people and the natural world. By refusing to acknowledge this simple fact, supporting this paradigm with our excessive lifestyles, and failing to offer direct resistance, we make ourselves accomplices in the greatest crime ever committed.

Time is running out—change must come, or eventually all will be lost. A belief in state sanctioned legal means of social change is a sign of faith in the legal system of that same state. We have absolutely no faith in the legal system of the state when it comes to protecting life, as it has repeatedly shown itself to care far more for the protection of commerce and profits than for its people and the natural environment. Clearly, the state itself causes and profits from many of the various atrocities against life that we must struggle against. To place faith in that same state as though it will act in the interests of justice and life is utter foolishness and a grave mistake.

Therefore, the E.L.F. will continue to fight to remove the profit motive from the killing of the natural environment, and to draw public attention to that which is deliberately concealed from them by the forces that control our lives and destroy our home.

We urge our sisters and brothers—let us strive to become the revolutionary force we've always spoken of being, and begin to take the control of our lives out of the hands of those who would destroy us.

NO COMPROMISE.

Happy New Year Bob Ferrando!

Defending the Earth

Earth Liberation Front (ELF) — Summary of Major Actions (through mid-2004)

1992: Founded in Brighton, England, by Earth First! members who refused to abandon criminal acts as a tactic when others wished to "mainstream" Earth First!

1994: Earth First! leader Judi Bari recommends that Earth First! mainstream itself in the United States, leaving criminal acts other than unlawful protests to Earth Liberation Front. Published in Earth First Journal.

October 1996: First confirmed actions by ELF in the US. Attacks have occurred more or less continuously since then. Total damages exceed $100 million.

2000
Jan. 23; Bloomington, Ind. Fire destroys a luxury home under construction at the Sterling Woods Development. Investigators find a cryptic message spray-painted in black on a sign near the house: "No Sprawl - ELF." An ELF statement obtained by the Environment News Service says, "The house was targeted because the sprawling development it is located in is in the Lake Monroe Watershed. This is the drinking water supply for the town of Bloomington, Indiana and the surrounding area. It is already being jeopardized by existing development and roads." Damages: $200,000.

March 24; Near Minneapolis, MN. Extensive damage to construction equipment along new highway route. Damages: $500,000.

April 30; Bloomington, Ind. At least six pieces of logging and heavy construction equipment are sabotaged and a trailer full of wood chips is set ablaze at a road construction site just outside the city. A communiqué from the Earth Liberation Front states its plan was to punish those developing wooded areas around Bloomington, which "have turned what was once forested land into parking lots, luxury houses for rich scum and expanded roads." Damages: $75,000.

July 21; Rhinelander, Wis. Vandals hack down thousands of experimental trees, mostly poplars, and spray-paint vehicles at a U.S. Forest Service research station. The Earth Liberation Front claims the attack was against bioengineering. Damages: $1 million.

Oct. 18; Shoals, Ind. Vandals find four pieces of heavy logging equipment in the Martin State Forest and cut hoses, slash seats, destroy gauges and pour sand in the engines, fuel tanks and radiators. They leave spray-painted graffiti including, "Earth Raper," "Go Cut in Hell," and "ELF." Damages: $55,000.

Nov. 27; Longmont, Colo. Arson hits one of the first luxury homes going up in a new subdivision. The Earth Liberation Front later sends a note, made of letters clipped from magazines, to the Boulder Weekly newspaper: "Viva la revolution! The Boulder ELF burned the Legend Ridge mansion on Nov. 27th." The underground group explains in a follow-up communiqué that the arson was driven by defeat of a statewide ballot measure to control growth. Damages: $500,000.

Dec. 9; Middle Island, N.Y. Fire erupts in a condominium under construction. The Earth Liberation Front claims responsibility, saying the homes were "future dens of the wealthy elite." The group, announcing "an unbounded war on urban sprawl," claims it checked for occupants - human and animal - in 16 condos before setting incendiaries in them. Damages: $200,000.

Dec. 19; Miller Place, N.Y. A house under construction goes up in flames. "Building homes for the wealthy should not even be a priority," the Earth Liberation Front writes in its communiqué. "Forests, farms and wetlands are being replaced with a sea of houses, green chemical lawns, blacktop and roadkill." Damages: $50,000.

Dec. 29; Mount Sinai, N.Y. Three luxury homes under construction are set ablaze, and a fourth is spray-painted with graffiti: "If you build it, we will burn it." The ELF issues a communiqué saying, "This hopefully provided a firm message that we will not tolerate the destruction of our island." Damages estimated at $2 million.

2001
Jan. 1; Glendale, Oregon. Fire ravages the offices of Superior Lumber Co. The arson is the third holiday conflagration of an Oregon timber firm in as many years. It summons investigators from local, state and federal law enforcement agencies. Damages: $400,000.

Feb 20; Visalia, California. ELF claims responsibility for a fire at a research cotton gin owned by Delta & Pine Land, a firm accused of ties with Monsanto's genetically-engineered seed program. Damages estimated at $700,000.

April 15; Portland, Oregon. ELF sets fire to cement trucks at Ross Island Sand & Gravel, using time-delayed fuses. Damages: $210,000.

May 21; Seattle, Washington. ELF burns an office and a fleet of 13 trucks at Jefferson Poplar Farms in Clatskanie, Oregon. Simultaneously, they burn down the office of Toby Bradshaw at the Univ of Washington. Total damages: $5 million.

Sep 8; Tucson, Arizona. Saying the attack was meant "as a warning to corporations worldwide", the ELF and ALF claim joint responsibility for an arson attack on a McDonald's restaurant. Damages: $500,000.

2002
Jan 29; St. Paul, MN. Fire at a Univ of Minnesota's Microbial and Plant Genomics lab, which was under construction. Damages: $250,000.

Mar 24; Erie, PA. Construction crane torched, in attempt to halt a local highway project. Damages: $500,000.

Aug 11; Irvine, PA. Attack on Forest Service research station. Damages: $700,000.

July-Oct; Richmond, PA. Numerous actions against SUVs in the Richmond area. Total damages estimated at nearly $100,000.

Dec. 2; Erie, PA. A mink farm barn was broken into and burned to the ground. No people or animals were hurt. Joint claim for responsibility by ELF and ALF.

2003
Jan. 1; Erie, PA. Four vehicles destroyed at a Lincoln-Mercury dealership. Damages: $90,000.

March 21; Washtenaw County, MI. Two nearly-completed luxury homes were burned down. The letters "ELF", along with anti-sprawl messages, were spray-painted at the site. Responsibility was later acknowledged by ELF. Damages: $400,000.

June 4; Macomb County, MI. Two more luxury homes under construction were burned down. Similar ELF-related messages were left at the site. Damages: $700,000.

Aug. 1; San Diego, CA. Fire destroys a 200-unit condominium project that was under construction, causing more than $50 million in damages. This was the largest and most costly action ever taken by ELF, and the largest in US history. A 12-foot banner found at the site said, "If you build it – we will burn it – the ELF's are mad." About 100 investigators, including members of the FBI, have been put on the case. Damages: $50,000,000.

Aug. 22; Los Angeles, CA. SUV's and Hummers destroyed at an auto dealership in West Covina, CA. SUV's damaged by graffiti it at least 3 other dealerships. Total Damages: $2.5 million.

Sept. 19; San Diego, CA. Four upscale houses under construction were destroyed by fire in Carmel Valley, CA. A banner left at the scene read "Development destruction. Stop raping nature. The ELFs are angry". Damages: $1 million.

Sept. 22; Big Rapids, MI. An unexploded time bomb was found at an unmanned pumping station of an Ice Mountain bottling station. The Nestle-owned facility has been subject to severe criticism for extracting underground water, purifying it, and reselling it under the Ice Mountain brand. The plant is licensed to pump out 400 gallons of ground water per minute. Local environmentalists have argued that the plant will deplete the local aquifer, disrupt the flow of surface waters, and potentially lower surrounding lake levels.

Oct. 8; Jemez Mountains, NM. Construction equipment of the US Forest Service damaged. Windows broken, tires slashed.

<u>2004</u>

Feb 7; Charlottesville, VA. Construction equipment at 30-acre development site targeted. One bulldozer set on fire and several other pieces of construction equipment have minor damage (broke windows and cut wires). Banner left at scene reads "YOUR CONSTRUCTION = LONG-TERM DESTRUCTION – ELF.

April 22; Snohomish, WA. Through media reports, the ELF Press Office has been made aware of Earth Liberation Front actions against urban sprawl April 20th and 21st. Although the ELF Press Office has received no communications about these actions from the persons responsible, a note found at the site of one of the fires was signed "ELF" and reportedly contained statements condemning suburban developments. In the absence of other information, this note does indicate a claim of responsibility for the fires and fire attempts by ELF activists. Damages: $1 million.

June 17; West Jordan, Utah. The ELF Press Office has been informed of a claim of responsibility in a fire in West Jordan, Utah on June 14th, 2004. The fire targeted Stock Building Supply and caused $1.5 million in damages.

ENERGY AND EQUITY

IVAN ILLICH (1973)

Degrees of Self-Powered Mobility

A century ago, the ball-bearing was invented. It reduced the coefficient of friction by a factor of a thousand. By applying a well-calibrated ball-bearing between two Neolithic millstones, a man could now grind in a day what took his ancestors a week. The ball-bearing also made possible the bicycle, allowing the wheel—probably the last of the great Neolithic inventions—finally to become useful for self-powered mobility.

Man, unaided by any tool, gets around quite efficiently. He carries one gram of his weight over a kilometer in ten minutes by expending 0.75 calories. Man on his feet is thermodynamically more efficient than any motorized vehicle and most animals. For his weight, he performs more work in locomotion than rats or oxen, less than horses or sturgeon. At this rate of efficiency man settled the world and made its history. At this rate peasant societies spend less than 5 per cent and nomads less than 8 per cent of their respective social time budgets outside the home or the encampment.

Man on a bicycle can go three or four times faster than the pedestrian, but uses five times less energy in the process. He carries one gram of his weight over a kilometer of flat road at an expense of only 0.15 calories. The bicycle is the perfect transducer to match man's metabolic energy to the impedance of locomotion. Equipped with this tool, man outstrips the efficiency of not only all machines but all other animals as well.

The invention of the ball-bearing, the tangent-spoked wheel, and the pneumatic tire taken together can be compared to only three other events in the history of transportation. The invention of the wheel at the dawn of civilization took the load off man's back and put it onto the barrow. The invention and simultaneous application, during the European Middle Ages, of stirrup, shoulder harness, and horseshoe increased the thermodynamic efficiency of the horse by a factor of up to five, and changed the economy of medieval Europe: it made frequent plowing possible and thus introduced rotation agriculture; it brought more distant fields into the reach of the peasant, and thus permitted landowners to move from six-family hamlets into one-hundred family villages, where they could live around the church, the square, the jail, and—later—the school; it allowed the cultivation of northern soils and shifted the center of power into cold climates. The building of the first oceangoing vessels by the Portuguese in the fifteenth century, under the aegis of developing European capitalism, laid the solid foundations for a globe-spanning culture and market.

The invention of the ball-bearing signaled a fourth revolution. This revolution was unlike that, supported by the stirrup, which raised the knight onto his horse, and unlike that, supported by the galleon, which enlarged the horizon of the king's captains. The ball-bearing signaled a true crisis, a true political choice. It created an option between more freedom in equity and more speed. The bearing is an equally fundamental ingredient of two new types of locomotion, respectively symbolized by the bicycle and the car. The bicycle lifted man's auto-mobility into a new order, beyond which progress is theoretically not possible. In contrast, the accelerating individual capsule enabled societies to engage in a ritual of progressively paralyzing speed.

The monopoly of a ritual application over a potentially useful device is nothing new. Thousands of years ago, the wheel took the load off the carrier slave, but it did so only on the Eurasian land mass. In Mexico, the wheel was well known, but never applied to transport. It served exclusively for the construction of carriages for toy gods. The taboo on wheelbarrows in America before Cortes is no more puzzling than the taboo on bicycles in modern traffic.

It is by no means necessary that the invention of the ball-bearing continue to serve the increase of energy use and thereby produce time scarcity, space consumption, and class privilege. If the new order of self-powered mobility offered by the bicycle were protected against devaluation, paralysis, and risk to the limbs of the rider, it would be possible to guarantee optimal shared mobility to all people and put an end to the imposition of maximum privilege and exploitation. It would be possible to control the patterns of urbanization if the organization of space were constrained by the power man has to move through it.

Bicycles are not only thermodynamically efficient, they are also cheap. With his much lower salary, the Chinese acquires his durable bicycle in a fraction of the working hours an American devotes to the purchase of his obsolescent car. The cost of public utilities needed to facilitate bicycle traffic versus the price of an infrastructure tailored to high speeds is proportionately even less than the price differential of the vehicles used in the two systems. In the bicycle system, engineered roads are necessary only at certain points of dense traffic, and people who live far from the surfaced path are not thereby automatically isolated as they would be if they depended on cars or trains. The bicycle has extended man's radius without shunting him onto roads he cannot walk. Where he cannot ride his bike, he can usually push it.

The bicycle also uses little space. Eighteen bikes can be parked in the place of one car, thirty of them can move along in the space devoured by a single automobile. It takes three lanes of a given size to move 40,000 people across a bridge in one hour by using automated trains, four to move them on buses, twelve to move them in their cars, and only two lanes for them to pedal across on bicycles. Of all these vehicles, only the bicycle really allows people to go from door to door without walking. The cyclist can reach new destinations of his choice without his tool creating new locations from which he is barred.

Bicycles let people move with greater speed without taking up significant amounts of scarce space, energy, or time. They can spend fewer hours on each mile and still travel more miles in a year. They can get the benefit of technological breakthroughs without putting undue claims on the schedules, energy, or space of others.

They become masters of their own movements without blocking those of their fellows. Their new tool creates only those demands which it can also satisfy. Every increase in motorized speed creates new demands on space and time. The use of the bicycle is self-limiting. It allows people to create a new relationship between their life-space and their life-time, between their territory and the pulse of their being, without destroying their inherited balance. The advantages of modern self-powered traffic are obvious, and ignored. That better traffic runs faster is asserted, but never proved. Before they ask people to pay for it, those who propose acceleration should try to display the evidence for their claim.

A grisly contest between bicycles and motors is just coming to an end. In Vietnam, a hyperindustrialized army tried to conquer, but could not overcome, a people organized around bicycle speed. The lesson should be clear. High-energy armies can annihilate people—both those they defend and those against whom they are launched—but they are of very limited use to a people which defends itself. It remains to be seen if the Vietnamese will apply what they learned in war to an economy of peace, if they will be willing to protect the values that made their victory possible. The dismal likelihood is that the victors, for the sake of industrial progress and increased energy consumption, will tend to defeat themselves by destroying that structure of equity, rationality, and autonomy into which American bombers forced them by depriving them of fuels, motors, and roads.

The Industrialization of Traffic

The discussion of how energy is used to move people requires a formal distinction between transport and transit as the two components of traffic. By *traffic* I mean any movement of people from one place to another when they are outside their homes. By *transit* I mean those movements that put human metabolic energy to use, and by *transport*, that mode of movement which relies on other sources of energy. These energy sources will henceforth be mostly motors, since animals compete fiercely with men for their food in an overpopulated world, unless they are thistle eaters like donkeys and camels.

As soon as people become tributaries of transport, not just when they travel for several days, but also on their daily trips, the contradictions between social justice and motorized power, between effective movement and higher speed, between personal freedom and engineered routing, become poignantly clear. Enforced dependence on auto-mobile machines then denies a community of self-propelled people just those values supposedly procured by improved transportation.

People move well on their feet. This primitive means of getting around will, on closer analysis, appear quite effective when compared with the lot of people in modern cities or on industrialized farms. It will appear particularly attractive once it has been understood that modern Americans walk, on the average, as many miles as their ancestors—most of them through tunnels, corridors, parking lots, and stores.

People on their feet are more or less equal. People solely dependent on their feet move on the spur of the moment, at three to four miles per hour, in any direction and to any place from which they are not legally or physically barred. An improvement on this native degree of mobility by new transport technology should be expected to safeguard these values and to add some new ones, such as greater range, time economies, comfort, or more opportunities for the disabled. So far this is not what has happened. Instead, the growth of the transportation industry has everywhere had the reverse effect. From the moment its machines could put more than a certain horsepower behind any one passenger, this industry has reduced equality among men, restricted their mobility to a system of industrially defined routes, and created time scarcity of unprecedented severity. As the speed of their vehicles crosses a threshold, citizens become transportation consumers on the daily loop that brings them back to their home, a circuit which the United States Department of Commerce calls a "trip" as opposed to the "travel" for which Americans leave home equipped with a toothbrush.

More energy fed into the transportation system means that more people move faster over a greater range in the course of every day. Everybody's daily radius expands at the expense of being able to drop in on an acquaintance or walk through the park on the way to work. Extremes of privilege are created at the cost of universal enslavement. An elite packs unlimited distance into a lifetime of pampered travel, while the majority spend a bigger slice of their existence on unwanted trips. The few mount their magic carpets to travel between distant points that their ephemeral presence renders both scarce and seductive, while the many are compelled to trip farther and faster and to spend more time preparing for and recovering from their trips.

In the United States, four-fifths of all man-hours on the road are those of commuters and shoppers who hardly ever get into a plane, while four-fifths of the mileage flown to conventions and resorts is covered year after year by the same 1.5 percent of the population, usually those who are either well-to-do or professionally trained to do good. The speedier the vehicle, the larger the subsidy it gets from regressive taxation. Barely 0.2 per cent of the entire United States population can engage in self-chosen air travel more than once a year, and few other countries can support a jet set which is that large.

The captive tripper and the reckless traveler become equally dependent on transport. Neither can do without it. Occasional spurts to Acapulco or to a party congress dupe the ordinary passenger into believing that he has made it into the shrunk world of the powerfully rushed. The occasional chance to spend a few hours strapped into a high-powered seat makes him an accomplice in the distortion of human space, and prompts him to consent to the design of his country's geography around vehicles rather than around people. Man has evolved physically and culturally together with his cosmic niche. What for animals is their environment he has learned to make into his home. His self-consciousness requires as its complement a life-space and a lifetime integrated by the pace at which he moves. If that relationship is determined by the velocity of vehicles rather than by the movement of people, man the architect is reduced to the status of a mere commuter.

The model American male devotes more than 1,600 hours a year to his car. He sits in it while it goes and while it stands idling. He parks it and searches for it. He earns the money to put down on it and to meet the monthly installments. He works to pay for gasoline, tolls, insurance, taxes, and tickets. He spends four of his sixteen waking hours on the road or gathering his resources for it. And this figure does not take into account the time consumed by other activities dictated by transport: time spent in hospitals, traffic courts, and garages; time spent watching automobile commercials or attending consumer education meetings to improve the quality of the next buy. The model American puts in 1,600 hours to get 7,500 miles: *less than five miles per hour*. In countries deprived of a transportation industry, people manage to do the same, walking wherever they want to go, and they allocate only 3 to 8 percent of their society's time budget to traffic instead of 28 percent. What distinguishes the traffic in rich countries from the traffic in poor countries is not more mileage per hour of lifetime for the majority, but more hours of compulsory consumption of high doses of energy, packaged and unequally distributed by the transportation industry.

The Energy Crisis

It has recently become fashionable to insist on an impending energy crisis. This euphemistic term conceals a contradiction and consecrates an illusion. It masks the contradiction implicit in the joint pursuit of equity and industrial growth. It safeguards the illusion that machine power can indefinitely take the place of manpower. To resolve this contradiction and dispel this illusion, it is urgent to clarify the reality that the language of crisis obscures: high quanta of energy degrade social relations just as inevitably as they destroy the physical milieu.

The advocates of an energy crisis believe in and continue to propagate a peculiar vision of man. According to this notion, man is born into perpetual dependence on slaves which he must painfully learn to master. If he does not employ prisoners, then he needs machines to do most of his work. According to this doctrine, the well-being of a society can be measured by the number of years its members have gone to school, and by the number of energy slaves they have thereby learned to command. This belief is common to the conflicting economic ideologies now in vogue. It is threatened by the obvious inequity, hurriedness, and impotence that appear everywhere once the voracious hordes of energy slaves outnumber people by a certain proportion. The energy crisis focuses concern on the scarcity of fodder for these slaves. I prefer to ask whether free men need them.

The energy policies adopted during the current decade will determine the range and character of social relationships a society will be able to enjoy by the year 2000. A low-energy policy allows for a wide choice of life-styles and cultures. If, on the other hand, a society opts for high-energy consumption, its social relations must be dictated by technocracy and will be equally degrading whether labeled capitalist or socialist.

At this moment, most societies—especially the poor ones—are still free to set their energy policies by any of three guidelines. Well-being can be identified with high amounts of per capita energy use, with high efficiency of energy transformation, or with the least possible use of mechanical energy by the most powerful members of society. The first approach would stress tight management of scarce and destructive fuels on behalf of industry, whereas the second would emphasize the retooling of industry in the interest of thermodynamic thrift. These first two attitudes necessarily imply huge public expenditures and increased social control; both rationalize the emergence of a computerized Leviathan, and both are at present widely discussed.

The possibility of a third option is barely noticed. While people have begun to accept ecological limits on maximum per capita energy use as a condition for physical survival, they do not yet think about the use of minimum feasible power as the foundation of any of various social orders that would be both modern and desirable. Yet only a ceiling on energy use can lead to social relations that are characterized by high levels of equity. The one option that is at present neglected is the only choice within the reach of all nations. It is also the only strategy by which a political process can be used to set limits on the power of even the most motorized bureaucrat. Participatory democracy postulates low-energy technology. Only participatory democracy creates the conditions for rational technology.

What is generally overlooked is that equity and energy can grow concurrently only to a point. Below a threshold of per capita wattage, motors improve the conditions for social progress. Above this threshold, energy grows at the expense of equity. Further energy affluence then means decreased distribution of control over that energy.

The widespread belief that clean and abundant energy is the panacea for social ills is due to a political fallacy, according to which equity and energy consumption can be indefinitely correlated, at least under some ideal political conditions. Laboring under this illusion, we tend to discount any social limit on the growth of energy consumption. But if ecologists are right to assert that non-metabolic power pollutes, it is in fact just as inevitable that, beyond a certain threshold, mechanical power corrupts. The threshold of social disintegration by high-energy quanta is independent from the threshold at which energy conversion produces physical destruction. Expressed in horsepower, it is undoubtedly lower. This is the fact which must be theoretically recognized before a political issue can be made of the per capita wattage to which a society will limit its members.

Even if nonpolluting power were feasible and abundant, the use of energy on a massive scale acts on society like a drug that is physically harmless but psychically enslaving. A community can choose between Methadone and "cold turkey"—between maintaining its addiction to alien energy and kicking it in painful cramps—but no society can have a population that is hooked on progressively larger numbers of energy slaves and whose members are also autonomously active.

In previous discussions, I have shown that, beyond a certain level of per capita GNP, the cost of social control must rise faster than total output and become the major institutional activity within an economy. Therapy administered by educators, psychiatrists, and social workers must converge with the designs of planners, managers, and salesmen, and complement the services of security agencies, the military, and the police. I now want to indicate one reason why increased affluence requires increased control over people. I argue that beyond a certain median per capita energy level, the political system and cultural context of any society must decay. Once the critical quantum of per capita energy is surpassed, education for the abstract goals of a bureaucracy must supplant the legal guarantees of personal and concrete initiative. This quantum is the limit of social order.

I will argue here that technocracy must prevail as soon as the ratio of mechanical power to metabolic energy oversteps a definite, identifiable threshold. The order of magnitude within which this threshold lies is largely independent of the level of technology applied, yet its very existence has slipped into the blind-spot of social imagination in both rich and medium-rich countries. Both the United States and Mexico have passed the critical divide. In both countries, further energy inputs increase inequality, inefficiency, and personal impotence. Although one country has a per capita income of $500 and the other, one of nearly $5,000, huge vested interest in an industrial infrastructure prods both of them to further escalate the use of energy. As a result, both North American and Mexican ideologues put the label of "energy crisis" on their frustration, and both countries are blinded to the fact that the threat of social breakdown is due neither to a shortage of fuel nor to the wasteful, polluting, and irrational use of available wattage, but to the attempt of industries to gorge society with energy quanta that inevitably degrade, deprive, and frustrate most people.

A people can be just as dangerously overpowered by the wattage of its tools as by the caloric content of its foods, but it is much harder to confess to a national overindulgence in wattage than to a sickening diet. The per capita wattage that is critical for social well-being lies within an order of magnitude which is far above the horsepower known to four-fifths of humanity and far below the power commanded by any Volkswagen driver. It eludes the under-consumer and the over-consumer alike. Neither is willing to face the facts. For the primitive, the elimination of slavery and drudgery depends on the introduction of appropriate modern technology, and for the rich, the avoidance of an even more horrible degradation depends on the effective recognition of a threshold in energy consumption beyond which technical processes begin to dictate social relations. Calories are both biologically and socially healthy only as long as they stay within the narrow range that separates enough from too much.

The so-called energy crisis is, then, a politically ambiguous issue. Public interest in the quantity of power and in the distribution of controls over the use of energy can lead in two opposite directions. On the one hand, questions can be posed that would open the way to political reconstruction by unblocking the search for a postindustrial, labor-intensive, low-energy and high-equity economy. On the other hand, hysterical concern with machine fodder can reinforce the present escalation of capital-intensive institutional growth, and carry us past the last turnoff from a hyperindustrial Armageddon. Political reconstruction presupposes the recognition of the fact that there exist critical per capita quanta beyond which energy can no longer be controlled by political process. A universal social straitjacket will be the inevitable outcome of ecological restraints.

Rich countries like the United States, Japan, or France might never reach the point of choking on their own waste, but only because their societies will have already collapsed into a sociocultural energy coma. Countries like India, Burma, and, for another short while at least, China are in the inverse position of being still muscle-powered enough to stop short of an energy stroke. They could choose, right now, to stay within those limits to which the rich will be forced back through a total loss of their freedoms.

The choice of a minimum-energy economy compels the poor to abandon fantastical expectations and the rich to recognize their vested interest as a ghastly liability. Both must reject the fatal image of man the slaveholder currently promoted by an ideologically stimulated hunger for more energy. In countries that were made affluent by industrial development, the energy crisis serves as a pretext for raising the taxes that will be needed to substitute new, more "rational," and socially more deadly industrial processes for those that have been rendered obsolete by inefficient overexpansion. For the leaders of people who are not yet dominated by the same process of industrialization, the energy crisis serves as a *historical imperative* to centralize production, pollution, and their control in a last-ditch effort to catch up with the more highly powered.

By exporting their crisis and by preaching the new gospel of puritan energy worship, the rich do even more damage to the poor than they did by selling them the products of now outdated factories. As soon as a poor country accepts the doctrine that more energy more carefully managed will always yield more goods for more people, that country locks itself into the cage of enslavement to maximum industrial outputs. Inevitably the poor lose the option for rational technology when they choose to modernize their poverty by increasing their dependence on energy. Inevitably the poor deny themselves the possibility of liberating technology and participatory politics when, together with maximum feasible energy use, they accept maximum feasible social control.

The energy crisis cannot be overwhelmed by more energy inputs. It can only be dissolved, along with the illusion that well-being depends on the number of energy slaves a man has at his command. For this purpose, it is necessary to identify the thresholds beyond which energy corrupts, and to do so by a political process that associates the community in the search for limits. Because this kind of research runs counter to that now done by experts and for institutions, I shall continue to call it counterfoil research. It has three steps. First, the need for limits on the per capita use of energy must be theoretically recognized as a social imperative. Then, the range must be located wherein the critical magnitude might be found. Finally, each community has to identify the levels of inequity, harrying and operant conditioning that its members are willing to accept in exchange for the satisfaction that comes of idolizing powerful devices and joining in rituals directed by the professionals who control their operation.

The need for political research on socially optimal energy quanta can be clearly and concisely illustrated by an examination of modern traffic. The United States puts between 25 and 45 percent of its total energy (depending upon how one calculates this) into vehicles: to make them, run them, and clear a right of way for them when they roll, when they fly, and when they park. Most of this energy is to move people who have been strapped into place. For the sole purpose of transporting people, 250 million Americans allocate more fuel than is used by 1.3 billion Chinese and Indians for all purposes. Almost all of this fuel is burned in a rain-dance of time-consuming acceleration. Poor countries spend less energy per person, but the percentage of total energy devoted to traffic in Mexico or in Peru is probably greater than in the United States, and it benefits a smaller percentage of the population. The size of this enterprise makes it both easy and significant to demonstrate the existence of socially critical energy quanta by the example of personal mobility.

In traffic, energy used over a specific period of time (power) translates into speed. In this case, the critical quantum will appear as a speed limit. Wherever this limit has been passed, the basic pattern of social degradation by high-energy quanta has emerged. Once some public utility went faster than 15 mph, equity declined and the scarcity of both time and space increased. Motorized transportation monopolized traffic and blocked self-powered transit. In every Western country, passenger mileage on all types of conveyance increased by a factor of a hundred within fifty years of building the first railroad. When the ratio of their respective power outputs passed beyond a certain value, mechanical transformers of mineral fuels excluded people from the use of their metabolic energy and forced them to become captive consumers of conveyance. This effect of speed on the autonomy of people is only marginally affected by the technological characteristics of the motorized vehicles employed or by the persons or entities who hold the legal titles to airlines, buses, railroads, or cars.

High speed is the critical factor which makes transportation socially destructive. A true choice among practical policies and of desirable social relations is possible only where speed is restrained. Participatory democracy demands low-energy technology, and free people must travel the road to productive social relations at the speed of a bicycle.

INDUSTRIAL SOCIETY AND ITS FUTURE

TED KACZYNSKI

(published September 19, 1995)

[1] INTRODUCTION

1. The Industrial Revolution and its consequences have been a disaster for the human race. They have greatly increased the life-expectancy of those of us who live in "advanced" countries, but they have destabilized society, have made life unfulfilling, have subjected human beings to indignities, have led to widespread psychological suffering (in the Third World to physical suffering as well) and have inflicted severe damage on the natural world. The continued development of technology will worsen the situation. It will certainly subject human beings to greater indignities and inflict greater damage on the natural world, it will probably lead to greater social disruption and psychological suffering, and it may lead to increased physical suffering even in "advanced" countries.

2. The industrial-technological system may survive or it may break down. If it survives, it MAY eventually achieve a low level of physical and psychological suffering, but only after passing through a long and very painful period of adjustment and only at the cost of permanently reducing human beings and many other living organisms to engineered products and mere cogs in the social machine. Furthermore, if the system survives, the consequences will be inevitable: There is no way of reforming or modifying the system so as to prevent it from depriving people of dignity and autonomy.

3. If the system breaks down the consequences will still be very painful. But the bigger the system grows the more disastrous the results of its breakdown will be, so if it is to break down it had best break down sooner rather than later.

4. We therefore advocate a revolution against the industrial system. This revolution may or may not make use of violence; it may be sudden or it may be a relatively gradual process spanning a few decades. We can't predict any of that. But we do outline in a very general way the measures that those who hate the industrial system should take in order to prepare the way for a revolution against that form of society. This is not to be a POLITICAL revolution. Its object will be to overthrow not governments but the economic and technological basis of the present society.

5. In this article we give attention to only some of the negative developments that have grown out of the industrial-technological system. Other such developments we mention only briefly or ignore altogether. This does not mean that we regard these other developments as unimportant. For practical reasons we have to confine our discussion to areas that have received insufficient public attention or in which we have something new to say. For example, since there are well-developed environmental and wilderness movements, we have written very little about environmental degradation or the destruction of wild nature, even though we consider these to be highly important.

[2] SOURCES OF SOCIAL PROBLEMS

46. We attribute the social and psychological problems of modern society to the fact that society requires people to live under conditions radically different from those under which the human race evolved, and to behave in ways that conflict with the patterns of behavior that the human race developed while living under the earlier conditions. It is clear from what we have already written that we consider lack of opportunity to properly experience the power process as the most important of the abnormal conditions to which modern society subjects people. But it is not the only one. Before dealing with disruption of the power process as a source of social problems we will discuss some of the other sources.

47. Among the abnormal conditions present in modern industrial society are excessive density of population, isolation of man from nature, excessive rapidity of social change and the breakdown of natural small-scale communities such as the extended family, the village or the tribe.

48. It is well known that crowding increases stress and aggression. The degree of crowding that exists today and the isolation of man from nature are consequences of technological progress. All pre-industrial societies were predominantly rural. The Industrial Revolution vastly increased the size of cities and the proportion of the population that lives in them, and modern agricultural technology has made it possible for the Earth to support a far denser population than it ever did before. (Also, technology exacerbates the effects of crowding because it puts increased disruptive powers in people's hands. For example, a variety of noise-making devices: power mowers, radios, motorcycles, etc. If the use of these devices is unrestricted, people who want peace and quiet are frustrated by the noise. If their use is restricted, people who use the devices are frustrated by the regulations. But if these machines had never been invented there would have been no conflict and no frustration generated by them.)

49. For primitive societies the natural world (which usually changes only slowly) provided a stable framework and therefore a sense of security. In the modern world it is human society that dominates nature rather than the other way around, and modern society changes very rapidly owing to technological change. Thus there is no stable framework.

51. The breakdown of traditional values to some extent implies the breakdown of the bonds that hold together traditional small-scale social groups. The disintegration of small-scale social groups is also promoted by the fact that modern conditions often require or tempt individuals to move to new locations, separating themselves from their communities. Beyond that, a technological society HAS TO weaken family ties and local communities if it is to function efficiently. In modern society an individual's loyalty must be first to the system and only secondarily to a small-scale community, because if the internal loyalties of small-scale communities were stronger than loyalty to the system, such communities would pursue their own advantage at the expense of the system.

68. It may be objected that primitive man is physically less secure than modern man, as is shown by his shorter life expectancy; hence modern man suffers from less, not more than the amount of insecurity that is normal for human beings. But psychological security does not closely correspond with physical security. What makes us FEEL secure is not so much objective security as a sense of confidence in our ability to take care of ourselves. Primitive man, threatened by a fierce animal or by hunger, can fight in self-defense or travel in search of food. He has no certainty of success in these efforts, but he is by no means helpless against the things that threaten him. The modern individual on the other hand is threatened by many things against which he is helpless: nuclear accidents, carcinogens in food, environmental pollution, war, increasing taxes, invasion of his privacy by large organizations, nationwide social or economic phenomena that may disrupt his way of life.

[3] INDUSTRIAL-TECHNOLOGICAL SOCIETY CANNOT BE REFORMED

111. The foregoing principles help to show how hopelessly difficult it would be to reform the industrial system in such a way as to prevent it from progressively narrowing our sphere of freedom. There has been a consistent tendency, going back at least to the Industrial Revolution, for technology to strengthen the system at a high cost in individual freedom and local autonomy. Hence any change designed to protect freedom from technology would be contrary to a fundamental trend in the development of our society. Consequently, such a change either would be a transitory one—soon swamped by the tide of history—or, if large enough to be permanent, would alter the nature of our whole society. Moreover, since society would be altered in a way that could not be predicted in advance there would be great risk. Changes large enough to make a lasting difference in favor of freedom would not be initiated because it would be realized that they would gravely disrupt the system. So any attempts at reform would be too timid to be effective. Even if changes large enough to make a lasting difference were initiated, they would be retracted when their disruptive effects became apparent. Thus, permanent changes in favor of freedom could be brought about only by persons prepared to accept radical, dangerous and unpredictable alteration of the entire system. In other words by revolutionaries, not reformers.

[4] RESTRICTION OF FREEDOM IS UNAVOIDABLE IN INDUSTRIAL SOCIETY

114. Modern man is strapped down by a network of rules and regulations, and his fate depends on the actions of persons remote from him whose decisions he cannot influence. This is not accidental or a result of the arbitrariness of arrogant bureaucrats. It is necessary and inevitable in any technologically advanced society. The system HAS TO regulate human behavior closely in order to function. At work people have to do what they are told to do, otherwise production would be thrown into chaos. Bureaucracies HAVE TO be run according to rigid rules. To allow any substantial personal discretion to lower-level bureaucrats would disrupt the system and lead to charges of unfairness due to differences in the way individual bureaucrats exercised their discretion. It is true that some restrictions on our freedom could be eliminated, but GENERALLY SPEAKING the regulation of our lives by large organizations is necessary for the functioning of industrial-technological society. The result is a sense of powerlessness on the part of the average person. It may be, however, that formal regulations will tend increasingly to be replaced by psychological tools that make us want to do what the system requires of us.

115. The system HAS TO force people to behave in ways that are increasingly remote from the natural pattern of human behavior. For example, the system needs scientists, mathematicians and engineers. It can't function without them. So heavy pressure is put on children to excel in these fields. It isn't natural for an adolescent human being to spend the bulk of his time sitting at a desk absorbed in study. A normal adolescent wants to spend his time in active contact with the real world. Among primitive peoples the things that children are trained to do tend to be in reasonable harmony with natural human impulses. Among the American Indians, for example, boys were trained in active outdoor pursuits—just the sort of thing that boys like. But in our society children are pushed into studying technical subjects, which most do grudgingly.

117. In any technologically advanced society the individual's fate MUST depend on decisions that he personally cannot influence to any great extent. A technological society cannot be broken down into small, autonomous communities, because production depends on the cooperation of very large numbers of people. When a decision affects, say, a million people, then each of the affected individuals has, on the average, only a one-millionth share in making the decision. What usually happens in practice is that decisions are made by public officials or corporation executives, or by technical specialists, but even when the public votes on a decision the number of voters ordinarily is too large for the vote of any one individual to be significant. Thus most individuals are unable to influence measurably the major decisions that affect their lives. There is no conceivable way to remedy this in a technologically advanced society. The system tries to "solve" this problem by using propaganda to make people WANT the decisions that have been made for them, but even if this "solution" were completely successful in making people feel better, it would be demeaning.

118. Conservatives and some others advocate more "local autonomy." Local communities once did have autonomy, but such autonomy becomes less and less possible as local communities become more enmeshed with and dependent on large-scale systems like public utilities, computer networks, highway systems, the mass communications media, the modern health care system. Also operating against autonomy is the fact that technology applied in one location often affects people at other locations far way. Thus pesticide or chemical use near a creek may contaminate the water supply hundreds of miles downstream, and the greenhouse effect affects the whole world.

119. The system does not and cannot exist to satisfy human needs. Instead, it is human behavior that has to be modified to fit the needs of the system. This has nothing to do with the political or social ideology that may pretend to guide the technological system. It is the fault of technology, because the system is guided not by ideology but by technical necessity. Of course the system does satisfy many human needs, but generally speaking it does this only to the extent that it is to the advantage of the system to do it. It is the needs of the system that are paramount, not those of the human being. For example, the system provides people with food because the system couldn't function if everyone starved; it attends to people's psychological needs whenever it can CONVENIENTLY do so, because it couldn't function if too many people became depressed or rebellious. But the system, for good, solid, practical reasons, must exert constant pressure on people to mold their behavior to the needs of the system. Too much waste accumulating? The government, the media, the educational system, environmentalists, everyone inundates us with a mass of propaganda about recycling. Need more technical personnel? A chorus of voices exhorts kids to study science. No one stops to ask whether it is inhumane to force adolescents to spend the bulk of their time studying subjects most of them hate. When skilled workers are put out of a job by technical advances and have to undergo "retraining," no one asks whether it is humiliating for them to be pushed around in this way. It is simply taken for granted that everyone must bow to technical necessity. And for good reason: If human needs were put before technical necessity there would be economic problems, unemployment, shortages or worse. The concept of "mental health" in our society is defined largely by the extent to which an individual behaves in accord with the needs of the system, and does so without showing signs of stress.

[5] TECHNOLOGY IS A MORE POWERFUL SOCIAL FORCE THAN THE ASPIRATION FOR FREEDOM

125. It is not possible to make a LASTING compromise between technology and freedom, because technology is by far the more powerful social force and continually encroaches on freedom through REPEATED compromises. Imagine the case of two neighbors, each of whom at the outset owns the same amount of land, but one of whom is more powerful than the other. The powerful one demands a piece of the other's land. The weak one refuses. The powerful one says, "OK, let's compromise. Give me half of

what I asked." The weak one has little choice but to give in. Some time later the powerful neighbor demands another piece of land, again there is a compromise, and so forth. By forcing a long series of compromises on the weaker man, the powerful one eventually gets all of his land. So it goes in the conflict between technology and freedom.

127. A technological advance that appears not to threaten freedom often turns out to threaten it very seriously later on. For example, consider *motorized transport*. A walking man formerly could go where he pleased, go at his own pace without observing any traffic regulations, and was independent of technological support-systems. When motor vehicles were introduced they appeared to increase man's freedom. They took no freedom away from the walking man, no one had to have an automobile if he didn't want one, and anyone who did choose to buy an automobile could travel much faster and farther than a walking man. But the introduction of motorized transport soon changed society in such a way as to restrict greatly man's freedom of locomotion. When automobiles became numerous, it became necessary to regulate their use extensively. In a car, especially in densely populated areas, one cannot just go where one likes at one's own pace; one's movement is governed by the flow of traffic and by various traffic laws. One is tied down by various obligations: license requirements, driver test, renewing registration, insurance, maintenance required for safety, monthly payments on purchase price. Moreover, the use of motorized transport is no longer optional. Since the introduction of motorized transport, the arrangement of our cities has changed in such a way that the majority of people no longer live within walking distance of their place of employment, shopping areas and recreational opportunities, so that they HAVE TO depend on the automobile for transportation. Or else they must use public transportation, in which case they have even less control over their own movement than when driving a car. Even the walker's freedom is now greatly restricted. In the city he continually has to stop to wait for traffic lights that are designed mainly to serve auto traffic. In the country, motor traffic makes it dangerous and unpleasant to walk along the highway. (Note this important point that we have just illustrated with the case of motorized transport: When a new item of technology is introduced as an option that an individual can accept or not as he chooses, it does not necessarily REMAIN optional. In many cases the new technology changes society in such a way that people eventually find themselves FORCED to use it.)

128. While technological progress AS A WHOLE continually narrows our sphere of freedom, each new technical advance CONSIDERED BY ITSELF appears to be desirable. Electricity, indoor plumbing, rapid long-distance communications ... how could one argue against any of these things, or against any other of the innumerable technical advances that have made modern society? It would have been absurd to resist the introduction of the telephone, for example. It offered many advantages and no disadvantages. Yet, all these technical advances taken together have created a world in which the average man's fate is no longer in his own hands or in the hands of his neighbors and friends, but in those of politicians, corporation executives and remote, anonymous technicians and bureaucrats whom he as an individual has no power to influence. The same process will continue in the future. Take genetic engi-

neering, for example. Few people will resist the introduction of a genetic technique that eliminates a hereditary disease. It does no apparent harm and prevents much suffering. Yet a large number of genetic improvements taken together will make the human being into an engineered product rather than a free creation of chance (or of God, or whatever, depending on your religious beliefs).

133. No social arrangements, whether laws, institutions, customs or ethical codes, can provide permanent protection against technology. History shows that all social arrangements are transitory; they all change or break down eventually. But technological advances are permanent within the context of a given civilization. Suppose for example that it were possible to arrive at some social arrangements that would prevent genetic engineering from being applied to human beings, or prevent it from being applied in such a way as to threaten freedom and dignity. Still, the technology would remain waiting. Sooner or later the social arrangement would break down. Probably sooner, given the pace of change in our society. Then genetic engineering would begin to invade our sphere of freedom, and this invasion would be irreversible (short of a breakdown of technological civilization itself). Any illusions about achieving anything permanent through social arrangements should be dispelled by what is currently happening with environmental legislation. A few years ago its seemed that there were secure legal barriers preventing at least SOME of the worst forms of environmental degradation. A change in the political wind, and those barriers begin to crumble.

[6] SIMPLER SOCIAL PROBLEMS HAVE PROVED INTRACTABLE

136. If anyone still imagines that it would be possible to reform the system in such a way as to protect freedom from technology, let him consider how clumsily and for the most part unsuccessfully our society has dealt with other social problems that are far more simple and straightforward. Among other things, the system has failed to stop environmental degradation, political corruption, drug trafficking or domestic abuse.

137. Take our environmental problems, for example. Here the conflict of values is straightforward: economic expedience now versus saving some of our natural resources for our grandchildren. But on this subject we get only a lot of blather and obfuscation from the people who have power, and nothing like a clear, consistent line of action, and we keep on piling up environmental problems that our grandchildren will have to live with. Attempts to resolve the environmental issue consist of struggles and compromises between different factions, some of which are ascendant at one moment, others at another moment. The line of struggle changes with the shifting currents of public opinion. This is not a rational process, nor is it one that is likely to lead to a timely and successful solution to the problem. Major social problems, if they get "solved" at all, are rarely or never solved through any rational, comprehensive plan. They just work themselves out through a process in which various competing groups pursuing their own (usually short-term) self-interest arrive (mainly by luck) at some more or less stable *modus vivendi*. In fact, it seems doubtful that rational, long-term social planning can EVER be successful.

[7] CONTROL OF HUMAN BEHAVIOR

152. Generally speaking, technological control over human behavior will probably not be introduced with a totalitarian intention or even through a conscious desire to restrict human freedom. Each new step in the assertion of control over the human mind will be taken as a rational response to a problem that faces society, such as curing alcoholism, reducing the crime rate or inducing young people to study science and engineering. In many cases there will be a humanitarian justification. For example, when a psychiatrist prescribes an anti-depressant for a depressed patient, he is clearly doing that individual a favor. It would be inhumane to withhold the drug from someone who needs it. When parents send their children to Sylvan Learning Centers to have them manipulated into becoming enthusiastic about their studies, they do so from concern for their children's welfare. It may be that some of these parents wish that one didn't have to have specialized training to get a job, and that their kid didn't have to be brainwashed into becoming a computer nerd. But what can they do? They can't change society, and their child may be unemployable if he doesn't have certain skills. So they send him to Sylvan.

[8] HUMAN SUFFERING

167. The industrial system will not break down purely as a result of revolutionary action. It will not be vulnerable to revolutionary attack unless its own internal problems of development lead it into very serious difficulties. So if the system breaks down it will do so either spontaneously, or through a process that is in part spontaneous but helped along by revolutionaries. If the breakdown is sudden, many people will die, since the world's population has become so overblown that it cannot even feed itself any longer without advanced technology. Even if the breakdown is gradual enough so that reduction of the population can occur more through lowering of the birth rate than through elevation of the death rate, the process of de-industrialization probably will be very chaotic and involve much suffering. It is naive to think it likely that technology can be phased out in a smoothly managed, orderly way, especially since the technophiles will fight stubbornly at every step. Is it therefore cruel to work for the breakdown of the system? Maybe, but maybe not. In the first place, revolutionaries will not be able to break the system down unless it is already in enough trouble so that there would be a good chance of its eventually breaking down by itself anyway; and the bigger the system grows, the more disastrous the consequences of its breakdown will be; so it may be that revolutionaries, by hastening the onset of the breakdown, will be reducing the extent of the disaster.

168. In the second place, one has to balance struggle and death against the loss of freedom and dignity. To many of us, freedom and dignity are more important than a long life or avoidance of physical pain. Besides, we all have to die some time, and it may be better to die fighting for survival, or for a cause, than to live a long but empty and purposeless life.

169. In the third place, it is not at all certain that survival of the system will lead to less suffering than breakdown of the system would. The system has already caused, and is continuing to cause, immense suffering all over the world. Ancient cultures, that for hundreds of years gave people a satisfactory relationship with each other and with their environment, have been shattered by contact with industrial society, and the result has been a whole catalogue of economic, environmental, social and psychological problems. One of the effects of the intrusion of industrial society has been that over much of the world traditional controls on population have been thrown out of balance. Hence the population explosion, with all that that implies. Then there is the psychological suffering that is widespread throughout the supposedly fortunate countries of the West. No one knows what will happen as a result of ozone depletion, the greenhouse effect and other environmental problems that cannot yet be foreseen. And, as nuclear proliferation has shown, new technology cannot be kept out of the hands of dictators and irresponsible Third World nations. Would you like to speculate about what Iraq or North Korea will do with genetic engineering?

170. "Oh!" say the technophiles, "Science is going to fix all that! We will conquer famine, eliminate psychological suffering, make everybody healthy and happy!" Yeah, sure. That's what they said 200 years ago. The Industrial Revolution was supposed to eliminate poverty, make everybody happy, etc. The actual result has been quite different. The technophiles are hopelessly naive (or self-deceiving) in their understanding of social problems. They are unaware of (or choose to ignore) the fact that when large changes, even seemingly beneficial ones, are introduced into a society, they lead to a long sequence of other changes, most of which are impossible to predict. The result is disruption of the society. So it is very probable that in their attempts to end poverty and disease, engineer docile, happy personalities and so forth, the technophiles will create social systems that are terribly troubled, even more so than the present once. For example, the scientists boast that they will end famine by creating new, genetically engineered food plants. But this will allow the human population to keep expanding indefinitely, and it is well known that crowding leads to increased stress and aggression. This is merely one example of the PREDICTABLE problems that will arise. We emphasize that, as past experience has shown, technical progress will lead to other new problems that CANNOT be predicted in advance. In fact, ever since the Industrial Revolution, technology has been creating new problems for society far more rapidly than it has been solving old ones. Thus it will take a long and difficult period of trial and error for the technophiles to work the bugs out of their Brave New World (if they every do). In the meantime there will be great suffering. So it is not at all clear that the survival of industrial society would involve less suffering than the breakdown of that society would. Technology has gotten the human race into a fix from which there is not likely to be any easy escape.

[9] STRATEGY

180. The technophiles are taking us all on an utterly reckless ride into the unknown. Many people understand something of what technological progress is doing to us yet take a passive attitude toward it because they think it is inevitable. But we don't think it is inevitable. We think it can be stopped, and we will give here some indications of how to go about stopping it.

181. As we stated in paragraph 166, the two main tasks for the present are to promote social stress and instability in industrial society and to develop and propagate an ideology that opposes technology and the industrial system.

183. But an ideology, in order to gain enthusiastic support, must have a positive ideal as well as a negative one; it must be FOR something as well as AGAINST something. The positive ideal that we propose is <u>Nature</u>. That is, WILD nature: those aspects of the functioning of the Earth and its living things that are independent of human management and free of human interference and control. And with wild nature we include human nature, by which we mean those aspects of the functioning of the human individual that are not subject to regulation by organized society but are products of chance, or free will, or God (depending on your religious or philosophical opinions).

184. Nature makes a perfect counter-ideal to technology for several reasons. Nature (that which is outside the power of the system) is the opposite of technology (which seeks to expand indefinitely the power of the system). Most people will agree that nature is beautiful; certainly it has tremendous popular appeal. The radical environmentalists ALREADY hold an ideology that exalts nature and opposes technology.

A further advantage of nature as a counter-ideal to technology is that, in many people, nature inspires the kind of reverence that is associated with religion, so that nature could perhaps be idealized on a religious basis. It is true that in many societies religion has served as a support and justification for the established order, but it is also true that religion has often provided a basis for rebellion. Thus it may be useful to introduce a religious element into the rebellion against technology, the more so because Western society today has no strong religious foundation. Religion, nowadays either is used as cheap and transparent support for narrow, short-sighted selfishness (some conservatives use it this way), or even is cynically exploited to make easy money (by many evangelists), or has degenerated into crude irrationalism (fundamentalist Protestant sects, "cults"), or is simply stagnant (Catholicism, main-line Protestantism).

Thus there is a religious vacuum in our society that could perhaps be filled by a religion focused on nature in opposition to technology. But it would be a mistake to try to concoct artificially a religion to fill this role. Such an invented religion would probably be a failure. Take the "Gaia" religion for example. Do its adherents REALLY believe in it or are they just play-acting? If they are just play-acting their religion will be a flop in the end.

It is probably best not to try to introduce religion into the conflict of nature vs.

technology unless you REALLY believe in that religion yourself and find that it arouses a deep, strong, genuine response in many other people.

It is not necessary for the sake of nature to set up some chimerical utopia or any new kind of social order. Nature takes care of itself. It was a spontaneous creation that existed long before any human society, and for countless centuries many different kinds of human societies coexisted with nature without doing it an excessive amount of damage. Only with the Industrial Revolution did the effect of human society on nature become really devastating. To relieve the pressure on nature it is not necessary to create a special kind of social system, it is only necessary to get rid of industrial society. Granted, this will not solve all problems. Industrial society has already done tremendous damage to nature and it will take a very long time for the scars to heal. Besides, even preindustrial societies can do significant damage to nature. Nevertheless, getting rid of industrial society will accomplish a great deal. It will relieve the worst of the pressure on nature so that the scars can begin to heal. It will remove the capacity of organized society to keep increasing its control over nature (including human nature). Whatever kind of society may exist after the demise of the industrial system, it is certain that most people will live close to nature, because in the absence of advanced technology there is no other way that people CAN live. To feed themselves they must be peasants or herdsmen or fishermen or hunters, etc. And, generally speaking, local autonomy should tend to increase, because lack of advanced technology and rapid communications will limit the capacity of governments or other large organizations to control local communities.

203. Imagine an alcoholic sitting with a barrel of wine in front of him. Suppose he starts saying to himself, "Wine isn't bad for you if used in moderation. Why, they say small amounts of wine are even good for you! It won't do me any harm, if I take just one little drink..." Well you know what is going to happen. Never forget that the human race with technology is just like an alcoholic with a barrel of wine.

APPENDIX A

OVERVIEW OF ENVIRONMENTAL GROUPS

Mainstream groups:

Michigan-
　　Environment Michigan (part of PIRGIM). Ann Arbor. (734) 662-6597.
　　East Michigan Environmental Action Committee (EMEAC). emeac.org
　　Friends of the Rouge. therouge.org

US-
　　Big 5:
　　Sierra Club. sierraclub.org
　　League of Conservation Voters. lcv.org
　　National Resources Defense Council (NRDC). nrdc.org
　　Environmental Defense Fund. edf.org
　　National Wildlife Federation (NWF). nwf.org

　　Others/International:
　　National Audubon Society. audubon.org
　　World Wildlife Fund (WWF). wwf.org, worldwildlife.org
　　Friends of the Earth. foe.org
　　The Nature Conservancy. tnc.org
　　The Wilderness Society. wilderness.org
　　Union of Concerned Scientists. ucsusa.org

More Activist/Radical Groups:
　　Rainforest Action Network. www.ran.org
　　Greenpeace. www.greenpeaceusa.org
　　Sea Shepherd Conservation Society. www.seashepherd.org
　　Earth First!. www.earthfirstjournal.org
　　Earth Liberation Front. No web site. Some details at: www.directaction.info
　　Rewilding Institute. www.rewilding.org

Related:
www.populationconnection.org (formerly 'zero population growth').

EARTH ALIVE

Journals:
    Resurgence. (UK). www.resurgence.org
    E magazine. www.emagazine.com
    Ecologist. (UK). www.theecologist.org
    Earth First! Journal. www.earthfirstjournal.org
    Fifth Estate. (Detroit). www.fifthestate.org
    Green Anarchy. Eugene, OR. www.greenanarchy.org

APPENDIX B

COPYRIGHT ACKNOWLEDGMENTS

Aristotle (ca. 350 BCE). Politics, On the Parts of Animals, On the Heavens, On the Soul. D. Skrbina, trans.

Bateson, G. (1968-1970). *Steps to an Ecology of Mind*. Harper and Row.

Bible (NKJV). Genesis 1, 9; Psalm 8. Thomas Nelson Publishers.

Foreman, D. (1991). *Defending the Earth*. South End Press.

Brennan, A. (1984). The moral standing of natural objects. *Environmental Ethics*, 6 (Cambridge Univ Press).

Carson, R. (1962). *Silent Spring*. Houghton Mifflin.

Devall, W. and Sessions, G. (1985). *Deep Ecology*. Gibbs Smith.

Feinberg, J. (1974). The rights of animals and unborn generations. *Rights of Animals* (Univ of Georgia Press).

Fox, W. (1984). Deep ecology: a new philosophy of our time? *The Ecologist*, 14(5/6).

Goodpaster, K. (1978). On being morally considerable. *Journal of Philosophy* (Journal of Philosophy Inc.).

Hardin, G. (1974). Lifeboat ethics. *Psychology Today* (Sussex Publishers, Inc).

Illich, I. (1973). *Energy and Equity*. Harper and Row.

Kaczynski, T. (1995). Industrial Society and its Future. (no copyright).

Leopold, A. (1949). *A Sand County Almanac*. Oxford Univ Press.

Lovelock, J. (1975). The quest for Gaia. *New Scientist* (Feb. 6).

Naess, A. (1973). The shallow and the deep, long-range ecology movement. *Inquiry*, 16 (Universitetsforlaget).

Nash, R. (1977). Do rocks have rights? *The Center Magazine* (copyright by author).

Plato (ca. 375 BCE). Phaedrus, Philebus, Timaeus, Critias, Laws. D. Skrbina, trans.

Radford, T. (2003). Goodbye cruel world. *The Guardian* (Oct. 2).

Roszak, T. (2002). Ecopsychology since 1992. *Wild Earth* (Summer).

Seymour, J. (1995). Age of healing. *Resurgence* (Nov-Dec).

Skolimowski, H. (1974). Ecological humanism. *Architecture Association Quarterly* (June-July).

Skolimowski, H. (1975). Knowledge and values. *The Ecologist*, 5(1).

Skolimowski, H. (1988). Eco-philosophy and deep ecology. *The Ecologist*, 18(4/5).

Spinoza, B. (1677). *Ethics*. D. Skrbina, trans.

Stone, C. (1972). Should trees have standing? *California Law Review*, 45.

Tilove, J. (1991). *Don't panic, but...* Ann Arbor News.

White Jr., L. (1967). The historical roots of our ecologic crisis. *Science*, 155(3767). American Assoc for the Advancement of Science.

www.ingramcontent.com/pod-product-compliance
Lightning Source LLC
Chambersburg PA
CBHW030902080526
44589CB00010B/110